The Maikop Treasure

A. M. Leskov

The Maikop Treasure

UNIVERSITY of PENNSYLVANIA MUSEUM
of ARCHAEOLOGY and ANTHROPOLOGY

Philadelphia

To Adyghea,
with love

DR. ALEKSANDR LESKOV, Professor, corresponding member of the German Archaeological Institute, is an archaeologist specializing in the Bronze and the Early Iron Ages of Eastern Europe. He has led expeditions to the south of Ukraine and the Northern Caucasus (Adyghea) and has authored many publications, including 20 books, albums, and catalogues. Leskov is the recipient of several grants, including a Fulbright Foundation Visiting Professorship of Ukrainian Archaeology (2005–2007), and is a Research Associate in the Mediterranean Section of Penn Museum and in the Program for the Archaeology of Ukraine, University of Pennsylvania.

Objects from the Museum für Vor- and Frühgeschichte are reproduced courtesy of the Director, Prof. Wilfried Menghin. Objects from the Antikenabteilung are reproduced courtesy of Dr. Gertrud Platz, Stv. Direktorin, Antikensammlung. Objects from the Metropolitan Museum are reproduced courtesy of Dr. Joan Aruz, Dept. of Ancient Near Eastern Art, Metropolitan. Excerpts from inventory books in the major museums quoted by permission.

Photograph on title page: Mountain lake in Adyghea; photograph by Dmitriy Slesarenko.

Publication of this work has been supported by a grant from the Samuel H. Kress Foundation.

LIBRARY OF CONGRESS CATALOGING-IN-PUBLICATION DATA

Leskov, Aleksandr Mikhailovich.
  The Maikop treasure / A.M. Leskov. — 1st ed.
     p. cm.
  Includes bibliographical references and index.
  1. Caucasus–Antiquities–Catalogs. 2. Black Sea Region–Antiquities–Catalogs. 3. Maikop culture–Catalogs. I. University of Pennsylvania. Museum of Archaeology and Anthropology. II. Staatliche Museen Preussischer Kulturbesitz. Antikenabteilung III. Museum für Vor- und Frühgeschichte (Berlin, Germany) IV. Metropolitan Museum of Art (New York, N.Y.) V. Title.
  DK509.L47 2008
  939'.5–dc22

                        2007049229

ISBN 13: 978-1-934536-04-9 (hardcover : alk. paper)

Manufactured in China on acid-free paper.

Table of Contents

Preface vi

Introduction 1

CATALOGUE 10

    University of Pennsylvania Museum of Archaeology and

        Anthropology, Philadelphia 14

    Antikenabteilung, Staatliche Museen, Berlin 105

    Museum für Vor- und Frühgeschichte, Berlin 167

    Metropolitan Museum of Art, New York 224

The Maikop Collection: A Historical Overview 226

Abbreviations 268

Bibliography 269

Index 284

Preface

Archaeological data is the only source for studying the period of history prior to the invention of writing. Tools and weapons, articles of daily life and ornaments, ruins of ancient cities and settlements, burial constructions and sanctuaries, artifacts made of wood, clay, glass, bone, various metals and alloys—all have proven to be almost limitless sources for studying civilizations of the distant past.

Every country has monuments that serve as symbols of its ancient history and culture. Egypt has its pyramids, Greece the Acropolis in Athens; likewise, Russia and Ukraine possess their own great monuments. For example, monuments of antiquity of incredible wealth and variety were found in Adyghea, the smallest of the republics of the Caucasus, located on the steppes and foothills of the left shore of the Kuban River. Mild climate, fertile soil, numerous freshwater creeks that flow into the Kuban, the proximity of the Black Sea, and the low mountain crossings connecting the steppes of the Black Sea area with Transcaucasia and the earliest civilizations of the Near East and Asia Minor—these are the factors that contributed to the unique territorial proximity of the richest monuments of different eras, beginning from the 3rd millennium BC and extending to the 14th century AD.

- The rich Medieval tombs (about 20 burial mounds altogether) of the Eurasian steppes were located in the Cossack village of Belorechenskaya, 20 km northwest of Maikop, the capital of Adyghea. The graves of Adyg nobility revealed Chinese and Iranian textiles, Venetian glass, Genoan silver, Central Asian ceramics, and Near Eastern precious objects.

- The richest Roman and Syrian imports from the last centuries BC were found in the Zubovskiy, Peschannoe, Vozdvizhenskiy, and Severskiy barrows (kurgans) built for wealthy Sarmatians, located in a 40–60 km radius around Maikop.

- Famous Scythian-Maeotian barrows exist in a 30–40 km radius around Maikop: Kostromskoy and Kelermes (7th–6th century BC), Ul'skiy (6th–5th century BC), and the Uliap sanctuary and the Kurdzhips and Karagodeuashkh barrows (4th century BC). These have gained renown for containing unique works of art from the ancient Near East (Urartu, Assyria, Iran), from ancient Greece, as well as high-quality Scythian art in the animal style. Monuments from the Maikop area are vital for studying the history of the Scythians, the best-known ancient people from Eastern Europe, closely connected to the Near Eastern and Ancient Greek civilizations and to the local

Maeotians, the ancestors of contemporary Adygs.

- In 1897 the richest barrow in Europe (with the exception of Greece) from the end of the 4th to the beginning of the 3rd millennium BC was discovered in Maikop. The gold and silver ornaments and vessels found there had been imports from Mesopotamia. The culture that extended throughout the North Caucasus, from the Caspian to the Black Sea, was named the Maikop culture after the location of this barrow. The centuries-old contacts between the bearers of the Maikop culture and the nomadic tribes of the Eastern European steppes, where Balkan imports are known, made it possible for us to compare the two most-investigated chronological systems—the Near Eastern and the Balkan. Based on these comparisons, we are able to synchronize the principal archaeological cultures of the south of Eurasia from the 4th to the 3rd millennium BC with the antiquities of the Near East and of the Balkan Peninsula. The monuments of the Maikop culture played a vital role in helping resolve the problems of chronology essential to the study of the ancient history of the Eurasian steppes.

The above examples attest to the role that monuments from the Maikop region play in world archaeology. Not coincidentally, many well-known Russian archaeologists from the 19th century onward conducted excavations between the Maikop region and the Taman Peninsula, the shores of which were studded with ancient Bosporan cities and whose steppes were densely covered with barrows of varying age. These barrows would be studied for a long time to come.

Over the course of nine years of active field operations in this territory (between 1981 and 1989) I fell in love with this rich land and its remarkable monuments and was sad to leave it behind when I emigrated to the United States. Never did I think that I would encounter Maikop antiquities again. The USSR's Iron Curtain policy prevented its archaeologists from access to American archeological literature, especially the periodicals. Thus we never knew of the acquisitions of Scythian artifacts made by New York's Metropolitan Museum in 1922 and the University of Pennsylvania Museum of Archaeology and Anthropology in 1930. The only indication that archaeological collections in New York and Philadelphia contained some items from southern Russia was a brief note in the exhibition catalogue *From the Lands of the Scythians* (Piotrovsky 1975).

My first glimpse of Scythian-type items from Maikop and other regions from the south of Russia, mentioned by Rostovtseff in his *Scythia and the Bosporus* (1925), came from a catalogue of treasures from the Berlin Museum (Antikenabteilung) by Greifenhagen, *Schmuckarbeiten in Edelmetall* (1970, 1975). And although the author indicated that some of these items have analogues in Philadelphia and New York, no one at the time thought that they all had belonged to a single collection, yet another part of which was in a collection in Berlin, at the Vor- und Frühgeschichte Museum. I visited Berlin for the first time in 1989 and saw for myself these items from the southern regions of the Russian Empire which had entered the German museums at the beginning of the 20th century. In 1995, the Henkel Foundation awarded me a special grant to study the Berlin collections.

In 2000 I visited the University of Pennsylvania Museum of Archaeology and Anthropology for the first time, where I saw truly remarkable artifacts that were clearly from the south of Russia and Ukraine. I shared my first impressions with Professors Holly Pittman, Renata Holod, and Donald White, and it was in the course of that now-memorable conversation that we conceived the idea of publishing a catalogue of this collection. The artifacts had been brought to the United States in 1915 and been given the name the "Maikop Treasure," under which they were published three times (1917, 1919, 1930) as part of the collection of a famous 20th century dealer, Ercole Canessa. After Canessa died, the generosity of Mr. William Hinckle Smith allowed the items in question to enter the collections of the Penn Museum in 1930. That same year, H. E. Fernald published in the *University Museum Bulletin* a brief notice concerning the acquisition, accompanied by photographs of several items. Over the next 70 years images of a few individual items made their way into the literature, but overall the largest archaeological collection from Russia and Ukraine located in the United States remained unpublished. The enormous time span of the collection (4,500 years—3000 BC–14th century AD), as well as its origin in these southern zones, which for a long time had served as a bridge connecting ancient Eastern civilizations with both the nomadic and the agricultural cultures of Eurasia—played important roles in persuading the Penn Museum to provide support for the production of a catalogue of the Maikop Treasure.

A year and a half of research both on the artifacts and in the Archives of the Penn Museum and the Metropolitan Museum, supplemented by my familiarity with the specialized literature, led me to conclude that the materials in the American collections are closely related to those that ended up in the two museums in Berlin (the Antikenabteilung in 1913 and the Vor- und Frühgeschichte in 1907). Furthermore, I concluded that at one time all of these constituted one great collection in the possession of the French collector Merle de Massoneau. The similar nature of the artifacts in the four museums made it necessary to publish them as one collection.

Again, the University of Pennsylvania supported my endeavor, and I went to Berlin, where my German colleagues arranged for me to examine the collections in both museums. Thus I had the opportunity to work closely with the items, as well as with museum archives (including inventory books, letters, old photographs and negatives, and newer publications regarding these collections). Only then did the true span of the planned publication become apparent, not only chronologically but also geographically, with artifacts coming from different cultures originating in the steppes and foothills of the Northwestern Caucasus, the Crimea, and Ukraine steppe.

The absence of essential archaeological data greatly hampered work on this book: Where did these items originate—in remains of settlements or in barrows, on the seashores, in the steppe, in the foothills, or in the mountains? How could we date them? Who excavated them and when? The reader will find answers to some of these questions in the pages that follow.

Let me note that the overwhelming majority of the items published here come from the looting of various barrows in the steppes of the south of Russia and Ukraine. De Massoneau assembled his collection over the course of 20 years, starting in 1890 when he began working in Russia. Our knowledge of the history of 19th century excavations in these regions, as well as the unique form and decorative patterns of some of the items, make the pieces easily recognizable and indeed allow us to establish that items from a single archaeological complex would frequently be divided among museums and private collectors, including de Massoneau. Other items in his collection were acquired after having been stolen from excavation sites, for example, from the famous Semibratnie barrows in the Taman Peninsula or from the royal Scythian barrow Kul-Oba near the city of Kerch.

Using the tools of modern research, it is now possible to provide reliable dates for the artifacts from de Massoneau's collection, to determine their cultural origins, and to pinpoint the provenance of individual items to one of the local cultures. Such cultural and chronological attribution of the items in this enormous collection (about 2,000 items, more than 330 inventory numbers) allowed us not only to supplement the typological characteristics of already known local groups, and thus to deepen our knowledge about the cultures of the Early Iron Age, but also to evaluate the mutual relations and influences among carriers of various archaeological cultures. This work helped clarify both common patterns and unique features in the development of the tribes' material and spiritual cultures. Thus we could propose a possible reconstruction of two rich complexes, one from the Maikop region (5th century BC) and another from the steppes of the Black Sea area in Ukraine (4th century BC).

In discussing this manuscript with my colleagues, I wondered on numerous occasions how to name the future book—a difficulty compounded by the great variety of objects from the different regions of the Black Sea area contained in de Massoneau's collection. Of the many suggestions that arose, the title used earlier, the "Maikop Treasure," emerged—not just because 90 percent of the artifacts are made of gold, but because of the scientific significance of the material in question, which extends far beyond the borders of Russia, Ukraine, and the states of Transcaucasia. These artifacts connect the antiquities of the Black Sea area with the Near East, Asia Minor, and the Balkans, effectively linking the centers of the most advanced civilizations of Antiquity and the Middle Ages. These artifacts are thus not so much material treasures, which, alas, tend to sow discord; rather they are spiritual treasures, which have always facilitated people coming together. In this sense, the name "Maikop" symbolizes monuments in which the multitude of various imports unites tribes and peoples of different cultures and time periods. "The Maikop Treasure" is thus the most appropriate title for the monographic publication of the world's largest collection of East European antiquities outside of Russia.

* * *

Many people and institutions have made possible the production of this study of the Maikop treasure—a rich collection that helps us to reconstruct the fascinating story of the ancient peoples of the Caucasus and the Ukrainian steppe. Objects from the Maikop treasure are held in four museums: Penn Museum in Philadelphia, the Metropolitan Museum in New York, the Antikenabteilung, Staatliche Museen, and the Museum für Vor- und Frühgeschichte, both in Berlin. I thank in particular Prof. Wilfried Menghin, Director of the Vor- und Frühgeschichte, and Dr. Gertrud Platz-Horster, Director of the Antikensammlung, Staatliche Museen, for their invaluable assistance and for permission to publish their holdings in one volume. Photographs of material from the Antikensammlung were taken by Johannes Laurentius, Ingrid Geske, and Isolde Luckert, and those from Vor- und Frühgeschichte by Claudia Plamp. The landscape photographs are by Dmitriy Slesarenko and Alexey Gusev and were provided with the assistance of Olesya Prasolova, adviser to the Press Service of the President of the Republic of Adyghea.

My initial time at the University of Pennsylvania was funded by Penn's Center for Ancient Studies, where I discussed the potential archaeological importance of the Maikop material. The good efforts of Holly Pittman and Renata Holod, both in Penn's History of Art Department, and of Donald White, then Curator-in-Charge of the Mediterranean Section of Penn Museum, helped me to pursue this work. During 2002–2003 I held the Rodney Young post-doctoral fellowship in the Museum's Mediterranean Section, which enabled me to begin the study of the Maikop Treasure. A grant from the 1984 Foundation allowed me to continue my analysis in 2003–2004 and to write the manuscript in Russian. I was supported during the academic year 2004–2005 and partly in 2006–2007 thanks to the generosity of the Penn Program for the Archaeology of Ukraine (Renata Holod and Holly Pittman, co-directors) through a grant from the Ukrainian Studies Fund to gather the illustrations, complete the documentation, and supervise the translation by Lada Onyshkevych, Ludmila Avilova, and Ilya Leskov. Dmitriy Rusanoff did the reconstructions for catalogue numbers 51 and 99. Karen Sonik edited the English text, providing a consistent and clear translation. I thank them all for their careful attention.

Nicholas Efremov-Kendall checked the figure descriptions and Lynn Makowsky, Keeper of the Mediterranean Section, supervised additional photography, funding for which was arranged by C. Brian Rose, Curator-in-Charge of the Mediterranean Section. Francine Sarin and Jennifer Chiappardi of the Museum's Photo Studio took the new photographs. Museum Archivist Alex Pezzati was very helpful in supplying archival materials and photographs, and Anita Fahringer of the Museum's Library provided assistance with my research. Walda Metcalf, Assistant Director for Publications in the Penn Museum, oversaw the transformation of the text into an actual book. Jennifer Quick, Penn Museum's Senior Editor, did further editing and designed the final book.

To all of these people I offer my thanks and appreciation.

Spring 2008
Philadelphia

Introduction

To properly tell the story of the so-called Maikop treasure, one must begin with a few words about the wealthy French collector M. A. Merle de Massoneau. The story of his life is the story of the origins of that vast and hitherto little-studied collection.

The founder of the Bank of the Orient in Paris, de Massoneau served for many years as the director of the Russian royal vineyards in the Crimea and the Caucasus. His position, which reflected both his significant material wealth and his high social status, necessitated regular trips between Yalta, where he lived in the Crimea, and the Caucasus and ensured his access to the finest artifacts on the market.

During the nearly twenty years he lived in Russia, from about 1884 to 1904, de Massoneau amassed a truly enormous, unique collection comprising a vast range of artifacts from sites in the south of the Russian Empire and the Crimea. Damm (1988:67) notes that important medieval materials were added from the tomb opened in Kerch on May 4, 1904. In 1907, the German scholar Robert Zahn wrote to inform the Berlin Antikenabteilung about de Massoneau's collection: "The collection contains various Greek and Roman antiquities, typical for the south of Russia. Furthermore, it seems to me that the wares made during the time of the great migrations (golden decorations, etc.) are very good, the Islamic ancient objects as well as the medieval objects from Circassian tombs (a large collection of weapons) are all very rich" (Vor- und Frühgeschichte Museum, Archives, case 1128.07).

The collection is currently divided among four known museums: the Classics (Antikenabteilung) and Prehistory departments (Museum für Vor- und Frühgeschichte) of the Staatliche Museen zu Berlin (hereafter the Berlin Museum); the Metropolitan Museum of Art in New York (hereafter the Metropolitan Museum); the University of Pennsylvania Museum of Archaeology and Anthropology (hereafter the Penn Museum); and the Römisch-Germanisches Museum in Cologne (hereafter the Cologne Museum). The artifacts of the latter are not published in this work, as relatively few items date to the pre-Scythian era. This last detail is not surprising given that the primary sites of excavation in Russia and southern Ukraine during the time de Massoneau was accumulating his collection were ancient Greek cities and kurgans.

The late 18th and the 19th century saw the uncovering of Olbia, located in the mouth of the southern Bug River; Chersonesus, on the southern tip of the Crimea; Panticapaeum, on the eastern side of the Crimean Peninsula; and Phanagoria, a town on the Taman Peninsula. At about the same time, extensive explorations were being conducted in the kurgans of southern Russia, with their rich artifacts dating to the Scythian period. These kurgans were located primarily in the Crimea, in the nearby steppes of the lower Dniepr River's left bank, and in the Northwestern Caucasus from Taman to Maikop, the capital of the Adyghea Republic. Further contributing to the profusion of ancient artifacts on the market were the contents of several extremely wealthy kurgans, including the Major Bliznitsa, Seven Brothers, and Karagodeuashkh in the northwest Caucasus, and the Nymphaion kurgans in the eastern Crimea, the excavations of which were just concluding when de Massoneau arrived in Russia.

The duration of de Massoneau's stay in Yalta was similarly fruitful, coinciding with the exploration of the most famous Scythian kurgans in the Crimea, including Golden, Talaevskyi, Dert-Oba, and Kulakovskyi (1890-95). Meanwhile, the Deev and Oguz kurgans, a little to the north in the steppes of modern Cherson, and the Shulgovka and Ushakovskie kurgans farther to the east, near the Sea of Azov and the lower Don River region, were being discovered. The richest finds of the time were made in the Maikop area.

Foremost among these finds was the Maikop kurgan itself, the most magnificent 3rd millennium BC burial ever seen outside of Greece; Ulskiy kurgan No. 1, at 15 m high the tallest in the area south of the Kuban River and containing the skeletons of 360 horses in its central part alone; and the rich kurgans of Kelermes, Kostromskoy, and Kurdzhips, with one sensational discovery following closely after another. The names of the excavators—A. E. Lutsenko, I. E. Zabelin, V. G. Tizengauzen, and N. I. Veselovsky, among others—were widely known throughout Russia and Western Europe. Thousands of gold and silver decorations, vessels, weapons, and horse trappings recovered from the south of Russia, among which were masterpieces of ancient Asian and ancient Greek art, contributed to a veritable archaeological boom. Newspapers and journals regularly reported more and more sensational discoveries, and collecting antiquities became a fashionable and prestigious activity.

Unfortunately, this "gold fever" led to an increase in grave robbing and to the appearance of a large number of artifacts on the black market. Private collectors found unlimited possibilities, and men such as Merle de Massoneau took full advantage.

In 1907, prompted by the unstable political situation in Russia after the 1905 revolution, de Massoneau divided his collection in preparation for selling it. The first portion, some 1,800-plus artifacts with a price tag of 95,000 DM (deutsche marks), was allocated to three sections of the Berlin Museum: Prehistory, contributing 45,000 DM, 42,500 DM of which came from Mr. von Diergardt (Damm 1988:65-66); Near-Asian, contributing 25,000 DM; and Classics, also contributing 25,000 DM. Given the state of the records, determining exactly how many items went to each department is problematic; what is known is that the Prehistory section took 956 items, while the Classics department acquired over 250 gold objects, in addition to two collections of ceramics, antique vases, and lamps (Greifenhagen 1970:figs. 18-28, 41). Artifacts from the pre-Scythian era represented only a small fraction of de Massoneau's total collection. Some 673 of the items acquired by the Prehistory department in 1907 were sold, in accordance with the will of von Diergardt, to Cologne's Römisch-Germanisches Museum in 1935-36; at least 200 of these date to the time of the great migrations of the 4th to 6th century AD and, though they are beyond the scope of the present volume, were the theme of a special publication (Damm 1988:65–210).

While the lot sold to the Berlin Museum in 1907 represented a significant part of his collection, de Massoneau himself retained a considerable number of artifacts. The story of how these found their way to the museum collections where they are now permanently housed, though it took another 23 years to unfold, is one well worth tracing as it allows us to reconstruct the bulk of de Massoneau's original collection.

The next major sale of artifacts de Massoneau had collected occurred in 1913, when Karapet, an Armenian merchant, offered up a collection of antiquities for purchase in Berlin. Ostensibly derived from the Chmyrev kurgan in the steppe on the left bank of the Dniepr River, this collection was carefully dissociated from the name of de Massoneau, who had supposedly already sold his collection, at considerable profit, to the Berlin Museum. The strategy proved successful: the Chmyrev kurgan was located far enough away from the Crimea and the Northwestern Caucasus, from which at least 90 percent of de Massoneau's artifacts were derived, that his connection with Karapet and this new lot of artifacts was not suspected. The Berlin Museum once again appeared on the scene, with the Classics section purchasing half the items available, thus becoming the largest repository of antique jewelry from southern Russia after the Hermitage in St. Petersburg (Greifenhagen 1970).

The second half of the collection offered by Karapet was acquired by Ercole Canessa, the most famous antique dealer of his time (Colosanti 1915). It is not known whether he undertook this purchase in Berlin or in Paris, where one of his galleries was located and where de Massoneau now lived. What is certain is that in 1914, with the outbreak of World War I, Canessa wisely moved his collections, including those objects purchased from Karapet, from Paris to Italy. Soon thereafter, the Italian government decided to allocate a special exhibition area for Canessa's collections in the Italian pavilion of the Panama-Pacific International Exposition in San Francisco (1915), and his artifacts traveled by sea from Genoa to America.

Before continuing the story of the Canessa collection upon its arrival in the United States, it is worth briefly noting the fate of those artifacts that remained in de Massoneau's possession.

In 1922, another significant part of his collection was put on the market. Published in a Paris catalogue as objects from the Cimmerian Bosporus (*Catalogue des Antiquités Greques, Romaines et Barbares* 1922), the collection was exhibited in 117 lots of gold, silver, bronze, ceramic, marble, and ivory objects originating in the eastern Crimea, the Taman Peninsula, and neighboring Kuban regions. How many of these items were actually sold is not recorded, but we are sure that de Massoneau retained some part of his original vast collection. On August 11, 1924, John Marshall, an agent of the Metropolitan Museum's department of Greek and Roman art, bought 32 gold plaques from de Massoneau's remaining collection (Marshall letter #58, Metropolitan Museum Archives). These plaques, which were not published in the 1922 Paris catalogue, were of six distinct types. The identification of these types and the discovery of comparable plaques in the other museums that purchased items from de Massoneau have proved vital to reconstructing the original collection.

The 1924 transaction with John Marshall was the last recorded direct sale of artifacts involving de Massoneau himself, so we shall trace the process by which those artifacts then in Canessa's possession reached the Penn Museum in 1930.

Canessa displayed his collection, especially the artifacts from de Massoneau, brilliantly at the 1915 San Francisco Exposition. The Scythian artifacts, shown in the U.S. for the first time, were published as "Treasures Found in a Scythian Tomb—Caucasus Region—Greek Work (6th century BC)" in the catalogue of Canessa's collection (Colosanti 1915). The catalogue entry briefly listed the items exhibited, identifying all of them in lot #2, with the exception of a silver cup said to belong to the "period of the Sacae" as Scythian.

After the close of the San Francisco exhibit, Canessa wrote to the Penn Museum in Philadelphia about the possibility of buying a number of items from him, as well as about some photographs he had sent to the Museum. Canessa first mentions certain Scythian objects offered to the Museum along with Greek and Roman antiquities in his letter of June 26, 1916, to Stephen B. Luce, then curator of the Mediterranean Section of the Museum. It seems that the Museum was not then able to purchase the artifacts, so in a letter dated July 10, 1916, Canessa asked Luce to return the photographs of the Scythian artifacts. Canessa then wrote on July 12 to say that he had received the photographs.

In 1917, Canessa again displayed his Scythian artifacts, this time in his New York gallery, characterizing them in *A Catalogue of Minor Art* (Canessa and Canessa 1917), lot #1, as treasures from a 6th century Scythian tomb. As described in the "Greek and Roman Goldsmith Work" section of the catalogue, this lot was identical to that published in the 1915 San Francisco catalogue. Once again, however, it failed to sell.

In 1919, E. Govett published the largest catalogue of the Canessa collection. The section on "Greek and Roman Gold and Silver Objects" opened with lot #78, which introduced the materials of interest to us as treasures from the Kuban in the Caucasus (southern Russia). The lists of items were divided into three sections—gold and silver wares, bronze objects, and objects of miscellaneous media (such as clay, stone, and glass)—again identical to those given in the 1915 and 1917 catalogues. While the entire lot (except the "Sacae" silver cup mentioned above) was still dated to the 6th century BC, the objects were no longer all purported to have come from a single complex (Govett 1919).

Canessa died in 1929, and a year later, in the last week of March 1930, the American Art Association and Andersen Galleries organized a sale of his collection in New York. In the catalogue released for the sale (Schumm 1930), under #120, a group of 6th century BC artifacts were identified as the "Maikop treasure." The introduction to the incomplete list of items (given alphabetically from A to P) states that they were discovered in 1912 in the Kuban in the Caucasus. In the catalogue's Foreword, which emphasized the most notable objects, the Maikop treasure (#120) is identified as coming from "the excavation of Scythia in 1912." The previously mentioned silver cup (listed in this catalogue under "O") was described as Sassanian. Given that Minns's *Scythians and Greeks* had been published in 1913, adding to the already extensive body of Russian and German scholarship

William Hinckle Smith (from *National Cyclopaedia of American Biography* [New York: James T. White & Company, 1944], Vol. 31, p. 496).

on Scythian artifacts, the meager and vague information offered in the 1930 (Schumm) and earlier catalogues (Colosanti 1915; Canessa and Canessa 1917; Govett 1919) is remarkable.

It is not surprising, then, that when the Penn Museum in Philadelphia was considering the acquisition of the so-called Maikop treasure, it engaged Yale professor M. I. Rostovtzeff, a specialist in the history, art, and archaeology of 1st millennium BC eastern Europe, to evaluate the collection. Rostovtzeff, who was by now at the top of the field of Scytho-Sarmatian archaeology, had published several important monographs, including *Antichnaya decorativnaya zhivopis' na Yuge Rossii* (1914); *Ellinstvo i Iranstvo na Yuge Rossii* (1918); *Skifia i Bospor* (1925); and *The Animal Style in South Russia and China* (1929), which remain pertinent even today. His examination of the objects led him to take two important steps: first, he repudiated the connection that had been suggested between the Scythian materials offered for sale and the Chmyrev kurgan and instead defined a Kuban origin for those objects manufactured in the Scythian Animal Style; and second, after personally examining the artifacts with Helen Fernald, a colleague from the Penn Museum, he recommended that the Museum purchase the "Maikop treasure." His memorandum on the value of the planned acquisition was sent to the Museum between March 25 and 28, 1930; the auction was scheduled for March 29 and Andersen Galleries was threatening to sell the collection piece by piece. With Rostovtzeff's evaluation and the generosity of William Hinckle Smith, a well-known businessman and Museum benefactor who, despite the economic crisis of the Great Depression, provided the funds for the purchase, the fate of this outstanding collection of Black Sea antiquities was settled.

With the exception of the Berlin Museum's sale of artifacts to Cologne in 1935–36, the final significant part of de Massoneau's collection thus found its permanent home in 1930. While we cannot be certain of the exact method he used to divide his collection, it is clear that, being a successful businessman, de Massoneau to some extent targeted specific buyers with shrewdly chosen artifacts. In the original 1907 sale to the Berlin Museum, for example, the Classics department gained a number of items from ancient towns in the northern Black Sea area and their necropoleis (Greifenhagen 1970:41–53), while the Prehistory department was similarly targeted with treasures from the time of the great migrations.

If tracing the division and sale of the original de Massoneau collection has been an arduous process, the attempt to prove the unity of a collection divided among four departments at three museums has proven even more so.

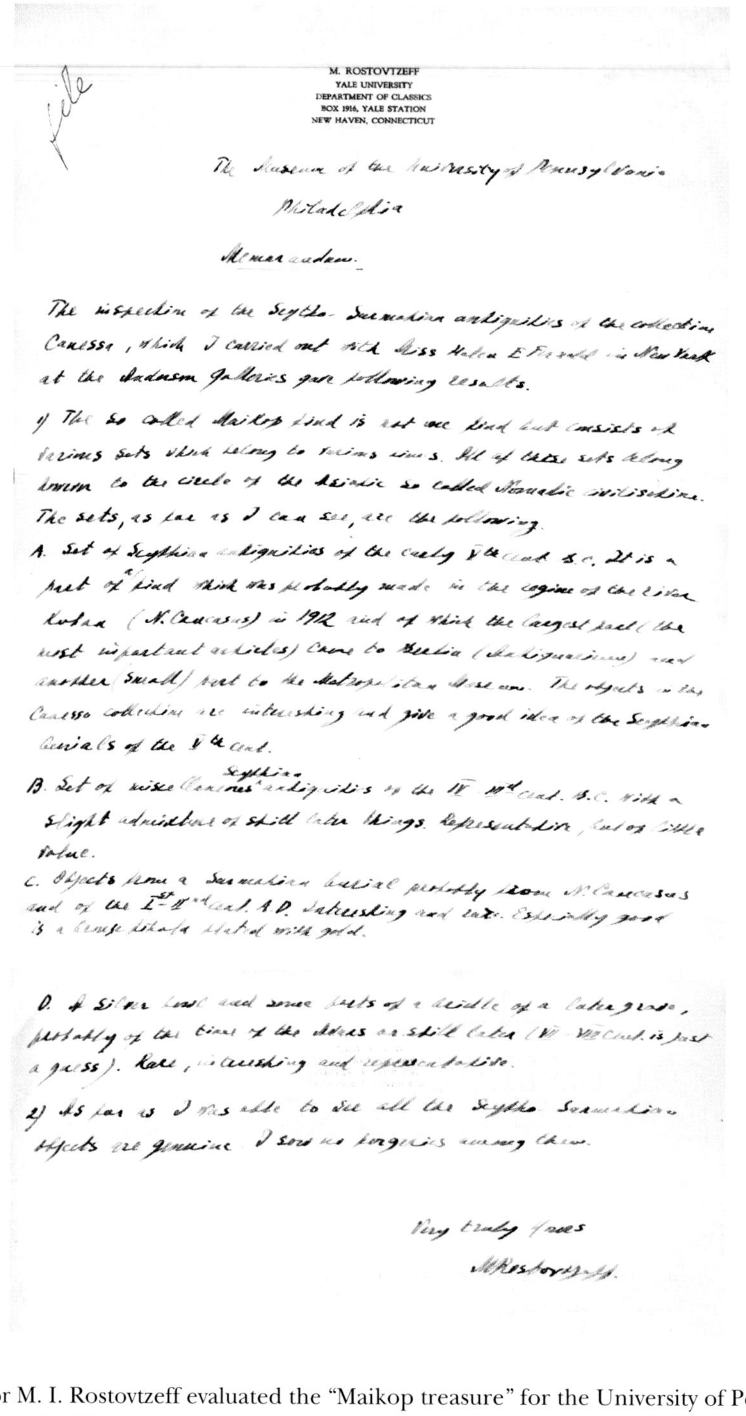

M. ROSTOVTZEFF
YALE UNIVERSITY
DEPARTMENT OF CLASSICS
BOX 1916, YALE STATION
NEW HAVEN, CONNECTICUT

File

The Museum of the University of Pennsylvania
Philadelphia

Memorandum.

The inspection of the Scytho-Sarmatian antiquities of the collection Canessa, which I carried out with Miss Helen E Fernald in New York at the Anderson Galleries gave following results.

1) The so called Maikop find is not one find but consists of various sets which belong to various times. All of these sets belong however to the circle of the Asiatic so called Nomadic civilisation. The sets, as far as I can see, are the following.

A. Set of Scythian antiquities of the early Vth cent. B.C. It is a part of a find which was probably made in the region of the river Kuban (N. Caucasus) in 1912 and of which the largest part (the most important articles) came to Berlin (Antiquarium) and another (small) part to the Metropolitan Museum. The objects in the Canesso collection are interesting and give a good idea of the Scythian burials of the Vth cent.

B. Set of miscellaneous Scythian antiquities of the IV–IIIrd cent. B.C. with a slight admixture of still later things. Representative, but of little value.

C. Objects from a Sarmatian burial probably from N. Caucasus and of the Ist–IInd cent. A.D. Interesting and rare. Especially good is a bronze situla plated with gold.

D. A silver bowl and some parts of a bridle of a later grave, probably of the time of the Avars or still later (VII–VIII cent. is just a guess). Rare, interesting and representative.

2) As far as I was able to see all the Scytho-Sarmatian objects are genuine. I saw no forgeries among them.

Very truly yours
M Rostovtzeff.

Yale professor M. I. Rostovtzeff evaluated the "Maikop treasure" for the University of Pennsylvania Museum in March 1930 and sent this memorandum recommending purchase of the collection. (Director's Office, Horace H. F. Jayne, University of Pennsylvania Museum Archives)

As early as 1925, when the Metropolitan Museum published the 32 gold plaques it had acquired from de Massoneau a year earlier (Alexander 1925), Dr. Zahn recognized that there were identical objects in the portion of the Berlin Museum's Classics collection purchased from Karapet in 1913. Of the six different types represented by the Metropolitan Museum plaques, four types had no fewer than 282 direct analogues to plaques held in the Classics section. Some time later it became apparent that these same four types of gold plaque were also represented in 38 of the several hundred items in the Maikop treasure acquired by the Penn Museum. The collection of the Berlin Museum's Classics department and that of the Penn Museum also share more than ten other types of golden wares.

A fraction of the at least 50 items dating to pre-Scythian, Scythian, and Sarmatian periods obtained by the Berlin Museum's Prehistory section were also being published, making them available to scholars worldwide for study and comparison. Sixteen such objects, comprising bronze details of horse trappings fashioned in the Scythian Animal Style, were published by Schmidt in 1927. Two objects published here do not belong to de Massoneau's collection, namely a plaque in the shape of a stag (Inv. No. 7036) from the Mavrogordato collection, and a part of some bimetallic (bronze-iron) object in the shape of a horse leg (Inv. No. 5826) from the Virkhov collection. Six of these 16 objects were published again by Potratz in 1960 (50:figs. X, XI) and 1963 (80:drawing 59). An additional example was published by Minns in 1942 (pl. III). To my knowledge, the rest of the items were never published; some of these disappeared during World War II and are now known only from the surviving old negatives and drawings in the Museum inventory (IIId 7016–7034).

In 1931, the similarity of a significant number of items belonging to the three different collections attracted Rostovtzeff's attention. He first suggested that the collections were all originally derived from a single "very rich discovery, made [he believed] in 1912 in the Kuban region, probably in the Maikop area, and subsequently sold to three (or more?) parties" (1931c:368), namely, the Staatliche Museen zu Berlin, the Metropolitan Museum of Art, and the University of Pennsylvania Museum of Archaeology and Anthropology. As support for the unity of these collections, Rostovtzeff noted especially the bronze details of a set of horse trappings in Berlin, which were instrumental in defining the Kuban origins of the items in this collection; on the basis of a black-figure skyphos in the Penn Museum, he indeed went so far as to assign a *terminus ante quem* of the first half of the 5th century BC to the Scythian items. In the course of my own close examination, it has become clear not only that the Philadelphia and Berlin collections contain many similar objects, but that the two collections contain items that in fact originate from a single complex.

In 1932, Rostovtzeff had the opportunity to stop for a day in Philadelphia to work with the Maikop treasure in more detail than had previously been possible. He summarized the results of this work in an undated letter, now in the Museum's Archives, sent to the Museum in the first week of February 1932. Rostovtzeff concluded that a number of bronze wares undoubtedly originating in the Kuban corresponded to the Scythian gold artifacts of the 6th and 5th century BC; at the same time he set apart a number of other items that were later attributed to the Bronze Age or pre-Scythian period. In comparing the Scythian gold objects with one another, Rostovtzeff further noted that some more closely paralleled objects from the Crimea and sites on the banks of the Dniepr River. While not excluding the possibility that these also originated in the Kuban, the differences in the color of the gold, technique of manufacture, and thickness of the plaques suggested that these items constituted their own group.

Rostovtzeff studied one final, relatively small group of Sarmatian objects, focusing especially on the strings of beads belonging to that and to earlier periods. Noting the presence among the beads of some Egyptian scarabs and figures of recumbent lions, he advised consultation with Egyptologists. Rostovtzeff had little experience with medieval objects and did not analyze them.

In conclusion, Rostovtzeff expressed his readiness to publish the Scythian and Sarmatian objects if the relevant photographs were sent to him. We do not know if he received the photographs he requested or if he wrote the article, which seems not to have been published.

In 1970 Greifenhagen published the first of a two-volume catalogue of gold and silver decorations from the Berlin Museum's Classics department. Of relevance here are materials bought from de Massoneau in 1907 (1970:figs. 18–28) and materials from Maikop bought in 1913 (figs. 29–38). The artifacts of the first volume, numbering more than 250, are typical of Greek towns in the northern Black Sea area and their necropoleis. Most of these objects also appear in local settlements of the Scytho-Sarmatian period. Only a few (about 10 types to be considered below) are characteristic not of Greek but rather of Scythian, Maeotian, or Sarmatian sites from the south of Russia.

In the second volume, Greifenhagen published 45 additional artifacts, mostly bronze with a few silver and iron, from the collection acquired by the Berlin Museum in 1913; 13 of these artifacts belong to the pre- and post-Scythian periods (1975:56, figs. 25–28, 31–34, 39–43).

Over the course of my work on the Maikop collection in the Berlin Museum's Classics collection, I discovered that significantly more items had been acquired from Karapet in 1913 than had been published by Greifenhagen. A number of these items had disappeared from the museum during World War II. Fortunately, brief information on them had been retained in the museum's inventory. According to this document, about 40 additional unpublished exhibits (comprising more individual objects) had been purchased; these were primarily of bronze, though some were also worked in stone, bone, glass, clay, silver, and gold. Most of the gold items were ornamental details, some manufactured in the pre-Scythian period and some worked in the Scythian Animal Style.

This unpublished material supports Rostovtzeff's observations regarding the unity of the collections in Philadelphia, New York, and the Classics department in Berlin, to which we may add the artifacts from the Berlin Museum's Prehistory department, especially the Scythian horse trappings. Apart from the four types of golden plaques on which Rostovtzeff's argument depended, we thus now possess a much larger corpus of material from the Scythian period, as well as from the pre-Scythian, Sarmatian, and medieval eras.

Over a hundred years ago, Merle de Massoneau began amassing the enormous collection that found the last of its permanent owners only in the 1930s. Museums in Berlin, New York, and Philadelphia, as well as Cologne, became owners of the largest collection of antiquities from Eastern Europe outside of Russia.

Today many revolutions have died down, two world wars have passed, the Soviet Union has come and gone, a Russia free of communism has returned to the world community, and Germany has been reunited after forty years and has entered the European community. Unfortunately, those objects created in antiquity and preserved for posterity in museums have not been spared the storms of history: many of the rich finds from the royal Scythian kurgans (Aleksandropol, First Mordvinovskyi, and Chmyrev) held in the Kharkov Museum of History, for example, disappeared during World War II, while a number of artifacts held in the museums of Ukraine and Germany were damaged by fire during the same war. On my first visit to the Prehistory section of the Berlin museum in 1989, I was extremely happy to discover a number of Bronze Age objects that had been held by the Cherson Museum of Local History prior to World War II; with the kind collaboration of the scholars from Berlin, these objects, bought from a private party, were returned to the Cherson Museum in the early 1990s.

The Berlin holdings of the Maikop collection were similarly affected: some objects were damaged by fire, others were broken, and still others disappeared altogether. Happily, both the Classics and Prehistory departments retained well-organized inventory books, compiled in 1907 and 1913, listing the damaged or missing objects' inventory numbers, brief descriptions with dimensions, and sketches, the quality of which is apparent upon comparison with those artifacts that survived. These inventory books thus offer not only valuable information on the lost objects but also guidance on their possible recovery. It is my hope that this volume, which publishes those lost items noted in the inventory books using archival information, existing photographs, negatives, and inventory sketches, will both restore a missing section of the archaeological record and ultimately lead to the recovery of those artifacts that have disappeared. The return of stolen art is an important moral and ethical problem of the modern day and one that must be fully addressed by organizations such as UNESCO, as well as by the scientific and cultural communities of the world.

I am an optimist, and I have some reasons for being one. There was little expectation after the World War II that the world would ever see again, for example, the treasures brought by Schliemann from legendary Troy. Through the efforts of the world community, this seemingly impossible task has been accomplished. I am convinced that the return of the Trojan treasure to its rightful owner, the Berlin museum, is a matter of time, and I hope it will happen soon. Similarly, I believe a day will come when we will rediscover those items that disappeared from de Massoneau's collection. It is on this positive note that I end this introduction to the world's largest collection of antiquities from the northern Black Sea region outside of Russia, a collection currently almost unknown to specialists in Russia, Ukraine, and Georgia, with the hope that it will serve as the starting point for a thoughtful analysis of this extraordinary collection of objects, appropriately termed the "Maikop treasure."

Catalogue

Of the three major parts of the Maikop collection, the Penn Museum holds the largest number of artifacts, with the greatest chronological range: from the 3rd millennium BC to the 14th century AD, from the Eneolithic and the Early Bronze Age to the Late Medieval period. This collection occupies a primary position in this catalogue and is described first, followed by items from the Antikenabteilung. Since some of the types of items in that collection are also present in Philadelphia, I have not repeated their descriptions but merely listed them. These lists do not take into account the dates of the items but follow the descriptions of all of the preserved items (after No. 55) and precede the items which disappeared during World War II. The Antikenabteilung items are better published than the other two parts, from the Berlin Museum für Vor- und Frühgeschichte and from the Penn Museum, due to the efforts of Greifenhagen in his two-volume Antikenabteilung catalogue, *Schmuckarbeiten in Edelmetall* (1970, 1975), in which he also included very short notes on some bronze and iron items.

A small number of finds were published from the other Berlin part (Schmidt 1927:pl. 9; Potratz 1960:pl. X, fig. 26, XI, figs. 28–31) and from the Philadelphia part (Colosanti 1915:2; Fernald 1930; Piotrovsky 1975:159–60). We are able to include illustrations of items which disappeared during the Second World War, thanks to quality drawings in the inventory books which were preserved at the Berlin museum from the beginning of the 20th century. Unfortunately, the 1907 inventory book of the Berlin Museum für Vor- und Frühgeschichte includes only drawings with no descriptions and only occasional dimensions (length or height). Potratz published some of the items from that collection without a scale, and Schmidt indicated only an approximate scale.

The Antikenabteilung's inventory book from 1913 was compiled notably better, with a good drawing of every item and a summary description, even if a very short one, and an indication of the item's dimensions. This work by the distinguished Keeper of the collection, Dr. R. Zahn, helped me considerably. Zahn began to describe the collection in 1913, immediately after it was accessioned by the museum, returning to that effort over the years. Notes in the inventory book about analogous items such as several gold plaques in the Metropolitan Museum of Art (accessioned in 1922) and in the Penn Museum (accessioned in 1930) could not have been made before 1930; thus, questions connected with the material of the Maikop collection continued to interest Zahn over the course of seventeen years.

The catalogue ends with a description of Maikop items in the Metropolitan Museum of Art, where a total of 32 gold plaques, of six different types, is preserved (Alexander 1925:180, fig. 7; Piotrovsky 1975:160, 15). But four of these plaque types from New York (totaling 30 plaques) are also represented in Philadelphia (cf. Nos. 62, 63, 65, 66) and are described in the Penn Museum chapter with an indication that analogous items exist in New York and in Berlin.

Several principles governed the preparation of this catalogue. Each part of the collection follows a chronological progression in the description of the material, regardless of the sequence of inventory numbers assigned to given items by a particular museum. Considering the distinctive character of the material in the two larger parts of the collection (in the Penn Museum and in the Antikenabteilung), the items made of bronze are listed first, followed by the gold, since horse trappings are in bronze while ornaments are largely represented by gold. These descriptions remain within the confines of a specific chronological period, the 5th–4th century BC, to which the bulk of the material belongs. The earlier material (Bronze Age, pre-Scythian period), as well as the later (Sarmatian period, Medieval period), is described in chronological order regardless of the item's material. Items not assigned a date are described last.

* * *

Neither of the two parts of the Maikop collection in Berlin is preserved in full, so in presenting the corresponding items in a collection, I describe the preserved items chronologically, followed by the items which have not survived.

Naming specific items was a challenge, as a name should reflect the essence of a given artifact. After assigning short descriptive names that reflect an item's particular feature, such as "shafted axe" or "socketed arrowhead," I include a detailed description. Descriptions of weapons or tools, however, are not sufficient for complex, simple, or primitive ornaments. While we can characterize the form and distinctive features of a given item (in contrast to a "flat axe" or a "shafted arrowhead"), it is difficult to convey in one or two words diadems, various pendants, earrings, and plaques that are present in the Maikop collection significantly more often than weapons and tools taken together. Maintaining consistency is particularly important in dealing with items of various functions and forms, made of various materials, and belonging to different historical periods separated by millennia. Thus I provide each item with a general name, often a one-word definition, then describe that item in detail.

Since many items were lost and their descriptions in the inventory books often have only one quantitative characteristic (length or height), I decided to provide only one dimension. It should not be difficult to imagine the item in its actual dimensions since the the length or the height is given.

Finally, both Berlin museum parts include separate items which are indisputably connected with de Massoneau's Maikop collection with regard to typology, culture, and chronology. They come from a few small collections (Count Keglevich, 2 items; Secret Adviser Von

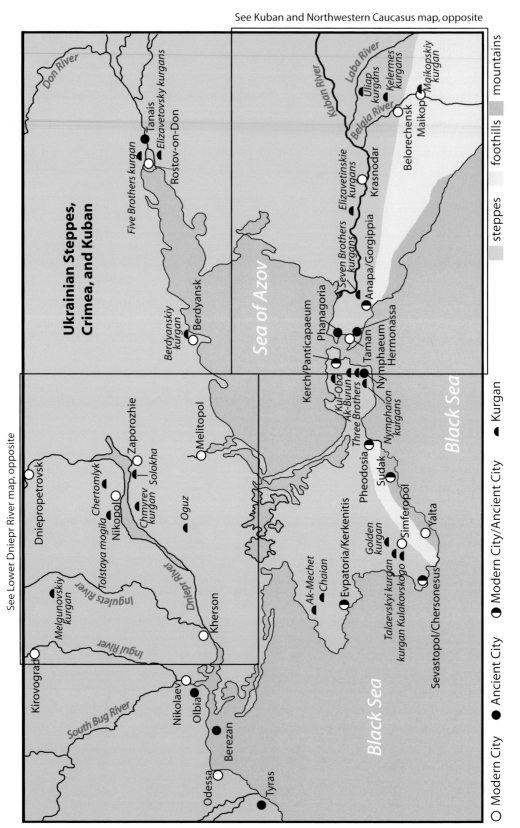

The famous barrows (kurgans) in the south of Ukraine and Russia.

Ukrainian Steppes, Crimea, and Kuban

See Kuban and Northwestern Caucasus map, opposite

See Lower Dniepr River map, opposite

Don River

Tanais
Elizavetovskiy kurgans
Five Brothers kurgan
Rostov-on-Don

Kuban River
Laba River
Uliap kurgdns
Belaia River
Kelermes kurgans
Mqikopskiy kurgan
Belorechensk
Maikop

Elizavetinskie kurgans
Seven Brothers kurgans
Krasnodar
Anapa/Gorgippia

Berdyanskiy kurgan
Berdyansk

Sea of Azov

Phanagoria
Kerch/Panticapaeum
Taman
Hermonassa
Nymphaeum

Zaporozhie
Chertomlyk
Solokha
Nikopol
Chmyrev kurgan
Oguz
Tolstaya mogila
Dnipropetrovsk

Melitopol

Kul-Oba
Ak-Burun
Three Brothers
Nymphaion kurgans

Pheodosia
Sudak

Black Sea

Ingulets River
Melgunovskiy kurgan
Ingul River
Dniepr River
Kherson

Kirovograd

South Bug River
Nikolaev
Olbia
Berezan

Odessa
Tyras

Ak-Mechet
Chaian
Evpatoria/Kerkenitis
Golden kurgan
Simferopol
Talaevskyi kurgan Kulakovskogo kurgan
Yalta
Sevastopol/Chersonesus

Black Sea

○ Modern City   ● Ancient City   ◑ Modern City/Ancient City   ◣ Kurgan

steppes   foothills   mountains

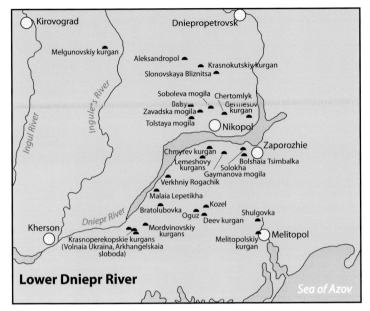

Lower Dniepr River

Kirovograd
Dniepropetrovsk
Melgunovskiy kurgan
Aleksandropol
Krasnokutskiy kurgan
Slonovskaya Bliznitsa
Soboleva mogila Chertomlyk
Baby Gerhesov
Zavadska mogila kurgan
Tolstaya mogila
Nikopol
Zaporozhie
Chmyrev kurgan
Lemeshovy Bolshaia Tsimbalka
kurgans Solokha
Gaymanova mogila
Verkhniy Rogachik
Malaia Lepetikha
Bratolubovka Kozel
Oguz Deev kurgan Shulgovka
Kherson
Mordvinovskiy
kurgans
Krasnoperekopskie kurgans Melitopolskiy Melitopol
(Volnaia Ukraina, Arkhangelskaia kurgan
sloboda)
Sea of Azov

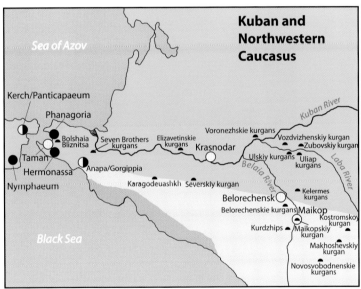

Kuban and Northwestern Caucasus

Sea of Azov
Kuban River
Kerch/Panticapaeum
Phanagoria
Voronezhskie kurgans
Vozdvizhenskiy kurgan
Bolshaia Seven Brothers Elizavetinskie Zubovskiy kurgan
Bliznitsa kurgans kurgans Krasnodar
Taman Ulskiy kurgans Uliap
Hermonassa Anapa/Gorgippia kurgans
Nymphaeum
Karagodeuashkh Severskiy kurgan Kelermes
kurgans
Belorechensk
Belorechenskie kurgans Maikop
Kostromskoy
kurgan
Kurdzhips Maikopskiy
kurgan
Black Sea
Makhoshevskiy
kurgan
Novosvobodnenskie
kurgans
Belaia River
Laba River

Graefe, 1 item) accessioned by the Berlin museums at the turn of the 20th century. In 1914, for example, the Antikenabteilung accessioned a bronze mirror of the "Olbian type" (No. 139), purchased from an unnamed Armenian dealer. De Massoneau's collection at the Antikenabteilung includes one complete, analogous mirror (No. 138), as well as a fragment of a handle of another mirror (No. 137), in the form of what may be a panther figure. The Berlin Museum für Vor- und Frühgeschichte includes 7 items from Mavrogordato's collection, 1 cheekpiece from Karu's collection, and 1 vessel from Kossnierska's collection. I have included these 12 items from the two museums in this catalogue because their unity with de Massoneau's collection seems beyond doubt. Finally, I included one more bronze cheekpiece from Karu's collection (No. 263) as a direct analogue for a Penn Museum cheekpiece (No. 38).

CAT. NOS. 1 (2nd from left), 2 (2nd from right), 3 (right), 4 (left)

University of Pennsylvania
Museum of Archaeology and Anthropology,
Philadelphia

1. Knife
    Inv. No. 30-33-95
    Bronze, cast, forged. L. 5.6 cm
    3rd millennium BC

This knife has a flat, double-edged, triangular blade with a pointed haft; both the cutting edges and point are worn and the missing edge at the base of one side of the blade gives it its current asymmetric appearance. Such knives were common in the Volga/Black Sea littoral steppes and the foothills of the Northern Caucasus from the 3rd to the early 2nd millennium BC. Though the simplicity of their form precludes an exact determination of their date (Markovin 1960:92, figs. 42:1–4) or a secure connection to a specific archaeological culture, the fact that the Maikop collection comprises mainly items from the Northern Caucasus and southern Ukraine suggests a connection to the Pit Grave (Iamnaia) or Maikop culture of the 3rd millennium BC.

2. Knife
    Inv. No. 30-33-93
    Bronze, cast, forged. L. 12 cm
    3rd millennium BC

This knife has a double-edged, leaf-shaped blade with a clear transition to its narrow haft; two ribs run from the tip to the base of the blade, articulating its raised central part. Such knives were typical of the Maikop culture (Munchaev 1975:401, fig. 56) in the last phase of its development, dating, according to current chronologies, to the third quarter of the 3rd millennium BC (Kushnareva and Markovin 1994:168–70).

3.   Knife-Dagger
      Inv. No. 30-33-94
      Bronze, cast, forged. L. 15.7 cm
      3rd millennium BC

This double-edged, elongated triangular blade has a clear transition to its short, broad haft; two ribs run from the tip to the base of the blade, articulating its raised central part.

Similar knives, running 17 cm or more in length, are generally categorized as "knife-daggers"; they are typical of the Maikop culture (Kushnareva and Markovin 1994:203ff) and are known from the Late Maikop period dolmens of the village of Novosvobodnaia (Rezepkin 2000:21–22, pl.. 28.16, 54.12, 64.7). This example should date to the same period, to about the third quarter of the 3rd millennium BC.

4.   Chisel
      Inv. No. 30-33-96
      Bronze, cast, forged. H. 8.7 cm
      3rd millennium BC

Trapezoidal plaque, four-sided in section, widening gradually to its curved tip, this chisel is sharp at both its base, which was attached to a wooden haft, and cutting edge. Similar tools, varying widely in size, are typical of the late period of the Maikop culture (though appearing also in earlier periods) (Munchaev 1975:402, fig. 50). The relatively small size of our example is comparable to that of the chisels recovered from Adyghea (Northwestern Caucasus) (Leskov 1991:nos. 6, 10) in burials dating to the later Maikop culture (third quarter of the 3rd millennium BC). This chisel likely dates to the same period.

5.   Macehead
      Inv. No. 30-33-117
      Stone, polished, drilled. H. 6.1 cm
      Mid-2nd millennium BC

This macehead is in the form of an upside-down pear with four hemispherical projections, each set off by a shallow groove at its base, arranged symmetrically around its upper part. The cylindrical socket was drilled from one side. Similar maces already appear in the first half of the 2nd millennium BC in the lower Don River region (Bratchenko 1976:142ff., figs. 75.5, 13), known especially from Late Catacomb or Ribbed Pottery culture sites of the second quarter of the 2nd millennium BC. Comparable examples have also been recovered, though not in association with any assemblages, from the Northern Caucasus (Markovin 1960:figs. 9.55, 13.100). One similar mace, though without the pear-shaped base, is part of the celebrated Borodinskiy treasure (currently dated to the 17th to 16th century BC) (Krivtsova-Grakova 1949:pls. xii.3, xvii.3). The *terminus ante quem* for this form ap-

CAT. NO. 5

pears to be the 13th century BC, when it appears in bronze rather than stone (Bratchenko 1976:147). Our example should thus date to the mid-2nd millennium BC, probably to the 15th or 14th century BC when this type was most common.

6.   Macehead
      Inv. No. 30-33-115
      Bronze, cast, carved. H. 4.7 cm
      Late 2nd–early 1st millennium BC

This cylindrical socket has four mushroom-shaped projections arranged asymmetrically around its upper part. These projections vary in both the diameter of their stems and the dimensions and decoration of their caps. One is incised with a cross; a second with a circle with a dot in the middle; a third with the same circle and vertical hatching along the edge of the cap; the fourth, the smallest, is devoid of ornament. The designs are deeply and somewhat carelessly cut. The base of the socket is articulated with a raised border, diagonally hatched to resemble a rope.

The carelessness of execution apparent in both casting and decoration distinguishes this object from other bronze maces, which are widely represented both at Late Bronze and Early Iron Age sites in Caucasia (Khachatrian 1963:fig. 8; Martirosian 1964:104, pls. ix.6,

CAT. NO. 6

xxxvi.17; Kuftin 1941:pl. cxv?) and 2nd to 1st millennium BC Koban culture sites in the mountains of the Central Caucasus (Tekhov 1971:figs. 23, 28.7; 1977:110–11, fig. 90; Kozenkova 1995:78–79, pl. xxi.7; Domanskiy 1984:figs. 31, 32). The form of this mace also seems unique among the spherical or pear shapes that are characteristic of Caucasia and the Northern Caucasus.

Inasmuch as bronze maces are not generally known from the steppe or forest steppe of Ukraine, the Crimea, the Don River region, or the Kuban, our example is probably a locally produced artifact, created in the Kuban under the influence of the Koban culture (a Central Caucasian culture named after a small Ossetian village), with the inexperience of the craftsman accounting for the irregularities in casting and form. As the greatest diffusion of pear-shaped maces with projections dates from the late 2nd to the early 1st millennium BC, our example is likely of comparable date.

7.   Horse Bit
     Inv. No. 30-33-79
     Bronze, cast. L. 21.5 cm
     7th century BC

This horse bit was formed from two links, each articulated with regularly spaced rows of rowels (these press against the lips of the horse to restrain it when the reins are pulled) running lengthwise, joined by the single rings at one end of each; the other end of each link terminates in two consecutive rings, the inner smaller than the outer.

Similarly ornamented bits are known from the Early Scythian period, although those bit ends are modified to form a stirrup shape (Galanina 1997:pls. 25, 330.17.77–80). This example, distinguished from earlier bits by the regular arrangement of the rowels (Valchak 2000:142–43), is best attributed to the end of the Novocherkassk period of the first half of the 7th century BC.

8.   Cruciform Bead
     Inv. No. 30-33-116
     Bronze, cast. H. 3.5 cm
     8th–mid-7th century BC

This bead is a cruciform shape with a cylindrical hole in its center; each of the four arms broadens toward the hemispherical cap at its tip. Similar beads, identified as weights by Kozenkova (1998:46–47, pl. xiii. 4), are typical of 8th century BC Koban culture sites. They are especially common in the Tliiskiy burial grounds (Tekhov 1977:figs. 112.13–27), though without the hemispherical caps at the ends of their arms. While this may suggest our bead has a closer relationship with Scythian cruciform beads and buttons, which are formed from four hemispheres arranged symmetrically around a larger central circle (Liberov 1965:pls. 23.23, 37–39), beads very similar to ours occur even at strictly Koban

CAT. NOS. 7 AND 8

burial grounds of the 8th to mid-7th century BC (Terenozhkin 1976:figs. 94.8–9). Our example should date to the same period.

9. Fasteners-Buttons (4 items)
   Inv. No. 30-33-121a–d
   Bronze, cast, carved. Diam. 1.5 cm
   8th–mid-7th century BC

These fasteners are hemi-spherical in form with a central convexity framed by a rhombus in the center of the front; four arcs extend to the base of the front from the

CAT. NO. 9

corners of the rhombus. There is a semicircular attachment loop on the reverse. The design on these buttons is typical of Novocherkassk-type artifacts, which are widespread in the 8th to mid-7th century BC (Kozenkova 1989:pl. xlii.2), and they appear at sites as far as Central Europe (Terenozhkin 1976:fig. 92). They likely date to this same period.

10. Long Beads (12 items)
     Inv. No. 30-33-75a
     Bronze, cast. L. 0.5–0.7 cm
     8th–early 6th century BC

These beads are in the form of squat, hollow cylinders. While the simplicity of their form precludes the assignment of a secure date, similar long beads are known at Early Iron Age and Early Scythian sites in the Northern Caucasus (Kozenkova 1989:pls. xlii.3, 5, xliv.6); our examples may thus be tentatively dated between the 8th and early 6th century BC.

CAT. NOS. 10 (left) AND 11

11. Long Bead
     Inv. No. 30-33-107
     Bronze, cast. L. 4.2 cm
     8th–mid-7th century BC

This long bead is in the form of a cylinder pierced lengthwise with broad, flattened ends and a thick relief line around its center. While bobbin-shaped pendants are characteristic of Koban culture, they differ from our example in their shorter length and use of a small suspension loop (Kozenkova 1998:47, pl. xiii.12–14; Tekhov 1977:figs. 112.29–30). As such items are not known from Scythian period complexes, our example likely belongs instead to the group of pre-Scythian artifacts contemporary with the Novocherkassk treasure of the 8th to mid-7th century BC that is also part of the Maikop treasure.

12. Pins (3 items)
     Inv. Nos. 30-33-84, -85, -86
     Bronze, cast. L. 13.1 (preserved portion), 10.5, 11.3 cm
     Late Bronze Age–pre-Scythian Period

These pins are in the form of a round shaft tapering to a point from a looped oval head. Though the head of one pin (Inv. No. 30-33-84) is broken, its bifurcation indicates it was similarly shaped. Comparable pins from the Fars/Klady burial grounds suggest a date of the 8th to mid-7th century BC (Leskov and Erlikh 1999:63, figs. 60.8, 9). While this form of pin is unknown in the Koban and Maeotian cultures of the Northern Caucasus, its presence at the proto-Maeotian burial site of Fars/Klady prevents us from attributing it absolutely to the steppes of the northern Black Sea littoral, where it already appears in the Late Bronze Age (Bočarev and Leskov 1980:pl.. 10.84; Leskov 1970:30–31, fig. 23.12). The close contacts between the tribes of southern Ukraine and the Kuban in the Late Bronze and Early Iron Ages indicate another possible region of origin.

CAT. NO. 12

13. Fasteners-Buttons (8 items)
     Inv. No. 30-33-120a–h
     Bronze, cast. L. 1.7–3.0 cm
     8th–mid-7th century BC

These fasteners are hemispheres of varying diameter, each with an oval attachment loop on the reverse. The simplicity of their form precludes the assignment of a secure date,

CAT. NO. 13

as similar buttons are equally wide-spread both at proto-Maeotian and Koban sites (8th to mid-7th century BC) (Leskov and Erlikh 1999:fig. 58.19; Kozenkova 1998:pl. xx.1–3), and at Scythian sites (4th to 3rd century BC) in Ukraine (Ilinskaia 1973:figs. 5.8-9, 8.3, 6, 21; Petrenko 1967:pl. 27.6, 7, 34, 36). As most of the items in this collection derive from the Kuban, where such buttons are almost unknown during the Scythian period, our examples likely date between the 8th and mid-7th century BC.

14. Arrowhead
    Inv. No. 30-33-89
    Bronze, cast. L. 4 cm
    8th century BC

CAT. NOS. 14 (left)
AND 15

This arrowhead is a narrow, triangular bilobate blade with sharp points on an elongated central socket that tapers from base to tip. Similar arrowheads are relatively rare among Northern Caucasian artifacts. They are preceded in the typological sequence by the forged and cast arrowheads from the latest Belozerskaia culture sites of the end of the Late Bronze or beginning of the Iron Age (Chernogorovka type sites) in the steppes of the northern Black Sea littoral (Dubovskaia 1993:fig. 79; 1997:fig. 13.5–6, 10a). A comparable arrowhead from burial complex No. 297 in the Klin-Iar III burial grounds, reliably dated to the end of the 8th century BC (Belinskii and Dudarev 2001:II, 81, fig. 4.3), suggests the probable date of our example.

15. Arrowhead
    Inv. No. 30-33-92
    Bronze, cast. L. 4 cm
    8th–mid-7th century BC

This arrowhead is a short, severely degraded bilobate blade on an elongated central socket that tapers slightly from base to tip; the blade likely originally had a rounded-rhomboidal form characteristic of Novocherkassk-type arrowheads. Such arrowheads, widespread in the Northern Caucasus (especially in the west) in the 8th to mid-7th century BC (Tereno-zhkin 1976:figs. 26.6, 27.3, 82.10–14), seem to have developed in the steppes of the lower Don River region and the Northwestern Caucasus (Erlikh 1994:73–75).

16. Bracelet
    Inv. No. 30-33-82
    Bronze, cast, forged. Diam. 6.7 cm
    8th–mid-7th century BC

CAT. NO. 16

This bracelet, made from a massive bronze shaft, triangular in section (flat on the interior, convex on the exterior), tapers slightly to tips that do not meet. Similar objects are widespread at Koban culture sites (Kozenkova 1998:pl. xvii.1, 12), from which they likely spread to proto-Maeotian sites. Examples from the Fars/Klady burial grounds of the 8th to mid-7th century BC are sufficiently similar to ours (Leskov and Erlikh 1999:63–64, figs. 61.1–8) to suggest that they date to the same period.

17. Plaques (2 items)
    Inv. No. 30-33-122a, b
    Bronze, cast. Diam. 1.5 cm
    8th–mid-7th century BC

These plaques are hemispherical in form with a round central convexity encircled by two bands of smaller convexities on the front; there is an attachment loop on the reverse. A

CAT. NO. 17

comparable plaque from the Berlin Museum's holdings of the Maikop collection (cf. No. 240, Inv. No. IIId 6898) seems connected with Novocherkassk-type artifacts, and similar objects have been found among 8th to mid-7th century BC horse trapping details also of the Novocherkassk type. Our plaques likely date to this same period.

18. Arrowhead
    Inv. No. 30-33-90
    Bronze, cast. L. 3 cm
    Late 7th–6th century BC

This arrowhead has a bilobate blade with ill-preserved edges and an oval-rhomboidal form on a central socket that tapers from base to tip; a barb with pointed tip projects down from near the base of the socket. According to Meliukova's detailed classification of Scythian arrowheads (1964:1–4), this example belongs to the first section (bilobate), second variant, second type (1964:18, fig. 1, pls. 6–7). Similar arrowheads from securely dated complexes of Scythian antiquity such as the Zhurovskie kurgans No. 401 and No. 487 and the Huliai-Horod kurgan No. 38 indicate our example should be dated between the late 7th and 6th century BC.

19. Arrowhead
    Inv. No. 30-33-91
    Bronze, cast. L. 3.7 cm
    Second half of 7th–6th century BC

CAT. NOS. 18 (left) AND 19

This arrowhead has a rounded-rhomboidal, bilobate blade with a central socket that tapers from base to tip; a barb with pointed tip extends down from near the base of the socket. This arrowhead is classified (cf. No. 18) in the first section, second variant, second type of Meliukova (1964) and so has secure analogues in well-dated complexes of the 7th to 6th century BC. The rhomboidal blade, which appears at sites in the northern Black Sea region and Northern Caucasus in the first half of the 7th century BC, continues in use into the 6th century BC. In the typological sequence, then, this arrowhead is likely older than No. 18 though the two could well have appeared in the same quiver assemblage.

20. Skyphos
Inv. No. 30-33-130
Clay, wheel-made, black glaze (much misfiring to red). H. 9.8 cm; Diam. 17.5 cm
Ca. 480–470 BC

This ceramic vessel, known as a kylix in such Russian publications as "Antichnye Gosudarst-va Severnogo Prichernomoria" [Classical states of northern Black Sea region] (Koshelenko, Kruglikova, and Dolgorukov 1984:pls. cxxxvii, 15–19, 41–44, 50, 51, 65), is characterized by a gently carinated lip, two handles (one survives) rising diagonally from the almost hemispherical body, and a short broad stem with a horizontally grooved base. Largely covered with black glaze, misfired to red in many locations, the lip, the groove on the base of the foot, the inner face of the handles, and the inside of the bowl (apart from a dot and circle in its center) are without decoration. The exterior is decorated with the same black-figure scene on both sides of the vessel: two women dressed in long garments and holding lyres sit one behind the other. Multi-petal palmettes, set on either side of the handles, flank each scene.

Identified as a black-figure Attic skyphos of the Lańcut Group by Beazley (1956:578, no. 54), this vessel was originally dated to 480 470 BC (cf. Piotrovsky 1975:158–59). Rostovtzeff (1931c:368) similarly attributed the skyphos to the first half of the 5th century BC. Archaeological excavations have confirmed this date through the recovery of one similar vessel from a 6th to early 5th century context (Chaikovskii 1992:no. 139) in Olbia and another, of approximately the same date, from Uliap kurgan No. 13 (Leskov 1990: fig. 45, Kat. 141). This latter find is especially interesting given that the majority of objects cataloged here derive from the same part of the Northwestern Caucasus.

This skyphos was first published in Schumm (1930:no. 120).

CAT. NO. 20

21. Red-figure Vessel Fragment
     Inv. No. 30-33-131
     Clay, wheel-made, black-
          glaze. H. 7.5 cm
     Late 5th century BC

This red-figure body sherd shows
the transition, marked by a horizontal band of ovolos, from the
shoulder to the neck of a vessel.
The sherd's surface is covered
with a black glaze that sets off the
red-figure upper bodies of two
young men confronting one another. It was first published in Piotrovsky (1975), where Bothmer
attributed the fragment to part
of a late 5th century BC Attic
pelike by the painter of Louvre
G539 (1975:158–59.12).

CAT. NO. 21

22. Cheekpieces (pair)
     Inv. Nos. 30-33-97, -98
     Bronze, cast. L. 10.5 cm, 9.4 cm
     5th century BC

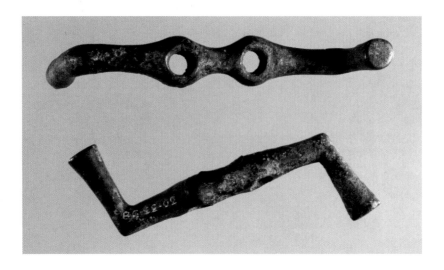

CAT. NO. 22

In these S-shaped cheekpieces the center of each round shaft swells to a figure 8, pierced with a hole in each loop, while the two ends, which turn up sharply in opposing right angles, terminate in identical thickened tips. Bronze and iron cheekpieces of this type are characteristic of the 5th century BC (Petrenko 1967:37, pl. 26.15) and are known from both the territory of European Scythia (Meliukova and Abramova 1989:pl. 35.13) and the Malie Semibratnie kurgans (State Hermitage, Classical department collection, Msbr.–42). Our examples may thus be securely dated to the 5th century BC.

  23. Cheekpiece
      Inv. No. 30-33-101
      Bronze, cast. Preserved L. 9 cm
      Mid-5th century BC

This cheekpiece is S-shaped; the center of the round shaft swells to a figure 8, pierced with a hole in each loop, and the surviving end, bent perpendicular to the shaft, has a broad, flattened form possibly representing a stylized bird's wing. The broken end undoubtedly took the same form.

CAT. NO. 23

   Similar cheekpieces are known from 5th century BC sites in the Kuban and Ukraine, and a practically identical cheekpiece exists in the Berlin holdings of this collection (No. 247, Inv. No. IIId 6913/14). The presence of comparable cheekpieces in both the Malie Semibratnie kurgans (State Hermitage, Classical department collection, Msbr.–44) and Ulskiy kurgan No. 11 (Gabuev and Erlikh 2001:112–25, figs. 4.1–2) confirms a mid-5th century BC date for our example.

  24. Plaque-Ornament
      Inv. No. 30-33-118
      Bronze, iron, punched, riveted. L. 11.5 cm
      5th century BC

CAT. NO. 24

This openwork plaque reveals a profile bird (facing right) holding a fish in its long curved beak and claws. Relief circles dot the head, body, and lower leg of the bird, while incised lines articulate the wing, which covers most of the body, and the tail. Diagonal hatching emphasizes the contoured outline of the fish, and there is a herringbone pattern on its tail. The eyes of both bird and fish are denoted by convex circles. Massive iron fasteners preserved on the head and leg of the bird and the head and tail of the fish are incongruent with the thinness and delicacy of the plaque, which seems otherwise suited to a soft foundation such as fabric or leather.

The subject of the plaque, a bird of prey grasping a fish, may be derived from depictions on classical coinage (Karyshkovskii 1982:83, 153, pl. xii.1). Gold plaques with similar depictions have been recovered from numerous 5th and 4th century BC Scythian sites (Mozolevskii 1980:105, figs. 44.4, 7–8), and four gold facings for a vessel bearing comparable representations form part of the Maikop collection held in Berlin's Antikenabteilung, Staatliche Museen (cf. No. 149, Inv. No. 30.221e 1–4) (Greifenhagen 1970:pl. 31). Bronze plaques depicting this theme have also been recovered from 5th to 4th century BC contexts in the Kuban (Malyshev and Ravich 2001:103ff., figs. 2.1–3). While our plaque differs noticeably from the comparanda in both the manner of its execution (it is punched rather than cast) and the specific rendering of the bird, it likely dates to the same period.

First published in *From the Lands of the Scythians* (Piotrovsky 1975).

25. Buckles-Buttons (4 items)
    Inv. No. 30-33-77a–d
    Bronze, cast. L. 1.7 cm, 1.9 cm, 2.0 cm, 2.2 cm
    5th century BC

These objects are in the form of a wolf's head profile (two items face left and two right) with a protruding ear and open maw. The smaller of the heads facing left is distinguished

from the others primarily by its jaw, which is rendered in relief rather than openwork. A horizontal attachment loop on
the reverse of each plaque secures it to the harness strap.

Fourteen similar buckles, in addition to other bronze
trapping details, were acquired by the Archaeological Commission from a private individual in the city of Maikop in
1903 (OAK 1906:169, figs. 331, 332) and transferred to the
Historical Museum in Moscow. Our 4 buckles were likely
part of the same complex—probably a burial looted in the
early 20th century AD—as the 14 now housed in Moscow and
dated to the 5th century BC on the basis of several plaques
among the trapping details (Moshinskiy 2003:36, fig. 64).
The recovery of several similar artifacts from a burial complex

CAT. NO. 25

in the village of Khosheutovo on the lower Volga River (Ochir-Goriaeva 2001:129–33, fig.
1), securely dated to the second quarter of the 5th century BC (Dvornichenko and Ochir-
Goriaeva 1997:99–115), supports this date for our buckles.

26. Buckles-Buttons (3 items)
     Inv. No. 30-33-77e–g
     Bronze, cast. H. 1.4 cm, 1.4 cm, 1.3 cm
     5th century BC

These buckles are in the form of a fragmentary head of a bird of
prey or bird-griffin in profile (two face right, one left); the protruding ear, disproportionately large eye, and open maw are all
executed in relief. Additional vertical relief lines emphasize the
neck, which is decorated with beaded ornament.

While the fragmentary condition of these buckles makes
it difficult to imagine the depictions in full (obscuring also the
means by which they were attached), what is preserved is similar
to the griffin depicted in No. 59 (Inv. No. 30-33-14.4). The beaded ornament on our examples is characteristic of the 5th century
BC though they may date as late as the early 4th century BC.

CAT. NO. 26

27. Buttons (5 items)
     Inv. No. 30-33-119a–e
     Bronze, cast. Diam. 2.6 cm
     5th century BC

These buttons are in the form of a hemisphere with a six-petal rosette set around a central
convexity on the front; the rosettes vary in the form of the lines separating their petals.

CAT. NO. 27

There is an attachment loop on the reverse of each.

Similar artifacts (cf. Antikenabteilung No. 141) are well known from 5th century BC sites in the forest steppe of Ukraine (Petrenko 1967:92–93, pls. 27.40, 46–48; Galanina 1977:50, pl. 28.9–10), and buttons of practically identical form have been recovered from Daghestan. Their occurrence with Archaic Scythian bronze arrowheads (Meliukova and Abramova 1989:pl. 112.38) in the Makhachkal region suggests they had already appeared in the 6th century BC, though they were most widespread during the 5th century BC. Our example is accordingly attributed to that period.

28. Mirror
    Inv. No. 30-33-129
    Bronze, cast, forged. Diam. 13.7 cm. L. 24.4 cm (with handle)
    5th century BC

This mirror takes the form of a disc with a polished front surface cast separately from its vertical handle, which is round in section and terminates in a ring. Trace marks on the disc suggest its edge was inserted into the split upper end of the handle before the mirror was hammered; this manufacturing technique is not otherwise known.

Mirrors with handles of this type are rare. The earliest example, a bronze disc attached with rivets to a vertical iron handle ending in a ring, is from an Archaic Scythian (late 7th–early 6th century BC) complex in kurgan No. 20 in Nartan (a village near the city of Nalchik in Kabardino-Balkaria in the Northern Caucasus) (Meliukova and Abramova 1989:218–19, pl. 86.34). Another typologically similar example from kurgan No. 26 at Kholodniy Iar in the Dniepr River forest steppe comprises a bronze disc cast together with the upper part of its vertical handle; the base of the handle, attached with rivets,

CAT. NO. 28

terminates in a ring. Dated by Pokrovska (1957:77) to the 5th century BC, it suggests the probable date of our mirror.

29. Pendant
    Inv. No. 30-33-76
    Bronze, forged. H. 5.5 cm
    5th century BC

This pendant is forged in three parts: the uppermost section, a flattened oval ring that widens toward its pointed, overlapping tips, has a second smaller oval ring, also with overlapping tips, looped through it; the lowest component, rolled from a flat wire, is curved

CAT. NO. 29

into a ring at its top linking into the central oval and forming a multi-looped spiral cone (broadening toward the base) below.

Similar conical pendants are known from the Maeotian second Ust-Labinskiy burial grounds (6th to 5th century BC) (Anfimov 1951:162, fig. 2.3), from Taurian sites in the mountains of the Crimea (6th to 4th century BC) (Leskov 1965:107, figs. 21.1, 15, 22.19, 25.11, 26, 32.1–2), and from the Late Koban burial grounds (Nesterovskiy, Isti-Su) in the Northern Caucasus (6th to 4th century BC) (Krupnov 1947:102–4, fig. 44.27; Artamonova-Poltavtseva 1950:33, fig. 9.4). The last have also yielded a headdress ring comparable to the upper part of our pendant (Kozenkova 1982:pl. xxiii.30, 33). The available comparanda thus indicate a date of the 6th to 4th century BC for this artifact, with a 5th century BC date being the most likely.

30. Cheekpieces (pair)
    Inv. No. 30-33-99a, b
    Bronze, cast. L. 6.4 cm
    5th–4th century BC

In these C-shaped cheekpieces, the center of each round shaft swells to a figure-eight, pierced with a hole in each loop, while the two ends curve up toward each other and terminate in spherical knobs.

The unusually small dimensions and shape of these artifacts are unparalleled among the bronze cheekpieces of the steppes and forest-steppes of the Dniepr and Don River regions, the Kuban, and even the Northern Caucasus. While C-shaped cheekpieces are known from 6th century BC Greek contexts (Donder 1980:pl. 43), these have three holes (one in the center and one at each end). Similar cheekpieces from Abkhazia and Georgia also have three holes, but

CAT. NO. 30

set in the central flattened part of the shaft (Bill 2003:108–9, fig. 20.4, pl. 3.21–22, 115.1–3). Two-holed, C-shaped cheekpieces comparable to ours but made of iron are known from the 5th century BC in the Northern Caucasus (Vinogradov 1972:134, fig. 2.10), continuing in use through the 4th century BC when they appear in the Kuban and Don River region (Maksimenko 1983:fig. 12.31). The examples found in the Kuban and Northern Caucasus seem generally to have been imported from Transcaucasia. Such cheekpieces also become widespread in Ukraine (Meliukova and Abramova 1989:96, pl. 36.10) and at contemporary Sarmatian sites in the 4th century BC (Moshkova 1963:37, pl. 21.4), remaining common into the later centuries BC (Polin 1992:figs. 11.27–28, 19.6–7; Smirnov 1984:figs. 23, 26.5, 36.5–6, 37.2, 38.7). Our examples likely date between the 5th and 4th century BC and may well derive from the Kuban, where bronze examples of this date are more common than in Ukraine.

31. Cheekpiece
    Inv. No. 30-33-100
    Bronze, cast. L. 8.6 cm
    5th–early 4th century BC

In this S-shaped cheekpiece, the center of each round shaft swells to a figure-eight, pierced with a hole in each loop, and the two ends turn up sharply in opposing directions.

CAT. NO. 31

Although S-shaped cheekpieces vary significantly in the shape of their tips, which are often thickened, those are undifferentiated. Judging from the S-shaped cheekpieces recovered from Ukraine, the Don River region, and the Kuban, this type belongs to the 5th and early 4th century BC (Petrenko 1967:pl. 26.3–4; Galanina 1977:26, pl. 11.13; Leskov 1990:180, no. 77). Our example should date to this same period.

32. Arrowhead
    Inv. No. 30-33-87
    Bronze, cast. L. 4.5 cm
    5th–4th century BC

This narrow, triangular, trilobate head has an elongated central socket. According to Meliukova's typology, this example belongs to the 4th type of trilobate arrowhead, widespread by the mid-5th century BC and most common in the 4th century BC (Meliukova 1964:pl. 7.10, 3, 4; pl. 8.5; pl. 9.1). Smirnov (1961) would attribute our example to his type 9 (48), which finds its closest analogues in the kurgans of the first half of the 5th century BC (figs. 16a.20–31), though similar artifacts in the Volga River and Ural Mountain regions occur later (pls. 18–33). Our arrowhead should thus be dated between the 5th and 4th century BC.

33. Arrowhead
     Inv. No. 30-33-88
     Bronze, cast. L. 3 cm
     5th–4th century BC

CAT. NOS. 32 (right)
AND 33

This narrow triangular, trilobate head has an elongated central socket. According to Meliukova's typology (1964:22, 24), this example belongs to the 10th type of trilobate arrowhead, already known in the 5th century BC. Based on the available comparanda (Meliukova 1964:pl. V, 8.9) it likely dates to the 3rd chronological group (5th to 4th century BC).

34. Bracelet
     Inv. No. 30-33-80
     Bronze, forged, engraved. Diam. 6.5 cm
     5th–4th century BC

This spiral bracelet, curving slightly more than two full turns, is formed from a twisted strand that is round in section except near the tips, which are square in section. The bracelet is decorated on its exterior near the tips with alternating groups of vertical and

CAT. NO. 34

horizontal hatched lines.

While no identical objects are known, a similar principle of ornamentation to that seen here is known from 5th to 4th century BC Maeotian sites in the Kuban (Leskov 1990: fig. 96, 98, 103–106; Meliukova and Abramova 1989:pl. 93.43, 45). Our bracelet likely belongs to the same period.

35. Bead with Masks
     Inv. No. 30-33-42
     Glass on a ceramic tube, applied handmade ornament. L. 2.7 cm
     5th–4th century BC

Twisted strands of opaque, multi-colored glass (white, yellow, and blue) overlay a ceramic tube. Three handmade, goggle-eyed, and large-nosed male faces are arranged around the bead (the noses of two are broken), and numerous round handmade convexities are applied above, below, and between the faces.

CAT. NO. 35

Similar beads, apparently Phoenician imports, are occasionally found at northern Black Sea and Northern Caucasian sites of the 6th to 5th century BC (Krupnov 1960:pl. LXIX.35) and the 4th century BC (Leskov 1974a:58, fig. 47; Leskov 1990:fig. 117–28). Our example likely dates between the 5th and 4th century BC.

36. Frontlet (?)
     Inv. No. 30-33-104
     Bronze, cast. L. 5.7 cm
     4th century BC

Harness ornament (?) in the form of a vertical, slightly curved plaque with a slit crosspiece at its base and the stylized head of a bird-griffin at its top. The head is characterized by a sharply curved neck, a short crest and protruding ear, a large eye with an articulated pupil, and a beak curving into a spiral. On the reverse there is a ring for attachment to the harness around a goat's neck.

While no identical analogues exist, two pendants that are similar in form but have different animal heads at their tops are known from the Antikenabteilung holdings of the Maikop collection (cf. Nos. 209 and 213, Inv. Nos. 30.223 and 30.224). Pendants with similar depictions of birds of prey do occur on other artifacts from both the Antikenabteilung (Nos. 171 and 218, Inv. Nos. 30.562 and 30.563a, b) and the Berlin Museum collections (No. 296, Inv. No. IIId 7024), though these lack the spiral-curved beak of our example. Overall, the form and style of this artifact seem typical of the Kuban variant of the Scythian Animal Style, suggesting a date of the 4th century BC.

First published in Fernald (1930:pl. III).

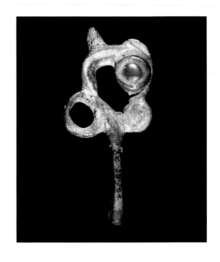

CAT. NO. 36

37. Harness Plaque
    Inv. No. 30-33-102
    Bronze, cast. L. 5 cm
    4th century BC

Wolf's head in profile faces left; the eye with articulated pupil, nose, chin, fur (visible from base of ear to first lower fang), and protruding ear are all in relief, while the triangular teeth within the closed maw are rendered in openwork for emphasis. There is a vertical attachment loop on the reverse. Notably, if the plaque is turned so the wolf's head is upside down, the head of a mountain goat executed entirely in relief becomes clear; its curved horn extends between the large, round eye and protruding ear. The skill and spatial artistry of the craftsman are remarkable: the ear is modeled and arranged to function effectively for both predator and prey. This duality is an important aspect of Scythian art.

Similar plaques are common at sites in the Kuban and are also known from both the Antikenabteilung (Nos. 214 and 215, Inv. Nos. 30.226a, b and 30.227a, b) and Prehistory Department's (No. 295, Inv. No. IIId 7023) holdings of the Maikop collection. All are dated on the basis of an identical plaque found in a securely dated 4th century BC complex excavated from a kurgan in the vil-

CAT. NO. 37 (2 views)

lage of Elizavetinskaia (Perevodchikova 1984:5ff., fig. 2.14).
    First published by Fernald (1930:pl. III).

    38. Harness Plaque
         Inv. No. 30-33-105
         Bronze, cast. L. 3.9 cm
         4th century BC

This flat plaque is in the form of the heavily stylized hind leg
and paw of a predator, with details in relief; there is a horizontal suspension loop on the reverse.

    Similar plaques are widely known from 4th century BC
Scythian kurgans in the steppe (Mantsevich 1987:108, cat. no.
91; 111, cat. no. 109; Alekseev, Murzin, and Rolle 1991:153,
cat. no. 20) and forest-steppe (Petrenko 1967:40 , pl. 30.1–2;
Ilinskaia 1968:fig. 34), and a comparable item in the Berlin Museum's holdings of the Maikop collection (No. 263, Inv. No.
IIId 6887) is listed as coming from the south of Russia. The
near absence of such plaques in the Kuban (only one reliable
example is known: Lappo-Danilevskii and Malmberg 1894:62,
fig. 39) suggests our example originated instead in the northern
Black Sea region during the 4th century BC, when such items were widespread there.

CAT. NO. 38

    39. Stamp
         Inv. No. 30-33-53
         Stone (?), carved, polished, drilled. H. 3.1 cm; Diam. 3.8 cm
         4th century BC

This stamp is in the form of a half-barrel with a small hole drilled through its length. The
base is concave and the broad, contoured stamping surface takes the form of a five-petaled

rosette, with a relief circle
set near its base, arranged
around a central concavity
that is itself cut with a ten-pet-
aled rosette (two levels of five
petals each). Each of the five
petals of the exterior rosette
slopes down from the central
rib running its length to the
deep incision that divides it
from the other petals.

CAT. NO. 39 (left), WITH IMPRESSION

While five-petaled rosettes are not known from the richest of the 5th–4th century BC Scythian complexes of Ukraine or the south of Russia, rosettes with six petals are common at 4th century BC Greek and barbarian sites in the Kuban, occurring both as independent items (Leskov 1990:182, cat. no. 105) and as ornaments on other artifacts (Artamonov 1966:pls. 304, 318). Our stamp may well date to this latter period, when rosettes of various forms were most common in the northern Black Sea region.

40. Gorgoneion Button
     Inv. No. 30-33-44
     Clay, punched, fired, gilded. Diam. 2.2 cm
     4th century BC

This thin, round plaque depicts Medusa's head encircled by a beaded band with borders in relief. Two pairs of holes in the middle of the reverse, one still containing traces of metal, originally held loops to sew the button to its foundation; the second pair of holes was apparently added to replace a broken loop held by the first.

Terracotta punched depictions of Medusa, often gilded, are characteristic of the mid-4th–early 3rd century BC, known from sites throughout the western Black Sea littoral, the Kuban, and the central Caucasus (Malyshev 1993:50, 51; Prokopenko 2001a:225). The beaded frame on our example is comparable to the double band of beading that edges a gilded gorgoneion from Uliap kurgan No. 11 (Leskov 1990:fig. 142, Kat. 174). Gorgoneia similar to ours and dating to the second half of the 4th century BC have also been recovered from complexes near Maikop, most notably from the Kurdzhips kurgan (Galanina 1980:88, no. 29) and from kurgan No. 15 in the village of Voronezhskaia (*OAK* for 1903, 1906:71, fig. 128). While gorgoneia continue to appear at sites of the 3rd–2nd century BC (Anfimov 1951:187, 189, fig.

CAT. NOS. 40 (top), 41 (left), 42 (right), 43 (bottom)

14.27), precluding the assignment of a secure date to our example, the overall composition of the Maikop collection makes a 4th century BC date the most probable.

41. Gorgoneion Button
    Inv. No. 30-33-45
    Clay, punched, fired, gilded (?). Diam. 2.4 cm
    4th century BC

This thin, round plaque (heavily worn and broken at one side) depicts Medusa's head encircled by two concentric relief lines; no traces of gilding are apparent. Two pairs of holes in the middle of the reverse originally held a loop for sewing the button to its foundation. This item likely dates to the same period as No. 40.

42. Gorgoneion Button
    Inv. No. 30-33-46
    Clay, punched, fired, gilded (?). Diam. 2.4 cm
    4th century BC

This thin, round plaque (heavily worn and broken at the top) depicts Medusa's head in a grooved frame that separates it from the plaque's broad edge; no traces of gilding are apparent. Two holes on the reverse originally held a loop for sewing the button to its foundation. This item likely dates to the same period as No. 40.

43. Gorgoneion Button
    Inv. No. 30-33-47
    Clay, punched, fired, gilded. Diam. 2 cm
    4th century BC

This thin, round plaque depicts Medusa's head encircled by a beaded frame; three additional rows of beading, probably representing hair, appear above the head. Two holes in the center of the reverse originally held a loop for sewing the button to its foundation. This item probably dates to the same period as No. 40.

44. Button
    Inv. No. 30-33-48
    Clay, punched, fired. L. 2 cm
    4th century BC

This round plaque, edged with a pseudo-beaded relief line, depicts the head of a helmeted Athena in relief in its central field. One hole, containing traces of a metal attachment loop, is preserved on the reverse.

Similar depictions of Athena appear on gold plaques from 4th century BC Scythian kurgans (Leipen 1971), and one recent discovery, from a later 4th century BC complex found at a Maeotian sanctuary in Tenginskaia village (Ust-Labinskiy district, Krasnodar region), is a partial depiction of the goddess on a fragment of a terracotta button (Erlikh 2002:15, fig. 5.12). Our example likely dates to the same period.

CAT. NOS. 44 (right) AND 45

45. Buttons (pair)
     Inv. No. 30-33-49a, b
     Clay, iron, punched, fired. Diam. 2.2 cm
     4th century BC

Two round plaques depict the head of a helmeted Athena. The first, with a beaded band framing the head, has two holes on its reverse to hold an attachment hoop. The second appears to have no border on its front, causing the head of Athena to appear somewhat larger, and has a half-oval iron attachment hoop preserved on its reverse. These depictions of Athena are comparable to that of No. 44 and undoubtedly belong to the same period.

46. Pendant
     Inv. No. 30-33-50
     Clay. H. 2.8 cm
     4th century BC

This pendant is in the form of the head of a female with a long slender neck; two braids diverging from the center of her high forehead frame her face and are topped by a tall, cylindrical headdress resembling a *kalathos*.

Similar pendants are common at 4th–3rd century BC sites in both the Northern Caucasus (Limberis and Marchenko 1992:50, pl. I.8; Prokopenko 1998:42 ff., fig. 1.18) and ancient Greece; the examples from Greece proper are more carefully

CAT. NO. 46

executed than those from the Greek colonies in the northern Black Sea region (Marshall 1911:pl. XLII.2169–71). Considering the composition of this portion of the Maikop collection, our example may well date to this same period.

47. Bracelet
    Inv. No. 30-33-81
    Bronze, forged, engraved. Diam. 6.1 cm x 6.6 cm
    Date unknown

This bracelet is curved from a twisted strand, round in section, with ends that do not meet. The simplicity of its form and the absence of ornamentation preclude the assignment of a secure date. While it may have come from a Maeotian complex, it is as plausibly dated to the Scythian period as to the Sarmatian.

CAT. NO. 47

48. Pendant or Headdress Ring
    Inv. No 30-33-75b
    Bronze, forged. Diam.3.0 x 3.5 cm
    Date unknown

This oval ring is curved from a thin, twisted strand, round in section, with overlapping pointed ends. The simplicity of its form precludes the assignment of a secure date; similar items have been recovered from pre-Scythian, Scythian, and Sarmatian sites.

CAT. NO. 48

49. Pendant or Headdress Ring
    Inv. No. 30-33-72
    Bronze, forged. Diam. 5 cm
    Date unknown

This circular ring is curved from a
thin, twisted strand that is round
in section; the thick, flattened tips
meet but do not join. The simplicity
of its form precludes the assignment
of a secure date; it may as well belong to the Scythian period as to the
Sarmatian.

CAT. NO. 49

50. Arrowhead
    Inv. No. 30-33-140
    Bronze, iron, cast, forged. L. 3.6 cm
    Date unknown

This bilobate (?) blade is positioned on a central socket. The form of the blade is obscured
by the iron armor (?) fragment in which it
is caught. The damaged state of this artifact
precludes the assignment of a secure date,
though it certainly belongs to the Scythian
period. If it were bilobate, as the surviving
fragment suggests, it should date no later
than the 6th century BC.

CAT. NO. 50

51. Ornament Detail Fragments
    Inv. No. 30-33-3a, b
    Gold, forged, filigree, enamel. L. 8.1 cm, 5.7 cm
    First half of 5th century BC

Each of two fragmentary curving plaques (the preserved edges curl inward) has a straight
horizontal base and a zigzagging upper border; the applied filigree decoration takes the form
of six-petaled rosettes and double columns of crescent-shaped leaves imitating tree trunks.
These plaques likely formed a single curved ornament measuring 16 cm in length (the right
third of the left half is missing) that would have been placed in the center (forehead part)
of a leather fillet for a woman or child or on a larger diadem which could have accommo-

dated two or three such ornaments. The narrow slits in the curving edges of the plaque were used in place of holes to attach the ornament to its foundation, and it was further secured with some sort of sticky mass. In its reconstructed form, the decorative scheme of the ornament would have comprised four rosettes, two in the center of the panel (one survives) and one at each end, and two imitation tree trunks, one placed between each side and central rosette (both survive). Each rosette is formed from six petals arranged around a central convexity, the whole enclosed in a circular border sandwiched between two small crescent-shaped leaves (curving away from it); the four pairs of leaves forming the imitation tree trunks are set with enamel inserts (partially preserved).

The date of this object may be determined on the basis of its ornament. While 4th century BC plaques occur with varying decorative

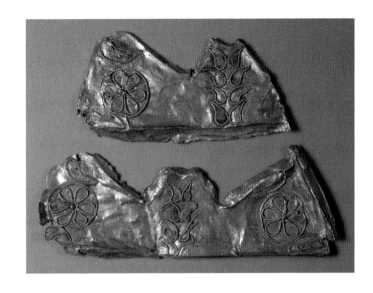

CAT. NO. 51; BELOW, WITH RECONSTRUCTION

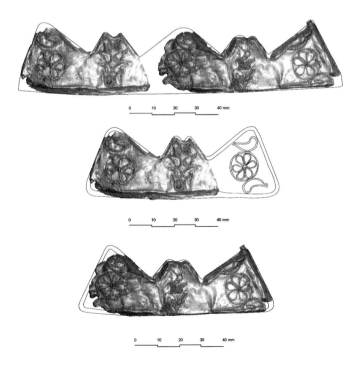

schemes, their ornaments are always punched. Only at 6th–5th century BC sites are applied filigree and granulated ornament common on plaques and other items. The available comparanda include a diadem from the Kelermes kurgan (Artamonov 1966:pls. 27, 28); a scabbard finial and pendant from Ostraia Tomakovskaia Mogila (Artamonov 1966:fig. 19, pl. 66); a flattened button and scabbard finial from Zolotaia Gorka kurgan (Artamonov 1966:figs. 22, 23); a scabbard finial from the Aleksandrovskiy kurgan (*Scythian Gold* exhibition catalogue [Reeder 1999:157, 47]); and a series of flat items from the Vettersfelde treasure, including the finial of a sword scabbard and gold pendants (Greifenhagen 1970:pls. 42.2, 43.2–3). These analogues indicate a date in the first half of the 5th century BC for our ornament.

> 52. Torque
>   Inv. No. 30-33-30a
>   Gold or electrum, forged, cast. Diam. 14 cm
>   5th century BC

This torque is a curved cast shaft that tapers from its center to tips that do not meet; the center is hexagonal in section, becoming rounder as it approaches the narrow tips. The relatively few torques known from the Sarmatian period are round or, very rarely, oval or triangular in section; this situation is essentially mirrored in the Scythian period (Meli-

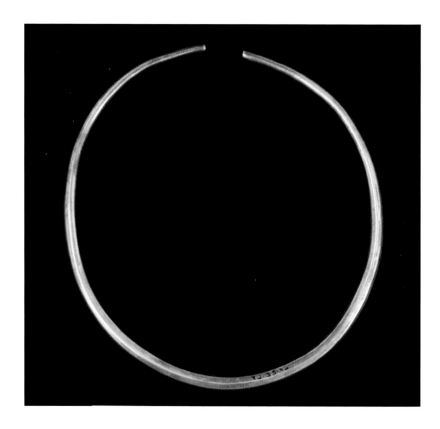

CAT. NO. 52

ukova and Abramova 1989:pls. 41.42, 53, 71.82, 93). Two gold torques, one rhomboidal in section from an early 5th century BC Scythian burial (Ilichevo) (Leskov 1968) and the other four-sided in section from an Early Scythian period burial in the forest-steppe region (around the Dniepr River) (Meliukova and Abramova 1989:pl. 41.20), suggest that a faceted section is a feature of the pre-4th century BC when torques are widespread. This conclusion is supported by the material both from the steppe and forest-steppe, where the few faceted torques are of known date no later than the 5th century BC (Petrenko 1978:41ff., pls. 28.1–2, 29.7); our example likely belongs to this same period.

53. Seal Ring
    Inv. No. 30-33-10
    Gold, cast, forged, engraved. Diam. 2.1 cm
    First half 5th century BC

This smooth-edged, rimless oval bezel continues into an oval hoop, round in section and noticeably wider in its lower part. The bezel is decorated with an engraved Siren moving to the right who clasps a lyre-type musical instrument to her breast; one long string is distinctly cut.

CAT. NO. 53 WITH
IMPRESSION

This ring's form has been variously categorized and dated. According to Boardman's typology of ring forms, it is type II in appearance and should date to the mid- or late-5th century BC (Boardman 1970:212–14, fig. 217, II). Neverov, who identifies the ring as having features characteristic of his types II and III, prefers a similar date of the middle to the third quarter of the 5th century BC (Neverov 1986:19). Richter, however, places rings with hoops that widen towards the bottom in an earlier period, ca. 550–480 BC (Richter 1968:46). The depiction on the bezel is similarly problematic as Sirens do not appear on ancient coins and are only rarely depicted on gems and rings; there are no such depictions on the approximately 500 ancient Greek rings in the Hermitage collection, and only three of the 1,648 such rings in the British Museum depict Sirens (Nos. 20, 35, and 202) (Marshall 1907:pls. I, XIII). Even those three examples, however, which all date to the 6th century BC, are very different from that depicted on our example.

Richter (1968, 1920) has noted that mythological figures (including Sirens) appear most commonly in the late 6th and early 5th century BC, with depictions decreasing over the course of the following period, ca. 480–330 BC, when Sirens are not depicted. As the one image that is even slightly similar to our example, a Siren in profile (facing left) on a gold ring from the Getty collection, dates to ca. 500 BC or slightly later (Spier 1992:no. 46), a date of the early 5th century BC for our example seems most likely. If accurately dated, this may be one of the earliest depictions of Sirens from a northern Black Sea context; it could as well have come from a Greek city-state as a Scythian elite burial of that period.

First published in Fernald (1930:pl. II).

54. Bracelet
Inv. No. 30-33-9
Gold, cast, forged, soldered, with filigree, engraved. Diam. 7 cm
First half 5th century BC

This bracelet curves from a thick shaft, originally with a socketed fitting bearing a ram's head at each end (one survives); the ram's head was soldered from two punched halves that were attached lengthwise with details in engraving. A band comprising loops of braided filigree wires framed by straight filigree wire was wrapped around the tip of the bracelet where it met the socket.

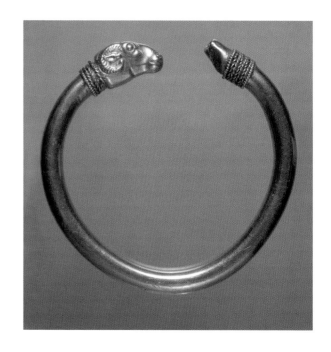

CAT. NO. 54

Similar socketed bracelets (and rhyta) are known from as early as the 6th century BC, though characterized by more modestly decorated and smaller sockets. These include a bracelet from the kurgan in Iemchikha village (Kiev province) (Petrenko 1978:56, pl. 46.3) dating to the second half of the 6th century BC and, of similar date, the gold rhyta from Semibratnie kurgans No. 2 and No. 4 (Anfimov 1987:92, 94, 112–13, 146, fig 4a), Uliap kurgan No. 4, and kurgan No. 13 in the village of Bolshaia Znamianka (in Zaporozhskaia Oblast) (Reeder 1999:243–44, no. 116). Longer and more heavily ornamented sockets with animal head terminals (lion or ram) occur on bracelets, torques, and rhyta from the later 5th century BC and became widespread in the 4th century BC (Artamonov 1966:fig. 135, pls. 201, 202, 263; Leskov 1972:pls. 32, 40). The recovery of rams' heads very similar to that on our bracelet on pendants, bracelets, and rhyta from 5th century BC contexts, most notably from the Nymphaion (Vickers 1979:pls. VIf, XVIIIc) and Semibratnie (Artamonov 1966:fig. 58) kurgans, suggests this artifact should be dated to the first half of the 5th century BC.

55. Earrings (pair)
    Inv. No. 30-33-7a, b
    Gold, forged, soldered, with granulation, filigree. H. 2.6 cm
    5th century BC

Each earring is in the form of a short cylinder atop a sphere; each is heavily decorated with granulation and filigree and suspended from a pseudo-beaded wire suspension loop. The cylinder, attached to the suspension loop with the small ring soldered to its lid, is ringed with pseudo-beaded wire along its top and bottom edges, while the sphere below, comprising two halves joined horizontally with a raised wire soldered along the seam, is encircled with a row of four granulated triangles (points toward the center seam) at both top and bottom. The base of each sphere is ringed with two ad-

CAT. NO. 55

ditional loops of pseudo-beaded wire, from the bottom of which hang a small pyramid (point downward) formed from four large granules.

Four similar earrings exist in the Antikenabteilung holdings of the Maikop collection (cf. Nos. 154 and 155) (Greifenhagen 1970:60, pl. 37.15–16), three of which differ from the Philadelphia pair primarily in their lack of central wire bands (soldered to the seam of the sphere in our example) and in the wider and more complex profile of the plaques forming the rings atop their cylinders. The fourth earring in Berlin (cf. No. 155), which does have a central relief band, is the closest to our example.

Although no ornaments of similar form are known from the 5th to 4th century BC sites of the northern Black Sea region, the use of granulation, especially in the form of triangles or pyramids, is much more widespread at sites of the 6th and 5th century BC than those of the 4th century BC. Greifenhagen's publication of some gold earrings heavily decorated with granulated triangles, said to derive from the south of Ukraine or the Kuban and attributed by him to the 5th century BC (1970:61, pl. 38.5), supports the assignment of such a date to our examples.

First published in Fernald (1930:pl. 1).

56. Ornament Detail
    Inv. No. 30-33-4
    Gold, punched (flowers), soldered, with filigree, granulation, braiding. L. 25 cm
    5th century BC

This short chain is square in section, with a cylindrical fitting soldered on its upper end, and a small sphere, from which three braided chains diverge, soldered to its lower end. The cylindrical fitting has a wire attachment loop on its flat, soldered top and pseudo-

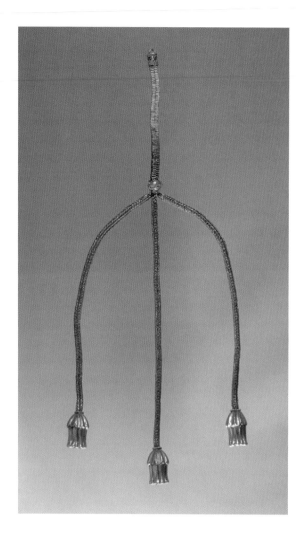

CAT. NO. 56, WITH DETAILS (right)

beaded wire with granulated triangles attached to it (points oriented to the cylinder's center) ringing its top and bottom edge. The small sphere at the other end of the chain is similarly decorated: its top, center, and base are all encircled with pseudo-beaded wire with granulated triangles (points oriented away from the wire) attached to it. Each of the three braided chains diverging from the base of the sphere is round in section and terminates in a pendant shaped like an unopened flower bud; the bud is soldered from two stamped halves. The inner foundation of the bud is partially obscured by the tips of the twelve petals below it, which are bent at right angles to the center; the base of the flower is ringed with pseudo-beaded wire.

Three identical segments not published here, originally part of a single ornament (complex pendant?) preserved in the Antikenabteilung holdings of the Maikop collection, are discussed by Greifenhagen (1970:58, pl. 34.2); both he and Zahn emphasize the rarity of four-sided chains while noting the existence of at least one comparable gold necklace. Greifenhagen mentions as well a similar chain with lion heads from Lycia (Froehner 1892: pl. 37) that is attributed to the Early Hellenistic period, though Greifenhagen (1970:59) favors an earlier date for it. In terms of decoration, the pseudo-beaded wire and granulated triangles decorating our ornament are very similar to those on the 5th century BC pair of earrings from this collection (cf. No. 55) and on the typologically similar ornament, comprising three braided chains with cylindrical fittings and small spheres (Meliukova and Abramova 1989:pl. 44.1) on a diadem from the Melgunovskiy kurgan (Pridik 1911). While the latter analogue is undoubtedly earlier, pseudo-beaded and granulated decoration is primarily known from 5th century BC sites (Artamonov 1966:fig. 19.22), and our example is best dated to this period.

57. Plaque–Appliqué
    Inv. No. 30-33-2b
    Gold, punched. H. 7.7 cm
    5th century BC

Plaque in the form of a wild boar's hind leg with details in high relief; the decoration of the leg combines Greek elements, including part of a palmette and a relief spiral, with Scythian traits: the boar's tail, done in relief and placed in the middle of the hip, is treated like the head of a bird (duck?). The upper edge of the plaque is folded over and pierced with two holes, and there are six holes along the edges of the front. The exact correspondence between the two holes on the reverse with the two uppermost on the front indicate that the plaque was fixed on the rim of a wooden vessel with two tacks (affixed from the inside of the vessel) that extended through the wood and the bent edge of the plaque. The remaining four holes also served to attach the plaque to the surface of the vessel.

Three similar plaques not published here, likely originally combined with this one to ornament a single vessel, exist in the Antikenabteilung holdings of the Maikop collection (Greifenhagen 1970:58, pl. 32.4) (cf. also No. 150, Inv. No. 30.221d 1-4), and more archaic, triangular gold appliqués stamped with

CAT. NO. 57

depictions of the hind legs of animals have been recovered from the Baby Kurgan in early- to mid-5th century BC contexts (Yatsenko 1959:58–63). The closest parallel to our example, however, is a gold plaque depicting a boar's leg with its tail on its hip from a quiver found in kurgan No. 5 in Arkhangelskaia Sloboda and dating to the turn of the 5th to 4th century BC (Leskov 1974:67, 77). On the basis of this comparanda, a date of the middle or third quarter of the 5th century BC seems the most appropriate for our example.

First published in the first *Canessa Collection Catalogue* (Colosanti 1915:2), where it was erroneously reconstructed as an ornament from the pointed end of a scabbard: the foundation of our plaque was not a flat surface, but was rather inserted into the hollow created by the folding of the plaque's upper edge.

58. Plaque–Appliqué
     Inv. No. 30-33-2a
     Gold, punched. H. 5 cm
     5th century BC

CAT. NO. 58

A panther's (?) head is rendered as if from above with details in relief. Its high forehead, with almost vertical ears, bulges over large, almond-shaped eyes, and the snout narrows slightly toward the wave-shaped wrinkles at its tip that set off its nostrils. The slightly convex jaws are dotted with hollow points that imitate whiskers, and there are two round bumps on the bridge of the nose above the eyes. The upper edge of the plaque is folded over and pierced with two holes, and there are seven holes, three along each side and one beneath the snout, along the edges of the front; traces of a gold tack are preserved in one hole. It was attached in the same manner as No. 57.

Three identical plaques in Berlin were studied by Greifenhagen (1970:58, pl. 32.5–6), who also noted a similar example from Thrace. Found in a mid-5th century BC context in the Goliamata burial grounds (near Duvankoi, close to Plovdiv) (Venedikov and Gerasimov 1973:64, fig. 227), this silver plaque-appliqué depicting a facing lion's head suggests a possible date for our example. Only one depiction of a facing panther's head is known from Scythian contexts (Leskov 1972:58, fig. 39); this example, from kurgan No. 5 in Arkhangelskaia Sloboda (Cherson region), was part of a late-5th century BC (or slightly later) complex. Our plaque should be similarly dated.

First published in Colosanti's 1915 catalogue (p. 2), where it was erroneously reconstructed as an ornament from the upper end of a scabbard (cf. No. 57).

59. Plaque
    Inv. No. 30-33-14.4
    Gold, punched. H. 3.2 cm
    5th century BC

In the form of an openwork, winged griffin facing left; details are added to the plaque in relief.
Its realistic leonine body is missing one foreleg
and most of the upraised tail, which likely met
the wing at its central point where there are
traces of a break. Its paws are rendered in relief
on the plaque's flat surface. Its head, neck, and
wing are those of a more schematically rendered
bird of prey; both neck and head, with the eye
and beak in relief, are bordered with beaded
ornament, and the wing, rising up to touch the
protruding ear of the griffin, is articulated with
parallel, slightly diagonal relief lines. There are
no traces of holes or loops on the plaque to indicate how it was attached.

CAT. NO. 59

While no exact analogues for this plaque are known, it is comparable in several details to other plaques both from the Maikop collection and from the Kuban. The form of
the wing, which curves up toward the ear, and the flat rendering of the paws are typical
of plaques purchased from de Massoneau by the Metropolitan Museum of Art (No. 315,
Inv. No. 24.97.57), the Antikenabteilung Museum (not published here; see Greifenhagen
1970:58, pl. 33.2), and the University of Pennsylvania Museum (No. 63, Inv. No. 30-33-
1.6–9). Gold plaques in the form of striding lions with paws depicted similarly to those
on our plaque have also been recovered from sanctuary No. 1 near the village of Uliap
(Leskov 1990:fig. 170). The rendering of the griffin's beak and the beading on its neck are
also characteristic of the 5th century BC, and it should likely be dated to this period.

    First published in Fernald (1930:pl. I).

60. Plaques (2 items)
    Inv. Nos. 30-33-14.2, 3
    Gold, punched. H. 3.1 cm
    5th–4th century BC

Plaques in the form of two openwork winged beasts, heraldically arranged, with plumed
heads articulated in relief and short tails. The facing animals stand on their hind legs, each
with one paw raised to press against the raised paw of the other and a wing behind it curling
up toward its head. The animals' lower paws appear in relief on the plaque's flat surface, and
their lower bodies are separated by a six-petal rosette (the lowest petal is missing) rendered

CAT. NO. 60

in relief. There are two holes for attaching the plaque to its foundation. The damaged and crumpled nature of this thin plaque precludes a secure identification of the beasts, but it is possible they originally took the form of sphinxes with human faces. The second plaque is extremely fragmentary.

While no direct analogues for this item are known, it is notable that figures in similar heraldic poses appear on diadems decorating 4th century BC Scythian headdresses (Leskov 1974:80, 91, figs. 124, 126), and the combination of an Eastern heraldic scene with a Classical Greek rosette, as on our example, is one that appears by the 5th century BC during the heyday of the Greco-Persian style in applied art. Our plaque thus likely dates between the 5th and 4th century BC, when the mingled Greco-Persian traditions so characteristic of Achaemenid art become common on artifacts from the Kuban.

61. Plaques (4 items)
    Inv. No. 30-33-13a–d
    Gold, punched. H. 2.6 cm
    5th–4th century BC

Each rectangular plaque is edged with a hatched (pseudo-beaded) line and with the frontal head of a horned and crested leonine griffin with upright ears in its central field. The griffin's horizontally hatched horns arise from its forehead before curving inward to meet at

CAT. NO. 61

their tops, creating an almost heart-shaped frame for the plumage that rises between them. There are four loops on the reverse for attaching each plaque to its foundation.

Eight identical plaques in the Antikenabteilung collection, not included here, were published by Greifenhagen (1970:59, pl. 36.10–13) as possible components of the Maikop collection. (His reservations about their derivation stemmed from worn museum numbers on them, but this Philadelphia example supports their attribution to de Massoneau's collection.) He dated the eight to between the 3rd and 1st century BC; such a late date, however, is not justified. Although no exact analogues are known, stylistically similar lion-griffins with the horns of goats and protruding ears are typical of 5th to 4th century BC Achaemenid art (Nikulina 1994:figs.

181.293–96, 448; Mitchell 1989:38, no. 11). Plaques from Chertomlyk (Artamonov 1966:figs. 104, 105, 107) and the kurgans of Mordvinovskiy and Verkhnerogachikskiy (Leskov 1974:42, 44, 46–47), which have similar hatched frames, also date from the mid-4th century BC or later. Our plaque is thus likely to date between the 5th and 4th century BC, when Greco-Persian influences are especially apparent in artifacts from the Kuban.

First published in Fernald (1930:pl. I).

62. Plaques (5 items)
   Inv. Nos. 30-33-1.1–1.5
   Gold, punched, soldered. H. 3 cm
   5th century BC

Five plaques in the form of a stag (three walk right and two walk left) with three birds' heads decorating its antlers and details in relief. The naturalistic rendering of the stags contrasts sharply with the stylized heads of the birds. There are several attachment loops on the reverse of each plaque.

Identical plaques not published here are preserved both in Berlin (14 items) (Greifenhagen 1970:58, pl. 33.1) and in the Metropolitan (4 items) (Alexander 1925:180f., fig. 7). Ten similar plaques, though with only two birds' heads on the antlers of each stag and with two or three holes instead of loops on the reverse, were recovered from the early 4th century BC Uliap kurgan No. 5 (Leskov 1990:fig. 156, no. 107). The loops on the reverse of the Maikop plaques, which may be an archaic feature, suggest our examples are better attributed to the 5th century BC.

CAT. NO. 62

First published in Colosanti (1915:2), where they were reconstructed as part of an arrangement of numerous gold plaques (including Nos. 63, 64, and 65) decorating a shirt purportedly found in a 6th century BC Scythian burial.

63. Plaques (4 items)
   Inv. Nos. 30-33-1.6–1.9
   Gold, punched, soldered. H. 2.6 cm
   5th century BC

Plaques in the form of a winged griffin (two walk right and two walk left) with a lion's body and the head of a bird of prey; each has several attachment loops on the reverse.

While identical plaques, not published here, are known from both Berlin (10 items) (Greifenhagen 1970:58, pl. 33.2) and the Metropolitan (4 items) (Alexander 1925:180f., fig. 7), no direct analogues have been recovered from excavation. Several details, however, aid in the dating of these objects: the treatment of the torso, the curving of the wing to-

CAT. NO. 63

ward the ear, the open jaw with visible teeth, and the pointed tips of the crest are all features characteristic of the Kuban variant of the Scythian Animal Style during the 5th century BC (Perevodchikova 1994:157f). The use of loops rather than holes for attachment supports an earlier date; attachment loops appear to be the more archaic feature.

First published in Colosanti (1915:2), where they were reconstructed as part of the same arrangement as Nos. 62 and 64–67.

64. Plaques (266 items)
Inv. Nos. 30-33-1.15, 1.16
Gold, punched, soldered. Diam. 0.4–0.7 cm
5th–4th century BC

Plaques are small hemispheres of varying dimension with attachment loops on the reverse. Though the simplicity of their form precludes the assignment of a secure date, it is worth examining the available comparanda. The largest collection of such plaques (not published here) may well be among the Maikop items in Berlin, where 842 plaques are represented (179 large and 663 small) (Greifenhagen 1970:60, pl. 37.6–7). Among the excavated materials, the earliest such plaques are from the late 7th to early 6th century BC Kelermes kurgans (Galanina 1997:pl. 31.313–14). While only single examples are known from Archaic sites in the Kuban and the Stavropol region (Meliukova and Abramova 1989:90–91), Greifenhagen (1970:60, fig. 54) noted the existence of a late 6th to mid-5th century BC complex from Hungary (burial from Zold khampushta) that contained more than a hundred similar plaques. They are noticeably better represented in the 5th century BC Ulskie kurgans (Leskov n.d.) and at 4th century BC Scythian sites, including kurgan Oguz (Leskov 1974:21, fig. 11), but are almost completely absent from 4th century BC Scytho-Maeotian sites in the Kuban. If our plaques originated in the Kuban, then they likely date to the 5th century BC; if they derive from the steppes of Ukraine or the Crimea, however,

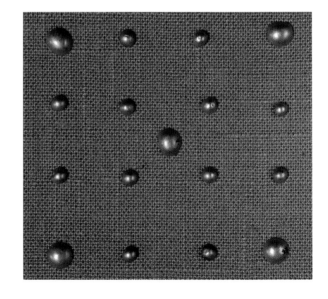

CAT. NO. 64

they are more likely to date to the 4th century BC.

First published in Colosanti (1915:pl. 2), where they were reconstructed as part of the same arrangement as Nos. 62, 63, and 65–67.

65. Plaques (6 items)
     Inv. No. 30-33-1.12
     Gold, punched, soldered. Diam. 1.6 cm
     5th century BC

Openwork plaques depict four heart-shaped volutes articulated in relief and arranged in a circular design around a central rhombus; the base of each volute forms one side of the rhombus, and four additional rhombi are set between the upper edges of the volutes. Four attachment rings are soldered on the reverse of each plaque.

CAT. NO. 65

There are a number of identical plaques, not published here, in the Antikenabteilung Museum (218 items) (Greifenhagen 1970:60, pl. 37.1) and the Metropolitan Museum (12 items) (Piotrovsky 1975:160, 15), and comparanda are also known from excavated contexts. The decorative elements of our plaques appear to have developed gradually in Asia Minor with close parallels known from the 7th century BC material from Ephesus (Greifenhagen 1970:27–28, fig. 8.1.4) and possibly also from an 8th century BC Urartian palace relief (Calmeyer 1976:fig. 43). The gold scabbards from the late 7th–early 6th century BC Kelermes kurgans (Galanina 1997:pl. 9.1c), possibly influenced by the Urartian material (Piotrovsky 1975:251f), are also notable for their similarity of ornament. While no such depictions are known from Ukraine or the Kuban after the Kelermes period, some 4th century BC Scythian kurgans (Reeder 1999:263, no. 126; Onaiko 1970:pls. xlii, 820a) have yielded larger and more heavily ornamented versions of these plaques: the volutes are more elongated, increasing the distance between them, and the intervening areas are filled with vegetal ornament such as rosettes, palmettes, and buds rather than simple rhombi. The plaques from the Maikop collection, which fall between the depictions on the Kelermes scabbards and the plaques from Oguz and Ryzhanivka in typology, likely belong to the 5th century BC.

First published in Colosanti (1915:pl. 2), where they were reconstructed as part of the same arrangement as Nos. 62–64 and 66–67.

66. Plaques (23 items)
     Inv. Nos. 30-33-1.13, 1.14
     Gold, punched, soldered. H. 1.6 cm (10 items), 1 cm (13 items)
     Second half 5th century BC

Cruciform plaques comprise five rhombi attached only at the corners: one in the center and

CAT. NO. 66

one forming each arm of the cross. Each rhombus is edged with a relief line and has a round convexity in its center. An attachment loop is soldered to the reverse of each plaque.

Identical plaques connected with the Maikop treasure are held in the Berlin museum (20 large and 20 small items) (Greifenhagen 1970:60, pl. 37.2–3) and similar plaques are also known from the Metropolitan Museum (10 items) (Piotrovsky 1975:160, 15). Among the excavated material the most important comparanda, comprising similar plaques complete with loops on the reverse (Mantsevich 1987:30, fig. 1), come from the central burial in the late 5th century Solokha kurgan (Alekseev 2003:259–60), with slightly later examples from the late 5th to early 4th century BC known from burial No. 2, kurgan No. 5, in Arkhangelskaia Sloboda. These latter are distinguished from our plaques by the use of holes rather than loops (a more archaic feature) for sewing. Additional plaques, formed from circles instead of rhombi and with holes instead of loops for sewing them to their foundations, are common in the 4th century BC; they have been recovered from kurgans of the Scythian elite in the steppes of Ukraine (Leskov 1974:46, 88) and from kurgan No. 11 in the group of "Chastie kurgans" on the central Don River (Puzikova 1995:album 8). On the basis of this evidence, our plaques seem to fit best in the second half of the 5th century BC. In terms of geographical derivation, it is notable that cruciform plaques comprised of rhombi are significantly more common in Ukraine than in the Kuban, where they are known from only two sites: the village of Tulskaia (south of Maikop) and the northern kurgan (4th century BC) in the village of Elizavetinskaia (Mantsevich 1957:30).

First published in Colosanti (1915:pl. 2), where they were reconstructed as part of the same arrangement as Nos. 62–65 and 67.

67.   Plaques (2 items)
      Inv. Nos. 30-33-1.10, 1.11
      Gold, punched, soldered. H. 2.6 cm
      5th century BC

Plaques in the form of two lotus-shaped palmettes are connected at their bases with a rhombus-shaped foundation; in the center of the foundation is another smaller rhombus, executed in relief and divided by a central line with a round convexity in its middle. Four attachment loops are soldered on the reverse.

Identical plaques not published here are held in the Berlin collection (19 items) (Greifenhagen 1970:58, pl. 33.4). Greifenhagen has noted that this form dates back to an Ionic type, but he

CAT. NO. 67

provided no direct examples. Lotus-shaped palmettes atop volutes are widely represented both in the Greek city-states of the northern Black Sea region and in the 4th century BC kurgans of the Scythian elite (Onaiko 1970:pl. xlii.505.b; Kazak 1995:no. 82). Unlike our examples, however, all the comparable artifacts known have small holes rather than loops (a more archaic feature) for sewing to their foundations. A date of the 5th century BC thus seems likely for our plaques.

First published in Colosanti (1915:pl. 2), where they were reconstructed as part of the same arrangement as Nos. 62–66.

68. Plaques (2 items)
     Inv. No. 30-33-24a, b
     Gold, punched, soldered. Diam. 0.6 cm, 0.7 cm
     5th century BC

In the form of a hemisphere edged with a relief line, the plaques vary both in dimension and in the manner in which they were attached to their foundations: one has two holes for sewing and the other has an attachment loop soldered to the central part of its reverse.

CAT. NO. 68

Similar artifacts, though lacking the relief border, are known from at least the Scythian Archaic period at sites in the Northwestern Caucasus (the Kelermes and Ulskie kurgans). While plaques with relief borders are less common, they occur in substantial numbers in the late 6th–mid 5th century BC Ulskie kurgans (Leskov n.d.). As no comparable objects have been recovered from 4th century BC sites in the Northwestern Caucasus, our examples are best dated to the 5th century BC.

69. Finial Fragments from Drinking Horns (3 items)
     Inv. Nos. 30-33-14.11–13
     Gold, iron, forged, soldered L. 1.7 cm, 3.3 cm, 3.5 cm
     5th–4th century BC

These heavily crumpled fragments were originally used as sockets for the tips of drinking horns. The animal head originally depicted on the end of each finial is currently impossible to identify; if the best preserved of these is any indication, however, it may have been a lion's head. Each finial was formed from two plaques, either soldered together or joined by iron tacks that also served to attach it to the horn's base.

The quality of the workmanship of these items is quite primitive, especially when compared to that of the finials from the Semibratnie kurgans (Anfimov 1987:92, 112–13) or Uliap kurgan No. 4 (Leskov 1990:fig. 187–90). It is even inferior to that of the finials from the Maikop collection in Berlin (not published here) (Greifenhagen 1970:pl.

CAT. NO. 69

36.1–5; Platz-Horster 2002:46–47, fig. 27). While the poor state of their preservation precludes a precise assessment of their date, they assuredly belong to the 5th or 4th century BC.

70. Tacks (2 items)
Inv. Nos. 30-33-14.22, 23
Iron, gold. L. 1.5 cm, 1.1 cm
5th–4th century BC

Tacks in the form of uneven, heavily corroded pins have a mushroom-shaped cap covered with a thin gold layer. These tacks may have served to attach finials to drinking horns or gold plaque-appliqués to wooden foundations. If so, they likely date between the 5th and 4th century BC.

71. Plaque
Inv. No. 30-33-14.6
Gold, punched. H. 3.8 cm
4th century BC

CAT. NO. 70

A thin openwork plaque is in the form of a schematically rendered rider astride a horse, both in profile facing right. The rider's right arm is raised and bent at the elbow, and he grasps a spear in his hand. Rectangular plaques with beaded frames from kurgan Kul-Oba bear similar depictions (Artamonov 1966:nos. 253–55), with the horse and rider sometimes supplemented with the figure of a rabbit. Unlike those examples, however, which were probably made in one of the

CAT. NO. 71

4th century BC Bosporan workshops, our plaque appears to be an example of local "barbarian" (non-Greek) work of the same period.

72. Plaque
     Inv. No. 30-33-14.1
     Gold, punched. H. 3.1 cm
     4th century BC

A thin openwork plaque is in the form of a clumsily rendered winged female figure with legs curving up and out into spirals; details are added in relief. Undoubtedly this is a representation of the "snake-footed goddess" thought to be the ancestor of the Scythians (Artamonov 1961:57–87); her face is characterized by a long straight nose, round eyes, a wide mouth, and a fringe of hair on her forehead. The raised wings blend into her head with its kalathos-type headdress, and breasts are clearly articulated on her chest. An additional small spiral links her spiral legs with the wings on each side. While the thinness of the plaque, which is partially bent and distorted, precludes an accurate judgment of the workmanship, the artifact is certainly of barbarian origin.

CAT. NO. 72

    Depictions of the snake-footed goddess are widespread at 4th century BC sites throughout the Bosporan Kingdom and Scythia (Grakov 1971:pl. xiv) and are even known from the Northwestern Caucasus in a 4th century BC kurgan in the village of Ivanovskaia (Anfimov 1987:127), but there are no close analogues to our depiction. The most comparable portrayal comes from the Aleksandropol kurgan of the second half of the 4th century BC (Artamonov 1961:fig. 15). It seems that all of the gold plaques bearing representations of the snake-footed goddess derive from a workshop in the Bosporan Kingdom and so necessarily contrast with ours, which belongs to the corpus of barbarian art widespread at Scythian-period (4th century BC) sites in the Kuban, especially in the steppes of southern Ukraine.

    First published in Fernald (1930:pl. I).

73. Plaques (2 items)
     Inv. Nos. 30-33-17, 18
     Gold, punched. H. 2.2 cm, 1.6 cm
     Second half 4th century BC

Each thin rectangular plaque, one mostly complete and one fragmentary, bears the representation of a standing female figure. The complete plaque, edged with either a slight

CAT. NO. 73

relief line or beading along the two short sides, shows a full-length female in very low relief. Her wings, which narrow toward the base, and garment, secured at the waist and falling in long folds to her heels, identify her as Nike, the goddess of victory. Her right hand is extended to the side, and her left hangs down, holding an elongated object that may be a sword or the wreath traditional to Nike. A hole pierces each corner of the plaque for attachment to what was probably a cloth foundation. Numerous such depictions of Nike are known both in ancient sculpture and on coinage, as on the gold stater of Alexander the Great (336–323 BC) (Zhuravlev 2002:no. 587). The fragmentary plaque, on which only the lower part of a female figure is discernible, was likely similar to the complete example. The figure is clad in a long garment secured at the waist and falling to the heels, and part of the right wing and the lowered right hand, which holds an unidentifiable object, are visible. The preserved short side is set off in relief, and one hole for attachment is preserved in the lower right corner.

The available comparanda, including a plaque bearing a similar depiction from the main burial in the Kurdzhips kurgan (Galanina 1980:92, no. 49, pl. vi), indicate that both these plaques should be attributed to the second half of the 4th century BC.

> 74. Plaque
>   Inv. No. 30-33-53
>   Gold, punched, soldered, with filigree. H. 1.2 cm
>   Second half 4th century BC

A plaque in the form of a two-sided lotus has a slightly raised six-petal rosette in its center. An attachment loop curves from a thin plaque soldered to the slightly concave section in the center of its reverse.

The size of this object suggests it originally functioned as part of either a complex pendant (Greifenhagen 1970:pl. 16.13) or a necklace of the Karagodeuashkh (Artamonov 1966:pl. 319) or Oguz (Chaikovskii 1992) type from the second half of the 4th century BC.

CAT. NO. 74

> 75. Button
>   Inv. No. 30-33-52
>   Clay, gilded, punched. H. 1.5 cm
>   Second half 4th century BC

This button is in the form of a two-sided lotus with a six-petal rosette in faint relief in its center. A pair of holes for sewing it to its founda-

CAT. NO. 75

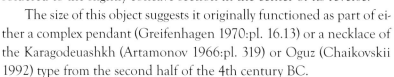

tion are set horizontally on the slightly convex central part of the reverse.

The date of this button is determined on the basis of comparable plaques from neck-laces of the Oguz (Chaikovskii 1992) and Karagodeuashkh (Artamonov 1966:pl. 319) type (cf. No. 74) and should therefore fall within the second half of the 4th century BC.

76. Plaques (3 items)
     Inv. No. 30-33-15a–c
     Gold, punched. Diam. 1 cm, 1.1 cm
     4th century BC

CAT. NO. 76

Three round plaques depict Medusa's head; on two of these she is shown with a slightly protruding tongue and a relatively straight hatched line above her fore-head indicating hair. Two holes, pierced from the front, take the place of ears and were used to attach the plaques to their foundations. On the third plaque, the Medusa's tongue is not visible and her hair swells from the center of the forehead before tapering off at the tips. Of the two holes replacing the ears, one is pierced from the front and one from the back.

Such artifacts are common at Scythian sites in Ukraine (Leskov 1974a:21.12; Onaiko 1970:pl. XLI) and very similar examples have been recovered from the 4th century BC Uliap kurgan No. 5 (Leskov 1990:fig. 172, no. 102). These plaques may thus be securely assigned to the 4th century BC.

77. Plaque (reconstructed from fragments)
     Inv. No. 30-33-134
     Gold, punched. L. 1.9 cm (preserved portion)
     4th century BC

CAT. NO. 77

A rectangular plaque is edged with a double relief line; a rabbit (facing right) occupies its central field, and there is a round hole for attachment, pierced from be-low, in the preserved lower left corner.

While the lower right section of the plaque is lost, precluding an analysis of the position of the rabbit's front paws, the overall depiction was likely comparable to that on similar plaques from Chertomlyk (Artamon-ov 1966:fig. 94) and Oguz (Kazak 1995:93, fig. 80), sug-gesting it should date to the 4th century BC (probably the latter half). As plaques bearing depictions of rabbits are not known from the Kuban, our example was likely recovered from a kurgan in southern Ukraine.

78. Plaque
    Inv. No. 30-33-20
    Gold, punched. H. 1.9 cm
    4th century BC

A triangular plaque is filled with relief granulation; each of the corners (two are broken) was originally pierced with a hole for attaching it to its foundation.

Similar plaques are common in 4th century BC Scythian kurgans in southern Ukraine (Artamonov 1966:fig. 104; Leskov 1974:figs. 11, 32, 36) and the Kuban, with the earliest example from the early 4th century BC Semibratniy kurgan No. 3 (Artamonov 1966:fig. 72). Two additional examples (one not published here) from the Berlin holdings of de Massoneau's collection (listed as from the south of

CAT. NO. 78

Russia) (Greifenhagen 1970:pl. 28.4) and one from Adyghea (recovered during the excavations of the Uliap kurgans) (Leskov 1990:fig. 179, no. 103) indicate that our plaque should be attributed to a 4th century BC site in the Kuban or southern Ukraine.

79. Plaque
    Inv. No. 30-33-14.9
    Gold, punched. L. 3 cm
    End 4th century BC

CAT. NO. 79

A thin openwork plaque takes the form of a recumbent winged griffin (?); while the damage to the animal's front torso and to the plaque itself precludes its secure identification, the depiction of the tail, which is raised and bent at the tip, is typical of predators such as griffins and lions. The animal's legs are tucked beneath it, and its head is turned back so the nose rests against the wing.

While similar depictions of griffins occur on plaques from a 4th century BC kurgan in the Darievka valley (Petrenko 1967:96, 98, pl. 19.41–42), the schematic and stylized treatment of the torso is more typical of objects from the end of the Scythian period, as from the 4th century BC Aleksandropol kurgan (Artamonov 1966:pl. 192, figs. 131, 133–34) or from the Sarmatian period (3rd to 2nd century BC) (Anfimov 1987:196). Our plaque thus likely dates to the late 4th or even the 3rd century BC.

80. Bracelet
Inv. No. 30-33-12
Gold, forged. Diam. 6.5 cm
4th century BC

A spiral bracelet is built of three coils curved from a narrow plaque triangular in section; the preserved end is flattened.

Similar bracelets with multiple coils are more typical of the Scythian than the Sarmatian period (Meliukova and Abramova 1989:pls. 41.42, 93, 71.82; Petrenko 1978:pl. 44.1–11), appearing already by the 5th century BC but most widespread during the 4th century BC. The relatively complex profile of our example, which is reminiscent of bracelets from 4th century BC sites in Ukraine (Reeder 1999:308, no. 158) and the Kuban (Anfimov 1987:158), indicates it should date to this same period.

CAT. NO. 80

81. Pendants (pair)
Inv. No. 30-33-8a, b
Gold, forged, soldered, with wire-drawing, filigree, and granulation. H. 1.8 cm
4th century BC

CAT. NO. 81

Pendants in the form of six-petal rosettes are soldered onto flat plaques; the petals and central circle of each rosette are set off in filigree. A wire attachment loop is soldered to the reverse of each pendant.

A comparable rosette from de Massoneau's collection was published by Greifenhagen (1970:52, pl. 28.12). While he did not describe the reverse, it likely had a suspension loop and served as a pendant, since a plaque would have been pierced with holes instead. Other rosettes of this type, often forming parts of complex ornaments, have been recovered from 4th century BC Scythian and Greek sites in the northern Black Sea region and from the south of Russia (Greifenhagen 1970:pls. 19.9, 16.3). Similar details on two necklaces dating to the second half of the 4th century BC (Reeder 1999:220–21, no. 101; Artamonov 1966:pl. 319), recovered from the Scythian royal kurgans at Oguz (in Ukraine) and Karagodeuashkh (in the Kuban), confirm a 4th century BC date for our pendants.

82. Sculptural Heads of Stags (2 items)
    Inv. Nos. 30-33-14.14, 15
    Gold, punched, soldered, with filigree, cutouts. H. 3.8 cm, 2 cm (preserved portion)
    Second half 4th century BC

Stags' heads comprised of two halves soldered together over a wooden (?) foundation possibly served as part of a diadem (Greifenhagen 1970:60, pl. 38.1–2). The antlers, cut from two flattened convex plaques soldered together in the middle and separated near the tips,

CAT. NO. 82

were inserted into two vertical holes framed by applied filigree circles set at the top of the head; another hole, set below the base of the antlers, may have held the ears. The eyes and nostrils are each articulated with wire circles, and a round, flat pendant was suspended from a loop threaded through each nostril (one survives). An oval hole at the base of the neck possibly allowed for the insertion of a nail or pin. The second plaque, missing both the antlers and the holes into which they were set, is distinguished from the first not only by its smaller size but also by the inferior quality of its workmanship; one of the two plaques comprising the ornament overlays the other in sections on its head and neck.

There is a similar stag's head, larger and better preserved than these, in the Antikenabteilung's holdings of the Maikop collection (cf. No. 179, Inv. No. 30.627). Greifenhagen (1970:60, taf. 38,1-2) suggested all three artifacts derived from a 3rd to 1st century BC context in the Taurian gubernia (which covered the Crimea, today's Khersonskaia Oblast, and most of today's Zaporozhskaia Oblast). This dating is clearly erroneous: two identical stags' heads from Kul-Oba (Stefani 1851:218, fig. xxxii.11) belong to the second half of the 4th century BC, and a similar item of the same period is known from the royal kurgan at Oguz (Leskov 1974a:19; Onaiko 1970:pl. xxxviii.451). The widespread distribution of these heads in the Crimea and the Cherson region contrasts sharply with their absence from sites in the Kuban; this suggests that they were manufactured somewhere in the European part of the Bosporan Kingdom in the second half of the 4th century BC.

Such artifacts seem often to have been affixed to diadems or headdresses, as indicated by the rectangular or round, flat bases on the Berlin and Kul-Oba examples (traces of a flat base appear on a Philadelphia example as well). The lack of such a base on the Oguz artifact and the existence of a similar cast stag's head that served as a pinhead (Stefani 1851:164, fig. xxiv.7), however, suggest that methods of attachment and foundations varied.

First published in Fernald (1930:pl. I).

83. Ornament
     Inv. No. 30-33-14.16
     Gold, punched, soldered, with filigree. L. 1.8 cm
     Second half 4th century BC

A hollow figure of a schematically detailed bird is composed of two halves soldered together. The wings are articulated with vertical relief lines and the wire circle soldered next to the beak links into the loop of a round, flat pendant with a filigree rim. A fragment survives of a second similar pendant.

While the poor preservation of the pendant precludes a definitive identification of its function, it may have been attached to a diadem or headdress; a headdress from Mord-

CAT. NO. 83

vinovskiy kurgan No. 1, for example, has a bird sitting on a flower at its peak (Leskov

1974:53, fig. 41). As both the Mordvinovskiy bird and the stags' heads of No. 82, which have identical pendants hanging from their noses, belong to the second half of the 4th century BC, our ornament should be attributed to the same period, probably originating in a Bosporan workshop.

84. Ornament
      Inv. No. 30-33-137
      Gold, punched, soldered. L. 1.5 cm
      4th century BC

CAT. NO. 84

A recumbent rabbit is composed of two punched plaques soldered together; the seam is clearly visible along the torso. Its head lies on its extended front paws, and its ears lie flat against its torso.

   The shape of the ornament suggests it was originally attached to a flat foundation, such as a 4th century BC pendant of the Ryzhanivka type (Onaiko 1970:pl. xxxvii.787e) or a pinhead of the Kul-Oba type (Artamonov 1966:pl. 249). In any case, none of the objects to which it might have been attached dates past the 4th century BC; as Nos. 82 and 83, our figurine was likely made in the workshops of the Bosporan Kingdom.

85. Ornament
      Inv. No. 30-33-14.10
      Gold, punched, stamped. L. 7.9 cm (preserved portion)
      4th century BC

A thin plaque is in the form of a narrow band with a straight base and a slightly wavy upper edge, bordered with a faint relief line from which five palmettes rise. The two outer palmettes, each with eleven petals, and the central example, with nine leaves, are rounded. The two intervening palmettes have elongated forms above small volute-shaped leaves: one has three lotus-shaped petals and the other takes the form of a tall vase broadening toward a wide mouth. Round holes of various sizes, pierced from both front and back, are scattered over the plaque's surface. The number of holes seems disproportionate to the delicate nature of the ornament, which was likely affixed to a headband with a leather foundation.

   Originally measuring 10 cm in length and bearing six palmettes (as visible in a photograph in Schumm [1930:Cat. No. 120k] and in the Penn Museum's card index in 1930, under No. 30-33-14), the band was damaged at some point between its acquisition in 1930 and 1962, when a negative (No. 92892) in the Museum's Photo Archives shows the ornament in its present form; the missing palmette was similar to the rounded ones in form.

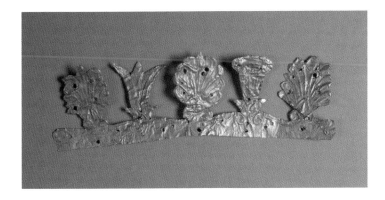

CAT. NO. 85

The form of its palmettes and the technique of its manufacture indicate this band should be dated to the 4th century BC.

86. Diadem (modern composite)
Inv. No. 30-33-5
Gold, cast, forged, punched, with cutouts, filigree, soldering, enamel (?).
L. 16.9 cm (preserved torque)
4th century BC (rosettes); Sarmatian period (torque)

The four composite rosettes attached to a semicircular fragment of a slim cast torque with soldered loops of varying widths were created from a mix of modern and ancient rosette forms (cf. Nos. 91, 130, and 133) and were added by a 20th century AD dealer (possibly Canessa himself, who first displayed the item in 1915).

Constructed in several layers, the rosettes are variously formed. Three of the four have a foundation comprising a clumsily cut five-petal rosette (4.4 to 4.6 cm in diameter) haphazardly pierced with eight to nine holes for the attachment of the central flower; these foundations were likely cut from a single sheet, possibly an appliqué for some sort of wooden vessel. The central flower, consisting of a regular 9- or 10-petal rosette edged with filigree, has a hole in the middle through which a tube bearing a small 6-petal rosette, also bordered with filigree, protrudes. One of these miniature rosettes is preserved here while fragments of the other two survive in the Museum's collection (Nos. 88 and 89, Inv. Nos. 30-33-14.15 and 30-33-14.17–20). The length of their tubes suggests that these miniature rosettes were attached to foundations such as the precious and complex pendants recovered from the richer sites connected with the art of the 4th century BC Bosporan Kingdom (Artamonov 1966:pls. 221–23, pls. 273, 304, 309, 315, 326–28). The fourth composite rosette has four layers, two of modern and two of ancient manufacture. The foundation (5.5 cm in diameter), which has eight clumsily cut petals (7 surviving), is a modern construction even if cut from ancient material. It is topped by an ancient rosette

CAT. NO. 86

with 13 petals (3 cm in diameter); each individual petal, as well as the rosette as a whole, is edged with filigree. A 5-petal rosette (2.5 cm in diameter), again of careless modern cut, sits atop the second and is pierced by a tube bearing a final ancient rosette (1.4 cm in diameter) edged with filigree.

The torque itself, with its slim form and tapering ends (one is preserved), likely belongs to the Sarmatian period, from the later centuries BC to the early centuries AD. Those rosettes of ancient manufacture included are, as noted above, likely of the 4th century BC. Both Canessa's account of this artifact as a Scythian diadem constructed under Greek influence and Harper's description of the four composite rosettes as fragments of gold diadems from a 5th century BC royal burial (Piotrovsky 1975:158.8) should thus be disregarded. Apparently the arrangement of the "flowers" was mixed up when they were reinserted on the torque, after the exhibit in New York. Thus, on the negative from the Museum's Photo Archives, NC35-22636, and in the publication of the exhibition catalogue on p. 158.8, the largest "flower" is placed in the middle whereas it is currently on the outside.

87.   Ornament Details (2 items)
      Inv. No. 30-33-22a, b
      Gold, punched, soldered, with filigree. Diam. 1.7 cm
      4th century BC

Each composite six-petal rosette has two layers attached by a tube rolled from a plaque and secured with soldering. The first ornament has a six-petal foundation: the tube that pierces its center terminates in a loop below it and is soldered to the center of a second six-petal rosette (one petal is lost) above it. The petals of the upper rosette take the form of long narrow rays with pointed tips that droop down toward the foundation; four circles are soldered in a square design to the convex cap in its center. Both the petals and central circles of the upper rosette are edged with filigree. Of the second ornament, only the six-petal foundation and tube remain; the form of the upper rosette is not known.

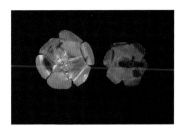

CAT. NO. 87

Similar ornaments are known not only from the Penn Museum portion of the Maikop collection (Nos. 86 and 88), but also from the Berlin holdings, not published here (see Greifenhagen 1970:pl. 37.8, 14), suggesting they all originated in a single region, likely in the area of Maikop. The excavated comparanda, which includes the richer pendants from the 4th century BC burials of the Scythian and Bosporan elite (Artamonov 1966:pls. 221–23, 304, 309), indicate our ornaments were manufactured in the same period in one of the jewelry centers of the Bosporan Kingdom.

88. Ornament Details (2 items)
Inv. Nos. 30-33-14.21a, b
Gold, punched, soldered, with filigree. L. 1.5 cm, 0.8 cm
4th century BC

CAT. NO. 88

Of these two seven-petal rosettes, the first ornament, of which four filigree-edged petals survive, has a round convex cap soldered to the center of the front and a small tube rolled from a thin plaque soldered to the center of its reverse. The second, more fragmentary ornament is similar to the first except in the shape of its petals, which are almost round; four of the petals are preserved, two *in situ*, and the small tube soldered to its reverse is broken in the middle of its length.

These should be dated to the same period as the ornaments of No. 87.

89. Ornament Details (4 items)
Inv. Nos. 30-33-14.17–20
Gold, punched, soldered, with filigree. L. 1.3–1.5 cm
4th century BC

CAT. NO. 89

Of these four compound ornaments two take the form of hemispherical six-petal rosettes, each with a small tube rolled from a thin plaque soldered in the center; the second rosette (whose tube is broken) has a thin suspension ring soldered to its edge that links into a wire loop holding a round, flat plaque bordered with filigree. The third ornament, of which only half is preserved, takes the form of a rectilinear (?) plaque with a small tube (similar to that on the two rosettes) soldered to it; the missing fragment may have been pierced with a loop for the suspension of the same type of round, flat plaque as on the second rosette. The fourth ornament, a ten-petal rosette, is similar to the other three in the short tube (now missing) that was soldered to the center of its reverse.

The second rosette, with its suspended plaque, and the rectilinear plaque are comparable to the items in Nos. 82 and 83, which are dated to the 4th century BC. The first rosette, though lacking a suspended plaque, is dated by analogy to the second, while the fourth ornament, the ten-petal rosette, is of a type widespread at 4th century BC (Leskov 1990:fig. 176). All four of these artifacts are thus likely from the same period.

90. Bands (2 items)
    Inv. No. 30-33-16a, b
    Gold, forged, cut out. L. 7.5 cm, 3.6 cm
    4th century BC

Of these two thin, unevenly cut plaques, the longer band, with one sharply zigzagging long side and one wavy one, has jagged short ends. Small flat-headed gold tacks (one preserved)

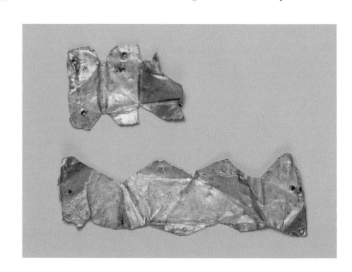

CAT. NO. 90

were inserted into the holes pierced from the interior along the edges of the band (three on each short side and one in the middle of each long side); they attached the band to a wooden (?) foundation, possibly a vessel. The second fragmentary band is more carefully worked. Its preserved short side is straighter, and both long sides take the form of more symmetric zigzags. There are two holes on the surviving short side and one more preserved on one of the long edges.

The undecorated and roughly worked appearance of these plaques makes it difficult to determine their date. Similar appliqués, though usually decorated in the Animal Style, were affixed to Scythian wooden vessels of the 5th to 4th century BC, while undecorated but much more carefully crafted bands were affixed to the wooden handles of whips from the 4th century BC kurgans of the Scythian elite (Reeder 1999:117, no. 14; 306, no. 156). As such bands are unknown from Sarmatian period or later contexts, our examples likely belong to the 4th century BC, when gold appliqués were most common in European Scythia.

91. Diadem (modern wire and tacks)
      Inv. No. 30-33-6
      Gold, forged, cut out (bands), punched (rosettes). L. 27.7 cm; H. 3.6 cm
      4th century BC (rosettes)

This composite ornament of modern construction, published in its final form in Colosanti (1915:2), was created from several unrelated ancient elements (cf. Nos. 86, 130, and 133): it consists of four individual bands with a composite six-petal rosette set in the center and at each end. The foundation was formed by overlapping and gluing together the short sides of the bands, which were further bound together with a modern wire threaded

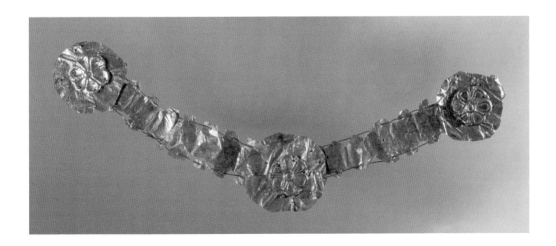

CAT. NO. 91

through both ancient and newly pierced holes. The composite rosettes were assembled in a similarly primitive fashion: the bases of the two on the ends are formed from round, flat plaques (4.2 and 3.8 cm in diameter) cut into four (?) petals, while that of the central one (slightly larger in diameter) has a more regular, rounded form. There are between five and ten holes scattered over each plaque, some connected to their original function and attachment. A smaller six-petal rosette (2.1 cm in diameter) is attached to the center of each plaque with glue and modern tacks. Each upper rosette has a round central convexity and petals edged with a relief line, but the one farthest left has concave rather than convex petals. All are pierced with holes of ancient origin for the attachment of these rosettes to their original foundations.

Dating the individual elements of this composite—which is made up of four bands, three round, flat plaques, and three rosettes of two different types—is problematic. Only the rosettes can be reliably dated to the 4th century BC on the basis of numerous analogues from Greek-Barbarian sites of that period in the Crimea, southern Ukraine, and the Kuban. The bands, however, are likely of the same period (cf. No. 90).

First published in Piotrovsky 1975 (p. 158.8, bottom).

92. Pendants (2 items)
     Inv. No. 30-33-27a
     Gold, punched, soldered, with granulation. H. 1.7 cm
     4th century BC

Pendants in the form of a hollow, elongated teardrop; the top of each is encircled by a horizontally grooved band and has a small, vertically grooved suspension ring attached to it. Deep vertical grooves also run lengthwise down each pendant's body to the base, which is ringed by a thin wire with four round granules forming a pyramid (pointing downward) soldered to it. The size of these pendants indicates they originally hung from a necklace.

Four identical pendants, published as artifacts from the south of Russia, are held in Antikenabteilung (No. 180, Inv. No. 30.632a–d) (Greifenhagen 1970:40, pl. 16.19). Although the collection from which these were acquired is not given, the lack of comparable items from the south of Russia in that collection strongly suggests that they, along with the two presented here, derived from a single necklace (cf. No. 93) acquired by de Massoneau for his collection. Similar ornaments from a burial ground near Krasnodar (Anfimov 1987:175) and from a necklace from the kurgan Bolshaia Bliznitsa (Artamonov 1966:pl. 309) indicate a 4th century BC date for these pendants.

93. Beads (103 items)
     Inv. No. 30-33-27b
     Gold, punched, soldered. L. 20 cm (string)
     4th century BC

CAT. NOS. 92 (2 pendants) AND 93

Each of these small, slightly compressed spheres has a faint rib along the center where the two halves were soldered together; together they form a string 20 cm long.

There are 117 identical beads in the Antikenabteilung's collection, not published here (Greifenhagen 1970:60, pl. 37.4–5, 13), that would have formed a string 23 cm long. As neither that nor the Penn Museum's string is independently long enough for a neck ornament, it is likely they originally formed a single chain at least 43 cm long with supplementary pendants (No. 92). Such beads are typical of necklaces of the 4th century BC.

94. Plaque Fragment
    Inv. No. 30-33-136
    Gold, punched. Diam. 1.8 cm
    Date unknown

This round, flat plaque is edged with a relief line; holes for sewing it to its foundation are preserved. The simplicity of its form and its damaged condition preclude a secure assessment of its date.

CAT. NO. 94

95. Plaque
    Inv. No. 30-33-14.24
    Gold, punched. L. 2.5 cm
    4th century BC

This thin, rectangular plaque is edged with a low-relief line and bears the faint depiction of a griffin (?) in its central field; the four irregular holes piercing its corners were used to sew it to a cloth foundation.

CAT. NO. 95

While the crumpled condition of the plaque makes it impossible to securely identify the animal depicted, the realistically rendered hind legs, the contour of the head, and the wings (raised to the level of the head) all suggest that it was a griffin of the type common in 4th century BC Scythian burials (Leskov 1974:fig. 81).

96. Plaque
    Inv. No. 30-33-25
    Gold, punched. Diam. 3.3 cm
    4th century BC

CAT. NO. 96

The convex side of this bowl-shaped plaque is bordered with two relief circles and has a hole through the center where an ornament (a rosette?) was originally inserted. After the imprint of the disc was made, the torn edges projecting beyond the lower rim were folded up against the concave side.

Although it cannot be independently dated, the plaque is comparable to Nos. 86–89 and 91 and so is tentatively dated to the 4th century BC.

97. Plaque
    Inv. No. 30-33-138
    Gold, punched. H. 0.6 cm
    Date unknown

In the form of a convex rhombus with a straight, flat base, this plaque carries in its central field the frontal face of an animal (?), of which only the two upright ears are clearly discernible. The relief lines between the ears may represent either eyes or teeth, and the small bumps at the top of the plaque may indicate a mane. The lack of holes or loops precludes a determination of the artifact's function or mode of attachment.

No analogues for this plaque exist, and while the standing ears resemble those of No. 61, which is executed in the Achaemenid style, this is insufficient for a secure assessment of its date.

CAT. NO. 97
(enlarged to show detail)

98. Plaques (2 items)
Inv. Nos. 30-33-14.7, 8
Gold, punched. H. 2 cm, 2.1 cm
4th century BC

These plaques are in the form of a seahorse with the head of a griffin. Sharp sawteeth running along the back of each profile head mirror those (partially broken) on the upper edge of the tail, which curves out from the spiral body. Two pierced holes allow the attachment of each plaque to its foundation.

Depictions of seahorses, including the heads on a pair of bronze cheekpieces from Uliap kurgan No. 5 (Leskov 1990:fig. 74, 79, no. 121), have been recovered from Scythian sites of the 4th century BC, the period of closest contact with the Greeks (Artamonov 1966:pls. 208–9, 256). Our plaques should be similarly dated.

CAT. NO. 98

The plaques were first published in *The Ercole Canessa Collection* (Schumm 1930:no. 120k), set, along with other plaques, on the vertical panel of a wooden sarcophagus of modern construction. The plaques' state of preservation has deteriorated significantly since then.

99. Horse Harness Ornament (?) with Pendants
    Inv. Nos. 30-33-111, 112, 113, 114
    Bronze, forged, punched. L. 6.5–7 cm (straight wires), 3.5 cm (connective
        pendant), 3 cm (short wires); W. 12 cm (base); H. 8.5–10 cm (plaques);
        Diam. 2.3 cm (circle)
    Later centuries BC

Reconstructed from the surviving details, this compound ornament comprised seven semi-oval plaques attached to a wire circle with sections of straight wire terminating in loops.

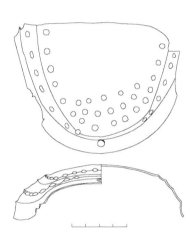

Three of the plaques were attached to long sections of wire that looped directly into the central wire circle, while the remaining three (two fragmentary) were on short sections of wire (one survives), each looped into one of the three hooks at the end of a single short wire also attached to the central wire circle. The wire circle, round in section, has flattened overlapping ends; the straight connecting wires, with the loops on the ends secured by spiral coils, were similarly round in section.

One of the plaques on the short wires, over half of which was preserved *in situ*, is flat and undecorated. The other plaques, appearing almost hemispherical because of their curved walls, were

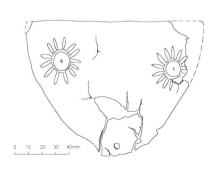

CAT. NO. 99, DETAILS OF INDIVIDUAL PLAQUES

decorated with simple, stamped ornament: two of the plaques on long wires bear in their lower corners indented circles with short relief lines radiating from them (resembling schematic suns), while the third plaque on a long wire, also preserved *in situ*, and the two remaining plaques on short wires, one whole and one in fragments, are each decorated with an arched band of punched indentations. One of these latter

CAT. NO. 99, DETAILS OF INDIVIDUAL PLAQUES

CAT. NO. 99 (reconstruction)

plaques has an additional row of indentations running along its base. The partial preservation of this ornament's elements *in situ* allows its reconstruction: if the central wire
circle was attached to a strap in a horizontal position, all plaques would have hung down
at an approximately equal length and jingled as they knocked against each other and
the horse's breastplate. The proposed strap may well have been a supplementary piece
attached to the horse's neck strap. This reconstruction is strengthened by the fact that
part of a bronze strap (cf. No. 100) appears in this same collection; it is denoted by the
same inventory number (No. 100, Inv. No. 30-33-113) and was likely part of this same
ornament. Such straps are also known from the Melitopol and Aleksandropol kurgans
(Ilinskaia and Terenozhkin 1986:148). An alternate reconstruction is also precluded by
the fact that none of the plaques had a suspension loop or holes suitable for attachment
to leather or wood.

     Horse burials in the kurgans of the 4th century BC Scythian elite often contained items such as small bells, crescent-shaped pendants, and plaques from neck ornaments (Meliukova 1981:49ff; Terenozhkin and Mozolevskii 1988:140ff). In Uliap kurgan No. 5 of that period, five horse heads were found accompanied not only by bits, cheekpieces, and frontlets but also by numerous beads that originally decorated the horses' necks (Leskov 1990:35, fig. 117–28). Notably, however, horse ornaments reached their pinnacle of development in a 2nd century BC ritual complex from Tenginskaia village in the Kuban; large eye beads, originally decorating a horse's neck, were recovered from the complex, along with half of a bronze breastplate. This last (39.5 cm long) was decorated with punched convexities and with triangular plaques and conical pendants dangling from wire loops on the base (Beglova 2002:297–304; Moshinskiy 2003:45, nos. 93, 94). This latter ornament is comparable in some respects to the one described here, with its applied ornamentation and attachment with straight wires terminating in loops secured with spiral coils. In the complex from Tenginskaia, there were also clearly defined ornaments for the bridle straps in addition to the beads on the horse's neck. The available comparanda, comprising 4th century BC material from Scythian kurgans in southern Ukraine and contemporary and later material from the Kuban and from Stavropol (Kazak 1995:14, fig. 1.1), suggest our ornament was connected with the Kuban of the later centuries BC.

100. Horse Breastplate Detail
    Inv. No. 30-33-113
    Bronze, forged. L. 14 cm; W. 5.2 cm
    Later centuries BC

This gently curved, rectangular band (broken on the left) has six small holes (pierced from the front) preserved along its lower edge. A fragment of wire with a loop at each end is

CAT. NO. 100

preserved in the far left hole; one loop served to attach the wire to the plaque and the other was attached to a pendant.

Similar breastplates have been recovered from horse burials (cf. No. 99), and ours likely derived from a similar context. This item, which has the same inventory number as the compound ornament of No. 99, was indeed attributed to the same complex as that ornament while still in de Massoneau's possession; the two items should probably be taken together and dated to the later centuries BC.

101. Torque
     Inv. No. 30-33-11a, b
     Gold, forged, soldered. Diam. 15.5 cm
     2nd–1st century AD

This spiral torque has three full coils curved from a tube 0.8 cm in diameter; the ends (one preserved) widen to a flat, soldered tip.

The absence of ornament complicates the assessment of its date. Torques with two or more coils are rare in the northern Black Sea region, and while a gold torque with more than two coils was recovered from a 4th century BC ritual complex in Adyghea (Leskov 1990:188, no. 197, cf. misprint and accurate image), circular objects (bracelets, necklaces, torques) curved from tubes are much more characteristic of the Sarmatian period than the Scythian (Anfimov 1987:227; Leskov and Lapushnian 1987:47, no. 169; 57, no. 150; 130, no. 151; 177). Our torque should thus be dated between the 2nd and 1st century AD.

CAT. NO. 101

102. Ornaments (2 items)
     Inv. No. 30-33-21a, b
     Gold, plaited, punched. L. 2.5 cm
     2nd century BC–1st century AD

Ornaments in the form of a small, three-linked chain with a flat disc hanging from a suspension loop; such ornaments are typical of 2nd century BC to 1st century AD Sarmatian sites in the Kuban and 1st century AD burials in Ukraine (Kazak 1995:146.5–6, 151.14; Simonenko and Lobai 1992), typically serving as suspended details for pendants of various forms (Leskov and Lapushnian 1987:pl. xxxii, figs. 58, 60, nos. 140, 167, 168, 171, 195; Anfimov 1987:179ff., 203). The late date at which they appear in Ukraine indicates that they were not typical of the Volga-

CAT. NO. 102

Ural region's Sauromatian-Sarmatian culture. Our examples should belong within the given range of the 2nd century BC and the 1st century AD.

103. Ornament
     Inv. No. 30-33-31
     Gold, bronze, cast, forged, plated. L. 8 cm
     2nd–1st century BC

On this gold-plated bust of a warrior holding a severed male head by the hair the warrior's straight hair frames a high forehead, large eyes beneath arched brows that meet at the bridge of the nose, and a broad nose; the plump slightly parted lips, emphasizing the small mouth, and the softened line of the jaw give his face a round aspect. A double-coiled torque rendered in relief encircles his neck, and the left side of his chest is set off in high relief, indicating his protective armor. The schematically depicted fingers of his right hand, which seem similarly protected, contrast sharply with the careful articulation of his oversleeve, defined with horizontal lines, and shoulder band and cuff, defined with vertical lines. The severed head he holds has features similar to his own. There are fragments of two shafts, one a horizontally projecting needle (4.5 mm in diameter) and the other presumably a vertically positioned receiver (5 mm in diameter), on the reverse; how these shafts were actually joined to each other is unknown and it is possible they served a function other than attachment per Fernald (1930:7).

No similar artifacts are known. While the image of a warrior holding a severed head recalls Herodotus's story of Scythian warrior customs (4.64), the clothing and other details of this specific rendering have nothing in common with the warrior images of Greco-

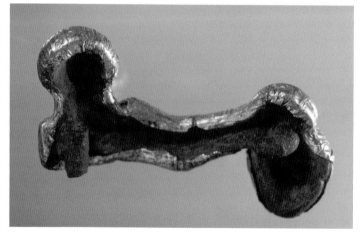

CAT. NO. 103

Scythian or Caucasian (Colkhido-Koban) art. We should, however, note that a fabulous
gold cap comes from the Maikop region (the Kurdzhips kurgan of the end of the 4th century BC) (Galanina 1980), with a depiction of two warriors, one of whom holds a decapi-
tated human head in his hand. On one of the bronze straps from the burial ground in the
village of Tli in southern Ossetia, an engraved depiction of a horseman was found with
a human head strapped to the harness (Tekhov 1977:99). The protective armor is more
reminiscent of Celtic depictions of such. Two examples—a 1st century BC bronze figurine
of a deity wearing protective armor from Bouray, in France (Schlette 1979:fig. 21), and a
2nd to 1st century BC horned deity with horizontally articulated oversleeves on a silver
cauldron from Gundestrup, in Denmark (Schlette 1979:126, figs. 31–33)—are especially
comparable to our figure in their attire. As the sacrifice of a man by decapitation was a
popular ritual among the Celts and is reflected in the Celtic sculpture of the 1st century
BC (Schlette 1979:120, fig. 28), it seems probable that this artifact was not in fact from the

northern Black Sea region, whence the rest of de Massoneau's enormous collection was derived, but was rather a Celtic antiquity of the 2nd–1st century BC acquired in France.

First published in the Colosanti catalogue (1915), where it was erroneously described as either a fibula (in the caption to its picture) or a buckle (in the list of items). It was published again in Piotrovsky (1975:159, no. 13), where it was tentatively and mistakenly identified as a "bizarre" bronze pin dating to the 1st century AD or later.

104. Ornament Detail
     Inv. No. 30-33-23a
     Gold, soldered, plaited. L. 5.5 cm
     2nd–1st century BC

This chain with a large ring in the middle of its length has a sphere suspended from a loop at each end.

Such ornaments commonly appear as part of Sarmatian period temporal pendants in the Kuban (cf. No. 102). They appear slightly later in the Crimea, where they are known from a rich 1st–2nd century AD Sarmatian burial (Kazak 1995:152, no. 16), and in the lower Don River region, where a comparably dated Sarmatian burial has yielded chains terminating in spherical beads rather than spheres (Alekseev 1991:110, no. 128). Our ornament is likely somewhat earlier than this comparanda, dating between the 2nd and 1st century BC.

CAT. NOS. 104 (right) AND 105

105. Ornament Detail
     Inv. No. 30-33-23b
     Gold, soldered, plaited, with filigree. L. 3.1 cm
     2nd century BC–2nd century AD

This fitting, oval in section, has a flat, soldered top ringed with plaited wire and three small chains diverging from its bottom end. Three *ovolos* formed from applied wire decorate its front, and there is a flat, horizontal attachment loop on its back. Of the three attached chains, only the middle one is fully preserved; its base is threaded with a long straight wire on which a small sphere soldered from two halves is secured, looping up to wrap in a spiral around its upper half. The fitting was originally part of a compound temporal pendant.

Chains with pendants are common in both the Scythian (4th century BC) and Sarmatian (2nd century BC to 2nd century AD) periods; the Scythian examples, however, typically had figural pendants (often duck or acorn shaped). Only in the Sarmatian period was it common for disc-shaped plaques or spheres to be attached to chains with a straight wire looped up and wrapped in a spiral (Petrenko 1978:pls. 19–21; Nekhaev 1987:132, fig. 58, 134, fig. 60). Our ornament thus likely dates between the 2nd century BC and 2nd century AD.

106. Bead
    Inv. No. 30-33-29
    Gold, iron, forged, soldered, with filigree L. 3.8 cm
    1st–3rd century AD

CAT. NO. 106

An elongated, barrel-shaped bead is covered with a gold layer and pierced lengthwise through its center with a wide, wire-ringed hole at either end.

Similar beads are known on necklaces from a rich 2nd–mid-3rd century AD burial in the ancient Greek necropolis of Gorgippia (Alekseev 1991:141, no. 183), and at least one comparable example, though slightly larger than ours, was recovered from the 1st to 3rd century AD Sarmatian burial grounds on the bank of the Krasnodar reservoir (Leskov 1990:fig. 221, no. 257). Our bead should thus be attributed to the early centuries AD.

107. Bead
    Inv. No. 30-33-28
    Iron, gold, forged. H. 1.2 cm
    1st–3rd century AD

A barrel-shaped bead is covered with a very thin gold layer. While such beads are not known from Scythian period sites on the Black Sea shore in the Caucasus or Ukraine, a bead of similar manufacture (iron covered with gold) in this collection (cf. no. 106) suggests this item should be dated to the Late Sarmatian period of the early centuries AD.

CAT. NO. 107

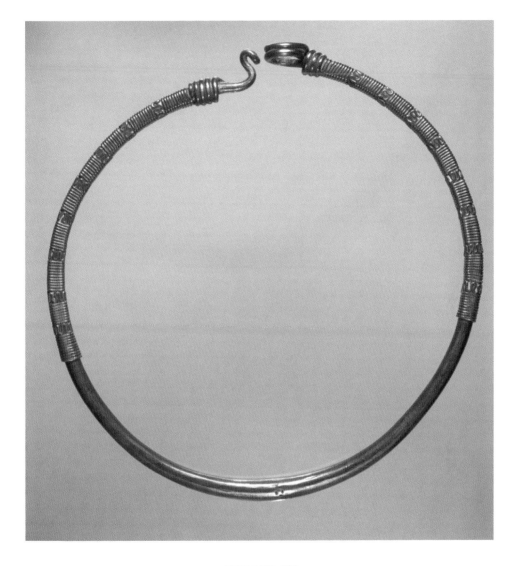

CAT. NO. 108

108. Torque
Inv. No. 30-33-30b
Silver, forged, with wire-drawing and plaiting. Diam. 16 cm
3rd–5th century AD

Curved from a shaft that is round in section in the center and tapers gradually toward narrow ends that are square in section. Each end was hammered out into the wire from which the two parts of the clasp—one a circle with two coils and one an S-shaped hook—were rolled. Two zones of ornament, each extending up a third of the length of the torque from the tips, are formed by coils of thin wire wrapped around the shaft in nine sections divided by eight short bands (created by pieces of the same thin wire) in the form of wavy lines.

While torques and bracelets with similar clasps are typical of the Late Sarmatian period in the steppes of the northern Black Sea region, the Crimea, and the Northern Caucasus (Meliukova and Abramova 1989:136, 143, pl. 55.28.56) and are found also in the necropoleis of the ancient Greek cities of the Bosporan Kingdom (Zhuravlev 2002: no. 329; Alekseev 1991:137, no. 175), no other example is so extensively adorned with coil decoration. Our torque is more comparable in that respect to fibulae with irregularly shaped coils from sites of the later 3rd to 5th century AD (Ambroz 1971:96ff., fig. 4.3,5), especially those from Abkhazia. Wire coil ornament in general is characteristic of ornaments and clothing details of the end of the Sarmatian period and beginning of the Middle Ages. This artifact thus likely dates between the 3rd and 5th century AD.

109. Amulet
       Inv. No. 30-33-54
       Bone, carved, polished, engraved. L. 5.7 cm; W. 0.6 cm
       4th century AD

CAT. NO. 109

An elongated pyramid is identically decorated on each of its four sides: a vertical row of six large circles, each with a dot in its center, is broken by an X-shaped incision between the second and third circles. The base of the pyramid is damaged and its decorative scheme is uncertain.

Pyramidal amulets with similar decoration are known from a 4th century AD context at Tanais, an ancient Greek city-state on the lower Don River (Böttger 2003:89ff., fig. 3.10, 123ff., fig. 8.6), and from a comparably dated complex in the lower reaches of the Dniepr River comprising Scythian, Sarmatian, and early medieval objects (Goshkevich 1913:117f., fig. 49). As such amulets are not known in the Kuban, despite the numerous Sarmatian period finds from that region, it seems likely they were connected with the sites of the ancient Germans, whose penetration of the East extended to the Don River. On the basis of this comparanda, our amulet should be attributed to a 4th century AD complex probably found in southern Ukraine.

110. Fibula
       Inv. No. 30-33-70
       Silver, forged, soldered. L. 4.2 cm
       7th–early 8th century AD

This is the curved back of a hinged, T-shaped fibula (front not preserved). The narrow, rectangular central shaft, articulated with a relief line along its middle, swells into an oval at one end and a large bell-shaped form terminating in a hinge at the other. The hinge is formed by a vertical shaft threaded through two long sockets (separated by a small space) and secured in place by the broad flat heads, rolled from thick plaques, at its ends.

CAT. NO. 110

   Similar fibulae are known from 7th to early 8th century AD sites in the Northern Caucasus (Kovalevskaia 1981:fig. 62.113), with the most comparable example coming from the burial grounds of Klin-Iar, which date from the second quarter of the 7th to the beginning of the 8th century AD (Flerov 2000:47–48, fig. 36.7). Our example should belong to the same period.

111. Fibula
      Inv. No. 30-33-69
      Silver, cast, forged, soldered, engraved. L. 4.5 cm
      7th century AD

This hinged, T-shaped fibula narrows gradually from the hinge (forming the upper stroke of the T) toward the elongated, semi-tubular receiver at its foot; the back is sharply curved and decorated at its widest part, adjacent to the hinge, with four dotted indentations in square formation framed above by a relief line and on either side by incised half-oval arcs. The hinge comprises a shaft threaded through two long sockets and secured by the small sphere soldered to each of its ends. A third small sphere is soldered onto the head of the fibula's pin, which projects out beyond the middle of the hinge.

   The shape of the fibula is clearly borrowed from the more massive Roman provincial versions, usually with heavily engraved backs, that developed in the Danube provinces in the 2nd to 3rd century AD and spread from there to the Rhine in the west and the Caucasus in the East (Ambroz 1966:74; Abramova 1995:140ff.). Local production of such items, albeit smaller in scale and only sparsely decorated, was established in the Northern Caucasus over

CAT. NOS. 111 (top) AND 112

time and fibulae similar to ours have occasionally been recovered from 7th century AD contexts. Kovalevskaia (1981:fig. 62.92) published one example from this period recovered from the Northern Caucasus, and Ambroz (1971:96–123, pl. I.46) published a similarly dated piece from Abkhazia. Our fibula should belong to this same period.

112. Fibula
     Inv. No. 30-33-71
     Bronze, forged, cast, soldered. L. 4 cm
     7th century AD

This hinged, T-shaped fibula tapers slightly from the hinge (forming the upper stroke of the T) toward the broad, flattened foot; the back is sharply arched and ribbed and the transition to the foot is set off in vertical relief. The hinge comprises a shaft threaded through two long sockets and secured by the small sphere soldered to each of its ends. A third small sphere is soldered onto the head of the fibula's pin, which projects out beyond the middle of the hinge.

   Similar fibulae are known from 7th century AD complexes in the Northern Caucasus (cf. No. 111) (Ambroz 1989:figs. 22.26,29.1). Our example should be attributed to the same period.

113. Earrings (pair)
     Inv. No. 30-33-33a, b
     Gold, forged, soldered, with granulation. H. 3 cm
     7th–early 8th century AD

These earrings are in the form of a hollow sphere with four smaller spheres soldered in a square formation to its upper surface. Oval suspension loops, curved from wire that is round in section, are soldered to the top of each earring and have tips that do not meet. Four small granules with a small hollow sphere set atop them were soldered in the lower curve of each suspension loop (preserved on one earring).

   Similar earrings (cf. No. 114) in bronze or gold are common among the Northern Cauca-sian artifacts of the Alani (7th to 8th century

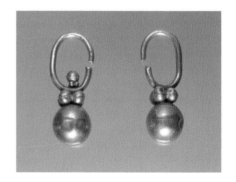

CAT. NO. 113

AD) (Kovalevskaia 1981:figs. 62, 113, 142–43). The most comparable pair, recovered from catacomb burial No. 20 in the Klin-Iar III burial grounds (Flerov 2000:35–36, figs. 32.6–7), was found in conjunction with not only a hinged T-shaped fibula (similar to No. 110) but also with various other objects that have direct analogues in this collection. As the Klin-Iar burial dates between the second quarter of the 7th and the beginning of the 8th century AD, our earrings should be dated within this same period.

114. Earrings (pair)
    Inv. No. 30-33-32a, b
    Gold, forged, soldered, with granulation. H. 4.5 cm
    7th–mid-8th century AD

CAT. NO. 114

While similar to No. 113, these earrings vary slightly in a number of details. The pendant here comprises a slightly larger hollow sphere with eight smaller spheres, here arranged in two rows of four, soldered atop it; the oval suspension loop, though still with tips that do not meet, is somewhat larger and the same secondary ornament set in its lower curve, four small granules topped by a small sphere, appears also on the exterior of the loop near the top of the curve.

Similar earrings (cf. No. 113) are known from the Northern Caucasus and belong to a single type, found in the mountain village of Kamunta (Northern Ossetia), that dates between the 7th and mid-8th century AD (Artamonov 1962:188).

115. Amulet
    Inv. No. 30-33-78
    Bronze, cast in a one-sided mold, polished, carved. L. 3.3 cm; H. 3.1 cm (max.)
    7th–mid-8th century AD

This amulet is in the form of a schematically rendered stag. Its front and lateral edges are polished, emphasizing its three-dimensionality, and long incised lines articulate its legs, eyes, and mouth. There is a suspension loop on its reverse.

Similar amulets appear in 5th to 9th century AD contexts in the Northern Caucasus, though they are most common at 8th to 9th century AD sites (Kovalevskaia 1981:87). The closest analogue to our amulet was recovered in conjunction with a coin of Emperor Heraklius II (AD 613–30) from the Klin-Iar III cata-

CAT. NO. 115

comb burial No. 20, which was dated by the excavator to no later than the mid-8th century AD (Flerov 2000:35–36, fig. 32.12). Our example should thus be dated between the 7th and mid-8th century AD.

116. Amulet
     Inv. No. 30-33-108
     Bronze, cast. Diam. 3.3 cm
     7th–mid-8th century AD

CAT. NO. 116

This amulet is in the form of a schematically rendered human figure with arms and legs outspread within a cog-shaped frame with 12 projections. A small suspension ring is attached to the frame above the figure's head.

According to Kovalevskaia's (1981:87, fig. 64) table on the chronology and development of amulets, our example belongs to the middle group and should date between the late 7th and 8th century AD. This date is consistent with that of a similar amulet, recovered from catacomb burial No. 20 (cf. No. 115) in the Klin-Iar III burial grounds (Flerov 2000:35–36, fig. 32.14).

117. Mirror
     Inv. No. 30-33-126
     Bronze, cast, polished. Diam. 5 cm
     7th–8th century AD

This mirror is in the form of a disc with a polished front surface; the reverse is clumsily decorated with a six-pointed star set between two concentric relief circles (one runs along the edge of the disc) and has a small suspension loop in its center.

Such mirrors are common at Alanian sites in the Northern Caucasus (Kovalevskaia 1981:figs. 62, 97, 117), with some securely dated examples known from late 7th to early 8th century AD complexes in the Klin-Iar

CAT. NO. 117

III burial grounds (Flerov 2000:42–45, fig. 39.27). While this type of mirror (Pletneva 1989:100ff., fig. 51) is also widely represented at mid-8th to early 9th century AD sites of the Saltovo-Maiatskaia culture (Pletneva 1998:fig. 73), our own example likely dates between the 7th and 8th century AD.

118. Mirror–Amulets (2 items)
       Inv. Nos. 30-33-127, -128
       Bronze, cast, polished. Diam. 3 cm
       Mid-7th–mid-8th century AD

These mirrors are in the form of a disc with a polished front surface; the reverse of each, edged with a relief line, has a suspension loop in its center.

CAT. NO. 118

Such objects are common at early medieval sites in the southern part of Eastern Europe, appearing at Alanian sites in the Northern Caucasus during the turn of the 7th to the 8th century AD (Kovalevskaia 1981:87) and at early sites of the Saltovskaia culture in the 8th to early 9th century AD (Kovalevskaia 1981:64). The closest analogue to our example was recovered from catacomb burial No. 20 in the Klin-Iar III burial grounds and dates between the early 7th and mid-8th century AD (Flerov 2000:35ff., fig. 33.2). This fits well with Pletneva's dating of such amulets (closest to her ninth type) to the 8th century AD (1989:99, fig. 49) and supports the attribution of our example to the mid-7th to mid-8th century AD.

119. Mirror
       Inv. No. 30-33-125
       Bronze, cast, polished. Diam. 6.3 cm
       8th–9th century AD

CAT. NO. 119

This mirror is in the form of a disc with a polished front surface. The reverse is decorated with four concentric relief circles and has a small suspension loop in its center.

While such objects (though with only three concentric circles) might have appeared already in the Late Sarmatian period (3rd century AD) in the Northern Caucasus (Meliukova and Abramova 1989:271, pl. 103.53), the only published example comes from an unknown complex near the mountain village of Koban (Northern Ossetia). Not a single example of such a mirror appears among the vast amount of material from the Northern Caucasus of this and the following period published in a special monograph on the early Alani by Abramova (1997). Mirrors decorated with three concentric circles only become common during the Early Medieval period, appearing at sites in the Northern Caucasus such as the burials from stages I–IV (last third of the 5th to the 7th century AD) in the Diurso burial grounds near Novorossiysk (Dmitriev 1982; Ambroz 1989:15, pls. 17.10, 4, 28, 19.7, 20.11, 21, 21.6). Such artifacts are also known in the Central Caucasus and Crimea from the end of the 5th to the 8th century AD (Kazanski and Soupault 2000). Mirrors decorated with four concentric circles (Pletneva 1981:fig. 73a) first appear alongside the earlier type (with three circles) at sites of the Saltovskaia culture during the 8th to early 9th century AD (Pletneva 1989:fig. 51.1), becoming more common over the course of this period (up to the early 10th century AD). Our example should be dated within this range.

120. Mirror
       Inv. No. 30-33-124
       Bronze, cast, polished. Diam. 10.6 cm
       7th–9th century AD

CAT. NO. 120

This mirror is in the form of a disc (less than a quarter is lost) with a polished front surface. The reverse is clumsily decorated with six concentric circles, three formed from relief lines (relief circle outermost) alternating with three formed from zigzagging lines, and it has a suspension loop in its center.

Although no identical artifacts are known, a comparable series of mirrors exists among the 7th–9th century AD artifacts of the Northern Caucasus (Kovalevskaia 1981:figs. 62, 79, 96, 97), and a somewhat similar example was recovered from catacomb No. 23 in the Klin-Iar III burial grounds of the second quarter of the 7th–early 8th century AD (Flerov 2000:47ff.). The increase in size (Kovalevskaia 1981:87) and deterioration in quality observed in Alanian mirrors in later periods, coupled with Pletneva's classification (1989:104, fig. 53) of a second form of mirror (7-10.5 cm in diameter) from Saltovo-Maiatskaia sites, suggest a date of 7th to 9th century AD for our example, which likely belonged to the Alanian or Saltovskaia culture.

94 The Maikop Treasure

121. Amulet
    Inv. No. 30-33-109
    Bronze, cast. Diam. 3.4 cm
    8th–9th century AD

CAT. NO. 121

This amulet is in the form of two flat, concentric circles connected by seven evenly spaced spokes. Six of the spokes protrude above the rim of the outer circle, and there is a suspension loop above the seventh.

Similar amulets are common at 6th–9th century AD sites in the Northern Caucasus. Our example, however, belongs to a specific type, described by Kovalevskaia (1981:87) as "wheel-shaped, seven-rayed amulets with a loop," that is characteristic of the 8th–9th century AD when amulets of varying forms are most widespread and appear especially in the Kuban, Karachaevo-Cherkessia, and Kabardino-Balkaria (Kovalevskaia 1981:87, figs. 64, 107, 108, 111, 125). This type probably dates back to the Alani of the Northern Caucasus, transmitted from that region to the Saltovskaia culture sites on the Don River periphery of the Khazar kingdom where it appears somewhat later (mid-8th–early 10th century AD) (Pletneva 1989:96, fig. 48). Our amulet likely belongs within the 8th to 9th century AD range.

122. Amulet
    Inv. No. 30-33-106
    Bronze, cast, soldered, forged. Diam. 4.9 cm
    8th–9th century AD

This amulet is in the form of a downward-facing crescent. The schematically rendered head of a snake hangs from the center and each of the two tips. A tall suspension loop is soldered to the reverse.

Although no direct analogues for this object are known, *lunulas* of gold or silver with inset stones have been recovered from Alanian sites of the 6th–7th century AD, with bronze examples appearing in the 8th–9th century AD (Kovalevskaia 1981:figs. 64.26-27, 64.55.85). The tradition of ornamenting such amulets with stone inserts

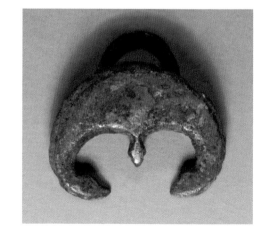

CAT. NO. 122

apparently made its way to the Saltovo-Maiatskaia tribes, as bronze lunulas similar to ours, likely dating between the 8th and 9th century AD (Pletneva 1998:fig. 41; 1989:111, fig. 58), have been found at their sites. Our amulet should thus likely be attributed to an 8th–9th century AD site in the Northwestern Caucasus.

123. Mirror
       Inv. No. 30-33-123
       Bronze, cast, polished. Diam. 15 cm
       10th–12th century AD

This mirror is in the form of a disc with a polished front surface. The reverse is edged with a relief line and has a large Celtic cross in low relief, formed from four uneven arcs and

CAT. NO. 123

divided in half by a straight relief line, filling its central field. There is a suspension loop in its middle.

Similar mirrors are known from 10th–12th century AD contexts at Late Alanian sites. One example, from the Zmeyskiy catacomb burial grounds of the 11th–12th century AD (Kuznetsov 1963:6–38, pl. iv.6), is ornamented with arcs. A slightly earlier example, also comparable to ours, is dated to the 10th or 11th century AD (Kovalevskaia 1981:227, fig. 94.142). Our mirror thus likely dates between the 10th and 12th century AD.

124. Two-Part Buckles (9 pairs)
       Inv. Nos. 30-33-55a,b, -56a,b, -57a,b, -58a,b, -59a,b, -60a,b, -61a,b, -63a,b, -64a,b
       Silver, cast, soldered, polished. L. 6.3 cm (connected pair); W. 1.3 cm
       10th century AD

These buckles are formed from two plaques that are triangular in section and have a small protrusion in the center of the slightly rounded short end. The other short end terminates in one case in a circular tongue on a short base and in the other in a ring-shaped receiver with a crosspiece at its base. The tongue would have been inserted at an angle into the receiver (holding the plaques perpendicular to each other) before both plaques were brought up into horizontal position, locking the tongue into place against the crosspiece of the receiver. Each plaque is decorated on the front with fantastic vegetal forms in low relief, probably executed during the casting process and subsequently polished, and has a pair of bronze attachment loops (one loop preserved) on its reverse.

Similar buckles, differing primarily in their lack of ornament, are preserved in both the Antikenabteilung's holdings of the Maikop collection (No. 195-97, Inv. No. 30.602-4) and in the Eastern Division of the State Hermitage (Inv. No. Kub. 173-175). Those in the Hermitage are said to be from the Maikop kurgans (Kozlov's collection) and are identified in file no. 3, Eastern Division (part 3:44–46) by Kramarovskii, keeper of that collection, as 10th century AD artifacts of the Hungarians, who had sites in the Kuban. Our buckles should be similarly dated.

CAT. NO. 124

First published in an exhibition catalogue by Piotrovsky (1975:159.14), where they were connected to a silver vessel and dated to the 8th to 9th century AD on the basis of scant evidence.

125. Two-Part Buckles (pair)
    Inv. No. 30-33-62a, b
    Silver, cast, soldered, polished, stamped. L. 6.7 cm (connected pair); W. 1.3 cm
    10th century AD

CAT. NO. 125

Buckles identical in form to No. 124 but with a different design on the plaque, with the circular tongue decorated with two uneven circles, each divided horizontally into two halves by the long central rib. Both halves of one circle and one half of the other are imprinted with a fine-toothed die. This half of the buckle was probably unfinished, as indicated by the incomplete ornamentation and lack of attachment loops on its reverse.

Dated to the 10th century AD (cf. No. 124).

126. Bracelet
    Inv. No. 30-33-40
    Glass, cast, molded.
        Diam. 6.8 cm
    11th–12th century AD

This bracelet is dark blue and triangular in section. Its overlapping tips are flattened and slightly broader than its central part.

A blue color and triangular section are characteristic of Byzantine bracelets, though those are typically somewhat larger (8–9 cm) in diameter (Shchapova 1997:87) than the one seen here. This example likely origi-

CAT. NO. 126

nated in Chersonesus in the 11th–12th century AD, when the production of Byzantine glass bracelets reached its peak.

127. Pendants (pair)
Inv. Nos. 30-33-73, -74
Silver, forged, soldered. H. 7 cm
13th–14th century AD

These balloon-shaped pendants, each curved from a thin, flat band, have tips that do not quite meet at the bottom. A narrow, tapering shaft, originally threaded with three spheres (each soldered from two halves) and one hemisphere, extends down from one tip and terminates in a circular, double-coiled stopper (originally covered by the hemisphere).

A similar gold pendant, with two pearls replacing the hollow spheres on its shaft (*OAK* 1898:44, fig. 231), was recovered from the Belorechenskie kurgans of the 13th–14th century AD. Notably, however, a similar technique for pendant manufacture was already known in the Saltovskaia culture of the 8th–early 10th century AD: a shaft extending down from a circle was threaded with beads and terminated in a rolled end hidden under a hemispherical plaque (Pletneva 1989:fig. 57; 1998:181, fig. 69). While our pendant likely dates from the period of the Belorechenskaya culture, then, it is possible the type had its beginnings in the Saltovskaia culture.

CAT. NO. 127

128. Buttons (3 items)
   Inv. No. 30-33-66a–c
   Silver, punched, soldered. H. 2.4 cm
   13th–14th century AD

These buttons are hollow ovals, each decorated with relief ornament and a narrow tube set at its top and bottom. A row of four vertically positioned rhombi, each with a straight relief line running from its vertical corners to the tubes at the oval's top and bottom, ring the center of each button. A loop was originally inserted into the tube at the top of each button and used to sew it on clothing.

Similar objects were recovered from 13th–14th century AD sites of the Belorechenskaya culture (Leskov 1990:fig. 216, no. 270). Our buttons belong to this same period.

CAT. NO. 128

129. Buttons (3 items)
   Inv. No. 30-33-65a–c
   Silver, forged, soldered, with filigree, granulation, engraving. H. 3.2 cm
   13th–14th century AD

These buttons are in the form of spheres (slightly damaged), each soldered from two halves. A band engraved with thin, diagonal lines is applied to the horizontal seam. There is a suspension loop atop each sphere and a small pyramid (point down) formed from four granules at its base.

While no exact analogues for these buttons are known (cf. No. 200 in the Antikenabteilung, Inv. No. 30.601a, b), they are typical in form and decoration (granula-

CAT. NO. 129

tion, filigree, and applied bands with engraved ornament) of artifacts from medieval sites in the Northern Caucasus (Kovalevskaia 1981:figs. 94.161, 162–200), especially those from the 13th to 14th century AD sites of the Belorechenskaya culture (Leskov 1991:64:313). As most of this collection is from the Maikop region and Northwestern Caucasus, where Belorechenskie sites were most widespread during the Middle Ages, our buttons may well derive from that culture and time period.

130. Ornament (?)
     Inv. No. 30-33-67
     Silver, punched, forged, soldered. Diam. 1.6 cm (wire circle)
     13th–14th century AD

This composite ornament is comprised of a wire circle with overlapping ends strung with six spherical buttons on suspension loops and two spherical beads. Each of the beads and buttons was soldered from two halves. The ornament is a modern creation assembled from various ancient elements (cf. Nos. 86, 91, and 133).

Identical buttons to those seen here occur at numerous sites of the Caucasian medieval period dating from the 7th (Alanian culture) to the 14th century AD (Belorechenskaya culture) (Kovalevskaia 1981:figs. 62.118, 119, 123; 94.53, 105, 193, 198;

CAT. NO. 130

Leskov 1991:66, no. 328). Spherical beads and wire circles are similarly common and there is no compelling reason to assume that any of the ornament's elements date outside of the medieval period. Considering the composition of this collection, it indeed seems likely that they should all be attributed to the Belorechenskaya culture and dated between the 13th and 14th century AD.

131. Bowl
     Inv. No. 30-33-132
     Silver, stamped, engraved. H. 3.5 cm; Diam. 14.2 cm
     13th–14th century AD

This large, flat-bottomed bowl has both interior and exterior decoration. The wall of the body slants out from the base to the midpoint and rises straight from there to the out-turned rim. An ornamental band beneath the rim on the exterior comprises the same motif, a combination of wavy lines with scrolls and trefoil flowers, repeated four times. The area between the lines is filled with stamped dots and hatched lines. Inside the bowl, on its base, is a round medallion bordered by two concentric circles connected with regularly spaced vertical hatch-lines; the running snow leopard partially obscured by the leaves and branches of a

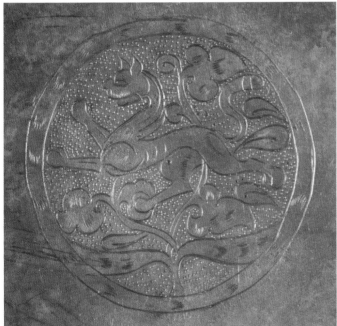

CAT. NO. 131
(detail at left)

tree is set against a background of stamped dots in the central field. The leopard's speed and agility are conveyed by the legs, which thrust forward; the lean, curved torso; the predatory head with protruding ears and open maw on a bent neck; and the raised, curving tail.

Bowls of similar form, while widespread throughout southern and western Siberia and the Northern Caucasus, are especially common in the Kuban (Kramarovskii 2001:246–49, 266–67). Several comparable items are known from 14th century AD Belorechenskie kurgans, with two pieces, one bowl and one goblet (Federov-Davydov 1976:figs. 132135–36), bearing very similar vegetal ornament to ours. The depiction of the snow leopard finds its closest analogue on a slightly earlier piece, a silver bowl found in 1898 in the Akmolinsk district (in modern Kazakhstan) and dated to "the period of Tartar rule" (Smirnov 1909:5, pl. ciii, no. 225) of the 12th to 13th century AD. Our bowl likely belongs to the later period and has been dated to the second half of the 14th century AD (the period of the Belorechenskie kurgans) (Kramarovskii 2001). Items of this type are now recognized as characteristic of the Golden Horde, with a wide diffusion in the Eurasian steppes in the 13th to 14th century AD.

First published in the catalogue by Piotrovsky (1975:159, 14), where it was incorrectly attributed to the 8th-9th century AD (in keeping with Canessa's 1930 identification of it, no. 120, N, O, as a Sassanian piece, though earlier catalogues of this collection, from 1915, 1917, and 1919, identified the bowl as Saka'n).

> 132. Saw or Single-Edge Sword Blade Fragment (?)
>   Inv. No. 30-33-110
>   Iron, gold, silver, forged, with encrustation. L. 21.9 cm; W. 3.4 cm
>   12th–14th century AD

This fragment is of a single-edged straight blade with a broken tip, originally triangular in section with a wide flat spine that narrowed to the sharp edge. The hilt (mostly broken), formed by cutting the back and edge of the blade, was a narrower but direct continuation of the blade. The careless notching of the back of the blade near its broken tip and the numerous transverse nicks contrast sharply with the traces of gold and silver encrustation on the entire surface of the blade. Part of a horse (?) with legs thrust forward in the middle of one side of the blade near its broken point is all that can currently be reconstructed of the original encrusted design.

Only a few iron artifacts with gold or silver encrustation are known from the northern Black Sea area, all belonging to the medieval period. These include iron stirrups encrusted with gold wire from the 11th to 12th century AD nomad burials on the bank of the Krasnodar reservoir (Noskova 1999:202–3, figs. 5.16, 7.18, 13.11) and an iron axe encrusted with silver (geometric designs and running animals) from a rich 13th–14th century AD nomadic burial in the Vornezhska province (Efimov 1999:93ff., fig. 3.1). This comparanda suggests

CAT. NO. 132

CAT. NO. 132 (details)

our blade should be dated between the 12th and 14th century AD, and may be associated with Golden Horde art.

133. Pendant (?)
        Inv. No. 30-33-34
        Gold, silver, stone (agate?), soldered, polished, drilled (stone),
            wire-drawing. L. 5.2 cm
        Scytho-Sarmatian or Middle Ages

This composite ornament is in the form of a wire circle tapering to its overlapping ends and strung with three pendants: a gold sphere soldered from two halves with a suspension loop soldered to its top; a silver sphere similar to the gold one in form and manufacture; and a spherical stone bead pierced with a wire that forms both its coil-wrapped suspension loop and its setting, a secure cage created by five extensions of the wire running from the base to the top of the bead. The ornament in its current state is entirely a modern creation, composed of various ancient elements (cf. Nos. 86, 91, and especially 130).

CAT. NO. 133

The gold and silver pendants are typical of the medieval period, found at numerous sites in the Northern Caucasus that date from the 7th to the 15th century AD. The stone bead is from at least five centuries earlier; such beads in gold mountings occasionally occur in 1st century AD contexts (Galanina 1980:87ff., pl. v) but are most widespread in the northern Black Sea region and the Kuban during the 5th to 3rd century BC. As for the wire circle, it may as well date to the Scytho-Sarmatian period as to the Middle Ages.

The steppe in Adyghea. Photograph by Alexey Gusev.

Antikenabteilung,
Staatliche Museen, Berlin

134. Cheekpieces (pair)
     Inv. No. 30.571a, b
     Bronze, cast. L. 16 cm, 14 cm
     8th-7th century BC

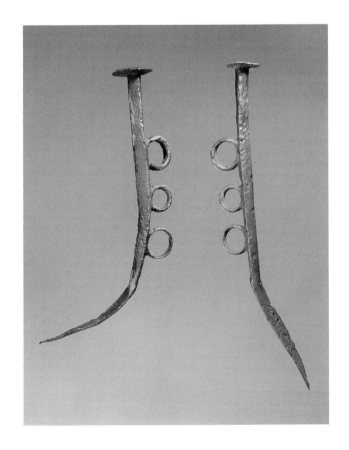

These cheekpieces are three-holed with a shaft that is rhomboidal in section and terminates at the top in a flat, round cap and at the bottom in a flattened, oval blade curving away from the three round loops. One is shorter due to a greater bend in its blade.

One cheekpiece is drawn in the inventory book, which compares it to objects that were acquired from de Massoneau in 1907: Inv. Nos. 11.863.304, 305. The latter is labeled in Russian "Fragments of un-

CAT. NO. 134

known function" on one side and the inscription "A6p" (clearly a Russian "6") 2254 above the number 2510 (both in red pencil in the same handwriting) on the reverse. In 1952, the Soviets returned part of the cheekpieces to the Antikenabteilung. There is also a penciled postscript in German: "Entweder [either] 30.571 oder [or] 11.863. 304, 305." These artifacts represent a classical variant of the cheekpiece type discovered (1939) in the Novocherkassk treasure (Iessen 1953:49ff.), which is most typical of the 8th–7th century BC.

135. Horse Bit
      Inv. No. 30.580
      Bronze, cast. L. 19 cm (preserved portion)
      8th–7th century BC

This severe bit is formed from two links (round in section), each articulated with two rows of sharp rowels (which press against the lips of the horse when the reins are pulled) on its inner side, joined by single rings at one end of each; the other end of each link terminates in two consecutive rings (one broken), the inner being much smaller than the outer.

The inventory book compares this artifact with material acquired from de Massoneau in 1907: Inv. No. 11.863.303; neither this object nor any representation of it survives. The drawing of this bit in the inventory book differs from the actual item described in that one outer ring is broken in the latter, so that it now measures 19 cm instead of the original 21 cm. Apparently the bit was acquired intact by the museum but later broken, likely during World War II. Similar double-ringed bits were recovered from the Novocherkassk treasure and are characteristic of 8th–7th century BC sites (Iessen 1953:49ff.; Leskov and Erlikh 1999:67–71).

First published by Greifenhagen (1970:56, fig. 28), whose description (based on the drawing in the inventory book) did not mention the missing outer ring on one link.

CAT. NO. 135

136. Mirror
      Inv. No. 30.583
      Bronze, cast, engraved. Diam. 7 cm
      6th century BC

CAT. NO. 136

This mirror is in the form of a disc with a polished front surface; the reverse, edged with a thick relief line, was engraved with three concentric circles which disappeared when corrosion was cleared from the mirror. Two of the circles bordered the circular traces of the handle, probably a handle-shaft, in the center of the mirror, while the third ran along the rim. The handle-shaft is characteristic of the Scythian Archaic period (6th century BC) (Kuznetsova 1987:35ff.).

First published by Greifenhagen (1970:56, fig. 30).

137. Panther (?) Figurine
   Inv. No. 30.581
   Bronze, cast. L. 5.2 cm
   6th century BC

The panther (?) has bent legs, a long tail, and a protruding ear. Interior details were lost when the figurine was cleaned of corrosion. It was originally set at the base of a mirror handle.

Such figurines are typical of "Olbian type" mirrors, common in the Northern Caucasus (Kuznetsova 1991) in the second half of the 6th century BC (Skudnova 1962), and most frequently take the form of panthers with half-bent legs; long, outward-curving tails; small protruding ears; and snouts terminating in slightly broadened tips (cf. Nos. 138 and 139). While both the head and tail (what remains appears to be curving outward) of our

CAT. NO. 137

figure are damaged, the bent legs are typical of the Scythian Animal Style from the time of the famous Kelermes Panther and suggest a date of the second half of the 6th century BC. Zahn's suggestion in the inventory book that this is a horse, taken up in Greifenhagen's publication (1970:55, fig. 9), should be disregarded; none of the over 80 "Olbian type" mirrors known features a horse on its handle.

138. Mirror
        Inv. No. 30.582
        Bronze, cast. H. 34.5 cm; Diam. 18.3 cm
        6th century BC

This mirror is in the form of a disc with a polished front surface. The reverse, edged with a high, straight rim, has a separately cast handle attached to one side with a semicircular bracket. The handle comprises a fluted shaft (3 flutes) terminating at each end with a rectangular capital topped by the figurine of an animal in profile: a recumbent stag, legs tucked beneath it, adjoins the disc of the mirror while a panther with bent legs and a backward-curving tail with a rolled-up tip is attached to the very base of the handle (upside-down when the mirror is upright). The stag is detailed with a recessed line indicating its mouth (?); an ear in relief laid back against its withers; and four circular indentations (representing prongs) in the antlers, which extend the length of the body and attach to the semicircular bracket above. The panther (cf. Nos. 137 and 139), rendered in a manner characteristic of the Late Archaic period, is more extensively detailed with small protruding ears; a small head with the snout articulated in relief; the suggestion of eyes beneath an overhanging forehead; and a slightly opened mouth indicated by a recessed line.

CAT. NO. 138

Two identical mirrors from Adyghea (between the towns of Krasnodar and Maikop), one found in the mountain village of Vochepshiy (Eskina 1995:108–12, fig. 1) and one in the farmstead of Kazazovo (Piankov and Tarabanov 1997:69ff., fig. 3.1), only add to the already extensive number of such mirrors compiled and published by Kuznetsova (1987:35ff; 1991). The discovery of mirrors of this type among the Greek material in the necropolis of Olbia dates them securely to the second half of the 6th century BC (Skudnova 1988:26, cat. 170, 112–13).

First published by Greifenhagen (1970:56, fig. 50).

139. Mirror
     Inv. No. 30.358 (acquired in 1914 from an unnamed Armenian merchant)
     Bronze, cast. H. 32.5 cm; Diam. 19 cm
     6th century BC

This mirror is in the form of a disc with a polished front surface; the reverse, edged with a high, straight rim, has a separately cast handle attached to one side with a semicircular bracket. The handle comprises a fluted shaft (two flutes) terminating at the base with a rectangular capital topped by a panther in profile (upside-down when the mirror is upright) and at the top with an oval placed horizontally above the shaft.

The relatively three-dimensional panther figurine is very similar to that of No. 138 (cf. also No. 137) and is characteristic of "Olbian type" mirrors (Skudnova 1988:26, cat. 87, 136, 174); such mir-

CAT. NO. 139

rors, which are especially common in the Northern Caucasus (Kuznetsova 1991), date to the second half of the 6th century BC.

140. Cauldron Fragment (2 items, 1 preserved)
      Inv. No. 30.626a, b
      Bronze, cast. L. 16 cm
      6th century BC

The rim fragment has a flat, wide edge topped with a (broken) handle in the form of a goat; while the goat is somewhat schematically rendered, some care was taken with the head. Its protruding ears delineated in relief, bulging eyes, open mouth with goatee beneath the lowered chin, and the creases on the hide between the ears and eyes, indicated with relief lines, identify this as one of the better examples of barbarian metal sculpture. Even the handle, of which only stubs remain on the goat's head and hindquarters, was integrated into the animal by imitating its long, curved horn. The cauldron itself was very large, as indicated by the only slight curvature of the surviving fragment, the width of the flat rim, and the thickness of the wall.

CAT. NO. 140

While cauldrons with vertical handles are first known from the Kelermes kurgans (the later group) of the late 7th to early 6th century BC (Galanina 1997:150ff., cat. 32, 33, 43, 53), it is only really in the 6th and 5th century BC that the largest of the Scythian cauldrons (both with and without animal-shaped handles) and cauldrons with goat-shaped handles appear (Shramko 1976:194ff., fig. 2.1; Rata 1966:351ff., fig. 1; Aricescu 1965:565ff., figs. 1–3; Terenozhkin et al. 1973:138ff., fig. 30.4; Alekseev et al. 1991:cat. 142). Goat figurines from cauldrons of the early group (ca. 6th to 5th century BC) are notable for their large horns (serving as handles), which curve up from the head and touch the torso at its hindmost part; those of the later group (5th–4th century BC) have comparatively small horns (Terenozhkin et al. 1973:fig. 30.4; Shramko 1976:fig. 2.1) that are either set only on the head or, as at Chertomlyk (Alekseev et al. 1991:cat. 142), curve up from the head to only the front part of the torso. Our example clearly belongs to the earlier group and should date between the 6th and early 5th century BC.

First published by Greifenhagen (1970:56, fig. 44).

141. Buttons (5 items, 2 preserved)
      Inv. No. 30.232a–e
      Bronze, cast. H. 2 cm
      5th century BC

These buttons are hemispheres, each with a grooved front surface and an attachment loop curved from a wide, flat plaque on its reverse.

Similar objects are known both from the Penn Museum holdings of the Maikop collection (No. 27, Inv. No. 30-33-119) and from Scythian period sites in Ukraine and the Northern Caucasus; these example should thus date to the 5th century BC (Petrenko 1967:pl. 27.46-48; Meliukova and Abramova 1989:pl. 112.38).

First published by Greifenhagen (1970:56, figs. 35, 37).

CAT. NO. 141

142. Cheekpieces (2 items, 1 preserved)
      Inv. No. 30.569a, b
      Bronze, cast. L. 12.3 cm
      5th century BC

The cheekpieces are S-shaped. The center of the round shaft swells to a figure 8, pierced with a hole in each loop, and the flattened ends curve up in opposing circles to form the stylized talons of a bird of prey.

Similar cheekpieces, widespread in the Kuban region, are also preserved in the part of the Maikop collection held by the Berlin Museum für Vor- und Frühgeschichte (No.

CAT. NO. 142

250, Inv. Nos. IIId 6907, 6917, 6923, and 286, Inv. No. 7029). They date to the 5th century BC.

First published by Greifenhagen (1970:56, fig. 24).

143. Cheekpieces (2 items, 1 preserved)
Inv. No. 30.572a, b
Bronze and iron, cast. L. 9.5 cm
5th century BC

These cheekpieces are S-shaped; the center of the flattened shaft swells to a figure 8, with a hole containing traces of iron bits pierced through each loop, and the two ends turn up in opposite directions, one tapering slightly to a rounded point and the other flattened to form a broad horse's hoof.

Similar cheekpieces (with a hoof at one or both ends) are common at 5th century BC sites

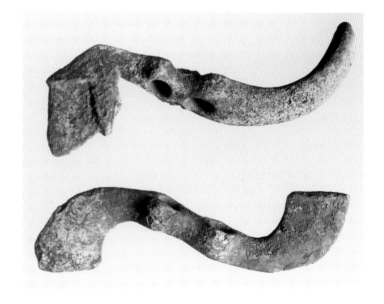

CAT. NOS. 143 (top) AND 144

in the Ukrainian forest-steppe (Petrenko 1967:36ff., pl. 26.6; Ilinskaia 1968:pls. XVI.2–3, XLIII, XLIV). The most comparable example, from the 5th century BC Semibratnie kurgans—though even in this case, the hoof is treated somewhat differently (Perevodchikova 2000:231–37, fig. 3.3)—supports such a date for these cheekpieces.

First published by Greifenhagen (1970:56, fig. 20).

144. Cheekpieces (2 items, 1 preserved)
    Inv. No. 30.573a, b
    Bronze, cast. L. 9.5 cm
    5th century BC

These cheekpieces are S-shaped. The center of the flattened shaft swells to a figure 8 with rounded rhomboidal borders pierced with a round hole in each loop, and the two ends, which turn up in opposing directions, terminate in broad, flat tips.

Such cheekpieces are common in the 5th century BC at both Scythian sites (Petrenko 1967:pl. 26.12; Ilinskaia 1968:pls. xxli.9, xxxv.11, liii.4) and sites throughout the Kuban.

First published by Greifenhagen (1970:56, fig. 19).

145. Cheekpieces (pair)
    Inv. No. 30.574a, b
    Bronze, cast. L. 12 cm
    5th century BC

These cheekpieces are S-shaped. The center of each flattened shaft swells to a figure 8 with rhomboidal loops, each pierced with a round hole, and the two ends, which turn up in opposing directions, terminate in broad, flat tips. Such cheekpieces are typical of the 5th century BC (cf. No. 145).

First published by Greifenhagen (1970:56, figs. 17, 18).

CAT. NO. 145

146. Finials (2 items, 1 preserved)
    Inv. No. 30.579a, b
    Bronze, cast. H. 8.2 cm
    5th century BC

These finials are in the form of a small, round shaft tapering from its flattened base to its rounded tip; both base and tip are set off with relief bands. There are five holes at the base, one along each narrow side (three total) and one on either side of the flat surface.

    While similar finials (pierced with four or five holes) are common at Scythian sites from the earliest period, they are all smaller in dimension than ours. Five identical finials (Gushchina 1962:66–69, fig. 24.1–5), though again of smaller dimensions, were acquired from a private collection by the Gosudarstvenniy Istoricheskiy Muzey (GIM), the State Historical Museum in Moscow, in 1929 and are dated to the 5th century BC; our example should belong to the same period.

    First published by Greifenhagen (1970:56, fig. 27).

CAT. NO. 146

147. Phiale
    Inv. No. 30.221a
    Silver, gilding, forged, die-formed, soldered. Diam. 16.2 cm
    5th century BC

This phiale is a low, flat bowl with a central omphalos encircled by a gilded relief band comprising three rows of leaves within a beaded border soldered inside it. The stylized head of a bird of prey skillfully engraved on one side of the bowl's interior is typical of the Scythian Animal Style of the steppes of Ukraine and the Kuban (Leskov 1990:18, fig. 23–24) and common on gold plaques of various purposes. The thickened rim, cut horizontally, protrudes slightly into the interior of the bowl.

    The closest analogue to this item, unquestionably a Greek import, is a phiale from the mid-5th century BC Semibratniy kurgan No. 2, which has a relief band of bearded Silenes encircling its omphalos (Artamonov 1966:fig. 53). While later phialai of similar form are known from 4th century contexts in kurgans in southern Ukraine and the Kuban and in Scythian royal kurgans in Solokha and Kul-Oba, these are much more extensively ornamented than our example, often with walls entirely covered in relief decoration (Artamonov 1966:pls. 157–59, 207, 210). The head of the bird of prey engraved on our example is similarly indicative of an early date, being most closely paralleled by a depiction on gold plating (for a wooden vessel) from the mid-5th century BC Zavadska Mogila kur-

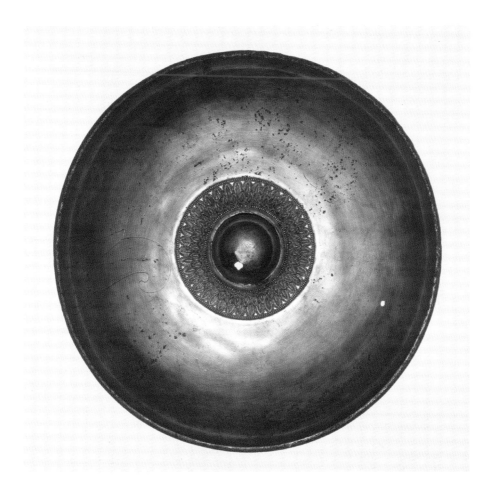

CAT. NO. 147; DETAIL OF ENGRAVING BELOW

gan No. 1 (in the Dniepropetrovsk Province) (Mozolevskii 1980:108, fig. 47.2); such plating is typical of the 5th century BC (Reeder 1999:165, nos. 52, 53). Notably, it is also during the 6th and 5th century BC that such heads are used as proprietary marks, scratched or engraved into various Scythian or Maeotian items of everyday purpose (such marks on common items are not known after this time) including a bronze mirror (Kuznetsova 1987, fig. 1a), a bone comb (?) (Skudnova 1954:306–17, fig. 3), and handmade pottery (Leskov 1985:81, figs. 31, 32, cat. 179). Regardless of whether the bird's head on our phiale was the proprietary mark of a Scythian owner or served some other purpose, it supports a 5th century BC date for this vessel.

First published by Greifenhagen (1970:56, pl. 29.1–2), who compared it to some silver phialai from the Chmyrev kurgan; that complex, however, certainly belongs to the 4th century BC (Onaiko 1970:19–20, pl. xiv).

148. Pectoral
Inv. No. 30.221c
Gold, forged, punched, with encrustation. L. 23 cm
5th century BC

This pectoral is in the form of a crescent-shaped plaque with rounded ends with three bands of relief ornament running along its length. The central band comprises thirteen diamond-shaped rhombi, seven containing two concentric rhombi alternating with six filled with inserts of light blue or green paste, laid corner to corner with a three-petal palmette facing outward at each end. The rows of ornament above and below the central band are identical, each comprising interlocking wavy lines that form a row of attached circles; a large round convexity is placed in the center of each circle and a smaller one is set both above and below each point of contact between the circles. Tiny holes for sewing the pectoral to its foundation are placed along its narrow unadorned border.

Pectorals are commonly recovered from 1st millennium BC sites, being especially well represented in Urartian (Merhav 1991:164–70, figs. 2–3, 5–9, 171–73, figs. 4–9) contexts—the 7th century BC example from Ziwiyeh, which depicts animals executed

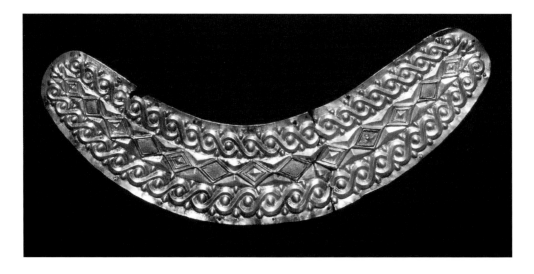

CAT. NO. 148

in the Median, Urartian, and Early Scythian styles is the most renowned example (Lukonin 1977:20ff.)—and at 8th and 7th century BC sites in the Northern Caucasus and Abkhazia (mainly bronze poitrels) (Dudarev 1991:pls. 15–16; Ivantchik 2001:figs. 111.5, 120.3, 121.1, 122.4, 123.11, 13, 124.11). However, they are not found at Archaic Scythian (7th to 6th century BC) sites in the Northern Caucasus or Ukraine. The colored paste applied to our pectoral may indicate a later date, as such inserts are known on gold ornaments from Late Archaic and Classical sites in the Kuban–Ulskiy kurgan No. 2/1909: a finial in the form of a horse head; plaques from the Metropolitan Museum's Maikop collection. The other ornamentation on the artifact (especially the rendering of the palmettes) supports a later date, finding its closest parallel on two gold pectorals (one small and one large) from the mid-5th century BC Thracian site of Goliamata Mogila, in Bulgaria (Vendikov and Gerasimov 1973:no. 215). These pectorals are similar not only in ornament, with the larger example being covered with convexities and rosettes in relief, but also in form, material, and mode of attachment, having two small holes on the edges for sewing. The comparison to the Goliamata Mogila material is compelling as some gold appliqués from the Maikop collection (Penn Museum No. 58) and Berlin (Inv. No. 30.221f 1–3) also find their closest analogues in that complex; it seems possible that they, along with this pectoral, derive from a single complex dating to the same period as Goliamata Mogila.

First published by Greifenhagen (1970:57, pl. 30.2), who noted comparanda for it but did not suggest a date.

149. Plaque-Appliqués (4 items)
 Inv. Nos. 30.221e 1–4
 Gold, punched, die-formed. L. 11.2 cm
 5th century BC

These plaques are in the form of irregular trapezoids, each depicting an eagle facing left and grasping a large sturgeon-like fish in its talons; the head of the eagle, bent almost at a right angle to the fish, lends some dynamism to the otherwise static composition. While the design was executed with a high-quality punch, it differs from similar items in its relatively high relief and the supplementary die treatment of the feet and feathers of the bird and the fins and tail of the fish. The upper edge of the plaque is folded over and pierced with two holes and there are four holes along each long edge of the front, many still containing small tacks with mushroom-shaped caps. The exact correspondence between the two holes on the reverse with the two uppermost on the front indicates that each plaque was fixed on the edge of a wooden vessel with two tacks (affixed from the inside of the vessel) that extended through the wood and the bent edge of the plaque. The remaining six holes also served to attach each plaque to the surface of the vessel.

While similar gold appliqués are known from Scythian kurgans in the Don River region, the steppe, and the forest-steppe of Ukraine (Korolkova 1998a:166–77), they are

CAT. NO. 149

generally lower in quality and smaller in dimension than those in the Maikop collection. Our plaques likely belong to the 5th century BC when plaques with punched depictions in the Scythian Animal Style were most highly developed. Both Semibratniy kurgan No. 4 (Artamonov 1966:pls. 118, 120–22), which has yielded appliqués with images of comparable quality to ours, and Zavadska Mogila kurgan No. 1, from which the two appliqués most similar to ours (they were attached to wooden bowls) derive (Mozolevskii 1980:106ff., figs. 44.4, 7, 8, 45–46), date to this period.

First published by Greifenhagen (1970:57, pl. 31).

150. Plaque-Appliqués (4 items)
    Inv. Nos. 30.221d 1–4
    Gold, punched. H. 13.4 cm
    5th century BC

This plaque is in the form of the hind leg of a stag (?) with details in high relief; the decoration on each leg combines Greek elements, such as a palmette on the hip, with Scythian ones: the stylized head of a bird of prey appears on both knee and hip. The upper edge of each plaque is folded over and pierced with two holes, and there are eight holes along the edges of the front, many still containing the original tacks. All four plaques, which seem intended for a single wooden vessel, were attached in the same manner as No. 149.

Four similarly decorated plaques, each depicting the hind leg of a boar and combining

Greek and Scythian decorative elements, are known from de Massoneau's collection; although three not published in this catalogue are currently held in Berlin (Greifenhagen 1970:pl. 33.1–2, 4) and one in Philadelphia (No. 57, Inv. No. 30-33-2b), they undoubtedly adorned a single vessel and may well derive from the same context as ours. Excavated comparanda also exist: one similar plaque in the form of a stag's leg, though lacking the combined Greek and Scythian ornament, is known from a 5th century BC burial (Meliukova and Abramova 1989: pl. 35.14), while another, from the early 5th century BC Baby Kurgan (Alekseev 2003:259; I. V. Yatsenko 1959:58ff., pl. iv.5), is more comparable but likely more archaic, being punched on a triangular plaque and lacking additional ornament. Our plaques likely date to the second half of the 5th century BC.

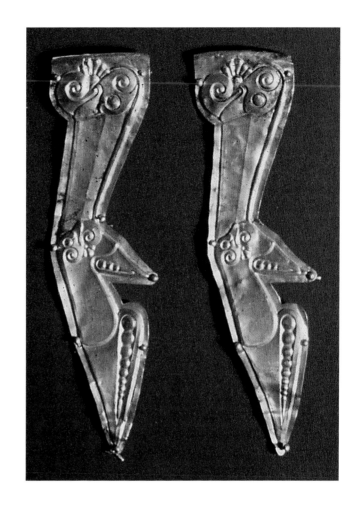

CAT. NO. 150

151. Plaque-Appliqués (5 items)
      Inv. Nos. 30.221g 1–5
      Gold, punched. H. 5.6 cm
      5th century BC

This plaque is in the form of the stylized head of a bird of prey (beak downwards) depicted in the Scythian Animal Style, each with a Greek palmette between the lower curve of the beak and the head. The upper edge of each plaque is folded over and pierced with two holes, and there are eight holes along the narrow unadorned border around the head on the front, several still containing tacks with miniature caps. These plaques were secured

CAT. NO. 151

to a wooden vessel in the same manner as No. 149.

Similar depictions of birds' heads are common in the 5th century BC, rendered on a bronze harness plaque from Semibratniy kurgan No. 2 (Artamonov 1966:pl. 115) and gold plaque-appliqués from both Zavadska Mogila kurgan No. 1 (Reeder 1999:167, no. 54) and the Ak-Mechet kurgans in the Crimea (Artamonov 1966:pl. 70), and are also known on gold plaques from sites dating to the turn of the 5th to the 4th century BC (Leskov 1972: pl. 34). Our examples belong to the same period.

First published by Greifenhagen (1970: 58, pl. 32.2).

152. Ornament Details (14 items)
    Inv. Nos. 30.221j 1–14
    Gold, punched, forged, soldered, plaited, engraved. L. 15.7 cm
    5th century BC

These thin, plaited chains terminate in a small ring at one end and a slightly larger ring at the other; a hollow ram's head (one missing) with a flat, round plaque soldered to its base is attached to each chain's larger ring with a small loop (soldered to the center of its base). These chains likely formed part of one larger ornament, possibly a diadem such as that found in the Melgunovskiy kurgan (Pridik 1911).

Similar rams' heads occur elsewhere in the Maikop collection, appearing as the finials on a bracelet in the Penn Museum (Inv. No. 30-33-9). Excavated comparanda, including

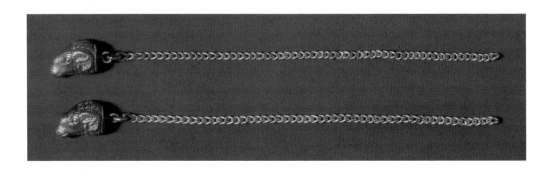

CAT. NO. 152

such heads from the 5th century BC Nymphaion kurgans (Vickers 1979:pls. vi.f, xviii.e) and comparable objects serving as rhyton finials from Semibratniy kurgan No. 4 (Anfimov 1987:113), indicate our chains likely belong to the mid-5th century BC.

First published by Greifenhagen (1970:58, pls. 33.3, 34.1), who suggested these chains were attached to an ornament for a horse or chariot (wagon).

153. Plaques (2 items)
    Misc. Inv. Nos. 7364–65=GL 370/371 bis (found in the Crimea; acquired in
        1878 from the collection of Count Keglevich of Vienna)
    Gold, punched. L. 1.5 cm
    5th century BC

These plaques are in the form of a profile lion (facing left). The tail curves up and back to form a figure 8 and there are four holes, two in the paws and two in the tail, for sewing each plaque to its foundation.

CAT. NO. 153

The 49 similar plaques excavated from tomb No. 4 in the Nymphaion necropolis in 1868 and sold to the Ashmolean Museum (Vickers 1979:10, 42, pl. 12a-b) represent the only known comparanda. The absence of comparable artifacts from the Crimea or the Taman Peninsula (the region from which Keglevich's collection derives), combined with the fact that the Nymphaion necropolis was looted prior to its 1868 excavation, suggests our plaques derive from that same site; they should date to the second half of the 5th century BC.

First published by Greifenhagen (1970:39, pls. 166–67), who dated them to the 4th century BC without citing any comparanda.

154. Earrings (3 items)
    Inv. No. 30.630a–c
    Gold, stamped, soldered, with granulation, filigree. H. 2.4 cm
    5th century BC

These earrings are in the form of a short cylinder atop a slightly elongated sphere, all heavily decorated with granulation and filigree. The cylinder, which has a small ring at its top to link into a suspension loop (not preserved), is ringed with pseudo-beaded wire along its top and bottom edges while the sphere below, soldered from two halves, is encircled with a row of four granulated triangles (points toward the center seam) at both its top and bottom. The base of the sphere is ringed with two additional loops of pseudo-beaded wire from the bottom of which hangs a small pyramid (point downward) formed from four large granules.

Similar earrings exist in the Maikop collection in both the Penn Museum (No. 55, Inv. No. 30-33-7a, b) and in this same collection (No. 155), all probably dating to the 5th century BC.

First published by Greifenhagen (1970:60, pl. 37.15), who attributed them to the south of Russia.

CAT. NOS. 154 AND 155 (right)

155. Earring
      Inv. No. 30.631
      Gold, stamped, soldered, with granulation, filigree. H. 2 cm
      5th century BC

Although similar in form and decoration to the earrings of No. 154, this earring lacks any suspension loops and has wire applied to the central horizontal seam of the sphere; this last feature is more reminiscent of the pair of earrings in the Penn Museum's holdings of the Maikop collection (cf. No. 55).

It should also date to the 5th century BC.

First published by Greifenhagen (1970:60, pl. 37.16).

156. Harness Plaque
      Inv. No. 30.228b
      Bronze, cast. L. 4.5 cm
      5th–4th century BC

This harness plaque is in the form of an openwork, profile elk's head (facing right) with a protruding triangular ear and an antler shaped like the beak of a bird of prey. Relief lines delineate the lower jawbone, the slightly open mouth, and the round eye, and engrav-

CAT. NO. 156

ing on the curved, elongated snout likely represented another bird's beak. There is an oval attachment loop on the reverse.

A very similar plaque in the Hermitage collection (unpublished), purchased in Maikop in 1906 and attributed to the 5th or 4th century BC on the basis of style, indicates the probable date of our piece.

First published by Greifenhagen (1970, 1975:Bd, I, 56, fig. 12).

157. Plaque-Buttons (3 items, 1 preserved)
   Inv. No. 30.234a–c
   Bronze, cast. H. 2 cm
   5th–4th century BC

These plaque-buttons are hemispheres with a semicircular attachment loop curved from a wide, flat plaque on the reverse.

Similar plaques (cf. No. 141) are common at 5th to 4th century BC Scythian sites.

First published by Greifenhagen (1970:56, fig. 36).

CAT. NO. 157

158. Cheekpieces (pair)
   Inv. No. 30.570a, b
   Bronze, cast. L. 10.6 cm, 9.4 cm
   5th–4th century BC

These cheekpieces are gamma-shaped and one is slightly smaller. Each round shaft swells to a figure 8, with a hole pierced through each loop, just before it bends sharply to the end that forms the long neck of its lion's head terminal. The other end terminates in a flattened tip. The lion has an open maw, and its fangs and ears are articulated in relief.

CAT. NO. 158

Two-holed cheekpieces with animal heads as terminals are most typical of 5th to 4th century BC complexes in the Kuban (Leskov 1990:cat. 67, 68, 121–24, figs. 70, 71, 74–79). Although no identical examples are known, our cheekpieces likely belong to the same period.

First published by Greifenhagen (1970:56, figs. 21, 22).

159. Cheekpiece
     Inv. No. 30.575
     Bronze, cast. L. 13.8 cm
     5th–4th century BC

The center of the shaft of this cheekpiece swells to a figure 8 with rhomboidal borders, with a round hole pierced through each loop. The flattened ends, which have a distinct zoomorphic aspect, are rendered in the Scythian Animal Style. One tip represents the head and neck of a lion-headed griffin with a paw extended to its lower jaw; an antler (?) curves in a circle above the round eye and beside the protruding ear. The other tip may represent a similarly featured and positioned predator or, when flipped upside down, can be seen as representing the head of a griffin with a round eye in relief and an open mouth, indicated by a recessed line, grasping the neck and lower jaw of a herbivore with a protruding ear, a horn curved in an oval loop, and a short, broad snout with a hole indicating the mouth. This second reading accounts better for the apertures in the representation but cannot be confirmed due to the corrosion of the metal.

CAT. NO. 159

This type of cheekpiece, as well as the style in which the lion-headed griffin is depicted, indicates a date of the 5th to 4th century BC.

First published by Greifenhagen (1970:56, fig. 23).

160. Finials (2 items)
     Inv. No. 30.591a, b
     Silver, cast. Diam. 1.8 cm, 1.6 cm
     5th–4th century BC

CAT. NO. 160

These finials are in the form of a truncated cone pierced vertically with a wide tubular hole, which likely secured the knots on some sort of strap. Zahn's identification of these as buttons or spindles (inventory book p. 88) is unconvincing given their small diameter and large holes.

Similar objects (cf. No. 175a, b) appear in Scythian warrior and horse burials as early as the 5th century BC but date primarily to the 4th century (Ilinskaia 1968:135ff.; 1973:42–63).

161. Whetstone
    Inv. No. 30.615L
    Stone, polished, with one-sided drilling. L. 16.3 cm
    5th–4th century BC

This whetstone is in the form of a long, polished bar, rectangular in section, with traces of gold casing on the upper third of its height. In the middle of its upper part is a drilled hole for suspension.

Both the form and gold casing of our example suggest a Scythian period date. Pre-Scythian (Chernogorovka-Novocherkassk) whetstones, while similar in form, are wider and more massive, and the gold casing, though first known on a late 6th to early 5th century BC whetstone from the celebrated Vettersfelde treasure (Greifenhagen 1970:63, pl. 43.4), is primarily known from very wealthy 4th century BC burials of the Scythian aristocracy in Chertomlyk and Kul-Oba, for example (Alekseev et al. 1991:107–8, fig. 72; Galanina and Gratsch 1986:no. 175-77). Our example thus likely dates between the 5th and 4th century BC.

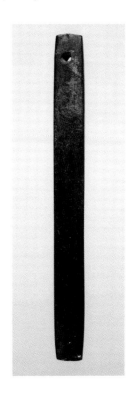

CAT. NO. 161

162. Torque
    Inv. No. 30.2211
    Gold, cast, forged. Diam. 21–21.5 cm
    5th–4th century BC

This torque is curved from a cast shaft, round in section, that tapers slightly toward its tips. While the simplicity of its form precludes the assignment of a secure date, similar torques are most typical of 4th century BC Scythian sites, with one comparable example

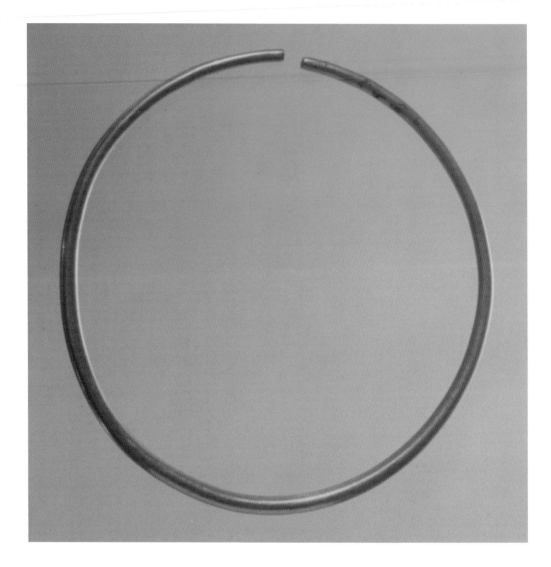

CAT. NO. 162

coming from Semibratniy kurgan No. 2 (second quarter to middle of the 5th century BC); our torque likely belongs within that range. This date is in keeping with the range set for all the items assigned Inv. No. 30.221 within this collection.

First published by Greifenhagen (1970:56, pl. 29.3), who did not suggest a date.

163. Drinking Horn (reconstruction)
       Inv. Nos. 30.221h (body), 30.221k-2 (band), 30.221i-1 (finial)
       Gold, forged, soldered, with filigree, pseudo-granulation, engraving. L. 23.5 cm
       5th–early 4th century BC

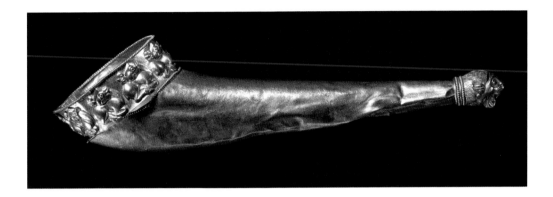

RECONSTRUCTION OF CAT. NO. 163

CAT. NO. 163, BAND (left) AND FINIAL

This conical drinking horn is reconstructed from three separate elements: a conical body, a lion's head finial, and a decorative band. The body of the horn, curved from a long plaque into a cone with a bend near its broad mouth, is ringed at its narrow tip by four bands, two smooth alternating with two that are pseudo-granulated, and at its wider mouth by a single band of pseudo-granulated wire. The reconstruction proposes the attachment of a small but carefully detailed lion's head, mouth open to reveal four sharp teeth and a protruding tongue, to the narrow end of the horn and a curving band (of identical diameter to the wide mouth of the horn) to its large open end, which was completely flat inside (for soldering?). The band, composed of nine identical plaques, was ringed at the top with pseudo-granulated wire (matching that on the horn) and decorated with recumbent elks; their heads are turned back so that their antlers, ending in heads of stylized birds of prey, lie along their hindquarters.

    Such a reconstruction is problematic. The horn described here lacks the elongated tube-socket used for the attachment of animal-head finials to such vessels. The tube-socket does appear on three more intact gold drinking horns from the Semibratnie kurgans (Anfimov 1987:92, 112–13) and on one from Uliap kurgan No. 4 (Leskov 1990:figs. 187–

90), growing more elongated in 4th century BC examples as the sockets move away from the head and require more reliable attachment (Reeder 1999:243–44; 312–14; Anfimov 1987:130). It is thus unlikely that the lion's head in this example was a part of the original artifact. The attachment of the decorative band is similarly problematic as it is identical in diameter to the mouth of the horn and the legs of the elks extend to the very edge of the band; a secondary band, not preserved, must have been used to secure the two.

The body of the horn, as noted in a recent publication of its reconstruction (Platz-Horster 2002:46, 47, fig. 17), is comparable to that of a gold drinking horn with a ram's head finial from the 5th century BC Semibratniy kurgan No. 4: in both cases the wide mouth is placed immediately after the bend. As this form runs counter to that typically used for gold and silver vessels from 5th–4th century BC sites in the Kuban, scholars have long suggested that the Semibratniy example, and ours by analogy, had an upper part (not preserved) formed from wood or horn (Aruz 2000:204, no. 143).

While the elk band has comparanda from the same period, including plaques with similar depictions recovered from Nymphaion kurgan No. 17 (Artamonov 1966:pls. 102, 105) and the Malie Semibratnie kurgans (*OAK* for 1880:96–97, pl. iv) (all of 5th century BC date), analogues have also been found in an early 4th century BC ritual complex at Uliap (Leskov 1990:fig. 154, 155, cat. 52.228). Our horn should thus be dated between the 5th and early 4th century BC.

First published by Greifenhagen (1970:pl. 35.1a, 3 and pl. 36.1, 3, 5), though not in its reconstructed form. Its later treatment by Vlasova (2002:139–41) is slightly erroneous as she attributes a short, curved, and truncated cone to both this item and to No. 164; in reality, only one such cone exists (belonging to No. 164), though it was published by Greifenhagen from both sides.

164. Drinking Horn (reconstruction)
       Inv. Nos. 30.221h-4 (body), 30.221k-1 (band), 30.221i-2 (finial)
       Gold, forged, soldered, with filigree, pseudo-granulation, engraving. L. 21 cm
       5th–early 4th century BC

This conical horn is reconstructed from three separate elements: a long, straight body, a lion's head finial, and a decorative band. The reconstruction proposes the attachment of a finial, comprised of a tube ringed by six alternating bands of smooth and pseudo-granulated wire with a lion's head terminal, to the narrow end of the horn and a band, formed from ten matching plaques decorated with recumbent elks (identical to No. 163), to the wide mouth. The lion in this example has an open mouth, revealing four sharp teeth and a protruding tongue, with additional details in incision and relief. The band of elks, ringed along the upper edge by pseudo-granulated wire, is soldered below to a circular metal base with walls of varying height that narrows toward its bottom. Contrary to the proposed reconstruction, this base could only have been attached to a drinking horn after a bend in the main body; the damage to the walls of the base and the lighter color of its

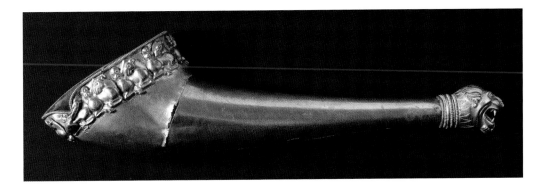

RECONSTRUCTION OF CAT. NO. 164

CAT. NO. 164, BAND (left) AND
FINIAL

metal walls indicates it was inserted into a now-lost section of the body that was attached to the straight cone.

This horn should be dated similarly to No. 163 to between the 5th and early 4th century BC.

In addition to the two reconstructed drinking horns in the collection, Nos. 163 and 164, two additional components from drinking horns or rhyta date to the same period. Both were first published by Greifenhagen (1970:59, pl. 35, 2a, 4–5, 2b, pl. 36, 2, 4).

164a. Rhyton or Drinking Horn (body)
    Inv. No. 30.221h-2
    Gold, forged, soldered, with filigree, pseudo-granulation. L. 17.3 cm

This body of a horn is in the form of a cone rolled from a plaque. It is slightly turned out at its wide upper edge and ringed at both ends with a band of pseudo-granulated wire.

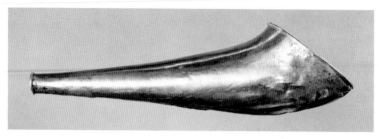

CAT. NO. 164A, B

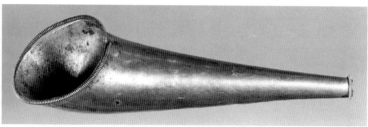

164b. Rhyton or Drinking Horn (body)
       Inv. No. 30.221h-3
       Gold, forged, soldered, with filigree. L. 16.5 cm

This body of a horn is in the form of a cone rolled from a plaque; it is slightly turned out at its wide upper edge and ringed at both ends with a band of wire.

165. Horseman Figurine
       Inv. No. 30.222b
       Bronze, cast, forged. L. 5.7 cm
       4th century BC

This figurine is in the form of a horse (the front legs of which are missing) and rider, who sits inclined slightly forward with his head thrown back. The rider has narrow shoulders with a large head atop a long neck. His face is distinct beneath the helmet-shaped hat set between his large ears. Bulging, deep-socketed eyes beneath distinct brows frame a long, thin nose set above a slightly parted mouth. He wears a *gorytos* (curved-bow case) at his waist and holds the reins of the horse taut in his hands. The horse itself, which has a small plume rising between its upright ears, has similarly distinct features on its slightly inclined head: large eyes are set above a slightly parted mouth. There is a projection, apparently denoting a binding, at the base of its tail, and the circular hoop beneath its belly likely attached the figurine to a horizontal pin.

This figurine is one in a series of nine, eight of which were originally held in this collection and one of which is preserved in the Hermitage (Inv. No. 2,735-288); this last was acquired from GAIMK—the State Academy of the History of Material Culture—in St. Petersburg in 1926 (along with many artifacts found in the 19th and 20th century AD). This series of nine originally comprised four complete figures (one from the Hermitage and three from Berlin) and five fragments (all from Berlin). Of these, three fragments are lost and the rest are published here. The four complete figurines are so similar in their details—including the pose of the horses, the detailing on the harnesses, the identical headgear and gorytoi of the riders, and the ring beneath each horse's belly (placed parallel or perpendicular to the rider) for the attachment of the figures to a horizontal pin—that they may well have come from a single complex that included the frag-

CAT. NO. 165

mentary figures as well. The fact that Berlin acquired its figurines in 1913 and the Hermitage in 1926 does not present an obstacle to this conclusion. It is well known that in 1925–28 many items discovered in the late 19th or early 20th century AD were acquired by the Hermitage from GAIMK, only finding their permanent home after the revolution. This was the case, for example, with the bronze bits from the 1908 excavations of N. I. Veselovskii in an Ulskiy Aul village, which were also acquired from GAIMK by the Hermitage in 1926. Indeed, the figures differ primarily in the weapons borne by the riders and in the minor details of attire.

The dating of these figures has undergone a significant revision since Rostovtzeff's 1922 publication of the Hermitage example as a 7th to 5th century BC artifact (pp. 35ff., pl. V.5). In this regard, the dating of these statuettes from the end of the 8th to the beginning of the 7th century BC, as proposed by J. Haskins (1952:340, with a footnote referring to Rostovtzeff, moreover), appears inexplicable. In 1931, when publishing one of the Berlin figurines, Rostovtzeff (1931b:54, pl. 5.6) narrowed this date to between the late 5th and 4th century BC. The form of the gorytos on these figures and the existence of many comparable toreutic artifacts from the 4th century BC (Meliukova and Abramova 1989:pl. 31.27–30) suggest that the range should be further narrowed to fall within the 4th century BC.

First published by Greifenhagen (1970:55, fig. 10), who erroneously described it as having a shield on its back; this detail is seen on a different figurine in the collection (No. 167b).

166. Horseman Figurine Fragment
     Inv. No. 30.222c
     Bronze, cast, forged. L. 3.6 cm
     4th century BC

CAT. NO. 166

In this figurine fragment of a horse and rider the head and neck of each are preserved. The narrow-shouldered rider has a long neck topped by a large head; both his helmet-shaped hat and facial features are well worn but clearly resemble those of No. 165. He is distinguished from the other statuettes in this series (cf. Nos. 165, 167a, b) in that his left hand holds both reins (the right only partially preserved) while his right holds a spear or javelin with a leaf-shaped tip. The horse is comparable to that of No. 165, having similar upright ears, large protruding eyes, and a slightly parted mouth holding the taut reins. There is a rectangular projection at the base of its neck.

Similar horsemen with spears or javelins in their raised right hands are depicted on 4th century BC gold plaques from the royal kurgan in Kul-Oba (Artamonov 1966:pls. 253, 255).

First published by Greifenhagen (1970:56, fig. 16).

167a. Horse Figurine Fragment
        Inv. No. 30.222d
        Bronze, cast, forged. L. 2.4 cm
        4th century BC

Only the head and neck of the horse are preserved from this fragmentary figurine. The clarity of detail is more remarkable here than in Nos. 165 and 166. A triangular plume rises between upright ears, and the deep relief circling the bulging eyes covers most of the head. Taut reins connected to cheekpieces (?) extend from either side of the slightly parted mouth, and there is a rectangular projection at the base of its neck.

The figurine is comparable in style and date to the other figurines published here (cf. Nos. 165, 166, 167b, 167c).

First published by Greifenhagen (1970:56, fig. 15).

CAT. NO. 167a

167b. Horseman Figurine (lost)
        Inv. No. 30.222a
        Bronze, cast, forged. L. 4.5 cm
        4th century BC

CAT. NO. 167b

This figurine, preserved only in the drawing and description in the inventory book, took the form of a horse and rider (facing right) similar to Nos. 165 and 166. The rider, who sits erect holding the reins, has a long neck topped by a large head beneath a tall, helmet-like hat; his bulging eyes frame a long, straight nose. A shield is secured on his back and a gorytos on his left side. The horse, its head slightly inclined, has similar bulging eyes and a slightly parted mouth; its ears stand upright and there is a rectangular projection at the base of its neck and another, possibly a binding, on its tail. Its pose, with forelegs thrust forward and hind legs bent at the knee and tucked beneath the belly, may indicate flight (or a fast run). The round hoop beneath the horse's belly likely attached the figurine to a horizontal pin.

The figurine is comparable in style and date to the other figurines in this series and is especially similar to No. 165.

167c. Horseman Figurine (lost)
Inv. No. 30.222
Bronze, cast, forged. L. 5.5 cm
4th century BC

This figurine, described from the photo in Rostovtzeff's publication (1931b:54, pl. 5.6), took the form of a horse and rider (facing left). The horseman, who sits erect astride the horse, has a long neck topped by a large head beneath a tall, helmet-like hat; his bulging eyes frame a long, straight nose above a slightly parted mouth. His hands are preserved only at the horse's shoulders, where taut reins are visible, and there is a gorytos on his left side. The horse, also with bulging eyes and protruding ears, has a rectangular projection on its neck. Its pose, with forelegs thrust forward and hind legs bent at the knee and tucked beneath the belly, may indicate flight or a fast run. The tail is broken off, but the hoop beneath its belly, likely for attaching the figurine to a horizontal pin, survives.

CAT. NO. 167c

While this figurine, published by both Rostovtzeff (1931b) and Potratz (1960:46ff.), is not explicitly described in the entry of the Keeper of the Collection, R. Zahn, on this series of figures (cf. 165–167b) as he discovered in the inventory book (p. 35), it is notable that he mentions three intact figures there while only describing two (a and b); figure c,

HERMITAGE FIGURINE

which comprises only a horse's head and the upper torso of a rider holding a spear, should be considered with the fragments d, e, f, and g, leaving one complete figure unaccounted for. The phrase following Zahn's note on the three intact figurines, "one raises his spear," supports the assumption that figure c is to be considered separately. This would mean that there were originally eight (rather than the seven explicitly described) statuettes in the collection (cf. No. 165), with a ninth represented by the figurine in the Hermitage (Inv. No. 2,735-288).

168. Harness Plaque
     Inv. No. 30.225
     Bronze, cast. H. 3.7 cm
     4th century BC

This plaque has a narrow, slightly curved base; below it is a large attachment ring and above it is a horse's head with the eye in high relief and mouth and nostrils rendered with a single relief line. The horse is further distinguished by a protruding, triangular ear, also articulated in relief, and a rounded projection on the back of its neck.

An identical harness plaque from a complex in the central Don River region is generally dated to the 4th century BC (Puzikova 1964:24ff., fig. 9.3), though the amphorae accompanying it indicate a date of as early as the second half of the 5th century BC (Puzikova 2001:135, fig. 22.1). Goncharova's stylistic analysis indicates that such plaques, which are markedly influenced by the Kuban variant of the Scythian Animal Style (central Don River region), are most consistent with a

CAT. NO. 168

date of the 4th century BC (2000:51–61, fig. 1.12).

First published by Greifenhagen (1970:56, fig. 14).

169. Harness Plaques (2 items, 1 preserved)
Inv. No. 30.230a, b
Bronze, cast. H. 5.5 cm
4th century BC

This cruciform plaque comprises five hemispherical convexities: one in the center and one at the end of each arm of the cross. There is a semicircular attachment ring on the reverse.

Similar plaques of varying dimensions are known from 4th century BC Scythian kurgans in the central Don River region (Liberov 1965:pl. 23.37–39; Savchenko 2001:182 ff., fig. 20.5) and seem to have their prototypes at 8th to 7th century BC Koban culture sites (Kozenkova 1998:46–47, pl. xiii.3–5). Our example thus likely belongs to the 4th century BC.

First published by Greifenhagen (1970:56, fig. 25).

CAT. NO. 169

170. Harness Plaque
Inv. No. 30.237
Silver, cast. L. 2.2 cm
4th century BC

This plaque is in the form of a recumbent mule (?) facing left with its legs tucked beneath its body. Both the pose and the features of the animal—including its long ears, small round eye, and mouth rendered in low relief—indicate that it is a peaceful herbivore. There is a semicircular attachment loop on the reverse.

There are no known analogues for this piece. While herbivores occasionally appear among the mainly predatory animal figurines in the Scythian Animal Style of the 5th to 4th century BC, the period of greatest diffusion of such animal art, these are generally depicted in poses of frozen movement (with heads turned back, legs drawn in, and torsos turned). Standing deer sometimes appear among 5th

CAT. NO. 170, 2 VIEWS

century BC finials (Ilinskaia 1968:38, pl. xxvi.12, 13, 15, 16), but they are not otherwise very similar to our example. In studying the Scythian Animal Style in the Ukrainian forest-steppe, Shkurko concluded that the art of the tribes of the central Don River region changed significantly in the 4th to 3rd century BC so that "the majority of predators loses its menacing, frightening appearance, changing into placid, peaceful animals" (1976:100, fig. 5.1–3). Our artifact may thus date to the 4th century BC.

171. Harness Plaque
      Inv. No. 30.562
      Bronze, cast. L. 5 cm
      4th century BC

This plaque is in the form of an openwork stag's head with an extended snout. Details—including lips, nostrils, oval eye, and triangular ear—are rendered in relief. A curved stag antler rises from the ear, terminating in the head of a bird of prey with a large round eye, protruding ear, and sharply curving beak. The other protrusion on the antler, round in section, may indicate a branch. Beneath the snout is a large attachment loop.

 Numerous analogues from 4th century BC kurgans in the Kuban, the closest of which was recovered from kurgan No. 19 in the village of Voronezhskaia (Moshinskii 2003:36, fig. 61; Zhuravlev 2002:no. 484), suggest the probable date of our example.

CAT. NO. 171

 First published by Greifenhagen (1970:56, fig. 13), who followed Zahn in erroneously describing it as the head of a bird of prey and a fish.

172. Frontlet
      Inv. No. 30.568
      Bronze, cast, engraved. L. 14.3 cm
      4th century BC

This frontlet is in the form of an open-work, S-shaped lion. It grasps the stag's head in its open mouth with its front paw, which is held against its chin, and its rear section is turned over and outward. The extensive detail engraved on both the lion and stag has been severely damaged by corrosion and is now barely visible. There is a horizontal attachment loop on the reverse.

Comparable depictions of lions, similar both in pose (Leskov 1990:no. 70, fig. 84) and the treatment of the head (Leskov 1989:no. 9, fig. 6), indicate that our piece is typical of the Scythian Animal Style in the 4th century BC Kuban.

First published by Greifenhagen (1970:56, fig. 29).

CAT. NO. 172

173. Cheekpiece
    Inv. No. 30.577
    Bronze, cast. L. 7.6 cm (preserved portion)
    4th century BC

CAT. NO. 173

This cheekpiece is gamma-shaped (broken). The flat shaft swells to a figure 8, pierced with a hole in each loop, just before the sharply bent end, which took the form of a flat plaque (only the base survives); the other end forms the long neck for its wolf's (?) head terminal. The wolf has a small head with a protruding ear, an oval eye, and an open mouth with a huge fang connecting its upper and lower jaws; one long arm extends from the base of the long neck, which is decorated with a round eye in relief and elongated oval beak representing the head of a bird of prey. The cheekpiece likely had an original length of 9 cm.

An example especially similar in its depiction of the predator's head was recovered from the 4th century BC Elizavetinskie kurgans (Perevodchikova 1987:44–58, fig. 3.12). Our cheekpiece belongs to the same period.

First published by Greifenhagen (1970:55, fig. 11).

174   Bells (3 items)
       Inv. No. 30.587a–c
       Bronze, cast. H. 7.1 cm, 7.2 cm, 7.2 cm
       4th century BC

These bells are almost cylindrical in form, each narrowing slightly toward the semicircular suspension loop at its top. There is a round hole for the attachment of a clapper (none survive) beneath each loop, and there are two narrow slits, set opposite each other, running lengthwise down each bell. One slit extends to the base of the bell, while the other is somewhat shorter.

Similar bells of varying sizes are common at Scythian sites from the late 7th–4th century BC, being larger in the earlier periods. These three, among the smallest known, likely date to the 4th century BC and were used independently as details rather than pendants for horse trappings.

First published by Greifenhagen (1970:56, figs. 47–49).

CAT. NO. 174

175. Finials (2 items)
       Inv. No. 30.592a, b
       Silver, gold, cast, forged. Diam. 1.6 cm
       4th century BC

Two truncated cones are covered with gold foil and pierced vertically with a wide tubular hole (obscured by corrosion). The shape and material of these objects, as well as their gold-foil ornamentation, sug-

CAT. NO. 175

gest they served as finials on the horse trappings of a rich warrior.

Such ornaments (cf. No. 160) are most commonly recovered from 4th century BC horse burials (as at kurgan Oguz) (Leskov 1974:20ff.).

176. Mirror
Inv. No. 30.605
Silver, cast. H. 22 cm; Diam. 17.5 cm
4th century BC

This mirror is in the form of a disc with a polished front surface. The reverse is edged with a low relief line (broken or unfinished), and the projecting handle tapers toward its broken base.

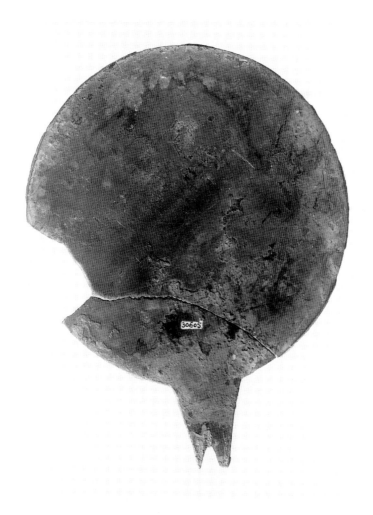

CAT. NO. 176

While the absence of a handle base precludes a secure identification of its type, the mirror certainly belongs to Kuznetsova's category of one-piece mirrors cast together with lateral handles (1987:35ff., fig. 3). It is probably of her fifth type, first sort (disc with rim), second variant, which dates to the 4th century BC. Such mirrors are relatively common at Scythian sites.

First published by Greifenhagen (1970:56, fig. 51).

177. Pendant
 Inv. No. 30.609
 Stone, gold, burnished, drilled. H. 2.4 cm
 4th century BC

CAT. NO. 177

This burnished, spherical stone bead is in a setting formed from four extensions of gold wire that run its length and intersect above the thin gold plating at its top and bottom. A small gold suspension loop, rolled from a thicker wire, is attached to the wire intersection point at the top of the bead.

A similar pendant in a gold setting is held in the Penn Museum holdings of the Maikop collection (No. 133, Inv. No. 30-33-34), and excavated examples are known from 4th–3rd century BC sites in the Kuban and northern Black Sea region and occasionally also from Roman period sites. Additional analogues from the Kurdzhips kurgan (Galanina 1980:87–88, pl. V) support a 4th century BC date for our piece.

178. Pendant
 Inv. No. 30.611
 Glass, molded, with applied ornament. H. 2.3 cm
 4th century BC

This pendant is in the form of a dark blue molded glass bird with eyes and lower torso defined with applied white and yellow lines. The tail and suspension loop are broken.

Similar figurines are known from 4th to 3th century BC Scythian-Greek sites in the southern part of Eastern Europe (Alekseeva 1982:pl. 47.35). One securely dated analogue from the Scythian royal kurgan in Melitopol of the second half of the 4th century BC (Terenozhkin and Mozolevskii 1988:104–5, figs. 116–18) confirms the date of our example.

CAT. NO. 178

179. Stag's Head Ornament
    Inv. No. 30.627
    Gold, stamped, soldered, with filigree and cutouts. H. 3.8 cm
    4th century BC

This stag's head ornament is composed of two plaques soldered together over a wooden (?) foundation and attached to a flat, rectangular base. Almost identical to the larger of the two stags' heads in the Penn Museum holdings of the Maikop collection (No. 82, Inv. No. 30-33-14.14), this example is distinguished primarily by its rectangular base and better state of preservation. The ears, which survive in this example, have rings attached to them; a disc on a loop dangles from each. Apertures along the edges of the flat plaque served to attach the ornament to its foundation, possibly a diadem or headdress.

Numerous such objects were made in workshops in the European Bosporus in the second half of the 4th century BC.

First published by Greifenhagen (1970:60, pl. 38.1–2).

CAT. NO. 179

180. Pendants (4 items)
    Inv. No. 30.632a–d
    Gold, stamped, soldered, with granulation, filigree. H. 1.6 cm
    4th century BC

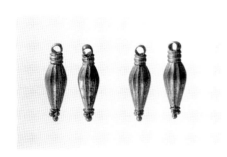

CAT. NO. 180

These pendants are in the form of a hollow, elongated teardrop. The top of each pendant is encircled by a horizontally grooved plaque and has a small, vertically grooved suspension ring attached to it. Deep vertical grooves run lengthwise down each pendant's body to its base, which is ringed by a thin wire with four round granules forming a pyramid (point downward) soldered to it. The size of these pendants indicates they originally hung from a necklace.

Two identical pendants exist in the Penn Museum portion of the Maikop collection (No. 92, Inv. No. 30-33-54) and may well derive from the same necklace as these four. The excavated comparanda include a 4th century BC gold example from the Krasnodar region that both indicates the probable date of ours and connects such pendants with the Kuban.

First published by Greifenhagen (1970:40, pl. 16, 19), who assigned them to the south of Russia based on the finds with which they were inventoried after World War II. The Philadelphia comparanda indicate these likely came from de Massoneau's collection.

181. Pendants (2 items)
     Inv. No. 30.633a, b
     Gold, stamped, soldered. L. 1.5 cm, 1.2 cm
     4th century BC

CAT. NO. 181

These pendants are small, horizontal tubes formed from a thin plaque. Each has a narrow, grooved plaque soldered vertically in the middle of its length that curves into a suspension loop at its top.

Though the simplicity of their form precludes an accurate assessment of their date, the appearance of fluted plaques on 4th century BC objects in the Maikop collection suggests these pendants may belong to the same period.

First published by Greifenhagen (1970:40, pl. 16.16–17), who noted they were among the materials attributed to the south of Russia; he linked them to this region as well.

182. Pins (2 items)
     Inv. No. 30.221n, o
     Gold, cast, forged, soldered, engraved. L. 17.5 cm, 18.9 cm
     4th century BC

These pins are in the form of a pointed shaft, rhomboidal in section, with a narrower, flattened base terminating in a spoonlike hollow. The smaller pin is distinguished from the other by the interpolation of a flat, winged griffin on a flat oval cap between the shaft and base. The griffin, facing left, is decorated with incised detail and the flattened base soldered to its head may have been a later addition. The purpose of these pins is unclear; similarly shaped items in the medieval period are thought to be earwigs (for cleaning the ears). They may, as Greifenhagen speculated (1970:59, pl. 36.6–7), have served a similar purpose in the Scythian period.

While the pins themselves have no known analogues, the striding winged griffin depicted on the one may be compared to the griffins on 5th to 4th century BC plaques

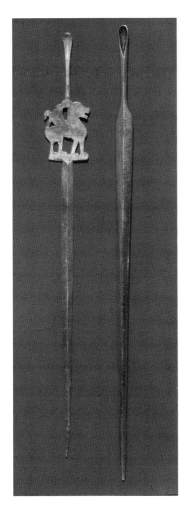

CAT. NO. 182A, B

CAT. NO. 182 DETAIL

from the Kuban and Ukraine. No exact parallels exist but the relatively flat torso and clarity of the lines used to render our griffin's snout and wings suggest a connection with the depictions from 4th century BC sites in the Ukrainian steppe. A winged griffin on a gold plaque from the Verkhnerogachikskiy kurgan (Leskov 1974:42, fig. 32, right) and a winged griffin on a bronze finial and lion on a gold plaque (Artamonov 1966:pls. 190, 192) from the Aleksandropol kurgan are all represented in the same flat manner as ours. This shift from three-dimensional to flatter animals also occurs in the Ukrainian forest-steppe and the central Don River region, being especially vivid in the mid- to late 4th century BC; our pins may well date to the same period.

First published by Greifenhagen (1970:59, pl. 36.6–7).

183. Plaque
    Inv. No. 1843, S. 68, 2,2=GL 371 (found in the Crimea)
    Gold, punched. L. 2.2 cm
    4th century BC

This rectangular plaque is edged with a hatched relief line and has a hole in each corner for sewing it to its foundation. A profile rabbit leaping to the left is rendered in relief in the main field.

The royal kurgan of Kul-Oba, from which many items were looted (Brashinskii 1967:29–53), has yielded 18 identical plaques now held in the Hermitage; one other, undoubt-

CAT. NO. 183

edly also from Kul-Oba, is in the British Museum collection (Artamonov 1966:fig. 94). Originally dated to the 5th century BC by Marshall (1911:237–38, pl. xl, no. 204–7), these plaques are now attributed to the second half of the 4th century BC; our example should belong to the same period.

First published by Greifenhagen (1970:39, pl. 16.5).

184. Plaque
   Misc. Inv. No. 7366=GL 372 (found in Crimea; acquired in 1878 from the
      collection of Count Keglevich of Vienna)
   Gold, punched. H. 3.1 cm
   4th century BC

CAT. NO. 184

This plaque in the form of a front-facing winged female, with details in relief, is a representation of the so-called snake-footed goddess, thought to be the ancestor of the Scythians (see Penn Museum No. 72). Her legs curve up in spirals, her arms take the form of wings curving up and in toward her kalathos-type headdress, and she wears a short, long-sleeved chiton flaring out into two divided sections below her belted waist. A seven-petal palmette appears in the space between her slit chiton and turned-out legs. Her slightly elongated face is characterized by a high forehead with a fringe of hair above large, round eyes, a straight nose, and plump lips. Six holes, three at the top and three at the bottom of the figure, served to attach the plaque to its foundation.

Similar depictions are known from Kul-Oba, but the two closest analogues include an item in Kiev, context unknown (Reeder 1999:233, no. 107), and one from the kurgan Bolshaia Bliznitsa, which dates to the end of the 4th century BC (Artamonov 1966:fig. 308). Both were probably made with the same punch in a workshop in Panticapaeum, the capital of the Bosporan Kingdom. Our plaque likely dates to the same period, around the second half of the 4th century BC.

First published by Greifenhagen (1970:39, pl. 16.1).

185. Torque Finial
   Misc. Inv. No. 11.863,58
   Gold, die-formed, engraved, with filigree, granulation, and enamel. L. 3 cm
   4th century BC

This finial is in the form of a lion's head on a socket that narrows towards its base, with details mostly in relief. The lion's mane comprises three rows of triangular tufts incised with lines representing individual strands, and there is a wire loop in its mouth. The socket

CAT. NO. 185

is ornamented with alternating bands of smooth and granulated wire of varying thickness with a broad band of ovolos formed from gold wire and filled in with light blue enamel interpolated near the base. The other end of the torque does not survive.

Similar finials are known on torques from Scythian royal kurgans (Solokha and Kul-Oba) (Mantsevich 1987:55ff., no. 33; Artamonov 1966:pl. 263) and elite burials (Talaevskyi kurgan, Arkhangelskaia Sloboda) (Mantsevich 1957:155ff., figs. 6, 8, 9; Leskov 1972:32, pls. 32, 40, 41). While the absence of finial tubes on our fragment precludes its secure classification with the shorter-socketed Solokha (Mantsevich 1987:57) and Kul-Oba torques (Alekseev 2003:262) of the last quarter of the 5th century BC (though the Solokha example and one of the Kul-Oba torques are from early 4th century BC contexts) (Alekseev 2003:260–61) or the longer-socketed examples from Talaevskyi (mid-4th century BC) and Arkhangelskaia (late 5th to early 4th century BC), the wire loop in the lion's mouth is similar to the Hercules knots in the mouths of the lions on the Solokha torque. Our artifact is likely from a kurgan in the Crimea or Ukrainian steppe and should date to the first half of the 4th century BC.

First published by Greifenhagen (1970:42, pl. 19.1–3). While accurately citing the discovery of torque finials in the form of lions' heads from Arkhangelskaia Sloboda, Greifenhagen erroneously indicated that socketed finials in the form of rams' heads were found there; such a finial, belonging to a rhyton rather than a torque, actually comes from the Gaimanova Mogila kurgan, also excavated in 1969.

186. Bracelet Finial
    Misc. Inv. No. 11.863,61 (found in the Taman Peninsula)
    Gold, die-formed, engraved, with filigree, granulation, and enamel. L. 3 cm
    4th century BC

This bracelet finial is in the form of a ram's head on a long, slim socket heavily decorated with filigree, granulation, and enamel. The socket was originally fitted on a plait form-

CAT. NO. 186 (ca. twice life-size)

ing the main body of a bracelet with ends that did not connect. The central field of the socket is decorated with applied wire S-shapes terminating in spirals alternating with narrow palm leaves; at either end are multiple roped and pseudo-granulated bands. The end adjoining the ram's head is also decorated with a broad band of ovolos filled with poorly preserved enamel.

A similar bracelet is known from the Penn Museum Maikop holdings (No. 54). Excavated comparanda, varying widely in dimension and the ornamentation of the socket, are widespread at 5th–4th century BC sites; the elongated and heavily decorated form of our socket distinguishes it from a group of earlier examples. Its closest analogue is a gold finial for a drinking horn from a mid-4th century BC cache in the Scythian royal kurgan Gaimanova Mogila (Alekseev 2003:276, app. 11; cf. Bondar 1975; Bidzilia 1971), which contained six gold and silver vessels and a drinking horn. This gold finial differs from ours only in the diameter of its socket. Our example should thus be dated to the second half of the 4th century BC.

First published by Greifenhagen (1970:42, pl. 19.4–5), who dated it to the 4th century BC.

187. Plaque
     Misc. Inv. No. 11.863,98
     Gold, punched. L. 2.5 cm
     4th century BC

CAT. NO. 187

This thin, rectangular plaque is edged with a faint relief border and pierced with a hole in each corner for attachment to its foundation. A reclining griffin, shown in profile facing right, fills the central field; the thinness of the plaque precluded the griffin from being more deeply punched so that the original position of its legs and curved tail cannot now be determined.

Similar plaques from complexes of the second half of the 4th century BC have been recovered from Chertomlyk (Alekseev 2003:267–68), from excavations near Kakhovka (Leskov 1974:78ff., fig. 77), and from the rich but looted kurgan Zholtokamena Mogila (Meliukova and Abramova 1989:pl. 38.36). Our plaque should belong to the same period.

First published by Greifenhagen (1970:50, pl. 27.1).

188. Plaques (2 items)
     Misc. Inv. No. 11.863,108
     Gold, punched, engraved. H. 1.8 cm
     4th century BC

CAT. NO. 188

These plaques are in the form of an eagle (?) with wings outspread, head turned to the right, and a body covered with columns of diagonal hatching, with punched details. Five holes were pierced at the top and bottom of each wing and in the center of the tail for sewing each plaque to its foundation.

Similar plaques are known from kurgan Karagodeuashkh, the Kurdzhips kurgan (Kuban) (Galanina 1980:90 ff., no. 40), kurgan Oguz and the Chmyrev kurgan (Ukrainian steppes) (Onaiko 1970:pls. 496, 500), and sites in the Kerch Peninsula (Kirilin 1968:182, fig. 3.4). With the exception of the Chmyrev kurgan, which dates to the third quarter of the 4th century BC, the other sites are from the last quarter of that century.

First published by Greifenhagen (1970:51, pl. 27.10).

189. Ornament
    Misc. Inv. No. 30.628
    Gold, stamped, soldered, with filigree. H. 2.4 cm
    4th–3rd century BC

This hollow sphinx, soldered lengthwise from two halves, stands with wings raised to touch the back of its head; each of the two hemispherical legs ends in a wide, flat base that is edged with dotted ornaments and pierced with two holes for attachment to a flat (?) surface, possibly a diadem or headdress. Two rings curved from fine wires, one with a disc-shaped pendant on a loop, are soldered to the sphinx's nose.

The style of this ornament indicates a date between the 4th and 3rd century BC.

First published by Greifenhagen (1970:61, pl. 38.3), who erroneously identified it as an earring. The holes in the ornament's base are clearly intended for sewing the ornament on in a vertical position.

CAT. NOS. 189 (bottom)
AND 190

190. Goat Ornament
    Inv. No. 30.629
    Gold, stamped, soldered, with granulation, filigree. L. 2 cm
    4th–3rd century BC

This hollow, recumbent goat is soldered lengthwise from two halves; the head, characterized by small, upright ears, bulging eyes framed by thin wire, and a small mouth delineated in low relief, is further distinguished by the two wire rings, each with a vertically grooved sphere on an elongated stem dangling from it, that are soldered to its nostrils. Granulated lines ring its head, neck, and hindquarters, and there is a granulated triangle on its forehead below the horns, which are made from a single filigreed wire and curve back and down to fall against its withers. A wide plaque curved into a loop replaces the tail and serves as a suspension ring.

The suspension loop indicates this was likely part of an intricate pendant, possibly part of a diadem or headdress, of the type common to Scythian-Greek sites of the 4th to 3rd century BC.

First published by Greifenhagen (1970:61, pl. 38.4), who identified it as a torque finial; such hollow miniature figurines, however, are unprecedented in this role.

191. Bowl
　　Inv. No. 30.584
　　Bronze, forged, with riveting, engraving. Diam. 8.5 cm
　　4th–2nd century BC

This hemispherical bowl has a slightly flattened base. The exterior has a rosette enclosed in a hatched band on its base and narrow petals that taper toward the bottom on its walls, while the interior has a protrusion in its center. At some point after it was made, four narrow plaques were riveted to the interior of the bowl at equal intervals; the better preserved of the two that survive rises above the lip of the vessel, revealing a round hole pierced from the exterior beneath its flat top. The purpose of these plaques is unknown.

The bowl's decoration is typical of ancient Greek items and widespread in the north-

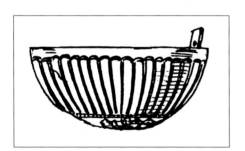

ern Black Sea region in the Greek and Roman periods. Our example is likely Bosporan work from the Hellenistic period (4th–2nd century BC) as ornamentation with petals is not characteristic of the Roman period (Kropotkin 1970:207–35, plates of bronze vessels).

First published by Greifenhagen (1970: 56, figs. 52–53).

CAT. NO. 191

192. Pendant
   Inv. No. 30.612
   Glass, molded, with applied ornament. H. 2.2 cm
   4th–2nd century BC

This pendant is in the form of a demon's head in yellow glass with hair in dark blue glass. The hair is combed up in the center to form a round suspension loop.

   Similar pendants and beads with human faces are widespread at Scythian-Greek sites in the northern Black Sea region from the 6th to 2nd century BC (Alekseeva 1982:33–34, pl. 47.23). As the closest analogue to ours comes from Tauric Chersonese and as such demonic depictions are most common in the Hellenistic period, our pendant likely dates between the 4th and 2nd century BC.

CAT. NO. 192

193. Phalerae (2 items)
   Inv. No. 30.595a, b
   Bronze, silver, forged, stamped. H. 8.5 cm, 7.1 cm
   3rd–2nd century BC

These fragmentary oval plaques of silver have edges folded over a bronze foundation and front surfaces decorated in relief. The main field, bordered with a roped band, has a small

CAT. NO. 193

oval with roped borders in its center and is divided in half by two wavy roped lines; each half is identically decorated with a seven-petal palmette extending out from the central oval. Hatched sections are used to articulate the petals of the palmette, lending visual integrity to the overall composition. The bronze foundations of these phalerae, which originally measured 10.5 cm in height, are severely damaged, precluding an assessment of their means of attachment.

Although similar phalerae are known from Sarmatian period sites, no close analogues to ours are known. Of the 114 examples most recently published in a compilation of Sarmatian phalerae (Mordvinceva 2001), only five are oval in form; three of these are from the Kuban (the Verkhniy farmstead, Akhtanizovskaia settlement, and the kurgans on Vasiurina hill), and two are from the lower Don River region (the Fedulovskiy treasure). The relief roping on the Akhtanizovskaia and Fedulovskiy phalerae (Mordvinceva 2001:71–73), the latter of which also has vegetal ornament somewhat similar to that on ours, suggests our examples date between the 3rd and 2nd century BC.

First published by Greifenhagen (1970:65, figs. 31, 32).

194. Beads (2 items)
    Inv. Nos. 30.221 m1–2
    Gold, punched, soldered, with filigree. Diam. 3.2 cm
    2nd–3rd century AD

These spheres are pierced vertically with a large hole and soldered crosswise from two halves. Pseudo-granulated wire rings the hole at the top and bottom of each bead and is applied over the central join. A row of small holes of unclear purpose is also pierced along one side of the join.

While gold beads do rarely appear in 4th century BC Scythian complexes (Petrenko 1978), they are typically small and undecorated and so have not been closely studied. Those from 2nd century BC Sarmatian sites, especially in the Kuban, are better known but are typically large and barrel shaped, often decorated with granulation and with smooth or pseudo-granulated wire edging their pierced holes (Anfimov 1987:200, 209). It is really in

CAT. NO. 194

the early centuries AD that beads similar to ours, typically smooth with applied wire and little granulated decoration, predominate. One large biconical example exists in the Penn Museum portion of the Maikop collection (No. 106, Inv. No. 30-33-29), while the excavated comparanda include a large oval bead from a 1st–3rd century AD Sarmatian burial (Leskov 1990:fig. 221, no. 257) and a necklace of large gold beads from a rich 2nd–3rd century AD burial in the necropolis of Gorgippia (Leskov and Lapushnian 1987:172, no. 262, fig. 86). The latter object is notable for the applied bands ringing both middle and holes of the two largest (centrally placed) beads. Our two beads likely derive from a plaited gold necklace originating in a 2nd to 3rd century AD complex (Anfimov 1987).

First published by Greifenhagen, who suggested that the large diameter of their pierced holes made them fit to serve as ornaments for horse trappings or a chariot (Greifenhagen 1970:59, pl. 36.8–9).

195. Two-part Buckles (8 items, 2 preserved)
    Inv. No. 30.602
    Bronze, cast, forged, soldered. L. 2.5 cm, 2.4 cm (4 cm when fastened)
    10th century AD

CAT. NO. 195

Two fasteners comprise a single buckle, each formed from two plaques that are triangular in section and have a small protrusion in the center of the slightly rounded short end. The other short end terminates in one case in a circular tongue on a short base and in the other in a ring-shaped receiver with a concave crosspiece covering the lower quarter of its area. The tongue would have been inserted at an angle into the receiver before both plaques were brought into horizontal position, locking the tongue into place against the concave crosspiece of the receiver. There is a pair of bronze attachment loops (one loop preserved) on the reverse of each plaque.

These fasteners are comparable in form to Nos. 196 and 197 and should be similarly dated to the 10th century BC.

First published by Greifenhagen (1970:56, figs. 42, 43).

196. Two-Part Buckles (16 items, 1 preserved)
    Inv. No. 30.603
    Silver, bronze, cast, forged, soldered. L. 2.8 cm
    10th century AD

CAT. NO. 196

One half of a buckle in two parts comprises a plaque, triangular in section, attached to a ring-shaped receiver with a crosspiece at its base that covers a quarter of its area.

The other end is slightly rounded with a small protrusion in its middle.

This fastener is comparable in form to Nos. 195 and 197 and should be similarly dated to the 10th century BC.

First published by Greifenhagen (1970:56, fig. 41).

197. Two-Part Buckles (19 items, 2 preserved)
Inv. No. 30.604
Bronze, cast, forged, soldered. L. 3.6 cm, 3.5 cm
10th century AD

CAT. NO. 197

These two fasteners belong to two different buckles, each comprising a plaque that is triangular in section and broadens slightly toward its tip, which is attached to a ring-shaped receiver with a crosspiece covering the lower third of its area. The form of the other half of each buckle appears in the inventory book (which mistakenly gives the material as silver, p. 89, instead of bronze). There are two attachment loops on the central vertical line on the reverse of each plaque and one of the fasteners was pierced with two holes beneath the receiver to further secure it to its foundation.

Similar fasteners in the Penn Museum part of the Maikop collection (Nos. 124 and 125, Inv. Nos. 30-33-63a, b and -62a, b) and in the Hermitage collection suggest a date of the 10th century AD for our examples (M. G. Kramarkovskii personal communication).

First published by Greifenhagen (1970:56, figs. 39, 40, which also mistakenly calls them silver).

198. Arrowhead
Inv. No. 30.589
Iron, forged. L. 8 cm
10th–12th century AD

CAT. NO. 198

This arrowhead is of the shaft type. The head is rhomboidal in section, tapering from flat base to pointed tip, and is set on an elongated shaft, round in section, which narrows slightly toward its base.

This item is typical of the steppes of the northern Black Sea region in the Northern Caucasus from the 10th to 12th century AD (Leskov 1991:no. 305).

First published by Greifenhagen (1970:56, fig. 26).

199. Pendant
      Inv. No. 30.599
      Silver, stamped, soldered. H. 4.8 cm
      11th–13th century AD

This almond-shaped pendant is comprised of two halves that were stamped from the interior and decorated before being soldered together. The outer surface, the upper three-quarters of which is covered with small bumps (as a walnut shell), is segmented by six relief lines running lengthwise from base to tip and is ringed by another small relief line at its top beneath a small suspension loop.

While no direct analogues for this item exist, its technique of manufacture indicates it belongs to the Middle Ages, between the 11th and 13th century AD.

CAT. NO. 199

200. Buttons (2 items)
      Inv. No. 30.601
      Silver, forged, soldered, with granulation, filigree. H. 2.5 cm
      13th–14th century AD

CAT. NO. 200

These buttons are in the form of a sphere soldered from two halves; a band comprising three diagonally hatched strips is applied to the horizontal seam. There is a small tube, to which a suspension loop was originally attached, formed from three coils of filigree wire at the top of each button and a pyramid (point downwards) formed from four granules at its base.

Similar buttons exist in the Penn Museum portion of the Maikop collection (cf. No. 129, Inv. No. 30-33-65a, b, c); they are all typical of the Belorechenskaya culture and date between the 13th and 14th century AD.

201. Harness Plaques (2 items, 1 preserved)
     Inv. No. 30.231a, b
     Bronze, cast. H. 3.1 cm, 2.9 cm
     Date unknown

These triangular plaques have a hemispherical projection in their centers and at each of their three points.
There are traces of an attachment loop on the reverse.

CAT. NO. 201

These items have no direct analogues at Scythian
or pre-Scythian sites; while bearing some resemblance
to the 4th century BC cruciform plaque of No. 169, precursors may in fact be in the pre-
Scythian crescent-shaped pendants of the 8th century BC (Terenozhkin 1976:48, figs. 19.7,
33.6, 42.5). A secure date cannot yet be assigned.
    First published by Greifenhagen (1970:56, figs. 33, 34).

202. Plaque-Buttons (4 items, 1 preserved)
     Inv. No. 30.235a–d
     Bronze, cast. Diam. 3 cm
     Date unknown

These buttons are hemispheres
with a flattened crosspiece (for
attachment) on their reverse.

    Similarly plain plaques
are common at sites throughout the northern Black Sea littoral and Northern Caucasus
during both the pre-Scythian
(8th to 7th century BC) and
Scythian periods.

CAT. NO. 202

First published by Greifenhagen (1970:56, fig. 38).

203. Button (?)
     Inv. No. 30.593
     Bone, carved, burnished. Diam. 1.4 cm
     Date unknown

This miniature truncated cone has an elegantly worked surface
pierced vertically with a wide, tubular hole. Its weight, 0.77 grams,
suggests it served as a small ornament such as a button or other

CAT. NO. 203

detail rather than as a spindle or finial.

This object is similar in form to Nos. 160 and 175, suggesting it may also belong to the 4th century BC; this date, however, cannot yet be confirmed.

204. Ornament Details (2 items)
Inv. No. 30.600a, b
Silver, forged, soldered. H. 1.6 cm
Date unknown

These ornament details are in the form of hollow open-work spheres with a small suspension hoop on one end and a tube, possibly for the suspension of a pendant, on the other. These may have served as end pieces for a necklace or other neck ornament.

These likely date to the medieval period.

CAT. NO. 204

* * *

Before continuing with the next section, which comprises items lost during World War II, we should note that there are 13 inventory numbers of various gold ornaments (Greifenhagen 1970:pls. 16.19; 32.45; 33.1, 2, 4; 34.2; 36.10–13; 37.1–3, 6–7, 13, 15–16) in the Antikenabteilung (Berlin) that have direct analogues in the portion of the Maikop collection in the Penn Museum. As all these items have been described in the chapter on the Philadelphia material, each cross referenced with the Antikenabteilung material, we will limit ourselves here to listing them with references to the Penn Museum material and to Greifenhagen's publication:

(1) Ornament: cf. No. 189, and Greifenhagen (1970:pl. 34.2). (2, 3) Plaque-Appliqués: cf. Nos. 190, 191, and Greifenhagen (1970:pl. 32.4–6). (4–10) Plaques: cf. Nos. 194–200, and Greifenhagen (1970:pls. 36.10–13; 33.1–2, 4; 37.1–3, 6–7). (11–12) Pendants and beads: cf. Nos. 225, 226, and Greifenhagen (1970:pls. 16.19; 37.4–5, 13).

Lost Items

205. Spearhead
Inv. No. 30.588
Bronze, cast. L. 12 cm
8th–7th century BC

This leaf-shaped, bilobate blade (its widest point is a third of the way from its base) has a central rib that continues on to form an elongated socket that is round in section and broadens gradually toward the base. Two holes on either side of the socket near its base

CAT. NO. 205

served to attach it to the shaft.

This type of spearhead is common at both pre-Scythian and proto-Maeotian sites and is widely represented in burials of the same date in the Kuban (Leskov and Erlikh 1999:44–45, fig. 51.1–2).

206. Arrowheads (5 items)
     Inv. No. 30.607
     Bronze, cast. H. 3.4 cm
     6th century BC

These arrowheads are socketed, with a trilobate blade and sharpened blade tips. The sockets on three of these items are damaged; one has a small spike on its base; and one, while undamaged and without a spike, is disproportionately long in the inventory book drawing. The elongated appearance of the fifth socket is more likely due to careless drawing than to any real discrepancy in length.

As trilobate blades appear in the late 7th–early 6th century BC (Meliukova 1964:19) and sockets with spikes are characteristic of the same period, our arrowheads likely date to the 6th century BC.

CAT. NO. 206

207. Buttons (6 items)
     Inv. No. 30.233a–f
     Bronze, cast. L. 2.2 cm
     5th century BC

CAT. NO. 207

Oval in form, each button has a grooved and rounded upper surface and an attachment loop curved from a wide, flat plaque on the reverse. One of these is drawn in the inventory book.

As the buttons in No. 141, these are characteristic of 5th century BC Scythian sites in the Kuban and Ukraine.

208. Rhyton Finial
     Inv. No. 30.598
     Silver, stamped, soldered. L. 7.2 cm
     5th century BC

This finial is in the form of a naturalistic ram's head (damaged). The sharply curving horns articulated with diagonal hatching curl out from the forehead to frame small protruding ears. It has almond-shaped eyes and a narrow mouth rendered with a horizontal line.

CAT. NO. 208

Similar ram's head finials are typical of the 5th century BC and include one example on a gold rhyton from Semibratniy kurgan No. 4 (second quarter of the 5th century BC). These are notable for their lack of the heavy decoration, in the form of granulation, filigree, or enamel insets on the tubular finials, that characterizes later rhyta. Our finial, which lacks a tubular receptacle, is thus likely part of this 5th century BC group. A modestly decorated gold rhyton with four bands of braided wire and a short finial from the Uliap sanctuary is an important transitional piece between the rhyta of the 5th century BC and those with more heavily ornamented tubular finials from the 4th century BC (Leskov 1990:no. 239, figs. 187–90). These are from both the Semibratnie kurgans (Galanina and Gratsch 1986:figs. 110, 111) and the Maikop collection (Greifenhagen 1970:pl. 35.3–5).

209. Frontlet
     Inv. No. 30.223
     Bronze, cast. H. 6 cm
     5th–4th century BC

This slightly curved plaque has a crosspiece near its base, bridging the slit through its lower length, and the neck and head of a mountain goat at its top. A twisted horn curves sharply to the base of the head and is set above almond-shaped eyes, with nostrils and closed mouth delineated in relief. There is a ring for transverse attachment to the harness on the reverse of the goat's neck.

Though there are no direct analogues for this item, similarly realistic depictions are characteristic of the 5th century BC Kuban variant of the Scythian Animal Style. Our frontlet thus likely dates between the 5th and 4th century BC.

CAT. NO. 209

210. Button (?)
     Inv. No. 30.229
     Bronze, cast. H. 2.6 cm
     5th–4th century BC

This button is in the form of a three-dimensional predator's head, characterized by protruding ears, round, bulging eyes, and an open maw with large teeth. There is an attachment ring on the reverse. The object's small dimensions suggest it served as a button or clothing ornament.

Despite the lack of close analogues and the difficulty in discerning the details of the object from the drawing, it likely dates between the 5th and 4th century BC.

CAT. NO. 210

211. Decorative Plaque
      Inv. No. 30.564
      Bronze, cast. L. 4.5 cm
      5th–4th century BC

CAT. NO. 211

This curved plaque terminates at one end with the head of an animal. Although tentatively identified by Zahn as a dolphin, the curving horn (?), possibly an attachment ring, instead suggests a caprid or other animal. Further details are not apparent.

The problematic reconstruction and lack of close analogues makes it difficult to securely date this plaque; however, what is visible of the depiction seems typical of a Kuban variant of the Scythian Animal Style. It thus likely dates between the 5th and 4th century BC.

212. Cheekpieces (pair?)
      Inv. No. 30.576a, b
      Bronze, cast. L. 12 cm
      5th–4th century BC

These cheekpieces are gamma-shaped. The round shaft swells to a figure 8, pierced with a hole in each loop, just before the sharply bent end in the form of a flat disc, and the other end takes the form of an openwork recumbent animal with bent legs and a protruding ear. Keeper Zahn recorded in his inventory book that though the flat disc was broken into five pieces, a lion's head executed in low relief on its surface was preserved. The second cheekpiece is not described in Zahn's inventory book.

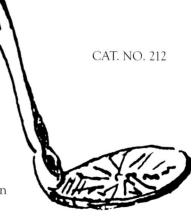

CAT. NO. 212

While gamma-shaped cheekpieces are common at 5th to 4th century BC Scythian-Maeotian sites in the Kuban, none of these bear relief ornamentation. The relief decoration recorded on our example, presented in the inventory book drawing of one of these artifacts, may thus represent an erroneous reconstruction.

213. Frontlet
       Inv. No. 30.224
       Bronze, cast. H. 5.4 cm
       4th century BC

This vertical, slightly curved plaque is slit lengthwise with two bumps at its base and the head of a predator at its top. The animal is characterized by a flat-lying ear (?); a large, round eye; and a nose and open jaw delineated with a single relief line and linked by a single fang. There is a lug for transverse attachment to the harness on the reverse of its upper part.

The treatment of the animal's head, especially the disproportionate size of the eye and the use of an apparently continuous relief line to depict the nostril and mouth, is comparable to that used in the 4th century BC Kuban variant of the Scythian Animal Style. The dating of our frontlet to this period is supported by the discovery of an identical plaque in one of the 4th century BC Elizavetinskie kurgans (Perevodchikova 1984:5ff., fig. 2.3).

CAT. NO. 213

214. Harness Plaques (2 items)
       Inv. No. 30.226a, b
       Bronze, cast. L. 5.4 cm
       4th century BC

These harness plaques are in the form of a profile wolf's head (facing left). The eye, nose, chin, fur (visible below base of ear), and protruding ear are all articulated in relief while the teeth are rendered in openwork for emphasis. There is a relief depiction, likely the head of a bird of prey, on its lower jaw and an attachment ring on the reverse of each. One of these is drawn in the inventory book.

The date of these and similar plaques in the Maikop collection (cf. No. 215 in this collection and No. 37 in the Penn Museum collection) is based on comparanda from the Elizavetinskie kurgans and one other analogue found in a 4th century BC complex (Perevodchikova 1984:5ff., fig. 2.14).

CAT. NO. 214

215. Harness Plaques (2 items)
     Inv. No. 30.227a, b
     Bronze, cast. L. 3.6 cm
     4th century BC

CAT. NO. 215

These harness plaques are in the form of a profile wolf's
head (one facing left, the other, right) with eye, nostrils, protruding ear, and base of the lower jaw articulated in relief
and teeth in openwork for emphasis. There is an attachment ring on the reverse of each
plaque. One of these is drawn in the inventory book.

   Though the predators rendered here have shorter snouts than those of No. 214 (and
No. 37 in the Penn Museum collection), they are similar in style and typology and should
also date to the 4th century BC.

216. Plaque-Buttons (3 items)
     Inv. No. 30.236a–c
     Bronze, gold, cast, plated. H. 2.8 cm
     4th century BC

CAT. NO. 216

These plaque-buttons are in the form of a cruciform rosette covered with thin gold plating; the four round, convex petals are attached to a central round convexity. Traces of an attachment loop
are preserved on the reverse of each button (?). One of these is
drawn in Zahn's inventory book.

   Though comparable plaques are known at 8th to 7th century
BC pre-Scythian sites (Leskov and Erlikh 1999:fig. 41.5), these are
never covered in gold. Similar but flat gold plaques, well represented
among the gold wares of the Maikop treasure (Greifenhagen 1970:pl. 37.2–3), are common
in 4th century BC Scythian and Maeotian burials in the Kuban, and similar bronze plaques,
generally lacking gold plating, are common at 4th century BC Scythian sites in the northern
Black Sea region (Petrenko 1967:pl. 27.9). Our example should date to this same period.

217. Decorative Plaque Fragment
     Inv. No. 30.238
     Bronze, cast. H. 4 cm
     4th century BC

This openwork plaque (partially preserved) is reconstructed as a symmetrical depiction of
a male figure within a ring; the man's arms and legs are extended and bent almost perpendicularly at the joints and there is a stylized head of a bird of prey comprising a round eye
with a spiral-curved beak between each knee and elbow (one preserved). The head of the

man is carefully detailed, contrasting with the schematic rendering of the body; a conical hat between protruding ears is set atop large, bulging eyes, a long, narrow nose, and a small mouth. The drawing in the inventory book is supplemented by a picture published by Rostovtzeff.

Similarly rendered heads are known both from this collection (cf. No. 165, Inv. No. 30.222b and Potratz's publication [1960:pl. xv.40]) and from the Hermitage (No. 2735–288). Additional comparanda include a plaque of a man standing atop lion heads and holding two birds of prey by the neck (No. 171, Inv. No. IIId 7015) and a bronze frontlet in the form of a man's head torn to pieces by a feline predator that was recently found by Erlikh during the excavations of the kurgans in Tenginskaia village (Kuban) (Moshinskii 2003:35, fig. 58). Numerous parallels for all these images occur in the art of the Colkhidian and Koban cultures; as a group, they extend back to the art of Luristan (Rostovtzeff 1931b:45–56). It is notable that objects from the Kuban combine Caucasian characteristics (especially facial type) with local Maeotian and Scythian features; this is manifested in their specific depiction of animals interacting with humans and of armor on warriors (gorytoi on the statuettes). Such Scythian elements on our plaque indicate a date of the 4th century BC.

CAT. NO. 217

First published by Rostovtzeff (1931b:53–54, pl. 1.3), who dated the fragment between the late 5th and early 4th century BC.

218. Harness Plaques (2 items)
Inv. No. 30.563a, b
Bronze, cast. L. 5.4 cm
4th century BC

CAT. NO. 218

These harness plaques are in the form of an openwork stag's head with an elongated snout and features rendered in relief, including a round eye, protruding ear, lips, and nostrils. The antler, which curves up from the base of the ear, terminates in the head of a griffin with a crest (?) and curved beak. An attachment ring is set beneath the eye of each stag. One of these is drawn in the inventory book.

While comparable objects are known from

this collection (No. 171, Inv. No. 30.562), from the portion of the Maikop collection in the Berlin Museum für Vor- und Frühgeschichte (No. 296, Inv. No. IIId 7024), and from the State Historical Museum in Moscow, the last recovered from a 4th century BC kurgan (No. 19) in Voronezhskaia village (Kuban), these typically have more elongated necks and one pronounced projection (branch?) on their antlers (Zhuravlev 2002:no. 484). The most similar artifacts to ours were recovered from the 4th century BC Sarmatian kurgan No. 3 in the village of Filippovka in Bashkir (Alekseev 2001:142, no. 116) and from the Sholok-hovski kurgan on the lower Don River (Maksimenko 1983:fig. 12.8).

219. Cheekpiece (?) Fragment
       Inv. No. 30.565
       Bronze, cast, engraved (?). H. 4.5 cm
       4th century BC

This openwork plaque is comprised of a flat base, rectangular in section, with three identical heads of predators jutting up from one side. The heads are on progressively more elongated and curved necks set so the teeth of each successive head rest on the nape

CAT. NO. 219

of the former. Each predator is characterized by protruding ears, oval eyes, and an open maw with large fangs joining the upper and lower jaw. The plaque has no visible means of attachment, suggesting it formed part of a gamma-shaped, two-holed cheekpiece; such cheekpieces were often decorated with similar openwork depictions.

The style in which the heads are rendered is characteristic of the Kuban variant of the Scythian Animal Style. Similar depictions are known both from this collection (No. 173, Inv. No. 30.577, and No. 221, Inv. No. 30.578) and from a securely dated 4th century BC complex in the Kuzhorskaia settlement (Kuban) (Leskov 1989:no. 24, fig. 17). The available comparanda, both from the Kuzhorskaia complex and from Veselovskii's excavations in the Elizavetinskaia settle-

ment (Rolle 1993:no. 71), support the identification of this plaque as a fragment of a 4th century BC cheekpiece.

220. Cheekpiece (?) Fragment
       Inv. No. 30.567
       Bronze, cast, engraved (?). L. 5.5 cm
       4th century BC

This openwork plaque, in poor condition, is comprised of a shaft, round in section, diverging at its upper end into three progressively more elongated branches or necks,

each terminating in the head of a predator. The lower jaw of each successive predator rests on the ears of the former. The heads are characterized by protruding ears, round eyes, and open maws with large teeth joining the upper and lower jaws. The fragmentary nature of this object precludes a secure assessment of its function; however, it may have been part of a two-holed cheekpiece of the type common in the 4th century BC.

The heads of the predators are stylistically similar to those of No. 219 (Inv. No. 30.565) and are typical of the 4th century BC.

CAT. NO. 220

221. Cheekpiece (?) Fragment
     Inv. No. 30.578
     Bronze, cast. L. 5 cm
     4th century BC

This partially preserved shaft terminates in an animal's head. Although a single relief line articulates both its nostrils and lips (cf. No. 168), its wide-open mouth and long fang, which serves as a crosspiece between the upper and lower jaws, suggest this is not the head of a peaceful herbivore or, as Zahn suggested, a horse. Its oval eye and large, crescent-shaped ear further indicate that Zahn's identification should be abandoned.

The specific treatment of the animal's mouth is paralleled in the 4th century BC Kuban variant of the Scythian Animal Style (Perevodchikova 1984:5ff., figs. 2, 4, 7; 1987:44ff., fig. 3.12). Our fragment should belong to the same period.

CAT. NO. 221

222. Arrowheads (6 items)
     Inv. No. 30.608
     Iron, forged. L. 2.2–2.5 cm
     4th century BC

These arrowheads are socketed, with trilobate, triangular blades. The form and dimensions are typical of Scythian-Maeotian examples of the 4th century BC (Meliukova 1964:25ff.).

Iron arrowheads are more typical of the Kuban and forest-steppes of Scythia than the classical steppes; the Uliap excavations further in-

CAT. NO. 222

dicate that iron examples are much more common at 4th century BC Maeotian sites than bronze ones (Erlikh 1992). Our example is typical of 4th century BC Scytho-Maeotian arrowheads in both form and dimensions.

223. Earrings (pair)
Inv. Nos. 30.221b 1–2
Gold, punched, soldered, with granulation, filigree. H. 12.3 cm
4th century BC

These earrings are in the form of a hollow crescent soldered from two halves with three rings, each holding a complex pendant on an elongated suspension loop, set at equal intervals along its bottom. The sinuous suspension loop attaches to the wire-coiled tip at one end and to the head of the hollow bird atop the tip at the other. Each crescent also has a hollow bird with a long neck and curved beak extending perpendicularly from its middle and a plaited

CAT. NO. 223

band with a row of granulated triangles (points toward the center) applied along the seams at its top and bottom. The three complex pendants hanging from the crescent are identical, each comprising a column formed from three round, convex plaques decorated with granulated triangles (points toward the center) on their upper surfaces and pierced with a central hole, also decorated with granulation, through which the wire chain attaching to the suspension loop was threaded. Each convex plaque had eight teardrop-shaped pendants suspended from rings soldered to its lower edge, with the bottom of each teardrop resting on the convex plaque below it to create a secure and unified whole. These were lost before World War II; the description is from full-scale photographs.

While crescent-shaped earrings (Petrenko 1978:29ff., pls. 18–19) are common in the steppes and forest-steppes of Ukraine, the majority of these lack supplementary pendants. Only three examples (Reeder 1999:266, no. 129) with multiple pendants are known, all decorated with filigree, granulation, duck figurines, and coiled ends similar to ours. Our examples are distinguished primarily by the bird figurine set in the middle of each and by their multilevel design. The convex plaques to which the teardrop-shaped pendants are attached are typically used as supplementary pendants on Archaic type crescent-shaped earrings (small, with meager ornament, no birds, and short hoops) dating as early as the 6th century BC in the Central Caucasus (Meliukova and Abramova 1989:pls. 86–74). One early to mid-5th century BC analogue (*OAK* 1909–10:152, fig. 219; Leskov n.d.) is from Ulskiy kurgan No. 4 while another, similar to the earrings described above but with granulated triangles on its convex plaque (Greifenhagen 1970:pl. 38.5), is from the south of Russia or the Kuban. Similarly ornamented crescent-shaped earrings appear by the 5th century BC and continue until the end of the 4th century BC (Petrenko 1978:29–30, pl. 19,3, 4, 10–11), found in both the steppes and forest-steppes of Ukraine and reaching their greatest diffusion in the 4th century BC. The overall dimensions, high hoops, abundant pendants, and rich granulated and sculptural (bird) decoration of our examples indicate they belong to the same period.

224. Pendant-Bead (?)
    Inv. No. 30.610
    Glass, gold, cast, with wire-drawing. L. 1.4 cm
    4th–2nd century BC

This bead is in the form of a light blue glass oval, pierced lengthwise, in a setting formed from four evenly spaced extensions of gold wire running from its top to bottom. The wire on the side of one of the holes may have been a suspension loop (cf. No. 177; also No. 133.3 in the Penn Museum collection). The gold cage of the bead indicates it served as a pendant rather than forming part of a set; beads in sets are never found in gold wire settings.

CAT. NO. 224

    The dating of similar pendants suggests our example should fall within the Hellenistic period (4th–2nd century BC).

225. Gorgoneia (4 items)
    Inv. No. 30.616
    Clay, molded, punched. Diam. 2.0–2.2 cm
    4th–2nd century BC

These four discs, three flat and one bean-shaped in section, include a Medusa's head framed by two rows of convexities set in the center of each.

    Similar gorgoneia exist in the Penn Museum portion of the Maikop collection (Nos. 40–43, Inv. Nos. 30-33-44 to 30-33-47), and excavated analogues are known not only from the 4th century BC Uliap burial grounds (Leskov 1990:no. 174,

CAT. NO. 225

fig. 142) but also from 3rd–2nd century BC burials (Leskov 1991, no. 270) and many other Hellenistic period sites. Our gorgoneia date within this same period.

226. Spindle Whorl
Inv. No. 30.617
Stone, polished, drilled. H. 5.8 cm
Date unknown

CAT. NO. 226

This spindle whorl is barrel-shaped and pierced lengthwise with a hole drilled, according to Zahn's entry in the inventory book (p. 91), from one side.

The appearance of similar spindle whorls in Scythian complexes dating between the 4th century BC and the 3rd century AD in the Eastern Crimea (Yakovenko 1970:fig. 15.1–8), in Maeotian settlements, and in Scytho-Sarmatian burials in the Kuban (Beglova 1989:150, figs. 3.8–9, 5.12–14; Meliukova and Abramova 1989:246, pls. 93.18, 99.69) precludes the assignment of a secure date.

Adyghea—the way from the foothills to the mountains. Photograph by Dmitriy Slesarenko.

Museum für
Vor- und Frühgeschichte,
Berlin

227. Adze
   Inv. No. IIId 6426 (found in the
      south of Russia)
   Bronze, cast. L. 17 cm
   13th–12th century BC

This adze is large, narrow, and six-sided in section, with a flat base and sides that flare gradually to the sharp cutting edge.

   This item belongs to a large group of massive adzes recovered from Late Bronze Age (13th to 12th century BC) contexts in both the steppes of the Dniepr River region (Leskov 1967:161ff., figs. 11.10, 12.1) and the Kuban (Sokolskii 1980:144ff., figs. 1.13, 2.16). The simplicity of its form makes a more specific assessment of our example's date difficult (Iessen 1950:171 noted that adzes tend to become larger over time); the four closest analogues to it, all from the Roztov bronze treasure (Iliukov 1999:61ff., fig. 1.3–6), date from the 13th to 12th century BC.

CAT. NO. 227

228. Finials (2 items)
      Inv. Nos. IIId 6924, 6925 (found in the south of Russia)
      Bronze, cast, hammered. H. 3.5 cm, 3.6 cm
      Late 2nd–early 1st millennium BC

CAT. NO. 228

These finials are in the form of a large shaft tapering slightly from base to tip and pierced lengthwise with a hole of consistent diameter. Each was hammered at the base to form a flat disc.

These are typologically similar to finials of the so-called Lukianovskiy type, which is common at late 2nd–early 1st millennium BC Belozerskaia culture complexes in the steppes of the northern Black Sea region (Otroshchenko 2001:178ff.; Vanchugov 1990:97ff., fig. 35.10). As no such finials are known from the eastern Ukrainian steppes, it is possible these items came from the northern Black Sea steppes rather than from the Northwestern Caucasus.

229. Axe
      Inv. No. IIId 6411 (attributed to Maikop in the inventory book;
          acquired in 1907 from the collection of P. Mavrogordato, deed 885/07)
      Bronze, cast, engraved. H. 16.1 cm
      Late 2nd–early 1st millennium BC

This axe is sinuous and double-curved with a sharp, rounded butt and a narrow, oval socket. Its central part, six-sided in section, flattens toward the sharp semicircular cutting edge. Ridges and engraving decorate the upper part of the axe: there are three ridges running lengthwise along the butt; the central part is divided vertically into three sections, each containing three or four hatched lines; and two diagonal hatched bands intersect to form an X on the broad cutting edge.

The form of this axe, originally considered typical of the Colkhidian culture of western Georgia (Dzhaparidze 1989:189ff., fig. 101.10), is also known in the Koban culture. Following Tekhov's 1950s–70s excavations of the Tliiskiy burial grounds in southern Ossetia, where the majority of such axes were found (Tekhov 1980–85), this type has generally been called Colkhido-Koban. While such axes rarely occur in the foothills of the Caucasus, individual examples do appear at 8th–mid-7th century BC sites there and in the steppe and even the forest-steppe zone of the northern Black Sea region. Our example likely

CAT. NO. 229

dates to this same period though this form appears in the foothills of the Caucasus and in Transcaucasia from the end of the 2nd millennium BC.

230. Jar
Inv. No. IIId 6601 (found in the south of Russia)
Buff clay, handmade, with burnishing, cogged stamp. H. 8 cm
Beginning 1st millennium BC

This long-necked jar has a gently out-turned rim, a spherical body, and a flat base. The broad decorative band on the shoulder, bordered at both top and bottom with a shallow grooved band, contains a main pattern of two intersecting zigzags (creating a central row of diamonds) formed from the shallow imprints of a cogged stamp.

The closest analogues to ours in both form and decoration come from the Kobiakovs-kaia-type sites studied by Sharafutdinova in the Kuban, mainly in the Krasnogvardeiskii region of the Republic of Adyghea (50 km north of Maikop), and dated by her to the beginning of the 1st millennium BC (Anfimov and Sharafutdinova 1982:139–47, fig. 4).

231. Jar
Inv. No. IIId 6602 (found in the south of Russia)
Buff clay, handmade, burnished. H. 6.5 cm
Beginning 1st millennium BC

This short-necked jar has a gently out-turned rim, a spherical body, and a flat, slightly indented base. The decorative band on the shoulder, bordered at both top and bottom with a pair of grooved lines, contains a pattern of diamonds and triangles formed from intersecting diagonal lines.

While the form and decoration of this vessel, as well as the quality of its burnishing, suggest it should be considered together with No. 230 and the vessels from Kobiakovskaia-

CAT. NOS. 232, 231, AND 230

type sites, it is also comparable to vessels from the early period of the Kizil-Koba culture, also dating to the beginning of the 1st millennium BC (Kolotukhin 1982:105ff., fig. 2.6).

232. Cup
    Inv. No. IIId 3086 (found in the Crimea; acquired through deed 1317/03
        in 1903 from the collection of A. Kossnierska)
    Reddish-buff clay (almost black in one place), handmade, burnished,
        poorly fired. H. 8 cm
    9th–8th century BC

The slightly out-turned rim slopes inward slightly before flaring into a rounded body with a flat base; the loop of the handle, flat in section, curves from the base to just above the height of the vessel before merging down into its rim.

In its form, firing, and quality of burnishing, this vessel is typical of Early Kizil-Koba material, which dates between the 9th and 8th century BC (Leskov 1965:98ff.; Kris 1981: pl. 27.1, 5; Kolotukhin 1982:105ff., fig. 3.7). Kossnierska's entire collection comes from the Crimea and the Northern Caucasus; the largest part, Bronze Age metal wares, was published by Motzenbäcker (1996). Judging by the drawings in the inventory book, the pottery collection comprised 23 vessels (22 of which disappeared during World War II) from various periods; the form and decoration of 10 of these may be connected with the

Kizil-Koba culture, allowing us to attribute them to Early Iron Age sites in the mountains and foothills of the Crimea.

233. Spearhead
      Inv. No. IIId 6418 (found in the south of
          Russia)
      Bronze, cast. L. 18.3 cm
      Early 1st millennium BC

This triangular, bilobate blade has a central rib, oval in section, that continues to form an elongated socket, round in section, that broadens gradually toward the base. The socket is decorated toward its base with two relief bands; between these, on either side, is an oval hole for attaching the shaft to the spear.

Spearheads of this type are characteristic of transitional period sites (between the Bronze and Iron Age) in eastern Georgia (Pitskhelauri 1979), finding their way thence to the eastern regions of the Northern Caucasus (Chechnya, Daghestan). The closest analogue to ours was recovered from the Serzhen-Iurt burial grounds of the Koban culture, dated to the 8th century BC by the Chernogorovka type stirrup-shaped bits and finials used for cross straps found there (Kozenkova 2002:80ff., pl. 27.11). As such spearheads are unknown in the western part of the Northern Caucasus, the Crimea, and Ukraine, our example was likely recovered from a transitional period site in the eastern part of the Northern Caucasus or Georgia.

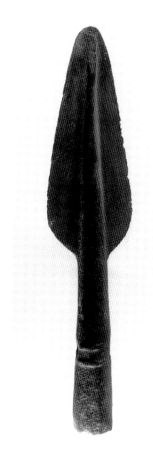

CAT. NO. 233

234. Spearhead
      Inv. No. IIId 6419 (found in the south of Russia)
      Bronze, cast. L. 13.2 cm
      8th–7th century BC

This triangular, bilobate blade has a central rib that continues to form an elongated socket, round in section, that broadens gradually toward its base; two holes, set on opposite sides of the socket near the base, were used to attach it to the shaft.

This form is typical of Early Iron Age sites in the Northern Caucasus; similar spearheads are known from 8th to 7th century BC proto-Maeotian sites in Adyghea (Leskov and Erlikh 1999:44–45, fig. 51).

CAT. NOS. 234 (right) AND 235

235. Spearhead
     Inv. No. IIId 6865 (found in the south of Russia)
     Bronze, cast. L. 9.7 cm
     8th–7th century BC

This triangular, bilobate blade has a central rib, rhomboidal in section, that continues
to form an elongated socket, round in section, that broadens gradually toward its base. A
hole, set in the socket near its base, was used to attach the blade to the shaft.

Such spearheads are typical of 8th to 7th century BC proto-Maeotian sites (Lovpache
1985:pl. XI.6).

236. Whetstone
     Inv. No. IIId 6809 (found in the south of Russia)
     Stone, polished, with one-sided drilling. L. 12.5 cm
     8th–7th century BC

This long, polished bar is rectangular in section and narrows toward the top. In the middle of its upper part is a drilled hole for suspension from a belt.

Well-polished whetstones from Early Iron Age warrior burials in the northern Black
Sea region and in 8th–7th century BC proto-Maeotian burial grounds in the Northern
Caucasus (Terenozhkin 1976:figs. 5, 6, 14ff.; Lovpache 1985:pl. X.1; Leskov and Erlikh
1999:61, fig. 59) suggest the probable date for our example. Very similar whetstones, how-

ever, are also known from 5th to 4th
century BC Scythian kurgans (cf. No.
237).

237. Whetstone
      Inv. No. IIId 6931 (found in
          the south of Russia)
      Stone, polished, with one-sided
          drilling. L. 11 cm
      8th–7th century BC (?)

This long, polished bar is oval in section
and narrows gradually toward the bottom. In the middle of its upper part is a
drilled hole for suspension from a belt.

     The simplicity of its form precludes
the assignment of a secure date to this
object. Comparable whetstones (cf. No.
236) are known both from the 8th to
7th century BC, with an example very
similar to ours being recovered from an
8th century BC burial from the Odessa
area (Cherniakov 1977:31ff., fig. 2.2),
and from Scythian period sites (perhaps
overshadowed by the whetstones in gold
casings from the Scythian royal kurgans)
(Galanina and Gratsch 1986:nos. 175–
77). Although this artifact is tentatively
assigned to the earlier period, a later Scythian date cannot be ruled out.

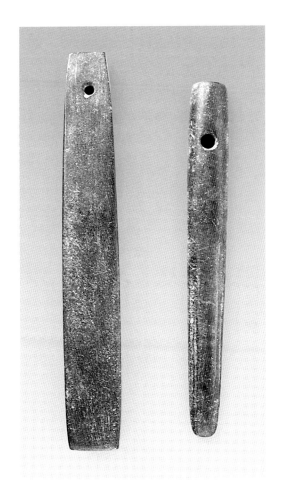

CAT. NOS. 236 (left) AND 237

238. Horse Bit
      Inv. No. IIId 6399 (found in Maikop; purchased through deed 885/07
          in 1907 from the collection of P. Mavrogordato)
      Bronze, cast. L. 18.1 cm
      Late 8th–mid-7th century BC

This severe bit is formed from two links, joined by single rings at one end of each. The
other end of each link terminates in two consecutive rings, the inner being only slightly
smaller than the outer. Running lengthwise on all sides of each link are regularly spaced
rows of cast rowels, which press against the lips of the horse to restrain it when the reins
are pulled.

CAT. NOS. 238 (bottom) AND 239

Double-ringed bits are typical of 8th to 7th century BC Novocherkassk treasure type sites (Iessen 1953:49–110) in the Northwestern Caucasus but are also found in the Black Sea steppe and forest-steppe. According to the development of such bits in the Northwestern Caucasus from single- to double-ringed (Leskov 1975b:68), our example, with its nearly identically sized outer rings, should belong to the end of the Novocherkassk period (late 8th to mid-7th century BC). Similar bits also occur in Early Scythian cultural assemblages (late 7th century BC). The ornamentation of our example suggests it belongs to a relatively late date (Valchak 2000:139ff.).

239. Horse Bit
    Inv. No. IIId 6899 (found in the south of Russia)
    Bronze, cast. L. 20.4 cm
    Second half 8th century BC

This severe bit differs from No. 238 primarily in the arrangement of the rowels and the dimensions of the two consecutive rings at the unattached end of each link. The inner rings are noticeably smaller than the outer in this example, and the rowels are arranged in bands rather than long rows.

According to the typological progression established for such bits, this example is slightly earlier than No. 238 but has a *terminus post quem* of the mid-8th century BC (Leskov 1975b:68; Leskov and Erlikh 1999:69–71; Valchak 2000:139ff.).

240. Plaque
Inv. No. IIId 6898 (found in the south of Russia)
Bronze, cast. Diam. 1.3 cm
8th–mid-7th century BC

CAT. NO. 240

This hemispherical plaque has a round boss, ringed by two concentric bands of circular convexities, in the center of its front. There is an attachment loop on the reverse.

Although the simplicity of its design hampers the assignment of a secure date, similar plaques are known both from the Penn Museum holdings of the Maikop treasure (No. 17, Inv. No. 30-33-122a, b) and from excavated complexes among elements of Novocherkassk-type horse trappings. In the inventory book description (p. 768) the plaque is discussed alongside double-ringed bits (cf. No 239) and should be similarly dated to the 8th to mid-7th century BC.

241. Horse Bit with Cheekpiece and Supplementary Weights
Inv. No. IIId 6912 (found in the south of Russia)
Bronze, cast. L. 21 cm (preserved portion)
First half of the 7th century BC

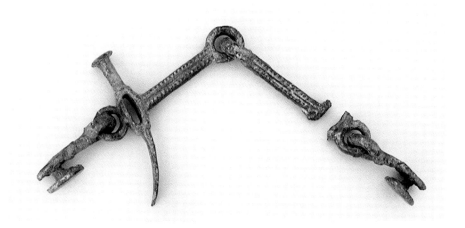

CAT. NO. 241

This severe bit is formed from two flattened links, each articulated along the length of its flat sides with two rows of rowels divided by a relief line, joined by the single rings at one end of each; the other end of each link terminates in a variation of the double ring (cf. Nos. 238 and 239), with the large oval hole of a perpendicularly placed cheekpiece (one survives) replacing the usual inner ring. The cheekpiece, with a flat cap at one end and a curved, hammered, and flattened tip at the other, is similar in form to the "classical" Novocherkassk type typically found with double-ringed bits. The reconstructed length of the bit is 28.6 cm and that of the surviving cheekpiece (the edge is damaged) is 9 cm. A supplemental weight in the form of a short, round rod with a bobbin at one end and a large ring at the other was looped into the outer ring of each link of the bit. These weights served as mobile pulleys for the reins, which would have been attached to the bobbins.

   This type of bit with cheekpiece is found only rarely; at the time of publication, only nine similar bits, half deriving from the Kuban, were known (Valchak 1993:23–29). The presence of such bits in a burial in the city of Endzhe (Popov 1932:101, fig. 88) and in kurgan No. 376 in the city of Konstantynovka (on the right bank of the Dniepr River in the forest-steppe zone) (Ilinskaia 1975:30ff., pl. XVI.6–10) allows us to date this bit to the first half of the 7th century BC.

   242. Finial (pole top)
        Inv. No. IIId 6607 (found in the
              south of Russia)
        Bronze, iron, stone, cast, ham-
              mered, polished. H. 19.4 cm
        6th century BC

This hollow, teardrop-shaped finial has seven evenly spaced, vertical slits that taper from base to tip. Two well-polished stone spheres, each 2 cm in diameter, rattle in its inner cavity when the finial moves. A three-dimensional panther's (?) head is set above the relief line ringing the top of the finial. Although worn, the upright ears, articulated in relief, and incised eyes and mouth recall a feline predator. At the base of the finial is the socket, square in section, with part of an iron shaft, rectangular in section, still protruding from it.

   Similar finials are common at sites in the Kuban and Sul River region (Ukrai-

CAT. NO. 242

nian left bank forest-steppe zone) and are classified by Perevodchikova (1980a:23–44, fig. 5) as type VII in form, dating from the 6th to early 5th century BC.

243. Finial (pole top)
Inv. No. IIId 6608 (found in the south of Russia)
Bronze, cast. H. 6.2 cm (preserved portion)
6th century BC

This fragment of a finial, with traces of five slits surviving, is topped by a panther's head (cf. No. 242) though it is not here set off with a relief band. The top of the finial thus serves as the animal's neck, with four grooves on both the neck and the back of the head apparently imitating the stripes characteristic of some feline predators. The sizeable snout of the animal allowed the craftsman to depict the wrinkles on its cheeks and to emphasize the mouth with its bared teeth.

Despite its missing bell, the form of the finial should likely be classified in Perevodchikova's type V (1980a:23–44), dating to the late 7th to 6th century BC, or type VII, dating from the 6th to early 5th century BC. Both types are commonly found in the Kuban and forest-steppe zone of Ukraine. It may thus be approximately dated to the 6th century BC.

CAT. NO. 243

244. Bell
Inv. No. IIId 6864 (found in the south of Russia)
Bronze, iron, cast, hammered. H. 9.8 cm
6th century BC

This large, single-cast bell is topped with a slightly elongated suspension ring; the iron crosspiece, to which an iron clapper (the end is broken) was attached with a loop, is preserved inside it.

While similar bells are found in 6th to

CAT. NO. 244

4th century BC Scythian complexes in the Kuban, the most comparable examples, larger in size (10–12 cm) and without side slits, are characteristic of the Scythian Archaic period; our bell thus likely dates to the 6th century BC (Leskov n.d.).

245. Dagger
    Inv. No. IIId 6315 (found in the Taman Peninsula; acquired through
        deed 389/07 in 1907 from the collection of P. Mavrogordato)
    Iron, hammered. L. 50 cm
    Late 6th–5th century BC

This dagger has a single-forged hilt that is cleft and flared at its base. The butterfly-shaped crossguard was separately forged, then set atop the blade with the hilt and forged again and the pommel was forged last.

CAT. NO. 245

This type of dagger or short sword, known as *akinak* to the Scythians, is assigned to Meliukova's (1964:53ff., pl. 20) second category, second type, based on its butterfly-shaped crossguard. It dates between the late 6th and 5th century BC.

246. Frontlets (2 items)
    Inv. Nos. IIId 7042.1, 2 (found in the Taman Peninsula)
    Bronze, cast. H. 5.2 cm, 4.8 cm
    First half 5th century BC

These two identical ornaments are each in the form of a slightly convex, rectangular plaque that widens toward the top where it merges into the base of the profile head of a bird of prey (one looks right, the other left). The long neck, round eye, and curved, predatory beak of each bird contrast with the stylized stag antlers and naturally rendered ears (ornamented with relief lines in one example) sprouting from its head. The rows of rectangular protrusions on the plaques themselves, four on one example and five on the other, are identified by Artamonov (1966:96, fig. 65, pl. 129) as the stylized plumage of bird wings. There are two perpendicular attachment loops on the reverse of each frontlet.

CAT. NO. 246

An additional frontlet of this type (now lost) was originally held in this collection (Inv. No. IIId 7034) (Schmidt 1927:pl. 9.1.9). The stag antlers on this missing frontlet are almost identical to those on three frontlets from Semibratniy kurgan No. 4, now held in the Hermitage collection. Given the compound and unusual form of these items and the fact that they have no other close analogues at Scythian period sites in Ukraine or the Northern Caucasus, it is possible that the lost Berlin frontlet originally formed a single complex with one of the three Hermitage examples and that all three Berlin front-lets derive from the Semibratnie kurgans. Looted as they were both prior to and during Tizengauzen's excavations in 1875, 1876, and 1878, it is entirely possible that Semibratnie artifacts made their way into de Massoneau's collection; they should then date to the second quarter of the 5th century BC.

First published by Potratz (1963:pl. 71).

247. Cheekpiece (2 fragments)
Inv. Nos. IIId 6913, 6914 (found in the south of Russia)
Bronze, cast. L. 5 cm, 4.9 cm
5th century BC

Of this cheekpiece, two fragments are S-shaped. The center of the round shaft (now broken) swelled to a figure 8, pierced with a hole in each loop, and there was a very broad, flattened form at each end. Assuming each hole was 0.7–0.9 cm in diameter and that the distance be-tween the holes measured 1.5–1.7 cm, the cheekpiece was originally 12.8–13.4 cm in length.

Similar cheekpieces in both iron (Ilinskaia 1968:60, pl. XLIII.4) and bronze (Petrenko 1967:37, pl. 26.12, 14) are typical of the 5th century BC, with identical examples known from one of the Malie Semibratnie kurgans (preserved in the Classical Section of the Her-mitage, MSbr-44) and from Ulskiy kurgan No. 11 (Gabuev and Erlikh 2001:112–25, fig.

CAT. NO. 247

4.1–2). Our example thus likely dates to the 5th century BC. Preserved in the Classical Section of the Hermitage, MSbr-44.

248. Cheekpiece
Inv. Nos. IIId 6918, 6819 (found in the south of Russia)
Bronze, iron, cast, hammered. L. 10 cm
5th century BC

This cheekpiece is S-shaped. The center of the round shaft swells to a figure 8, pierced with a hole in each loop, and the two ends, with identical bulging tips, turn up in opposing right angles. An iron ring from the horse bit to which it was originally attached wraps around the cheekpiece between the two holes.

Similar cheekpieces in both bronze and iron are typical of 5th century BC European Scythia (Petrenko 1967:37, pl. 26.15; Meliukova and Abramova 1989:pl. 35.13). Although a similar form in bronze with caps added on its ends continues into the 4th century BC (Mozolevskii 1973:187–234, fig. 30), our example should date to the 5th century BC.

CAT. NO. 248

249. Cheekpiece
     Inv. No. IIId 6910 (found in the south of Russia)
     Bronze, cast. L. 11.3 cm
     5th century BC

This cheekpiece is S-shaped. The center of the short, flattened shaft swells to a figure 8 with rhomboidal borders, with a round hole pierced in each loop; the two ends, which turn up sharply in opposing directions, have a zoomorphic aspect. One tip, bent almost perpendicular to the shaft, is rendered as the muscular hind leg of an animal (broken at the end) with a tail running along it, while the other, less sharply bent, represents the head and upper torso of a lion with details in relief. The animal's front paw extends to touch the bottom of the open jaw. The heart-shaped ear is typical of the Scythian Archaic period and unknown in the 4th century BC.

CAT. NOS. 249 (top) AND 250

Similar cheekpieces are known from the 5th century BC. The upper end of our example, shaped to resemble a lion's torso, has an analogue in Semibratniy kurgan No. 4
(second quarter to mid-5th century BC) (Galanina and Gratsch 1986:nos. 88, 89), while
its lower part and general S-shaped form (collection of V. I. Glazov, accessioned in 1913
and preserved in the Classical Section of the Hermitage, no. 2522-2) is paralleled by a pair
of cheekpieces from the Taman Peninsula (5th century BC) (Galanina and Gratsch 1986:
no. 86). A 5th century BC date for our example is confirmed by the recovery of an identical cheekpiece from one of the Malie Semibratnie kurgans kept in the Classical Section of
the Hermitage (MSbr-26).

250. Cheekpieces (pair)
       Inv. Nos. IIId 6907, 6917,
           6923 (found in the south
           of Russia)
       Bronze, cast. L. 11.3 cm, 8.1
           cm (preserved portion)
       5th century BC

These cheekpieces are S-shaped. The
center of each flattened shaft swells
to a figure 8, pierced with a hole in
each loop, and the ends curve up in
opposing circles to form the stylized
talons of a bird of prey (one of the
cheekpieces is broken at one end).

   Similar cheekpieces are found at
5th century BC Scythian sites from
the Ukrainian forest-steppe (Galanina
1977:pl. 17.15) to the Crimea (Yakovenko 1974:104ff., fig. 42).

   First published by Schmidt (1927:
pl. 9.2.7).

CAT. NO. 250A, B

251. Mirror
       Inv. No. IIId 5192 (found in the south of Russia; acquired from the
           collection of P. Mavrogordato)
       Bronze, cast, riveted. L. 7.8 cm
       5th century BC

This fragment comprises the short handle of a mirror, oval in section, with two horse
protomes at its top and a thick, circular disc at its base. The horses, each with head

slightly lowered and facing outward, are not identical: the mouth of one is parted, while only a line represents that of the other. The top of the handle, decorated with relief bands on both sides, was flattened and slit at the top for the insertion of the disc-shaped mirror (a fragment survives), which was further secured by two rivets set vertically in the handle's upper part.

While the prominence of horse, lion, and bull protomes in architectural contexts throughout Achaemenid Iran suggest this mirror should date between the end of the 6th and the 5th century BC, it is notable that no comparable mirrors have been recovered from Iran proper. The closest comparanda, connected with Asia Minor (a part of the Achaemenid Empire) (Oliver 1971:113–20), comprise

CAT. NO. 251

some unusual bronze mirrors with horse heads looking in opposite directions at the base. Our mirror was likely produced in Transcaucasia, an Achaemenid province in which many Achaemenid-style artifacts were manufactured, and later transported to a contemporary site in the Kuban. Achaemenid-influenced objects of this type are most typical of the 5th century BC in the art of the Kuban.

252. Cheekpieces (pair)
     Inv. Nos. IIId 7031, 7041 (found in the Taman Peninsula)
     Bronze, cast. L. 17.8 cm
     5th–4th century BC

These cheekpieces are S-shaped. The center of each round shaft swells to a figure 8 with rhomboidal borders, with a hole pierced in each loop, and the two ends turn up sharply in opposing directions. One end, bent almost perpendicular to the shaft, flares slightly toward the tip; the other end, flattened and less sharply bent, terminates in the stylized representation of a horse's hoof.

Bronze cheekpieces of this size are unusual; while over 20 Scythian cheekpieces occur within the Maikop treasure (as published here), none of the surviving examples are of this length. The inventory book (p. 786) does indicate the existence of a now-lost identi-

CAT. NO. 252

cal cheekpiece (Inv. No. IIId 7031) measuring 17.8 cm in length and attributed to the
Taman Peninsula. Despite the nine items intervening between the two entries, it seems
likely that the lost cheekpiece and this one originally formed a pair. Similar cheekpieces
are common at 5th to 4th century BC Scythian sites (Ilinskaia 1968:75ff., fig. 36, pl.
XVI.2–3).

First published by Potratz (1963:pl. 18).

253. Cheekpiece
      Inv. No. IIId 6915 (found in the south of Russia)
      Bronze, cast. L. 12.8 cm
      5th–4th century BC

The center of the round shaft of this cheekpiece swells to a figure 8 with rhomboidal borders, with a hole pierced in each loop. One end widens slightly at its flattened tip while
the other, which curves gently down, takes the form of a horse's leg.

Similar cheekpieces are known from Semibratniy kurgan No. 2 (Hermitage, Classical Section, SBr II-58), one of the Malie Semibratnie kurgans, and the Elizavetinskie
kurgans (Ku 1913, 4/152,426; Ky 1914 1/9,11,18). An additional pair, with one end terminating in the leg of a horse (Artamonov 1966:fig. 151), was also recovered from Bols-

haia Bliznitsa, a late 4th century BC royal kurgan. Our example thus likely dates between the 5th and 4th century BC. In the old archival photograph there is an image of an unknown item (L. 5.3 cm), Inv. No. IIId 5826, along with the cheekpiece described here. A small part of its iron shaft, round in section, was preserved, ending in the carefully modeled lower part of a horse's leg and hoof in cast bronze. This bimetallic item came from the collection of R. Virkhov but is not connected with his excavations in the Koban burial-ground in northern Ossetia. Judging from Deed 1455/02, this item was acquired by the museum in 1902, having entered Virkhov's collection during his sojourn in the Caucasus. This is likely a part (end) of a cheekpiece. It is also likely that it was examined by German colleagues, who placed it alongside this cheekpiece (No. 253). This photograph apparently led to a mistake by Schmidt, who published this fragment as belonging to de Massoneau's collection (1927:pl. 9.2/3).

First published by Schmidt (1927:pl. 9.2.8).

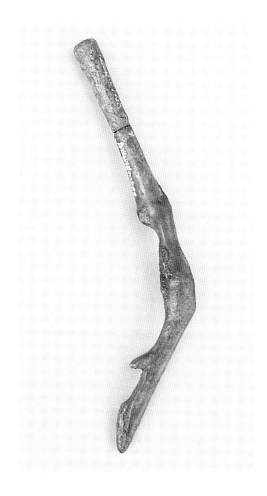

CAT. NO. 253

254. Cheekpiece
Inv. No. IIId 6911 (found in the south of Russia)
Bronze, iron, cast, hammered. L. 8.8 cm (preserved portion)
5th–4th century BC

This S-shaped cheekpiece is in the form of a recumbent animal. The short shaft swells to a figure 8, pierced with a hole in each loop, near one of the ends, which turn up sharply in opposing directions. One tip forms the long neck of the animal (broken at the head) with an outstretched paw that probably touched its lower jaw in a manner typical of predators. The other end takes the form of the animal's lowered hindquarters, with its back paws pressed up against its belly (the shaft). An iron ring from the horse bit to which it was

CAT. NO. 254

originally attached is wrapped around the cheekpiece between its two holes.

At some point between its acquisition (1907) and publication (Schmidt 1927:pl. 9.2.5), the museum reconstructed this cheekpiece, attaching a plastic griffin's head to the surviving neck and torso. Although accepted as late as 1963, this reconstruction was erroneous, being based on models from the most archaic of Scythian sites. Potratz's 1963 publication of this item was confused: (1) the cheekpiece was in de Massoneau's collection but was not found on his property: de Massoneau's estate was in Massandre, near Yalta on the south coast of the Crimea, where to this day not a single item in the Scythian Animal Style has been found; (2) referring to Schmidt's article, Potratz wrote that the cheekpiece is preserved in the Antikenabteilung, Staatliche Museen, Berlin (1963:80, fig. 59), although Schmidt indicated it was in the Museum für Vor- und Frühgeschichte.

The rendering of a griffin's head with a horn framing its eye is typical only of late 7th to mid-6th century BC artifacts and three-holed bone cheekpieces from the Scythian Archaic period: this two holed-cheekpiece, however, has a *terminus post quem* of the late 6th century BC, when such griffins were no longer being depicted. It is more likely that the missing head on this example took the form of the head of a stag of the type used on a pair of very similar bronze cheekpieces from a 4th century BC context in Uliap kurgan No. 2 (Leskov 1990:nos. 67, 68, fig. 70—further notable as it confirms that such cheekpieces are typical of the Kuban variant of the Scythian Animal Style), or, as noted above, of a preda-tor. The legs on this animal terminate in what appear to be paws rather than hooves, and the outstretched foreleg, often pressed against the lower jaw, is typical of depictions of predators. Cheekpieces in the form of zoomorphic figures or elements are characteristic of the Kuban variant of the Scythian Animal Style. This example thus likely dates between the 5th and 4th century BC.

255. Plaque
Inv. No. IIId 6906 (found in the south of Russia)
Bronze, cast. L. 2.5 cm
5th–4th century BC

This hemispherical plaque is flattened. The rounded
front surface takes the form of an animal head with
large oval eyes under arched brows, a projecting snout,
and heart-shaped ears laid flat against its head. There
is a perpendicular attachment loop on the reverse.

While no identical plaques are known, the ears are
rendered similarly to those on objects of an Early Scythian tradition, known from 5th (and maybe very early
4th) century BC sites in the Kuban. As bronze plaques,
pendants, and buttons decorated in the Scythian Animal Style are most typical of the 4th century BC, however, our plaque cannot be more precisely dated than
to between the 5th and 4th century BC.

CAT. NO. 255

256. Buckle
Inv. No. IIId 7002 (found in the south of Russia)
Bronze, cast. L. 3.3 cm
5th–4th century BC

This buckle is in the form of an openwork standing bear, in profile facing right, rendered
in high relief with a well-articulated torso. There is a break on the front surface of the
animal's back and, under that same break on the reverse, another round break from a projecting detail. It is likely there was originally a
hook attached here and that this object served
as a buckle with the bear at its base.

Bears are not typical of the Scythian art of
the northern Black Sea steppe or the Kuban
but are found in the forest-steppe of Ukraine,
probably deriving from the central Don River
region or the eastern part of the Volga River
and Ural Mountain region. They are most
common, and often depicted similarly to
this, on artifacts of the Ananynskaia (Zbrueva
1952:135ff., pls. XVI.10, XXIX.8) and Sauromatian cultures (Smirnov 1964:216ff., figs.
10.13, 33, 48.26, 74.7, 10) and are also found

CAT. NO. 256

in the central Don River region (Liberov 1965:fig. 2.173, 174, 197; Puzikova 2001:fig. 29.2–3). Our buckle thus likely dates between the 5th and 4th century BC.

This artifact is a notable addition to the small but significant group of Northern Caucasian objects closely connected, whether imported or locally made, to contemporary cultures of the Don River and Volga River to Ural Mountain regions (Zbrueva 1952:pl. xxxix.6, 8). Smirnov (1964:26ff., fig. 50.1a, 81) linked this material to the Sauromatian advance into the Northern Caucasian steppes (beginning in the 6th to 5th century BC).

257. Cheekpiece
    Inv. No. IIId 6908 (found in the south of Russia)
    Bronze, cast, engraved. L. 12.1 cm
    4th century BC

This cheekpiece is gamma-shaped. The round shaft swells to a figure 8 with rounded rhomboidal borders, with a hole pierced in each loop, just before its sharply bent end, which takes the form of a stylized tridactylous foot of a bird of prey. The engraved head of a stylized bird of prey is set at each joint of the foot and at the transitions to the claws.

CAT. NO. 257

This type of cheekpiece is typical of the Kuban variant of the Scythian Animal Style and common throughout the Kuban from the Taman Peninsula to Maikop. Though listed in the inventory book as coming from the south of Russia (other items are similarly attributed), this cheekpiece certainly originated in the Maikop region or the Kuban. This assertion is supported by Nekhaev's 1984 recovery of identical cheekpieces from Kuzhorskaia village (a suburb of Maikop) (Nekhaev 1987:90, fig. 17) and the kurgans in Elizavetinskaia village (Korovina 1957:174ff., fig. 9.4) and close analogues from Abkhazia (near the town of Sukhumi) (Voronov 1975:218ff., figs. 9.16, 10.12). The available comparanda indicates a 4th century BC date for our example.

258. Cheekpiece Fragment
    Inv. No. IIId 6362 (found in the Taman Peninsula; acquired through
        deed 389/07, from the collection of Mr. Karu)
    Bronze, cast, engraved. H. 7.4 cm (preserved portion)
    4th century BC

This cheekpiece fragment is gamma-shaped, originally with a flattened shaft and two holes framed by rounded rhomboidal borders (one is preserved). One end, bent almost perpendicular to the shaft, survives in the form of an openwork disc with 19 short, protruding rays emphasized with engraving and a 7-petal palmette on its base. Four animal heads with engraved features (shown from above) set on long, curved necks form the interior pattern of the disc.

CAT. NO. 258

    Though no direct analogues for this cheekpiece are known in the Kuban, the depictions on the cheekpiece are characteristic of the 4th century BC Kuban variant of the Scythian Animal Style, when flatly rendered animals heavily decorated with engraved ornament are common (Galanina and Gratsch 1986:nos. 276, 279, 284, 285; Nekhaev 1987: figs. 7.12, 18).

259. Cheekpiece
    Inv. No. IIId 6610 (found in the south of Russia)
    Bronze, cast. L. 11.5 cm
    4th century BC

CAT. NO. 259

This cheekpiece is gamma-shaped. The round shaft swells to a figure 8, pierced with a hole in each loop, near the base of the flat openwork plaque (mostly lost) forming the upturned end of the cheekpiece. The surviving end terminates in the head of a predator with an open maw and clearly delineated fang, set off from the shaft by a horizontal relief band.

This was likely one of a group of gamma-shaped cheekpieces with their plaques, bent almost at right angles, depicting the heads of predators (birds or animals) or the stylized feet of birds of prey with claws curved in a circle (Moshinskiy 2003:36, fig. 63). This type was common in 4th century BC complexes in the Kuban, found at kurgans in the Voronezhskaia, Elizavetinskaia, and Kuzhorskaia villages.

260. Harness Plaque
      Inv. No. IIId 6905 (found in the south of Russia)
      Bronze, cast. H. 3.5 cm
      4th century BC

This flat round plaque is in the form of a panther's (?) head with details in relief. It is characterized by small semicircular ears (one survives) rising slightly above the forehead, deep-set eyes beneath an overhanging forehead, and deeply wrinkled cheeks imitating, along the base of the plaque, bared teeth (the mouth itself is absent). There is a vertical suspension loop on the reverse.

In the inventory book (p. 769) this object was published on the same page as No. 254, a cheekpiece in the form of a recumbent stag. The recovery of three similar plaques with a pair of cheekpieces in the form of recumbent stags from Uliap kurgan No. 2 (Leskov 1990: nos. 85, 69) suggests that our example and No.

CAT. NO. 260

254 may indeed have come from a single complex. Both the plaques and the cheekpieces discussed above are characteristic of the Kuban variant of the Scythian Animal Style, indicating their likely origin in that region. The date of this plaque specifically may be narrowed, based on the discovery of an identical plaque from a securely dated complex at the Shuntuk mountain village near Maikop (Ilinskaia and Terenozhkin 1983:53.1), to the 4th century BC.

First published by Schmidt (1927:pl. 9.2.4).

261. Cheekpiece (?) Fragment
Inv. No. IIId 6922 (found in the south of Russia)
Bronze, cast, engraved. L. 5 cm (preserved portion)
4th century BC

This flat openwork plaque with engraved detail is almost round in section near the transition to the (broken) shaft. The horizontally hatched band along the round edge of the plaque may represent an animal's tail pressed against its hindquarters, and the lines engraved along the plaque's inner edges lend it additional depth and volume.

Although its function cannot be securely identified, the similarity of this object's form and style of engraving to a cheekpiece from a complex of

CAT. NO. 261

bronze items found at the Shuntuk mountain village near Maikop (Ilinskaia and Terenozhkin? 1983:53.3) suggests it was originally part of a 4th century BC cheekpiece deriving from the Kuban.

262. Cheekpiece (?) Fragments (2 items)
Inv. Nos. IIId 6920, 6921 (found in the south of Russia)
Bronze, iron, cast, hammered. L. 9.5 cm, 7.5 cm
4th century BC

These fragments are in the form of flat, slightly convex openwork plaques, each almost round in section at its break. Each plaque is bimetallic, an unusual feature among the Maikop artifacts, and comprises two strips: an upper bronze one and a lower iron one. Although the upper edge of the larger example is broken, it is still better preserved than the smaller.

CAT. NO. 262

These plaques are, as No. 261, comparable to the cheekpieces from Shuntuk (Ilinskaia and Terenozhkin 1983:53.3), suggesting they were also originally fragments of 4th century BC cheekpieces from the Kuban. The inclusion of such bimetallic objects in the Kuban variant of the Scythian Animal Style is supported by the existence of a bimetallic cheekpiece (?) fragment from the south of Russia, also held in the Museum für Vor- und Frühgeschichte (Inv. No. IIId 5826). This bimetallic fragment (L. 5.3 cm) comprises a round iron shaft ending in the cast bronze representation of the lower part of a horse's leg and hoof. Acquired from the collection of R. Virkhov in 1902 (deed 1455/02), it probably entered his collection during his stay in the Caucasus.

263. Harness Plaque
     Inv. No. IIId 6887 (found in the south of Russia)
     Bronze, cast. L. 4 cm
     4th century BC

This flat plaque is in the form of the heavily stylized hind leg of a predator with details in relief. There is a horizontal suspension loop on the reverse for attachment to the harness.

While comparable objects are known both from the Penn Museum portion of the Maikop collection (No. 38, Inv. No. 30-33-105) and from 4th century BC Scythian kurgans in the Ukrainian steppe and forest-steppe (Chertomlyk, Solokha, and Vovkivtsi, among others) (Mantsevich 1987:108, no. 91; 111, no. 109; Alekseev, Murzin, and Rolle

1991:153, no. 20; Ilinskaia 1968:fig. 34), such plaques are not generally known from the Kuban despite the vast increase in material recovered from that region in the last half-century. A single example, a plaque similar in form to the one from Karagodeuashkh kurgan (MAR N13) (Lappo-Danilevskii and Malmberg 1894:62, fig. 39), provides an insufficient basis for including the Kuban in the zone where such harness plaques were widely used. The one similar bronze plaque (Inv. No. IIId 6358) reputed to have come from the Taman Peninsula, acquired by the Berlin Museum in 1907 (Deed 389/07) from the Karu collection (which included items from the Crimea and Nikopol region as well as the Kuban), may well be from the Crimea or Nikopol region instead and so cannot confirm the existence of such plaques in the Northwestern

CAT. NO. 263

Caucasus. This example is thus dated to the 4th century BC on the basis of the Scythian material and probably derives from the northern Black Sea region.

264. Plaque Fragment
  Inv. No. IIId 6933 (found in the south of Russia according to inventory book)
  Bronze, cast, engraved. H. 5.2 cm
  4th century BC

This fragment of a flat openwork plaque is in the form of the frontal head and upper body of a man holding in his right hand a bird of prey (in profile) by the neck. The bird's beak, which curves down in a spiral, presses against the side of the man's head, hiding his ear. The figure has a high forehead, covered with straight hair and topped with a short cap; large, bulging, round eyes; a heavily worn nose; and a small, barely indicated mouth above an elongated chin. There is an engraved circle on the right side of his chest and a diagonally hatched band encircles his neck, representing a twisted torque; additional diagonally hatched bands edge his torso, the lower line of his right arm (the left is broken), and the inner outline of the neck and beak of the bird he holds in his hand, suggesting depth and volume. Fine, highly conventional engraving is used to render both his fingers and the eye and beak of the bird. Though the greater part of this plaque is missing, it may be reconstructed from the depiction of a similar bronze plaque (Inv. No. IIId 7015) in the inventory book (p. 784).

Our plaque, according to the inventory book, derives from Kartalinia (Kartalini), a part of historical Georgia; this attribution is echoed in the description in deed 1128/07 (recording the museum's acquisition of de Massoneau's collection), which groups it with a complete plaque that was packed in the same box and thought to derive from the same locale. While the latter complete plaque has not survived, a photograph (N1381) from the museum's photo archive (fig. 38a) offers a sense of its appearance.

It comprised an openwork rectangular plaque (11.5 cm in length) depicting a standing, facing male figure holding an identical monster in each of his widespread and half-bent arms. Each monster's narrow torso is bent at the middle, melding with the man's hips, and each takes on the form of two necks extending from this central point, one rising up to terminate in the head of a bird of prey with a spiral beak and the other extending down and terminating in the head of a lion with an open maw. The birds of prey are held by their necks with their beaks pressing against the

CAT. NO. 264

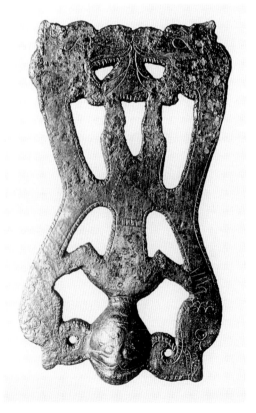

CAT. NO. 264 REPRODUCTION (2 views)

side of the man's head while the lower jaws of the lions, which face each other in heraldic fashion, are secured beneath his feet. Though it is better preserved, the man's head is comparable to our example in its features, having a long, straight nose; a slightly jutting chin; and hair, delineated in relief, combed up and to the sides from the center of the forehead. Hatched bands are used to articulate his twisted torque, his belt, and much of the outline of his body, as well as to delineate the figures of the monsters. The primary difference between this plaque and ours lies in the placement of the man's hands, which are lower down on the necks of the monsters in our example; this congruity supports the theory that both plaques derived from a single complex.

The heraldic pose (Nekhaev 1987: 82, fig. 7) of the lions is characteristic of the 4th century BC; such a date is confirmed by the rendering of the monsters' heads (lion and bird of prey), which are typical of the Kuban variant of the Scythian Animal Style. This is notable given the find spot of these plaques in Transcaucasia. While Scythian Archaic period (7th to early 6th century BC) artifacts from Georgia and Armenia are found in these territories, left behind by nomads of the northern Black Sea region setting out for incursions into the Near East, our objects were certainly made several centuries later. Given that the head of the male figure is very close in style to the art of the Central Caucasus, it seems likely both plaques discussed here were made in the Northwestern Caucasus of the 4th century BC, where objects incorporating Scythian and Koban features were fairly typical (Perevodchikova 1994:168).

265. Frontlet

Inv. No. IIId 6377 (acquired from the collection of P. Mavrogordato)
Bronze, cast. H. 4.2 cm
4th century BC

This frontlet is in the form of a short rod with a flat base, hemispherical in section, that curves into a ring (for attachment to the harness) at the top; a stylized animal head is attached on the side of the ring opposite the rod. The head of the animal, cast in a two-sided mould (traces of casting are also visible on the rod), is characterized by a large eye, indicated with a semicircular groove; a raised protruding ear; and a closed mouth marked with a faint groove.

Acquired by the museum from the Odessa collector P. Mavrogordato (deed 855/07), the inventory book records this item as coming from Gurzuf, on the southern shore of the Crimea (then inhabited by the Taurian tribes). This derivation is unconvincing as not a single other item in the Scythian Animal Style is known from

CAT. NO. 265

that region. Mavrogordato's collection contained many objects from the Northwestern Caucasus and northern Black Sea littoral in addition to his Crimean material, and he may well have mistaken the find spot of this item in the process of selling his large collection to the museum (among the finds from the Mavrogordato collection from the northern Black Sea steppes, cf. No. 267). While the Gurzuf origin of this noseband ornament is doubtful, it also must be noted that this is the only item of the Scythian period which made its way into the inventory book among plentiful medieval material coming from the Gurzuf burial ground. This allows us to consider that this noseband ornament came from the territory of Scythia, of which the southern shore of the Crimea was never a part.

While noseband ornaments of similar form are common at 4th century BC Scythian sites, the animal depicted on our example lacks horns, long ears, and a beak-like tip for its snout, all features characterizing the other known comparanda. The closest analogue to ours derives from a 4th century BC kurgan in Koshevatoie village (Petrenko 1967:pl. 29.12).

266. Belt Buckle
    Inv. No. IIId 6743 (found in Kerch)
    Bronze, cast. H. 5.5 cm (preserved portion)
    4th–3rd century BC

CAT. NO. 266

This belt buckle is in the form of an expressive but schematically rendered warrior (missing a foot) astride a horse (missing its hindquarters and front hooves) galloping to the left. The face of the rider is featureless and the horse has only a round hole for its eye and a cleft indicating its slightly parted mouth. The horseman wears a broad belt over wide trousers that are tucked into his boots and a gorytos (?), represented by a small bulge at his hip; his right arm is raised and, though broken at the wrist, probably held a spear (in a pose comparable to that of the riders with spears on the gold plaques from kurgan Kul-Oba) (Moshinskiy 2003:31, nos. 44, 45). The large hook extending from the front of the horse's chest and bent towards the reverse of the fragment joined this segment to the rest of the buckle.

While the clothing and military trappings of the horseman have numerous parallels among 4th century BC toreutic artifacts, items depicting mounted Scythian warriors are quite sparse in this period. The dearth of such buckles in Scythian burials indicates this

piece may derive instead from one of the numerous Greek complexes in Kerch. One similar buckle from that region, of iron covered in gold, depicts two riders joined in battle
and dates between the 4th and 3rd century BC (Koshelenko, Kruglikova, and Dolgorukov 1984:pl. LXXXII.6). Another analogue, this one from the Crimea (a chance find in
Simferopol) (OAK for 1889:26, fig. 11), takes the form of a rider on a galloping horse and
dates "no earlier than the 3rd century BC" (Guliaev 1969:124, fig. 16). On the basis of this
comparanda, our example should date between the 4th and 3rd century BC.

267. Phalera
    Inv. No. IIId 7109 (art of the Taganrog treasure acquired from the
        collection of P. Mavrogordato)
    Silver, gilding, iron, stamped, engraved, die-formed, riveted. Diam. 12 cm
    2nd century BC

A roundel with a convex central field is ringed by two concentric raised and diagonally
hatched bands, the inner one of which is slightly higher than the outer, and bordered

CAT. NO. 267

with a flattened flange decorated with a zigzagging band and punched dots in the triangles created along the edge. The central field contains a horse protome, depicted primarily in profile though the head and one of the forelegs have a frontal aspect, surrounded by punched dots. The horse is skillfully delineated with a splendid mane; a handsome head with an almond-shaped eye, a nervous nostril, and a slightly parted mouth; hair indicated by rows of short hatch marks; and a relief line, likely a harness detail, tapering from the mouth to the eye. Four rivets are fairly evenly spaced along the border of the central field; the fragments of iron plaques preserved in these locations on the reverse indicate these rivets served to attach this object to its foundation.

This phalera is undoubtedly one of the six known from the lost Taganrog treasure that (according to Spitsyn) fell into the hands of Romanovich and was eventually (in 1907) acquired by Mavrogordato; this item made its way thence into the Berlin Museum collection, where it was ascribed (inventory book, p. 797) to Maikop. Mordvinceva (2001:64) assigned the Taganrog treasure to her Group 4, the "Black Sea region pictorial style," mostly originating in the Greek cities of the northern Black Sea region and probably dating to the 2nd century BC (see Smirnov 1984:74-75).

268. Bead
      Inv. No. IIId 6420 (found in Maikop)
      Glass, cast, colored. H. 2 cm
      3rd-1st century BC

CAT. NO. 268

This small, pierced brown glass bead is in the form of a compressed and slightly distorted sphere; a row of six small yellow rings circles its middle and the surface is further decorated with several large, intersecting dark yellow and grey circles
Though classical period beads from the northern Black Sea region have been the subject of a major study by Alekseeva (1975-1982), examples with ornamentation identical to ours are not included there and the specific color of our bead has few parallels. As Alekseeva's (1975:69, pl. 14.95) 90th type, dated to the 2nd century BC, seems the most comparable in decoration and color, our example likely dates between the 3rd and 1st century BC.

269. Belt Buckle
      Inv. No. IIId 7106 (found in the Taman Peninsula)
      Bronze, cast. L. 4.6 cm
      1st-2nd century AD

This rectangular openwork buckle has a recumbent sphinx, oriented to the left with head facing front, in its center; though the degradation of the metal has severely damaged the

CAT. NO. 269

face and torso of the sphinx, its raised wing with the tip lifted towards its head is clearly visible. There is a short hook with a bent (outward) tip in the center of the left crosspiece for attaching the other half of the buckle.

Buckles of this type, dating between the 1st and 2nd century AD, are known from Panticapaeum (Koshelenko, Kruglikova, and Dolgorukov 1984:346, pl. LV.3). Our example likely belongs to the same period.

First published by Rostovtzeff (1931a:46–55, pl. 1.2), who dated it between the 2nd and 3rd century BC and published it with five other buckles from the same museum. Rostovtzeff mistakenly considered that the buckles he published were a gift to the museum (p. 46); this does not apply to de Massoneau's collection, as it was purchased for some very serious money.

270. Pin
    Inv. No. IIId 6728 (found in the Taman Peninsula)
    Silver, almandine, hammered, burnished (stone), with encrustation,
        filigree. L. 2.5 cm (preserved portion)
    Late 4th–early 5th century AD

This nail-shaped pin, broken at the tip, has a flat, round head topped with a burnished hemispherical almandine in its center. The head is edged with pseudo-granulated filigree wire.

Similar bronze pins, with round gold caps carrying red glass inserts, were found in the late 4th to early 5th century AD Kerch crypt No. 145 (Zasetskaia 1979:fig. 2.4, app. 15; Zasetskaia maintains that, since its head cannot be hammered this item should not be termed a nail or a tack). Our example should be dated to the same period.

CAT. NO. 270

271. Medallion
    Inv. Nos. IIId 6669, 6970 (found in the Taman Peninsula)
    Bronze, glass, stamped, soldered, burnished (glass). Diam. 4.8 cm
    5th–6th century AD

This round medallion (reconstructed from two fragments) is edged with a gilded bronze band, with a four-petal rosette rendered on its front surface; the petals and their intervening leaves are also edged with gilded bronze bands and inset with colored glass. The large center of the rosette is a bulging brown oval, ringed by four crescent-shaped petals

CAT. NO. 271

(three survive) containing inserts of the same color (two survive). Four leaves (three survive) inset with green glass (one insert survives), alternate with the petals. The area between the medallion's border and the rosette likely also contained a glass or other colored filler. Of the inserts, only the prominent central oval rose above the medallion's surface; the rest were the same height as their gilded bronze partitions. The round convex cap from a bronze tack, with traces of a suspension loop attached to its end, is preserved on the reverse of the ornament.

The form of the object suggests it dates to the medieval period though no exact parallels are known. The closest analogues appear among 5th century AD artifacts from Abkhazia and in the form of similar (encrusted) fibulae from 5th to 6th century AD Northern Caucasian contexts (Prokopenko 2001b:70–74, fig. 2.5), suggesting the probable date of our medallion.

272. Bead
     Inv. No. 6637 (found in the Taman Peninsula)
     Silver, gilding. L. 1.4 cm
     5th–6th century AD

This bead has 14 facets and is pierced lengthwise with a large hole (diam. 0.7 cm). The size of the hole indicates this bead was, along with others, attached on the twisted metallic strand, round in section, of a headdress ring.

Such headdress rings as that described here are widely known among early medieval sites of the Northern Caucasus. Kovalevskaia dates one similar example to the 6th century AD (1981:179, fig. 62.69), while a gold analogue from the lower Don River region and another from Kerch, both from the late 4th or 5th century AD, support Kamenskiy's attribution (1987:254ff., fig. 1.1) of a comparable silver ring from a burial near Krasnodar to the 5th to 6th century AD. While our bead likely belongs to that same period, the discovery of numerous similar earrings in the burial grounds of Diurso near Novorossisk

CAT. NO. 272

(Dmitriev 1982:69ff., figs. 5.26, 6.3, 8.6, 9.1, 12.7) indicates that such objects appear as late as the 8th century AD.

273. Strap Ornament
Inv. No. IIId 6638 (found in the Taman Peninsula)
Silver, gilding, stamped, riveted, engraved. L. 2.8 cm
5th–mid-7th century AD

This ornament is in the form of a flat, double-layered square fitting attached with a lug to a flat plaque in the form of a fish tail; the tail is edged with a diagonally hatched band and its interior surface filled with engraved semicircles that imitate fish scales. There are two tacks at the top of the fitting intended to secure a leather strap between the two layers.

Slightly larger plaques, otherwise comparable in material (silver), form, and ornament, were recovered from the early 5th century AD Kachinskiy complex in western Ukraine (Kukharenko 1982:234–43), which contained a rich variety of women's silver ornaments and silver horse trappings. These plaques served as strap decorations on the horse trappings. Similar strap ornaments are known both from the Mokraia Balka burial grounds in the town of Kislovodsk, in contexts dating to the second half of the 6th to first quarter of the 7th century AD (Afanasiev 1979:43ff., fig. 2.43–44), and in Crimean crypts from the late 4th to mid-5th century AD and from the first half of the 7th century AD (Zasetskaia 1979:5–15, fig. 5.33, 34; Veimarn 1979:34–37, fig. 1.15). Our example thus likely dates between the 5th and mid-7th century AD.

CAT. NOS. 273 (right) AND 274

274. Pendant
Inv. No. IIId 6639 (found in the Taman Peninsula)
Silver, glass, stamped, soldered, with filigree, burnished (glass). H. 1.7 cm
6th–mid-7th century AD

This flat, leaf-shaped pendant (tip down) has a suspension loop (broken) in the center of its wide top. The central field, surrounded by a low rim edged with pseudo-granulated filigree wire, is filled with an insert of burnished, colorless glass.

Similar pendants (for necklaces) from the Northern Caucasus published by Kovalevskaia (1981:fig. 64.7) date from the 6th to mid-7th century AD. As the color of their inserts and the quality of their metal (red glass and gold in the publication) do not seem to affect the date, it is likely that our example dates to the same period.

275. Facings (2 items)
    Inv. Nos. IIId 6667, 6668 (found in the Taman Peninsula)
    Silver, stamped, riveted. H. 3.5 cm
    8th–9th century AD

CAT. NO. 275

These facings are in the form of an openwork isosceles triangle. The top of each triangle resembles a fish tail, with two symmetrical and opposing crescents (facing down) sprouting from the peak. Short tacks with mushroom-shaped caps are preserved at each corner of the facings.

Although they have no direct analogues, these may be tentatively identified as medieval strap ornaments; they are sufficiently similar to the "horned" buckles from the Saltovskiy burial grounds of the Khazar culture (Pletneva 1967:fig. 44.65–66) to suggest they date to the 8th to 9th century AD, when materials from the Saltovo-Maiatskaia culture are common in the Kuban.

276. Strap Plaque
    Inv. No. IIId 7098 (found in the Taman Peninsula)
    Bronze, cast. H. 4 cm
    10th–11th century AD

This plaque is in the form of a large central circle ringed by three evenly spaced circles of similar size. Each outer circle is separated from the central one by a rectangular bar with a round bump at each of its tips. There is a round hole in the center of each circle, to which hemispherical inserts (one preserved) were attached.

An identical but better-preserved item (now lost) is known from this same collection (cf. No. 310, Inv. No. IIId

CAT. NO. 276

7097). Similar plaques have been described by Fedorov-Davydov (1966:59, fig. 10.1, type I.A.I.) as used to join the three straps of a horse's harness. Our example corresponds to Fedorov-Davydov's (115) Category I, with pins from Section A, triple-tipped, and dating to the 10th–11th century AD.

277. Headdress Ring
    Inv. No. IIId 6732 (found in the Taman Peninsula)
    Silver, hammered, soldered, with filigree. Diam. 5 cm
    11th–12th century AD

Restored from five sections this headdress ring is curved from a rod, round in section, with ends that meet. There is a wire coil with eight loops, formed from wire twisted to imitate rope, soldered near the midpoint of the ring and a similar coil, with six loops, near one of the ends.

The differences between this item as described here and as drawn in the inventory book (1907–1908, p. 744, IIId 6732) are notable. In the inventory book, its form is that of a headdress ring (dimensions not given) glued from two fragments with only one coil and ends that do not meet; in its central part (in approximately the location of the second coil described above), there seems to be a biconical bead with filigree ornament soldered from thin plaques ("Blechperle" in the inventory book). At some later point (possibly during World War II), the ring was damaged, losing its central bead and exposing the second coil beneath it, and then restored in its current form. An explanation for why the ends of the ring now meet, however, is less forthcoming; it is possible that the section joining the two tips was in the museum collection in 1907 but was only restored after the completion of the inventory book entry.

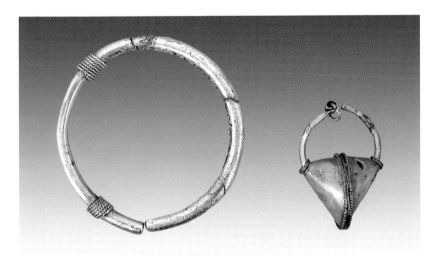

CAT. NOS. 277 (left) AND 278

The loss of the bead included in the inventory book drawing hampers the dating of this item: while headdress rings with additional wire coils occur at Sarmatian period (first centuries AD) sites in the southern part of Eastern Europe in the steppes between the Volga and Dniepr Rivers, the Northern Caucasus, and the Crimea, examples with attached biconical beads secured on supplementary wire coils occur significantly later at 11th to 12th century AD Polovetsian sites in the steppes (Federov-Davydov 1966:39, fig. 6.IV). The attribution of such a late date to our example is supported by the recovery of a similar silver ring with biconical bead from the Kuban, in the same zone from which the part of de Massoneau's collection published here is derived (Leskov 1991:no. 313).

278.   Earring
       Inv. No. IIId 6733 (found in the Taman Peninsula)
       Silver, hammered, soldered, with filigree. H. 3.1 cm
       12th–14th century AD

This earring is in the form of a wire ring, round in section, strung with a hollow bead in the form of an equilateral triangle soldered from two thin-walled halves, each edged with twisted filigree wire along the seam. One tip of the earring, flattened and rolled into a loop, had a wire ring attached to it into which the hook (now broken) on the other tip linked.

Similar earrings are common in medieval Northern Caucasian contexts, with ten comparable examples not published in this volume appearing in de Massoneau's collection alone (Inv. No. IIId 6523–6532), and are also typical of newly discovered 12th to 14th century AD medieval complexes in the Kuban (Garanina, Limberis, and Marchenko 2001:152, pl. 4.3–4). Our earring should be dated to the same period.

279.   Handle (?)
       Inv. No. IIId 6916 (found in the south of Russia)
       Horn, sawn. L. 18 cm
       Date unknown

CAT. NO. 279

This handle is formed from part of a horn, lightly polished around the point and minimally worked.

As this object was listed together with No. 27 in the inventory book (p. 770), it is possible they came from the same 5th to 4th century BC context, but this cannot be confirmed.

280. Pendant
     Inv. No. IIId 6964 (found in the south of Russia)
     Horn, carved, sawn, drilled. L. 17.1 cm
     Date unknown

This horn pendant has two suspension holes (drilled from both sides) near the sawn-off base. The decorative zone, containing four incised zigzagging bands, is bordered at the top by two straight horizontal bands just below the suspension holes and at the bottom, just past the midpoint of the pendant, by four straight horizontal bands.

Two similar but undecorated horns appear in the inventory book in close connection with 5th to 4th century BC bronze cheekpieces of the Scythian type (cf. Nos. 279 and 253, 282 and 257). While this example may belong to the same period, such a date cannot currently be confirmed.

281. Pendant
     Inv. No. IIId 6965 (found
         in the south of Russia)
     Horn, carved, sawn, drilled.
         L. 13.9 cm
     Date unknown

This horn pendant has two suspension holes (drilled from both sides) near the sawn-off base. The two adja-

CAT. NOS. 280 (right) AND 281

cent decorative zones, marked off by incised horizontal lines, extend from just below the suspension holes to the midpoint of the pendant. The upper zone is filled with partially intersecting, vertically and horizontally incised lines while the lower contains parallel and slightly inclined vertical lines. The incising was carelessly executed with a thin chisel.

The date is undetermined.

282. Work Tool (?)
       Inv. No. IIId 6909 (found in the south of Russia)
       Horn, sawn, polished. L. 23.7 cm
       Date unknown

This horn work tool has a sawn-off base, heavily ground on the exterior of the curving tip. The grinding suggests it was used as a tool (in leatherwork?) though the polishing of two-thirds of its length (from the bottom up) and the careful treatment of its interior surface at the base indicate it may have served as a handle instead.

CAT. NO. 282

This item is presented together with No. 257 in the inventory book, suggesting that they may derive from the same 4th century BC context (cf. No. 279). Currently, however, this cannot be confirmed.

Lost Items

283. Handle
       Inv. IIId 7035 (found in the south of Russia)
       Bronze, cast. Dimensions unknown
       Pre-Scythian period

This handle is in the form of a socket, tapering slightly toward the base and terminating in the head and torso of a mountain goat with a long neck, two semicircular horns, and a goatee. The goat is further characterized by round eyes rimmed with a relief line, short, projecting ears, and a wide relief band that seems to mark the transition between the head and neck. Its front legs are also delineated in relief, bent at the knees and tucked along the handle serving as its torso. There are two round holes in the base of the socket for attachment to a whetstone. The description is based on the inventory book and an old photograph.

The style in which the goat is rendered indicates it came from Luristan, where similar objects, many summarized and published by Potratz (1968:14–15, pls. XI.56–57, XII.58, 60, 61), appear in early 1st millennium BC contexts. This object is unusual in de Massoneau's collection, from which imported items dating from the end of the Bronze to the beginning of the Iron Age are absent. If it indeed derives from the south of Russia, it may be the first item from Luristan found in this region.

CAT. NO. 283

284. Plaque
    Inv. No. IIId 7036 (found in Tiligulskoe village; acquired from the
        collection of P. Mavrogordato)
    Bronze. L. 7.4 cm
    5th century BC

This plaque is in the form of a flat, openwork elk's head (facing left). The elk has a large hooked nose, a projecting ear, and a low antler comprising two stylized heads of birds of prey joined by a palmette; its round eye, nostrils, mouth, the base of its lower jaw, and its projecting ear are all articulated in relief. The reverse of the plaque and the means by which it was attached are not

CAT. NO. 284

preserved. The description is based on the inventory book and an old photograph.

Ten or so similar but individually detailed plaques, serving as quiver, gorytoi, or armor decorations (Chernenko 1970:190ff.), are known, dated on the basis of close parallels from securely dated 5th century BC sites in the Ukrainian steppe and forest-steppe.

First published by Schmidt (1927:pl. 9.1.2), who mistakenly attributed it to de Massoneau's collection, and later published by Potratz (1960:pl. X, fig. 23).

285. Harness Plaque
Inv. No. IIId 7016 (found in the Taman Peninsula)
Bronze, cast. H. 6 cm
5th century BC

CAT. NO. 285

This plaque is in the form of a stag's head with features and details in relief. The front and back branches of the long, sweeping antlers form stylized heads of birds of prey. Existing comparanda suggest there was likely a horizontal attachment loop on the reverse to secure it to the harness.

A number of similar plaques have been recovered, including examples from Semibratniy kurgan No. 4 (second quarter of the 5th century BC); a comparably dated plaque from one of the Malie Semibratnie kurgans (Perevodchikova 1987:44ff., fig. 2.2; Galanina and Gratsch 1986:no. 7); and a slightly later example from Ulskiy kurgan No. 11 (second half of the 5th century BC) (Leskov 1991:no. 137), which differs from our plaque and the Semibratniy example in the shortness of the stag's neck. While additional analogues are known from 5th century BC complexes in the central Dniepr River region (Petrenko 1967:93, pl. 31.2, 4, 7), the closest parallel to Kuban harness plaques of this type comes from the Krivaia Luka burial grounds in the Volga River region and belongs to the Sauromatian culture of the 5th century BC (Meliukova and Abramova 1989:pl. 66.21).

First published by Schmidt (1927:pl. 9.2.6) and later by Potratz (1960:pl. XI, fig. 29), though the latter showed it in an incorrect position (set horizontally instead of vertically).

286. Cheekpiece
Inv. No. IIId 7029 (found in the Taman Peninsula)
Bronze, cast. L. 12 cm
5th century BC

CAT. NO. 286

This cheekpiece is S-shaped. The center of the flattened shaft swells to a figure 8, pierced with a hole in each rounded rhomboidal loop, and the ends curve up in opposing circles to form the stylized talons of a bird of prey.

Two similar pairs of cheekpieces from de Massoneau's collection are known, with one set, attributed to the south of Russia, held in this collection (No. 250), and the other pair (one now lost) held by the Antikenabteilung, Staatliche Museen, Berlin (No. 142, Inv. No. 30.569a, b). Comparable cheekpieces have also been excavated from 5th century BC steppe and forest-steppe contexts in Ukraine; our example should be similarly dated.

287. Decorative Plaque
Inv. No. IIId 7032 (found in the Taman Peninsula)
Bone, sawn, drilled, carved. L. 9.3 cm
5th century BC

This plaque is in the form of a recumbent dog (?) oriented left with its head turned back and resting on its slightly bulging front hip. Its face is characterized by narrow eyes, protruding ears, and an open maw with bared teeth. The body is gracefully curved, terminating in a slim, hanging tail with a thickened tip. Both pairs of legs are visible, one overlying the other; the schematic rendering of the forelegs, indicated by two narrow lines terminating in more realistic paws, contrasts with the more naturalistic portrayal of the hind legs. Additional detailing comprises both relief, with a line emphasizing the animal's powerful neck and an oval on its front hip, and incision, with a carved scroll on its lower jaw, a backwards S on its front hip, and two curved lines on the joint of the hind legs. There is a round attachment hole in the center of the back hip.

CAT. NO. 287

While depictions of dogs (wolves) are common at 5th century BC sites in the forest-steppe of the Don River region (Shkurko 2000:304ff., pl. I), especially in the Volga area (the habitation zone of the Sauromatians and later the Sarmatians), they only appear in the steppes of the northern Black Sea region at the turn of the 5th to the 4th century BC (Leskov 1972:57–58, pls. 35, 38), and even then only sparsely. This imagery is further atypical of the Kuban variant of the Scythian Animal Style, though a few items have been found in the Northern Caucasus that are typical of Sauromatian art (Smirnov 1964:fig. 81). While our specific depiction is notable for the relief line that appears to divide the neck into two planes, a feature known from classic examples of the Archaic period Scythian Animal Style (the Kelermes Panther, the Kostromskoy stag), its other ornamental details, executed in carving, are characteristic of a later period. Inasmuch as Sauromatian antiquities are generally dated between the 6th and 5th century BC, our plaque should likely be attributed to the 5th century BC.

First published by Minns (1942:15, pl. III.i), who dated it to approximately 500 BC.

288. Decorative Plaque
    Inv. No. IIId 7033 (found in the Taman Peninsula)
    Bone, sawn, drilled, carved. L. 9.8 cm
    5th century BC

This plaque is in the form of a recumbent dog (?) oriented right with its head turned back and resting on its slightly bulging front hip. This plaque differs from the previous one (No. 287) only in a few details: it has a slightly more curved torso, a shorter tail (possibly broken off), hindquarters lacking in ornamentation, and two attachment holes (one above the other) on its front hip.

It should be dated to the 5th century BC.

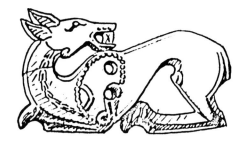

CAT. NO. 288

289. Harness Plaques (pair)
    Inv. Nos. IIId 7017, 7018 (found in the Taman Peninsula)
    Bronze, cast. L. 2.7, 3.1 cm
    5th–4th century BC

These plaques are in the form of an openwork profile goat (one faces left, the other, right) with semicircular horns curving from the forehead to the base of the neck. While the upper body of each goat is typical of standing animals, the front and back legs bend at the knee, connecting at the hoof like recumbent figures. There was likely an attachment loop on the reverse of each.

While the closest parallel to these plaques comes from a 4th century BC kurgan located near Maikop in the mountain village of Shuntuk (Ilinskaia and Terenozhkin 1983:53.11), another analogue was found in the 5th century BC Khosheutovskiy complex in the lower Volga River region (Moshinskiy 2003:38, no. 69). Our examples thus likely date between the 5th and 4th century BC, when nomads of the northern Black Sea region (from the Volga to the Dniepr River) used such plaques as horse trappings.

First published by Schmidt (1927:pl. 9.1.7, 10).

CAT. NO. 289

290. Plaque
  Inv. No. IIId 7027 (found in the Taman Peninsula)
  Bronze, cast. Dimensions unknown
  5th–4th century BC

This openwork plaque is in the form of a misshapen elongated oval pierced with holes in one half and with added detail in the form of hollows and convexities. The subject of the plaque and the manner in which it should be viewed are open to debate: it is set vertically in the inventory book (p. 785) with the openwork section at the top, while in Schmidt's publication (1927:pl. 9.2.1) the openwork section was set at the base.

The problem of "zoomorphic transformations" and multiple meanings in the Scythian Animal Style was initially studied by Kantorovich (2002) and is especially relevant in the attempt to unravel the imagery of this plaque. In the inventory book, the base is shown with a flat, setoff section (unlike Schmidt's photograph) that allows the lower part of the

CAT. NO. 290

plaque to be seen as a bird with profile head facing right and the openwork section rising above the head to be seen as a variety of heads of birds of prey (generally found on stag antlers). It seems preferable, however, to place this plaque horizontally with the massive flat section to the left and representing the hindquarters of a recumbent feline predator with long tail turned in a circle and with the interpretation of the openwork section, with its numerous holes and details in relief, left open to the imagination. The overall plaque might then depict an animal curled in a circle.

It dates between the 5th and 4th century BC.

291. Plaque
      Inv. No. IIId 7019 (found in the Taman Peninsula)
      Bronze, cast. Dimensions unknown. L. 3 cm (?)
      4th century BC

CAT. NO. 291

This plaque is in the form of an openwork recumbent animal oriented to the left with its head turned back to rest on its hindquarters; its legs are tucked beneath it and there is an attachment loop at its base on the left. The drawing in the inventory book and the dimensions of the adjacent plaque (No. 289, Inv. No. IIId 7018, measuring 3.1 cm) suggest it is 3 cm in length.

Although no direct excavated analogues are known, a similar plaque is known from this collection (cf. No. 292, Inv. No. IIId 7020) and comparable depictions are known from a plaque-"rod" for intersecting straps recovered from the 4th century BC kurgan Strashnaia Mogila in the Dniepr River steppes (Meliukova and Abramova 1989:pl. 36.6). The overall style of our plaque is typical of the same period.

First published by Schmidt (1927:pl. 9.1.4).

292. Plaque
      Inv. No. IIId 7020 (found in the Taman Peninsula)
      Bronze, cast. L. 3 cm (?)
      4th century BC

This plaque is in the form of an openwork recumbent animal oriented to the right with its head turned back to rest on its hindquarters. Its legs are tucked beneath it, and there is an attachment loop at its base on the right. The dimensions are estimated based on the measurements of Nos. 289 and 291.

Though this plaque is rendered similarly to No. 291, it was less clearly drawn in the inventory book and never pub-

CAT. NO. 292

lished, making it impossible to pair the two. Stylistically, this example also belongs to the 4th century BC, a date confirmed by material from the Dniepr River steppe (Meliukova and Abramova 1989:pl. 36.6).

293. Plaque
    Inv. No. IIId 7021 (found in the Taman Peninsula)
    Bronze, cast. Dimensions unknown
    4th century BC

This plaque is in the form of a stylized seated male (?) rendered in profile (facing right), though both soles of his feet are visible. His head, covered by an animal mask (?), rests on his knees. There are two protruding lugs on his reverse and a round attachment loop beneath his buttocks.

The plaque described above appears almost unique; the only known comparanda is a noseband ornament (or frontlet) in the form of a standing male figure with animal head (likely a mask) recently found by Erlikh in a mid- to late 4th century BC kurgan in Tenginskaia village in the Kuban (Moshinskiy 2003:35, nos. 59–60). The depictions on both our plaque and this ornament are certainly connected with some sort of religious ritual, though the indefinable nature of the animal head precludes a more specific identification of what is going on; the masks may depict images of totemic animals of particular clans.

CAT. NO. 293

Known depictions of male figures (both of face and figure), whether Greek or barbarian, generally date to the 4th century BC. Our plaque likely belongs to the same period. While Greek products are mainly typical of the steppes of the northern Black Sea region (in Ukraine) and the closest environs of Panticapaeum (Kul-Oba, on the Kerch Peninsula, Bolshaia Bliznitsa in the Taman Peninsula), most local barbarian objects depicting humans are connected with the Kuban. The Colkhido-Koban influence in our example is clear.

First published by Schmidt (1927:pl. 9.1.1) and later by Potratz (1960:pl. X, fig. 26).

294. Plaque
    Inv. No. IIId 7022 (found in the Taman Peninsula)
    Bronze, cast. Dimensions unknown
    4th century BC

This plaque is in the form of an openwork recumbent animal oriented to the left with its head turned back to rest on its hindquarters, and its legs tucked beneath it. It is distin-

CAT. NO. 294

guished from Nos. 291 and 292 primarily by the absence of a visible attachment loop (this may have been on the reverse).

Both the style of the depiction and the recovery of a similarly rendered animal on a plaque-"rod" for intersecting straps from the 4th century BC kurgan Strashnaia Mogila in the Dniepr River steppes (Meliukova and Abramova 1989:pl. 36.6) indicate a 4th century BC date.

First published by Schmidt (1927:pl. 9.1.8).

295. Harness Plaque
     Inv. No. IIId 7023 (found in the Taman Peninsula)
     Bronze, cast. Dimensions unknown
     4th century BC

This plaque is in the form of a wolf's head in profile (facing left). The eye with articulated pupil, nostrils, corner of the mouth, and slightly drooping projecting ear are all articulated in relief, while the triangular teeth within the closed maw are done in openwork for emphasis. The stylized head of a bird of prey is set between the corner of the lower jaw and the ear, with contours rendered in relief.

CAT. NO. 295

   Similar plaques are known from both the Antikenabteilung (No. 214) and Penn Museum (No. 37, Inv. No. 30-33-102) holdings of the Maikop collection and from the 4th century BC Elizavetinskie kurgans (Rostovtzeff 1929:pl. XI.4). Our plaque should date to the same period.

   First published by Schmidt (1927:pl. 9.1.5) and later by Potratz (1960:pl. XI, fig. 28).

296. Harness Plaque
     Inv. No. IIId 7024 (found in the Taman Peninsula)
     Bronze, cast. Dimensions unknown
     4th century BC

This plaque is in the form of an openwork stylized head of a stag (?). The almond-shaped eye (?) in the center of the plaque is set above an attachment ring and abuts a projecting ear with edges delineated in relief on one side and a snout (broken) on the other. Above the eye rises the long, curved neck of a bird of prey, characterized by a projecting ear, round eye, and sharply curved beak. While the break in the plaque precludes a secure identification of the main animal, similar plaques depict stylized stag antlers with tips in the form of heads of birds of prey (Moshinskiy 2003:36, no. 62; Nekhaev 1987:84, no. 17). Our example thus may well represent a stag's head with the curved head of the bird of prey above it representing a variation of the usual antlers.

CAT. NO. 296

Similar plaques are known both from the Antikenabteilung holdings of the Maikop collection (cf. No. 171 with a stag snout) and from 4th century BC kurgans in the Kuban: kurgan No. 19 in Voronezhskaia village yielded four harness plaques similar to ours, three with stag snouts and one with that of a bird of prey (*OAK* for 1903; 1906:74, figs. 140, 141, 148). The Voronezhskaia plaques are especially notable because of the supplementary branches in the form of birds' heads extending from the main antler (1906:fig. 144), comparable to the head of the bird of prey that replaces the antler on our example. Additional analogues recovered from a sanctuary in Tenginskaia village (Kuban) suggest the date of these plaques may be further narrowed to the second half of the 4th century BC (Erlikh 2002:7–16, fig. 4.1–6).

297. Cheekpiece (?) Fragment
   Inv. No. IIId 7025 (found in the Taman Peninsula)
   Bronze, cast. L. 5.1 cm (preserved portion)
   4th century BC

This fragment is comprised of the upper part of the round shaft (the break occurred at a hole), which terminates in the head of a predator with a curved goat's horn. This combination, known as a "lion-headed griffin of the Achaemenid type," is characterized by a large, round eye, an open mouth rendered in relief, and a small, projecting ear. The base of the long neck is ringed by a relief band from which an arm with a sharp-clawed paw extends to touch its lower jaw. An analogue in the portion of the Maikop collection held in the Antikenabteilung Museum (No. 159, Inv. No. 30.575) indicates this example was likely two-holed.

Similar cheekpieces are held in the Krasnodar Historical-Archaeological Museum (Perevodchikova 1984:5ff., fig. 4.2), with a fragment also known from

CAT. NO. 297

the kurgans in Elizavetinskaia village (Perevodchikova 1987:44ff., fig. 3.4), indicating a date of the 4th century BC.

First published by Schmidt (1927:pl. 9.2.2).

298. Frontlet
Inv. No. IIId 7026 (found in the south of Russia)
Bronze, cast. H. 4.3 cm
4th century BC

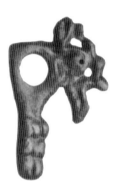

CAT. NO. 298

This frontlet is in the form of a short, flat shaft with a base set off in relief; the broad top, pierced with a circular hole (for attachment to the bridle), is abutted by a stylized openwork griffin's (?) head. While the protruding ear, round eye in relief, and curved beak are all typical of a bird of prey, the vertical crest on its head is suggestive of a griffin.

Similar noseband ornaments are common at 4th century BC Scythian sites in the steppe and Dniepr River forest-steppe, with the largest group possibly recovered from the fill of kurgan Chertomlyk (dating no earlier than the mid-4th century BC) (Alekseev, Murzin, and Rolle 1991:85, fig. 55, no. 17), but are not known from the Kuban. Thus, while our example may be dated to the 4th century BC, it cannot currently be attributed to the Taman Peninsula.

First published by Schmidt (1927:pl. 9.1.6).

299. Cheekpiece
Inv. No. IIId 7028 (found in the south of Russia)
Bronze, cast. Dimensions unknown
4th century BC

This cheekpiece is gamma-shaped. The round shaft swells to a figure 8, pierced with a hole in each loop, near the base of the flat openwork plaque set almost perpendicular to the shaft at one end, and terminates in a sharp-clawed, openwork paw (?) at the other end. The plaque takes the form of the upper torso and head of a recumbent lion with an open maw and engraved details.

CAT. NO. 299

Identical lions are known from horse trapping details, as on noseband ornaments and a cheekpiece from Kuzhorskaia village and a frontlet from Uliap kurgan No. 2 (Nekhaev 1987:82, 83, 91, nos. 9, 11, 23), indicating our example should be considered typical of the Kuban variant of the Scythian Animal Style and dated to the 4th century BC.

300. Frontlet
 Inv. No. 7030 (found in the south of Russia)
 Bronze, cast. H. 4.7 cm
 4th century BC

This frontlet is in the form of a vertical shaft, semicircular in section and tapering significantly from top to bottom. The shaft terminates in a seven-petal palmette at its base and has a circular hole (for attachment to the bridle) in its broad top, which is abutted by the stylized head of a bird of prey with a long, spiral-curved beak.

CAT. NO. 300

Similar noseband ornaments are known from excavated sites: while the 4th century BC kurgans in Voronezhskaia village (Perevodchikova 1987:48, fig. 3.11) have yielded one analogue, the closest parallel comes from a sanctuary (second half of the 4th century BC) in Tenginskaia village in the Kuban (Erlikh 2002:7–16, fig. 4.8). Our example should date to the same period.

First published by Schmidt (1927:pl. 9.1.3) and later by Potratz (1960:pl. XI, fig. 30).

301. Belt Buckle
 Inv. No. IIId 7104 (found in the Taman Peninsula)
 Bronze, die-formed, soldered. L. 6.5 cm
 1st–2nd century AD

This belt buckle is in the form of a circular openwork frame curved from a single long

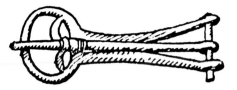

CAT. NO. 301

shaft, the ends of which flare out from the back of the frame, forming a long, almost triangular base and terminating in rings through which a crosspiece is threaded. In the center of the crosspiece is another long shaft (identically attached) that projects beyond the front edge of the circular frame and serves as the base for the tongue of the buckle; a special bracket covers the tongue at the base of the frame, limiting its mobility.

Similar buckles, made of silver, bronze, or iron, are widespread at Sarmatian period sites in southern Ukraine, the Crimea, the Kuban, the center of the Northern Caucasus, and the 1st to 2nd century BC Greek necropoleis of the Bosporan Kingdom (Viazmitina 1972:33ff., fig. 66.7; Meliukova and Abramova 1989:pls. 55.13, 111.29–30; Leskov 1991:no. 228; Koshelenko, Kruglikova, and Dolgorukov 1984:pl. CLV.1, 4). Our example should be similarly dated.

302. Belt Buckle
     Inv. No. IIId 7105 (found in the Taman Peninsula)
     Bronze, cast. Dimensions unknown
     1st–2nd century AD

This rectangular openwork buckle has a standing lion in high relief in profile to the left, with its head in a three-quarter view and rising slightly above the frame in its center. There is a hook, bent outward, in the middle of the left crosspiece for attaching the other half of the buckle.

This buckle was published with five similar examples from the museum, including one from this collection (cf. No. 269), by Rostovtzeff (1931a:46–55, pl. 1.5), who dated them to the 2nd to 3rd century AD. The analogues recovered from Panticapaeum (Koshelenko, Kruglikova, and Dolgorukov 1984:346, pl. CLV.3) indicate that a 1st–2nd century AD date is more likely.

CAT. NO. 302

303. Belt Buckle
     Inv. No. IIId 7102 (found in the Taman Peninsula)
     Bronze, cast, die-formed. L. 7.5 cm
     2nd century AD

This belt buckle is in the form of a semicircular openwork frame cast together with the plaque adjoining it on its flattened side. The tongue of the buckle was attached in the

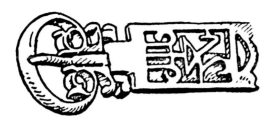

CAT. NO. 303

transverse slit of the plaque. A rectangular openwork guard containing the insignia of the Bosporan king Tiberius Iulius Eupatorius (reigned AD 154–170) is attached to the plaque on the side opposite the tongue.

Similar insignia to that represented here are well known from sites in the Bosporan Kingdom and its neighboring regions (the Kuban and Crimea). Direct analogues for the depiction in the openwork guard were published by Solomonik (1959:132ff., nos. 72, 76, 78, 79, 80) and Treister (2000:118–23, fig. 1.1, 3, 4), with the latter noting that in the Bosporus, "around the middle of the 2nd century AD, under the influence of the Roman military costume, the manufacture of belt plates with the royal insignia was organized, probably in the royal workshops...imitating the wares from Upper Germany and Rhaetia." This analysis is confirmed by the most comprehensive studies of these insignia (Solomonik 1959; Drachuk 1975; S. A. Yatsenko 2001), which indicate that buckles bearing Tiberius Iulius Eupatorius's imperial mark on the guard date between the mid- and late 2nd century AD.

First published in 1909 by Ebert (1909:71, fig. 5.4).

304. Belt Buckle
  Inv. No. IIId 7103 (found in the Taman Peninsula)
  Bronze, cast. Dimensions unknown
  2nd–3rd century AD

This rectangular openwork half of a buckle has a small projecting ring in the center of one short end intended to link with the hook terminating the missing half of the buckle.

While the absence of close analogues for this fragment alone precludes the assignment of a secure date, it is grouped with six other items in the inventory book (p. 796), five of which appear to be buckles dating to the 2nd to 3rd century AD (cf. Nos. 269, 301–303, 306); the last (No. 305), which appears to end in a hook, seems likely on the basis of its contours and dimensions to be the other half of the buckle described here.

CAT. NOS. 304 (right) AND 305

This item should thus date between the 2nd and 3rd century AD.

305. Belt Buckle
     Inv. No. IIId 7107 (found in the Taman Peninsula)
     Bronze, cast. Dimensions unknown
     2nd–3rd century AD

This rectangular openwork half of a buckle has a small projecting hook in the center of one short end, intended to link with the ring terminating the missing half of the buckle (No. 304), and a slight semicircular bulge in the center of the opposite side. Two consecutive holes within the frame on this opposite side, the first rectangular and the second semicircular (fitting within the bulge), likely secured the guard for the attachment of the strap. The main field of the buckle contains an openwork depiction of a so-called Sarmatian *tamga* insignia, similar to the royal insignia (only a triangle is missing from the middle part) of the Bosporan king Tiberius Iulius Eupatorius.

Similar insignia to that represented here, used both for branding livestock (Solomonik 1959:27, fig. V.2, 79ff., no. 35) and as ornaments for strap finials (Solomonik 1959:133, no. 76; Drachuk 1975:pl. XII, nos. 899, 900, 901; pl. XIII.11, 12, 13), are mainly found in the Bosporus and the Tanais region. A date of 2nd to 3rd century AD is quite secure.

306. Belt Buckle
     Inv. No. IIId 7101 (found in the Taman Peninsula)
     Bronze, cast, die-formed. L. 7.5 cm
     2nd–3rd century AD

This buckle is in the form of a semicircular openwork frame cast together with the plaque adjoining it on its flattened side. The tongue of the buckle was attached in the transverse slit of the plaque. A rectangular guard for the attachment of the strap is attached to the plaque on the side opposite the tongue.

CAT. NO. 306

A similar buckle from Panticapaeum, differing only in its openwork guard, dates to the 2nd to 3rd century AD (Koshelenko, Kruglikova, and Dolgorukov 1984:pl. CLV.9). Such a date for our example is confirmed by the publication by Treister of additional examples (2000:118ff., fig. 1.4–5), those with scrolls on the guard to secure the belt, dating to the 2nd century AD.

First published by Ebert (1909:71, fig.5.5).

307. Buckle

> Inv. No. IIId 6665 (found in the Taman Peninsula)
> Silver, cast or die-formed. Dimensions unknown
> 3rd–5th century AD

This buckle is in the form of a semicircular openwork frame with a tongue, triangular in section, tapering toward a tip projecting beyond the rounded front edge of the frame.

CAT. NO. 307

While its simplicity of form and the absence of a guard precludes the assignment of a secure date, this buckle appears closest to Kovalevskaia's (1979:15) variant II, buckles with semicircular frames lacking guards. It is distinguished from the rest of this group by the triangular section of its tongue but likely dates similarly to between the 3rd and 5th century AD. That said, the possibility that it belongs to a slightly later period (Kovalevskaia's next chronological group dates to the 6th to 7th century AD) cannot be ruled out.

308. Pinhead (?)

> Inv. No. IIId 6671 (found in the Taman Peninsula)
> Bronze, almandine, hammered, burnished (stone), with encrustation,
>   carving. Dimensions unknown
> End 4th–beginning 5th century AD

This flat, round head of a nail-shaped pin (?) is edged with a hatched band and with an almandine insert in its center. Although the absence of information on the reverse of this fragment precludes a secure identification of its purpose, it is sufficiently similar to Nos. 270 and 309 to be identified as a pinhead.

CAT. NO. 308

If this is indeed a pin fragment, it should be dated similarly to analogues from Kerch crypt No. 145 to the late 4th or early 5th century AD (Zasetskaia 1979:fig. 2.4, app. 15).

309. Pins (3 items found)

> Inv. Nos. IIId 6729, 6730, 6731 (found in the Taman
>   Peninsula)
> Silver, glass, hammered, burnished (glass). Dimensions
>   unknown
> End 4th–beginning 5th century AD

This nail-shaped pin, broken at its lower end, has a flat, round head topped with an insert of burnished red glass in its center; the head is

CAT. NO. 309

edged with a hatched band. Two similar but very fragmentary pins are also held in the collection.

This item is comparable to Nos. 207 and 308 and should be similarly dated to the end of the 4th or beginning of the 5th century AD.

310. Strap Plaque
       Inv. No. IIId 7097 (found in the Taman Peninsula)
       Bronze, cast. Dimensions unknown
       10th–11th century AD

This strap plaque is of the same form and function as No. 276 but here better preserved, having all four of its hemispherical inserts.

It dates between the 10th and 11th century AD.

CAT. NO. 310

311. Strap Plaque
       Inv. No. IIId 7099 (found in the Taman Peninsula)
       Bronze, cast. Dimensions unknown
       10th–11th century AD

CAT. NO. 311

This strap plaque is comprised of a small central ring from which three identical and evenly spaced branches, each formed from three hemispheres, diverge. The central ring passes through the first hemisphere on each branch, which is divided from the second by a projecting semicircular divider. The second and third hemispheres of each branch are separated by two rectangular bars flanking a flattened circle delineated in relief.

While the quality of its drawing in the inventory book (p. 795) and the lack of a description there precludes a more detailed account of this item, it is clearly comparable to two other strap plaques in this collection (cf. Nos. 276 and 310) and should be similarly dated to between the 10th and 11th century AD.

312. Buckle Frame
       Inv. No. IIId 6666 (found in the Taman Peninsula)
       Silver, cast or die-formed. L. 6.6 cm
       Date unknown

This buckle frame is in the form of an openwork oval, round in section and narrowing toward the tips, which nearly meet in the center of one long side where the tongue would have been. The frame slopes inward on the long side opposite the tips.

CAT. NO. 312

The lack of frames comparable in dimension and shape among the vast corpus of published bronze and silver buckles from Ukraine and the south of Russia is problematic, suggesting our example may have been deformed; while Sarmatian period (Viazmitina 1972:133ff., fig. 66.1, 3, 6) and medieval (Fedorov-Davydov 1966:46ff., fig. 7.3) iron buckles of superficially similar form, with oval frames and tongues running lengthwise, do exist, the medieval examples at least were used in horse trappings and are not valid comparanda. A secure date thus cannot be assigned for this object.

313. Facings (2 items)
     Inv. Nos. IIId 6672, 6673 (found in the Taman Peninsula)
     Gold, stamped, soldered, riveted. Dimensions unknown
     Date unknown

Two identical facings are each in the form of a figure 8 with a hollow in each loop and with a projection containing a rivet at its top and bottom. In the drawing, the central part of each of the links in the figure 8 surface is set off, although not clearly, by convexities and concavities.

As the precise form of the facings is unknown, a secure date cannot be assigned.

CAT. NO. 313
(2 views)

314. Plaque
     Inv. No. IIId 6674 (found in the Taman Peninsula)
     Gold, stamped, soldered. Dimensions unknown
     Date unknown

CAT. NO. 314

This rectangular plaque is hemispherical in section and flat on the reverse. There is transverse fluting on the rounded front surface and a hole in the center of each short end for attachment to the foundation, likely a strap.

The lack of close analogues precludes the assignment of a secure date.

The Metropolitan Museum of Art, New York

315. Plaque
Inv. No. 24.97.56
Gold, stamped, soldered, with filigree, encrustation, glass, or stone (lost).
    H. 3 cm
5th century BC

This plaque is an openwork winged lion, moving right with its head turned back, on a thick pedestal. Details, including two rows of vertical hatching on the pedestal; long lines on the wing, which curves up toward the head; the musculature of the torso; and the toes on each paw, are articulated in relief. Both the tail, which is made of ribbed wire that curves up sinuously and forms a small circle on the lion's hindquarters, and ear, comprising a low rim for an insert, are soldered and the plaque is pierced with four small holes for attachment to fabric or leather.

CAT. NO. 315

While no direct analogues for this plaque are known, it is comparable in some respects to a 5th century BC gold plaque representing a winged griffin from the Penn Museum's Maikop holdings (No. 59, Inv. No. 30-33-14.4); its major difference is in the use of holes for attachment rather than the loops that are more common on the Maikop plaques (commonly griffins or stags), but it is also more elaborately manufactured, with soldering, filigree, and encrustation used in addition to stamping. Although encrusted gold articles are typical of late 7th–6th century BC sites in the Kuban, known both from the Kelermes kurgans (late 7th–early 6th century BC) and from Ulskiy kurgan No. 1 (late 6th century BC), our plaque is more typical in style to that of the 5th–4th century BC (Artamonov 1966:fig. 71).

Excavated comparanda include a gold plaque from Nymphaion kurgan No. 17 in the form of a walking winged lion with its head turned back and its tail, which curves up onto its hindquarters, ending in the head of a bird of prey (Artamonov 1966:pl. 101), and similar but wingless lions from the mid-5th century BC Semibratniy kurgan No. 2 (Artamonov 1966:pl. 111). Our plaque is thus attributed to the early to mid-5th century BC. First published by Piotrovsky (1975:160.15).

316. Plaque
       Inv. No. 24.97.57
       Gold, stamped. H. 3 cm
       5th century BC

Openwork lion with the head of a bird-griffin on a thick pedestal formed by large claws picked out in relief above a row of vertical hatching; the head is turned back to rest on its spine, and the muscular torso and thin, sinuous tail, which curves up onto its back, are both articulated in relief above the spindly, almost birdlike forelegs and the slightly more muscular hind legs. The plaque is pierced with five small holes for attachment to cloth or leather.

CAT. NO. 316

Six identical plaques from the district of Maikop were purchased in 1908 by the Imperial Archaeological Commission (Pharmakowsky 1999:24, 148, fig. 10), suggesting the probable origin of this piece. In terms of date, this item should belong to the same range as No. 1, though the differences in the color of the gold and the manufacturing technique suggest that this example is slightly later, probably dating to the mid- to late 5th century BC. First published by Smirnov (1909:pl. CXIX.45).

* * *

In addition to the two plaques described in this section, the Metropolitan Museum of Art holds thirty additional plaques of four different types, all of which are represented in the collection at the Penn Museum and are described in the entries for Nos. 62, 63, 65, and 66 (Inv. No. 30-33-1.1, 2, 5, 4). These four types of plaques also appear in the Antikenabteilung in Berlin, and have been previously published by Greifenhagen (1970:58, 60; pls. 33.1–2, 37.10).

The Maikop Collection:
A Historical Overview

The University of Pennsylvania Museum of Archaeology and Anthropology houses 133 items from the Maikop treasure dating between the 3rd millennium BC (Early Bronze Age) and the 14th century AD. The Staatliche Museen zu Berlin's Classical Antiquities section possesses 106 inventory numbers, acquired in the 1907 purchase directly from de Massoneau and in the 1913 purchase from Karapet, with artifacts ranging in date from the 8th–7th century BC (Early Iron Age) to the 14th century AD. (As 13 inventory numbers in the Antikenabteilung are identical to the gold ornaments from the Penn Museum collection, they are not published here.) Three more items, 11863.303–305 (a pair of three-holed cheek-pieces and a two-ring bit), were lost during World War II. Setting the preserved and described pair of cheekpieces (No. 134, Inv. No. 30.571a, b) and horse bit (No. 135, Inv. No. 30.580) against those that were lost, it becomes unclear which particular set of cheekpieces and bit has survived (1907 inventory book: Inv. No. 11.863.303-305, or 1913: Inv. Nos. 30.571a,b and 30.580). The portion of the Maikop collection in the Pre-History section, comprising 88 inventory numbers acquired in 1907, has a chronological span extending from the 13th–12th century BC (Late Bronze Age) to the 14th century AD (High Middle Ages). Those items from de Massoneau's collection currently housed in the Berlin Museum's Near Eastern department and Cologne's Römisch-Germanisches Museum are not treated in this publication.

The final and smallest portion of the Maikop collection, 6 inventory numbers (to which are assigned 32 gold plaques) bought in Paris in 1922, is held by the Metropolitan Museum of Art in New York. Thirty of the plaques in this museum belong to four types already known from the Philadelphia and Berlin collections and so are not included in this catalogue (see the Penn Museum Collection Nos. 61, 62, 64, and 65). The remaining two, manufactured in the Scythian Animal Style, are original in appearance and are published here.

This book therefore publishes 316 of the 333 separate inventory numbers available (comprising many more artifacts), omitting those 17 duplicated elsewhere in the dispersed collection. A chronology of those materials included in this catalogue, summarized in

Table 1, is analyzed below in order of the earliest to latest artifacts.

Only 13 inventory numbers are attributed to the Bronze Age, the earliest period represented in the Maikop collection. Three of these items, all in the collection of the Berlin Museum's Prehistory department, are from collections other than de Massoneau's: an axe (No. 229) is from the collection of P. Mavrogordato, and two jars (Nos. 230, 231) were acquired from the collection of A. Kossnierska. While this number may seem small, it should not be surprising; during the time that de Massoneau was amassing his collection, the sites of ancient Greek cities and large Scythian kurgans were the primary targets of both excavation and plunder in the south of Russia.

The pre-Scythian period is represented by a mere 23 inventory numbers. Among these are several items from other collections: a two-ring bit from the collection of Mavrogordato (No. 238), and a cup from Kossnierska (No. 232); further, the whetstone handle (No. 283) is clearly an import from Luristan. Those periods succeeding the Scythian, to which 200 inventory numbers (approximately two-thirds of the collection) are attributed, are as poorly represented as those preceding it: the Sarmatian period has 20 inventory numbers, the Early Middle Ages have 22, and the High Middle Ages have 21. An additional 19 inventory numbers are of uncertain date.

The Bronze Age

The 13 inventory numbers attributed to this period date from the 3rd to the 1st millennium BC and are quite typical of the Bronze Age archaeological cultures of the North Pontic steppes and the North Caucasian piedmont. To the Maikop culture, which occupied large tracts of the steppe and piedmont regions in the 3rd millennium BC, may be attributed three handled knives and one chisel (Nos. 1–4), all of relatively characteristic form. To the late Catacomb culture or the Ribbed Pottery culture may be attributed a pyriform stone macehead (No. 5), a type that continued to be manufactured, though later in bronze, into the 13th century BC. The late Catacomb culture spread over the steppes and forest-steppes of the Don and Dniepr river basins in the second quarter of the 2nd millennium BC, or to the North Caucasus archaeological culture, which demonstrate a large degree of cultural unity after the disappearance of the Maikop culture.

The last three centuries of the 2nd and the early centuries of the 1st millennium BC are typified by a spectacular increase in the quality and quantity of metallurgy and metalworking in the North Pontic steppes, spurred by multilateral contacts with the peoples of the Volga-Ural regions, the Northern Caucasus, and the Carpatho-Danubian basin (Bočarev and Leskov 1980). Although one chisel from the Maikop collection (No. 227) undoubtedly dates to this period, the fact that numerous hoards of metal artifacts including objects not only of local Pontic manufacture but also items typical of the Volga-Ural, Kuban, and Carpatho-Danubian regions makes the site of origin difficult to assess. Similarly, the two Late Bronze Age finials (No. 228) are of the Lukianovskiy type known both

Table 1. Chronological Structure of the Maikop Collection

	Original items/total	Bronze Age	Pre-Scythian period 8th–7th c. BC	Scythian period 7th–3rd c. BC	Sarmatian period 1st c. BC–4th c. AD	Early Medieval period 5th–9th c. AD	High Medieval period 10th–14th c. AD	Not established
Philadelphia–Penn Museum	133/133	6	11	77	9	13	10	7
Berlin–Museum of Berlin, Department of Classical Antiquities	93+2/106	–	3	77+2	2	–	6	5
Berlin–Museum of Prehistory and Ancient History	88/88	7	9	42	9	9	5	7
New York–Metropolitan Museum	2/6	–	–	2	–	–	–	–
TOTAL	316+2/333	13	23	198+2	20	22	21	19

in the northern Black Sea steppes and farther west, in southwestern Ukraine and Moldavia, regions closely connected with Carpatho-Danubian metal production. One other artifact from this period, a cast bronze macehead (No. 6), was likely locally produced in the Kuban under the influence of the Koban culture.

We clearly see the difficulty of identifying the probable origins of the artifacts of the Maikop collection. Although the collection mostly derives from Maikop, it contains objects linked to or characteristic of other regions, such as the North Pontic steppes west of the Don River. Among the meager Late Bronze Age finds are also some of Transcaucasian origin; these include one spearhead of east Georgian manufacture with relief bands decorating its long socket (No. 233), a type that does not occur farther west than Daghestan and Chechnya, and one axe of the Colkhis type (No. 229), most common in the Caucasus but known from sites as far west as Akkermen near Odessa (Terenozhkin 1976:34, pl. 34, fig. 8), that was recovered from the town of Maikop.

In the 1980s, also in the region of Maikop, several dwelling sites were discovered that yielded pottery complexes dating from the beginning of the 1st millennium BC. Such complexes of burnished tableware richly decorated with incised and corded ornament had formerly been known only from the excavations at the Don River estuary (Sharafutdinova 1980), recovered by Miller in the course of his 1920s excavations at the Kobiakovo hillfort (1926:71–142, figs. 25, 26, 28). Miller's discovery of burnished pottery differing sharply from the ordinary kitchenware of the late Srubnaia (Timber-grave) culture (Krivtsova-Grakova 1955:99ff.; Leskov 1975a) led to the designation of a new archaeological culture, the Kobiakovo (Sharafutdinova 1980), and to the theory that the people of this culture migrated from the Kuban River region. Excavations conducted by Sharafutdinova and Anfimov on the Kuban confirmed this hypothesis, raising the question of what impelled this migration (Anfimov and Sharafutdinova 1982:139–47).

Unfortunately, the archaeological contexts in which this burnished ware was found have yielded primarily sherds, with complete vessels practically unknown. The two complete jars (Nos. 230 and 231) preserved in the collection of the Museum für Vor- und Frühgeschichte are thus invaluable artifacts for the study of the Kobiakovo material culture. Given that the Maikop collection as published contains not a single other artifact typical of the lower Don River region in general and of the Kobiakovo sites located there specifically, the two complete burnished jars almost certainly derive from the right bank of the lower Kuban River, where a number of Kobiakovo sites have been found.

As for the ultimate origins of the Kobiakovo culture itself, no compelling theory has yet been put forth. The collection of burnished pottery from the Kuban and lower Don River regions remains limited, and vessels of similar form and decoration are widely known among the various cultures in the south of Eastern Europe, from Koban culture sites in the east (Krupnov 1960) to Sakharna-type sites in Moldova (Smirnova 1977:94–107) and Kizil-Koba culture sites in the Crimean piedmont. The final artifact presented in this section belongs to the last of these groups, the Kizil-Koba culture, and takes the form of a burnished cup (No. 232) from the collection of Kossnierska. Typical of the Kizil-Koba culture of the early 1st millennium BC, it has been published in this book together with the jars of the Kobiakovo culture.

In summary, only four of the finds presented in this section date from the Early Bronze Age; the remainder belong to the Late Bronze Age or even Early Iron Age, with the Colkhidian-type axe (No. 229), the east Georgian spearhead (No. 233), and the Kizil-Koba cup (No. 232) especially being transitional in form; while emerging in the Late Bronze Age, these were certainly produced and used into the Early Iron Age.

The Pre-Scythian Period

In the pre-Scythian period, those artifacts typical of the Bronze and Early Iron ages disappeared in the south of Eastern Europe, to be replaced by artifacts of the Novocherkassk type (8th–7th century BC). The instability of this period, marked by raids of the nomadic tribes from the North Pontic steppes on Asia Minor and the Near East, even up to the borders of Egypt, allowed the development of unique artifacts of interest to scholars of both Eastern Europe and the ancient Near East. The Cimmerians and the Scythians, the first peoples of Eastern Europe to appear in the written records of the Near East, are mentioned in the written sources of Assyria and Urartu, in various books of the Bible, and in the histories of ancient Greece. The publication here of those artifacts relevant to them in the Maikop collection is thus especially important.

While it is now impossible to reconstruct the original associations and exact archaeological contexts of those finds from this period preserved in both departments of the Berlin Museum and in the Penn Museum (totaling 23 inventory numbers), the typical artifact assemblage recovered from burials of the Novocherkassk type indicates that our objects are likely a collection of disparate finds recovered from various sites on the left bank of the Kuban River in the region that yielded the majority of Novocherkassk-type artifacts (Leskov and Erlikh 1999; Erlikh 1994; Dubovskaia 1997; Lovpache 1985:18–20, pl. 8–15; Sazonov 1995:84–107). The 24th inventory number (IIId 7035) corresponds to the whetstone bronze handle, identified as a Luristan import. In collections of Luristan bronzes, similar finds are dated between the 9th and the 7th century BC. The predominance of large, clearly identifiable objects such as weapons (6 inventory numbers), whetstones (2 inventory numbers), and harness details (13 inventory numbers) in the collection, coupled with the absence of pottery from this period, contrasts sharply with the typical assemblage recovered from an excavated Novocherkassk site, over half of which typically comprises pottery and ornaments. The accidental nature of the Maikop acquisitions is further demonstrated by the fact that the collection contains four pairs of two-ring bits (No. 7, No. 135, Nos. 238, 239), but only one pair of the accompanying three-holed cheekpieces (No. 134). That said, as in the ratio of spearheads to arrowheads (four to two), the Maikop collection in some respects actually reflects the archaeological situation: the predominance of spearheads over arrowheads among the artifacts recovered from proto-Maeotian cemeteries, coeval with the Novocherkassk treasure, is well known.

Differences already seem apparent in the artifact assemblages recovered from proto-Maeotian cemeteries of this period in the Kuban, where spearheads significantly outnumber arrowheads, and those recovered from the coeval graves in the steppe and on the border of the Ukrainian forest-steppe in the Dniepr basin.

In the latter region, comprising the North Pontic zone, ten rich burials of warrior horsemen are known; all are secondary burials set in earlier Bronze Age kurgans, including Zolnoe, Butenki, Nosachevo, Kvitki, and Olshany in Ukraine (Terenozhkin 1976; Skoriy 1999:79–98); the kurgans near Nekrsovskaia village; and the Obryvsky kurgan on the lower Don River (Terenozhkin 1976:54ff.). Arrowheads seem to have figured much more prominently in these graves, with each containing a set of them, mostly of bronze but also of iron and bone. No cemeteries have yet been discovered in this zone.

While part of the difference between the excavated assemblages in these zones may have to do with social status, with only one rich kurgan, that of Uashkitu (Erlikh 1994), known from the Kuban against the ten known from the North Pontic zone, it is significant that in the period following this one, marked by the fully developed Maeotian culture in the Kuban and the flourishing Scythian culture in southern Ukraine, the contrast between the artifact assemblages from the graves of the two cultures is even more conspicuous. The Maeotian burials typically contain spearheads and swords of various types rather than arrowheads, while the Scythian burials of nearly all the males and a significant number of females invariably contain bronze arrowheads. This contrast in the standard weaponry of the two regions has served as the basis for various theories on the differing structures and organizations of the Scythian and Maeotian armies (Erlikh 1992:16ff.). The Maikop collection contains very few arrowheads, unsurprising given that the majority of the objects published here derive from the Kuban.

The Scythian and Sarmatian Periods

In discussing the Scythian artifacts in the Maikop collection, which total 198 inventory numbers, it is necessary to first note the uneven chronological distribution of the material (see Table 2).

Only 11 inventory numbers belong to the Archaic period, with most representing objects from the everyday lives of the nomads: bronze arrowheads (Nos. 18 and 19, No. 206), a harness detail (No. 244), a cauldron fragment (No. 140), two finials (pole tops) (Nos. 242 and 243), and a mirror with a handle-shaft (No. 136). The last of these, of a type typically procured from China via Central Asia or Siberia, is typical of the nomads of the Eurasian steppes. The three remaining inventory numbers from this period are all partial or whole examples of "Olbian-type" mirrors. The extensive territory over which such mirrors were distributed, ranging from Hungary in the west to the Urals in the east, makes it unlikely that they were all produced at a single production center, even one as developed as the

Table 2. Chronological Structure of the Maikop Collection, Scythian Period

	Archaic period–late 7th–6th c. BC	5th c. BC	5th–4th c. BC	4th c. BC	4th–2nd c. BC	TOTAL
Philadelphia–Penn Museum	2	25	11	37	2	77
Berlin–Museum of Berlin, Department of Classical Antiquities	6	17	13	35+2	6	77+2
Berlin–Museum of Prehistory and Ancient History	3	12	7	19	1	42
New York–Metropolitan Museum	–	2	–	–	–	2
TOTAL	11	56	31	91+2	9	198+2

ancient Greek city of Olbia. The most likely sources of these mirrors are the Greek workshops in the colonies of the North and West Pontic zones, whence they were distributed to the Sauromatians, the Maeotians, the Scythians, and their neighbors to the west.

The majority of the items from the Scythian period in the Maikop collection, 178 inventory numbers, date from the 5th and 4th century BC. This predominance of Classical Scythian artifacts over those from the Archaic Scythian period sadly reflects an archaeological reality: in the period when de Massoneau was amassing his collection, Archaic Scythian sites were few and far between. Despite the extensive fieldwork conducted in the south of Eastern Europe in the past four decades, the situation has changed little even today, and our understanding remains very limited of the Scythian and Maeotian cultures of the late 7th and 6th century BC, when the participants in the Scythian campaigns in the Near East returned to the North Pontic lands. Splendid discoveries made in the Central Caucasus piedmonts and Stavropol krai, first by Petrenko (1978), are far from sufficient to solve a number of historical problems closely connected with Herodotus's description of Scythia in the period before the Persian invasion of the North Pontic steppes under King Darius I.

Given that the bulk of objects in this section, as well as in the collection overall, date between the 5th and 4th century, it is useful here to review the archaeological background to these artifacts. Unlike Archaic Scythian period sites, the sites of this period densely occupy both the North Pontic zone and the Kuban. They comprise primarily kurgans in the Crimean and Ukrainian steppes and kurgans and ground cemeteries, as well as dwellings, hillforts, sanctuaries, and hoards, on the Kerch and Taman peninsulas and on the left bank of the Kuban. A number of cities and settlements of the ancient Greek Bosporan

Kingdom are located on the Kerch and Taman peninsulas. The vast majority of the Maikop collection as collected by de Massoneau derives from Kerch and the territory between Taman and Maikop.

The objects themselves are an assorted lot, though it is immediately obvious that the collector focused his attention on objects of gold and bronze. Interestingly, de Massoneau's first sale to the Berlin Museum in 1907 included few artifacts of gold (this assessment is limited to those objects acquired by the Classical and Prehistory sections). When considering only those objects likely to derive directly from Scythian or Maeotian sites, this number dwindles to four inventory numbers: a torque finial in the form of a lion's head (No. 185); a bracelet finial in the form of a ram's head (No. 186); a rectangular plaque with a griffin in its central field (No. 187); and two plaques in the form of eagles with outspread wings (No. 188).

The second portion of de Massoneau's collection, divided among the Classical department of the Berlin Museum and Ercole Canessa's gallery (the latter collection ultimately acquired by the Penn Museum), was of a very different character: over half of the inventory numbers are made of gold or silver.

The disparity in the richness of the 1907 and 1913 collections sold by de Massoneau is due to the composition of each collection. The most valuable artifacts in the 1907 collection were the early medieval finds from the stone sepulchers in Kerch, which were transferred from the Berlin Museum's Prehistory section to Cologne's Römisch-Germanisches Museum and which are not treated here. The focus of the 1913 collection, conversely, was the rich Scythian-Maeotian material with which we are concerned.

Aside from the material composition of these 5th and 4th century BC artifacts, they may also be classified according to their functions: (1) weapons and tools, (2) harness elements, (3) ornaments and utensils from daily life, and (4) vessels and vessel embellishments. The results of this classification are presented in Table 3.

It is immediately obvious that two of the most important types of artifacts among those noted above, weaponry and pottery, are the worst represented. The scarcity of Scythian and Maeotian weapons in the collection, totaling only five inventory numbers, is not indicative of their lack of importance in Scythian or Maeotian society but is rather linked to collector demand: since iron is typically in much worse condition than bronze in archaeological contexts, looters tended to ignore even complete iron artifacts when raiding a site. One corollary of this phenomenon has been that modern excavators digging at sites plundered in the 19th century AD typically recover iron artifacts, and iron weapons first of all, in the course of their work.

The prominence of bronze and iron artifacts in Scythian and Maeotian sites is unsurprising given that both cultures flourished during a period of rapid developments in mass production, ferrous metallurgy, and ironworking. The products of Bronze Age casters and coppersmiths were superseded by mass-produced bronze arrowheads, spearheads, and javelin heads. A trend from elaborate and complex shapes to standardized and simple ones is also evident in this period, a natural development in a professional craft and likely also a corollary of mass production. In the 6th century BC, Scythian swords and akinaks (short

Table 3. Chronological Distribution of Categories of Material Culture, 5th–4th c. BC

	Weapons, whetstones			Horse harnesses			Ornaments, utensils			Vessels		
	5th c. BC	5th–4th c. BC	4th c. BC	5th c. BC	5th–4th c. BC	4th c. BC	5th c. BC	5th–4th c. BC	4th c. BC	5th c. BC	5th–4th c. BC	4th c. BC
Philadelphia–Penn Museum	–	2	–	2	2	3	25	7	37	2	–	–
Berlin–Museum of Berlin, Department of Classical Antiquities	–	1	1	5	7	20	10	2	12	7	2	–
Berlin–Museum of Prehistory and Ancient History	1	–	–	9	7	21	1	–	2	–	–	–
New York–Metropolitan Museum	–	–	–	–	–	–	2	–	–	–	–	–
TOTAL	1	3	1	16	16	44	38	9	51	9	2	–

swords) were supplied with sophisticated guards and pommels, but these became were increasingly simplified as time passed. Similarly, in the Kuban, Scythian akinaks were widely used in the Archaic period but were later superseded by the relatively simple Maeotian swords, which were especially widespread in the 4th century BC (Erlikh 1992:4–5).

Also ill represented in the Maikop collection is a category of artifact typically ubiquitous at ancient sites: pottery. Despite abundant finds of various shapes and sizes of pottery in 6th to 4th century BC Maeotian burials, early collectors seem to have been uninterested in pots. It is no accident that de Massoneau's collection, extensive as it was, contained not a single clay pot of local Scythian or Maeotian production; two lone ancient Greek vases, now in the Penn Museum collection (Nos. 20 and 21), represent the clay pottery of this period.

The metal vessels or vessel embellishments from this period are better represented, comprising 9 inventory numbers and including a silver phiale (No. 154); five sets of gold appliqués for wooden vessels (Nos. 57 and 58, Nos. 149, 150, and 151); a ram's head finial from a silver drinking horn (No. 208); and several components of gold drinking horns (Nos. 163 and 164). The central parts of two more drinking horns are also present in the collection. Initially, there were likely four drinking horns with practically identical central parts; however, the finials and upper parts of two surviving horns have not survived. A bronze bowl (4th–2nd century BC) is the tenth metallic vessel of the Scythian period in de Massoneau's collection. These vessels, as valuable as they are, undoubtedly originated in 5th or 4th century BC graves of the Scythian and Maeotian nobility; as such, they are extremely unlikely to have been found in isolation and were probably part of a rich assemblage of such objects from the grave of a wealthy (but not royal) figure. In Zavadskaia Mogila kurgan No. 1, for example, a kurgan in southern Ukraine excavated by B. N. Mozolevskiy, at least five wooden vessels decorated with gold appliqués were recovered (Mozolevskiy 1980:86ff., pls. 45–46). The funerary goods in Semibratniy kurgan No. 2 were even richer, including three gold drinking horns, a silver rhyton of Achaemenid manufacture, and Greek silver vases (Artamonov 1966:pl. 117; Anfimov 1987:92ff.). In the same vein, the ritual area of Uliap kurgan No. 4 contained three bronze vessels, a silver phiale, gold plaques and a torque, a gold drinking horn, and a gilded silver rhyton decorated with Pegasus protomes (Leskov 1990:39ff.). Given these assemblages and the fact that the metal vessels and vessel embellishments in the Maikop collection all date to approximately the 5th century BC, it is probable that at least some of them derive from a single site, perhaps belonging with other artifacts in the collection. Such drinking horns were likely used in the 4th century BC as well, with one prominent example deriving from Uliap kurgan No. 4: though typologically characteristic of the 5th century BC, it was recovered from a 4th century BC context. Notably, there are two additional cone-shaped elements from such horns in the Berlin Museum's Antikenabteilung (see No. 164a, b, Inv. Nos. 30.221h-2, -3) and there are three gold finials from drinking horns in the Penn Museum's collection (No. 69, Inv. Nos. 30-33-14.11–13). It is unclear whether these once constituted two horns or more as the finials in Philadelphia are so poorly preserved they cannot be reliably dated to the same period (5th century BC) or definitively identified as deriving from the same association as the two reconstructed drinking horns in the Antikenabteilung collection (Nos. 163, 164).

While the reconstruction of the original relationships and associations between the artifacts in the Maikop collection remains very inexact, we may be certain that though the artifacts published here are divided among three museums (with a further division between the Classical and Prehistory departments of the Berlin Museum), such relationships do exist. Some artifacts assigned different inventory numbers and sometimes even scattered across two or even three different museums would have been recovered from a single archaeological context or assemblage. This unity of the overall collection is highlighted by the division of sets of artifacts between the Penn Museum and the Berlin Museum's Classics section: such sets include the gold appliqués for two separate wooden vessels (Nos. 57 and 58; not republished in the Antikenabteilung collection), several gold earrings (No. 55, Nos. 154 and 155), and various elements of a complex gold pendant (No. 56; not republished in the Antikenabteilung collection). The seven types of plaques appearing in both collections, four types of which are also found in the Metropolitan Museum of Art in New York (see Table 4), further reinforce this unity.

As noted above, however, reconstructing specific archaeological assemblages from within the overall Maikop collection is a more difficult task, requiring an analysis of the objects' dates, inventory numbers, and style, as well as a comparison with the composition of excavated assemblages.

In the Classics section of the Berlin Museum those artifacts said by de Massoneau to have come from a single grave were marked with a single inventory number, 30.221, with letter indexes ranging from *a* to *v*. The dealer who sold these objects to the Berlin Museum (Karapet) stated they came from the Chmyrev kurgan (in the Zaparozhye region in Ukraine); it was not until Rostovtzeff had seen the collection that the Kuban provenance of the majority of finds became clear. Unfortunately, some of these items, despite de Massoneau's assertion, cannot have been recovered from a single assemblage, typically because they lack a secure 5th century date (such as Nos. 162, 182, 194, and 223). Judging from the data available in the museum, the earrings disappeared before World War II (Petrenko 1978:9-30, pl. 19). Thus, the field of artifacts from the Berlin Museum's Classics section that may have derived from a single context is narrowed to include the following main objects: the silver phiale (No. 147); a gold pectoral (No. 148); three sets of gold appliqués for wooden vessels (Nos. 149–51); 14 gold chains from a single ornament (No. 152); and four sets of elements from gold drinking horns (Nos. 163 and 164). Based on their dates and stylistic characteristics, the sets of objects divided among the Berlin Museum's Classics section and the Penn Museum should be added to this collection of items: these include the two sets of earrings (No. 55; Nos. 154 and 155); two additional sets of gold appliqués for wooden vessels (Nos. 57 and 58); the complex gold pendant (No. 56); and 340 of the seven types of gold plaques (see below for a discussion of these) in the Maikop collection, which would have been sewn on garments or funerary materials placed in wealthy burials (Table 4).

Table 4. Plaque Types

	Deer	Griffin	Framed lion-griffin	Lotus-shaped	Cruci-form	Open-work	Buttons	TOTAL
Philadelphia—Penn Museum	5	4	4	2	23	6	305	349
Berlin—Museum of Berlin, Department of Classical Antiquities	14	10	8	19	40	218	842	1151
New York—Metropolitan Museum	4	4	–	–	10	12	–	30
TOTALS	23	18	12	21	73	236	1,147	1,530

When we examine the composition of this reconstructed assemblage, we cannot but be struck by what is lacking: while precious vessels and a few personal ornaments are evident, the important categories of horse trappings and weapons are completely omitted. The category of personal ornaments may be rounded out somewhat by the inclusion of four additional items from the Penn Museum collection that are stylistically and chronologically in keeping with the rest of the assemblage: a gold torque (No. 52); a gold seal-ring bearing the image of a siren (No. 53); a gold bracelet (No. 54); and a gold headdress ornament, likely for a woman or child (No. 51), that suggests the assemblage being reconstructed may derive from a woman's grave.

Unfortunately, the categories of horse trappings and weapons cannot be as easily supplied. Those horse trappings in the Maikop collection that do date to the 5th century BC are mostly simple in form and ornamentation, very different from the rich sets of harness components recovered from elite contexts, such as the Semibratnie kurgans, of this period. The 5th century BC weapons in the Maikop collection are similarly incongruous with our reconstructed assemblage, comprising only a few modest bronze arrowheads.

At this point we have advanced as far as is possible in reconstructing a potential assemblage from within the overall Maikop collection, and we are now ready to take the final step in the process, comparing the reconstruction with actual excavated assemblages of similar date and geographical origin.

The late 6th and early 5th century BC Ulskie kurgans, the 5th century BC Semibratnie kurgans, and the kurgans near Nymphaeum on the Kerch Peninsula offer a number of artifacts for comparison to those in the Maikop collection.

One artifact type found in the kurgans of each of these groups is the gold plaque, recovered from the rich Scythian burials where it was sewn on personal garments or funerary materials. There is a definite chronological progression in the quantity of such plaques found in burial contexts.

The best-preserved of the Semibratnie burials—kurgans No. 2, No. 4, and No. 6—are all attributed to tribal leaders and warriors based on the height of the kurgans, which reach up to 18 m, the rich horse burials accompanying them, and the abundant weaponry they contain. Precious objects are similarly abundant, taking the form of vessels and personal adornments, including torques, necklaces, bracelets, rings, and amulets (Artamonov 1966:36–39). There are still relatively few gold plaques. Kurgan No. 2, the best preserved, contained 171 plaques of 13 different types, while kurgan No. 6 contained 113 plaques of four types; even fewer plaques were recovered from the remaining kurgans (E. V. Vlasova, keeper in the Classical Department of the Hermitage, personal communication).

Among the Nymphaion kurgans, the situation is much the same. In kurgan No. 17, the best preserved among the group, 106 plaques of 13 different types were found, while in kurgan No. 24, another rich burial, only 16 plaques in total were recovered (Artamonov 1966:34–36, confirmed by Vlasova). Both these burials belonged to wealthy warriors. The women's burials at Nymphaeum provide a slightly different picture: kurgan No. 1, containing a female skeleton, was furnished with personal ornaments including a gold necklace, earrings, rings of electrum, and "not less than 84 golden plaques" (Vickers 1979:9; 2002:8); kurgan No. 4 similarly contained "not less than 49 plaques" (Vickers 1979:10; 2002:9). In several of the other women's burials, however, including kurgans No. 2, No. 3, and No. 5, no such plaques were recovered despite the presence of various other precious personal ornaments. This same situation is apparent in the late 6th and early 5th century BC Ulskie kurgans, in which gold plaques are more common than in the Archaic Kelermes kurgans but less common than in the later Semibratnie kurgans. The same regularity has been established in the Ukrainian steppes.

In total, of the 92 burials dating from the late 7th to 5th century BC, only 6 kurgans, primarily from the 5th century BC, have yielded gold plaques intended to be sewn on garments and these only in small numbers (Murzin 1984:12–46, app. 2, 114–23). Kurgan No. 371, from the necropolis on Berezan Island, is the chronological exception, being securely dated to the second half of the 6th century BC and containing over 30 gold button-shaped plaques (Kaposhina 1956:230, fig. 14).

It is only in the late 5th century BC that the situation changes and we begin to get burials containing large numbers of these gold plaques, used for such diverse purposes as headdress or cloth ornaments and decorations for funerary veils. A late 5th century BC kurgan excavated by Otroshchenko in the Zaporozhie region yielded hundreds of gold button-shaped plaques. Among Scythian burials from the turn of the 5th century BC, the greatest number of gold plaques is evidently from the side grave in kurgan No. 5 at Arkhangelskaia Sloboda: more than 500 gold plaques of eight different types were recovered (Leskov 1972:29–32, pls. 31–41). The undisturbed side grave of the royal Solokha kurgan yielded a comparatively paltry 300 gold plaques, similarly dated, belonging to nine types (Mantsevich 1987:63–68). In the Kuban, no single burial of this period has yielded anywhere near the 1,530 gold plaques, 1,147 of them button shaped, in the Maikop collection. Further, button-shaped plaques are relatively rare at 5th century BC sites in the Kuban.

In the 4th century BC, the situation changes somewhat: button-shaped plaques are practically unknown in the Kuban but appear in large quantities in royal Scythian burials in Ukraine, especially in those dating to the second half of the 4th century BC. The Chertomlyk kurgan is perhaps the most impressive example, yielding over 2,500 plaques of which over 1,000 are button shaped (Alekseev 1986:70, 71, 162). Notably, however, the fact that button-shaped plaques comprise only 40 percent of the total number of gold plaques even at Chertomlyk, whereas they comprise 75 percent of the total number of plaques in the Maikop collection (Table 4), suggests that the examples in the Maikop collection must be attributed to more than one archaeological context.

This conclusion is supported by a closer analysis of the gold plaques in the Maikop collection, which include 73 cruciform plaques. Of these 73 plaques, 43 are composed of rhombs, a sub-type known only from Scythian sites in the Ukrainian steppe; the remaining 30 are composed of squares, a sub-type known only from the Kuban (Mantsevich 1987:30–31). With the button-shaped plaques, then, the Maikop collection contains a total of 1,190 plaques that should be attributed to the Ukrainian steppes rather than the Kuban; it is only the remaining 340, divisible into 6 categories, that fit within the context of later 5th century BC sites in the Kuban, and it is consequently only these 340 plaques that may belong to the assemblage reconstructed above. An excavated assemblage from the early 4th century BC kurgan No. 5 at Uliap supports this possibility, as it contained approximately 300 plaques of 12 types (Leskov 1990:S.35, figs. 143–45, 147, 148, 156, 160, 172, 173, 179, 180; Korovina 1957:187).

The discussion of one specific type of artifact, the gold plaque, which likely formed part of this first reconstructed assemblage, has elucidated more than the mere composition of the assemblage, primarily precious vessels and personal adornments. It has also indicated a more specific date for the assemblage, the second half of the 5th century BC, and suggested its probable geographical origin in the Kuban. From this information we may deduce additional points. In the period and region specified, only the Semibratnie kurgans, where the local elite buried their dead during the 5th century BC formation of the Sind state (Anfimov 1987:91), have yielded artifacts culturally and chronologically comparable to our reconstructed assemblage.

Indeed, the primary difference between the Semibratnie artifacts and ours is in the number of Greek artifacts in evidence. The Semibratnie kurgans contained significant numbers of Greek objects, indicating close relationships with such cities of the Bosporan Kingdom as Hermonassa, Phanagoria, and Gorgippia. As reconstructed, however, our assemblage contains only one item, the silver phiale (No. 147), with Greek associations. Even if we add to our reconstruction the early 5th century BC skyphos (No. 20), this hardly improves the situation. We are left to conclude that our reconstructed assemblage cannot have come from a site near the Bosporan Kingdom or it would contain a significantly larger number of Greek artifacts. It is more likely to have come from the side grave of a large kurgan near Maikop, east of the Taman Peninsula, and probably comprised the funeral goods of a wealthy woman buried in the side grave of a large kurgan. In order to confirm the origin of the reconstructed association, specific tasks must be carried out: the police archives of the late 19th and early 20th century must be searched, with special attention paid to files pre-dating 1912. In that period, the looters must have discovered and plundered a previously untouched side burial. Unfortunately, we have found no information on legal excavations or on the looting of a rich kurgan published in the scientific journals or popular magazines of the time; it is only the police reports from the administrative districts between the Taman Peninsula and Maikop that often contained information on illegal excavations, confiscated finds, or records of purchases deposited in museums.

The suggested date for the assemblage, placed in the second half of the 5th century BC, is supported by the fact that the majority of the finds (340 plaques of six types) belong to this period; of the rest, some of the items belong to the first half of the 5th century BC and one type of plaque, the walking stag, finds its closest analogue in the early 4th century BC Uliap sanctuary No. 5 (Leskov 1990:S.33–36, fig. 156).

Having tentatively identified and attributed one 5th century BC assemblage from the many artifacts in the Maikop collection, we are left to consider an issue raised in the process, namely, the origin and association of the 1,190 plaques that are characteristic of 4th century BC Ukrainian steppes. It is important to recognize the chronological and geographical dichotomy shaping up here among the Scythian objects in the Maikop collection: many of those objects dated to the late 5th century derive from Maeotian sites in the Kuban, while many of the objects dating to the middle of the 4th century BC are more characteristic of Scythian sites from the steppes of southern Ukraine. Artifacts in the latter category, which may form a second archaeological assemblage, include the 1,190 gold plaques (see Table 4); a stag's head (No. 179), a sphinx figurine (No. 189), and a goat ornament (No. 190), intended for attachment to a diadem or headdress; two gold pins (No. 182); and a pair of gold earrings (No. 223), which find their closest analogue in the 4th century BC Chmyrev kurgan (Petrenko 1978:30, pls. 19, 12–13).

All of the artifacts proposed for the second assemblage find their closest analogues among the objects recovered from the richest of the 4th century BC royal Scythian kurgans, including Chertomlyk, Oguz, and Chmyrev (Rostovtzeff 1931c:367–68). It is interesting to note that Karapet, the dealer who sold the second part of the de Massoneau collection to the Berlin Museum in 1913, asserted that the objects he was selling derived from the Chmyrev kurgan. This derivation, mentioned in the Berlin Museum's inventory book, was later rejected by Rostovtzeff after he identified objects that were clearly from the Kuban.

It is only now, in the course of this study, that we recognize that both Karapet and Rostovtzeff were partially correct. The portion of the collection sold by Karapet, part of which was purchased by the Berlin Museum's Classical section and part of which ultimately came to Philadelphia, comprised artifacts deriving from at least two major assemblages differing in chronological and geographical origin. It seems increasingly probable that the second and later assemblage of objects, dating to the 4th century BC and deriving from a Scythian site in Ukraine, was indeed recovered from the Chmyrev kurgan as the dealer asserted in 1913.

Two richly furnished graves for men, with associated horse burials, have already been recovered from the Chmyrev kurgan; there could easily have been another side grave for a woman contained within it, looted prior to its excavation with the resulting artifacts ending up in the hands of de Massoneau. Future excavations will be able to clarify whether such a grave indeed existed and, if such a one is found, the most probable source for many of the artifacts in the Maikop collection will have been identified. In any case, it is certain that those artifacts tentatively attributed to this second assemblage, including the 1,190 gold plaques (see Table 4) and various articles of jewelry, well correspond to the funeral goods of a noble woman, such as might have been buried in one of the huge kurgans of the Scythian elite of this period. Independent of the exact number of valuable objects comprising the reconstructed association, there is no reason to doubt that a large number of artifacts recovered from two chronologically and geographically distinct sites were sold to one person. This would explain, among other things, why de Massoneau purchased over 1,000 identical button-shaped plaques of practically no value as display items. Other artifacts, both gold ornaments and bronze elements of horse equipment, are represented by one or two items each, sold in the quantity they had been discovered to the owner of the richest collection of archaeological objects from the monuments of southern Russia and Ukraine.

This reconstructed assemblage represents a vital contribution to our knowledge of a period hitherto defined primarily by the materials recovered from the Semibratnie and Uliap kurgans.

Having reconstructed two probable assemblages from among the 5th and 4th century BC artifacts in the Maikop collection, we are left with a significant number of remaining objects, primarily elements from horse trappings or equipment (see Table 3). A total of 76 inventory numbers belong to this latter category of artifact, with the vast majority (70 inventory numbers, 68 of bronze and 2 of bone) executed in the Kuban variant of the Scythian-Maeotian Animal Style. These objects are important not only because they are a significant addition to the corpus of Scythian and Maeotian horse equipment currently known but also because they represent a range of dates from the 5th to the 4th century BC and thus offer us the opportunity to examine the manner in which Scythian and Maeotian art, and the Animal Style in particular, developed over time.

Previous scholarship on the subject of the Scythian Animal Style and relevant excavations in the Kuban have fortunately laid the groundwork for this study: these include E. V. Perevodchikova's doctoral dissertation (1980b); large-scale excavations headed by the author at the Uliap complex in the 1980s; Nekhaev's (1987) excavations of the same period near Kuzhorskaia; and Erlikh's work (2002) at sites near Tenginskaia village.

The majority of artifacts in the Animal Style were manufactured from gold or bronze, with gold used primarily for flat and stamped objects and bronze used primarily for cast items. The most popular technique for objects in the latter category was lost-wax casting, which allowed the production of three-dimensional pieces. Stamped gold artifacts typically served as personal ornaments, sewn on leather or textiles, and much less rarely used as appliqués for wooden vessels. From as early as the Archaic Scythian period (the Kelermes kurgans, as well as the Melgunovskiy kurgan and the kurgan near Kostromskaia village), burials of the Scythian nobility contained large casements designed for the adornment of such items as a wooden shield, sword sheath, quiver, and gorytos. But in the 5th and 4th century BC Scythian-Maeotian sites in the Kuban, not a single casement of this type has been reported. Cast bronze objects, on the other hand, typically served as elements of horse equipment—cheekpieces, frontlets, noseband ornaments, harness plaques, and various ornaments.

In attempting to trace the manner in which the Scythian-Maeotian Animal Style changed over different periods, preliminary observations indicate that developments did not correspond exactly with the current historical periodization. While the Archaic Scythian period was already characterized by a well-developed Animal Style, strongly influenced by Iranian, Urartian, and Ionian elements, the composition of the Maikop collection suggests that there are at least three stylistically different groups of artifacts discernible at 5th and 4th century BC sites in the Kuban, with the middle group serving as a transitional type. As seen in Table 2, artifacts from the 4th century BC far outnumber those from the turn of the 5th or 4th century BC. This trend is magnified when we look specifically at elements of horse equipment (see Table 3), which are the most likely to be executed wholly in the Animal Style.

Previous research, specifically that carried out by Perevodchikova, has already elaborated two separate groups in the Scythian Animal Style aside from the Archaic type found at 7th to 6th century BC sites: the Semibratniy type of the 5th century BC, named for the Semibratnie kurgans and characterized especially by the realistic rendering of animals on horse harnesses and other equipment, and the Elizavetinskaia type, named for the kurgans discovered in that village and characterized especially by the wide application of chasing on flat details of horse equipment (Perevodchikova 1980b; 1984:5–15; 1987:44–58).

There are further differences between the Semibratnie and Elizavetinskaia types than outlined above. Artifacts in the former style, exemplified by the realistically sculptured frontlets in the Maikop collection (No. 246), are smoothly shaped, lacking major features typical of the earlier Kelermes phase, an archaic tradition that survives in some monuments of the 5th century BC Scythian Animal Style from the Ukrainian steppe (Mozolevskiy 1980:fig. 83, 11–13). Chasing is not yet apparent; instead, details of the images are rendered in relief. Numerous harness plaques of this period, manufactured in the same style, are known from Semibratniy kurgan No. 4 and Ulskiy kurgan No. 11 (Maslenitsina 1993:65, figs. 1, 3, 7), as well as from the Maikop collection (No. 285). Artifacts in the latter style, aside from the frequent use of chasing, also indicate the development of new forms: S-shaped cheekpieces decorated with sculptured animals or animal parts disappear, superseded by gamma-shaped cheekpieces decorated at one end with the image of an animal's head or claws, typically executed in openwork with details in chasing. Cheekpieces bent at a right angle had already appeared in the 5th century BC (they are known from the Semibratnie kurgans, Ulskiy kurgan No. 11, the coeval Nymphaion kurgans near

Kerch from the Ukrainian steppes, among others), but these earlier examples were not ornamented.

Early scholarship on the subject also noted that the Semibratniy Animal Style was influenced by features from Achaemenid art (Rostovtzeff 1922; Artamonov 1966:81; Perevodchikova 1987:48), while the Elizavetinskaia type was influenced by Colkhido-Koban art, specifically by its ornamentation style. In Colkhido-Koban art, dating from the late 2nd to early 1st millennium BC, borders were rendered in thin, often double lines, with additional hatching in the main field. Traits of the Koban culture are identifiable in the pre-Scythian and Archaic Scythian periods in the Northwestern Caucasus and are especially apparent in the second half of the 4th century BC, the period to which the Elizavetinskie kurgans date. Materials of the Elizavetinskaia type of the Animal Style have been recovered by Erlikh (2002:7–16) from Maeotian sites near the village of Tenginskaia, by Veselovsky (*OAK* for 1903:75, figs. 139–53), from the kurgans near Voronezhskaia, and from the kurgans near Kuzhorskaia (Nekhaev 1987:82ff., Nos. 9, 10, 15, 21–25); they are also known from the Maikop collection (see Nos. 257, 258, 295, and 296).

The number of differences that developed between the Animal Style as seen at Semibratnie and as seen at Elizavetinskaia may seem odd, given that there is a separation of only a century between the two sites. This intervening span, however, saw a number of historical developments: the extent of interaction between the Greeks and their barbaric neighbors rapidly expanded all over the northern shores of the Black Sea; classical production and trade centers shifted from Olbia to the Crimean and Taman peninsulas; the Achaemenid Empire grew in power and had a marked influence on the Kuban basin; and the Bosporan Kingdom appeared and developed a strong relationship with the Sindo-Maeotian sites of the Northwestern Caucasus. The importance of this last development is evident at the early 4th century BC site of Uliap, where five sanctuaries and two cemeteries (containing some 300 burials in total) have yielded numerous Greek imports, including vessels of precious metal, two panathenaic amphorae, a set of Greek table pottery near unique in its variety, and various gold ornaments (Leskov 1990). Evidently, Greek influence extended also to Maeotian pottery: in the Uliap collection alone there are at least ten types of vessels clearly imitating Greek models (Beglova 1995:12).

Given the distance of the sites of the middle of the Kuban from the urban centers of the Bosporan Kingdom and the Black Sea shore, it seems clear that the influence of the Bosporan Kingdom gradually extended from the late 5th century BC until it reached sites far beyond its own territory. The marked Iranian influence in the 5th century BC Kuban, indicated by widespread Achaemenid artifacts (Perevodchikova 1994:130ff.), inevitably had an effect on the Maeotians as well, especially given the close relations between the Bosporan Kingdom and the Achaemenid Empire in the 4th century BC. A final development should be noted here: in the early 4th century, cultural contacts with the tribes of the Koban culture which were settled in the mountains and piedmont region of the central Caucasus are vividly reflected in the depiction of human representations and the use of chasing to render details. The century-long span between the Semibratnie kurgans and those at Elizavetinskaia, given the range of influences to which it was subject, was thus quite sufficient to induce the development of the Animal Style from its manifestation in the Semibratnie artifacts to that evident in the Elizavetinskie artifacts.

The extensive changes that occurred between the two periods, however, are such that a transitional period seems warranted. And indeed, this is what we find in the archaeological record. A comparison of the finds from Uliap with those of the earlier Semibratnie and the later Elizavetinskaia Animal Styles allows us to determine the transitional role of the Uliap material in the typological sequence. The combination of sculpted images with incised or chased detailing is typical of Uliap cheekpieces (Leskov 1990:cat. nos. 63–68, 121–24, fig. 68–79). One example, a pair of cheekpieces from Uliap kurgan No. 5, has seahorse terminals with chased detail on their crests (Leskov 1990:cat. no. 121, fig. 74–79). Similarly, both S-shaped and gamma-shaped cheekpieces are known from the site: four pairs of the former, four pairs of the latter (these have chased detail), and one pair of straight cheekpieces with panther's head terminals at one end and an openwork oval at the other, possibly representing the panther's rear (Leskov 1990:cat. no. 122, fig. 75).

The established chronology of the Animal Style in the Scythian period is thus marked by three major points of development, beginning with the Semibratnie kurgans (Nos. 2, 4, and 5), dated between the second and third quarter of the 5th century BC (Artamonov 1966:36ff.), continuing to the Uliap kurgans with their transitional material, dated from the turn of the 5th century BC to the first decades of the 4th century BC (Leskov 1990:28ff.), and ending with the Elizavetinskie kurgans, dated, along with the kurgans at Voronezhskaia and Kuzhorskaia, to the 4th century BC (Artamonov 1966:39ff.). The dating of this latter group was aided by Erlikh's well-reasoned attribution of the Tenginskaia sanctuary to the second half of the 4th century BC (Erlikh 2002:14–15). The rarity of artifacts from the Uliap period, with examples primarily existing in the State Hermitage collections (Perevodchikova 1984:5–15, figs. 2–5), underlines the importance of their existence in the Maikop collection (Nos. 25, 26, 158, 253, 254, 255, 260, 289, 291, 292, 294, and 299). The fact that the Maikop collection, as published here, indeed contains examples of all three types noted above makes it a most significant source for the study of the Animal Style specifically.

Interestingly, as in the Maikop collection (Table 2), the artifacts from the 4th century BC, the period of the Elizavetinskie kurgans, are much more numerous than those of the 5th century BC, the period of the Semibratnie kurgans, and the turn of the 5th century BC, the period of the Uliap kurgans. The quantitative domination of Animal Style artifacts from the 4th century BC in the Kuban forces our attention to other regions where Scythian artifacts are also found: in the lower and middle Don River region, the Ukrainian forest-steppe, and southwestern Ukraine and Moldova 4th century BC sites have not yielded many Scythian Animal Style artifacts.

While undecorated 4th century BC bronze cheekpieces are known from the very beginning of the 4th century BC in the North Pontic steppes (Solokha) (Mantsevich 1987:108ff., cat. nos. 95, 106, 121, 133), finds from later 4th century BC Scythian royal kurgans in that region, including Chertomlyk, Oguz, and Melitopol, indicate the ultimate dominance of the utilitarian horse harness in Scythia. Modest iron bits and cheekpieces are combined with bronze frontlets shaped like sculpted animal heads and similarly modest flat harness details, often with bird's heads (beaks pointing down). The other bridle components are rings and finials. Only the richest kurgans, such as Oguz and Chmyrev, contained horse burials furnished with iron bits and cheekpieces and accompanied by gold and silver frontlets and harness plaques of the same shape as bronze examples.

The variety of shapes and lavish decoration of the pieces of horse equipment from Kuban sites of the second half of the 4th century BC should be stressed; this elaboration dates back to at least the 5th century BC, the period of the Semibratnie kurgans, when horse equipment from the Kuban is visibly richer than that from Scythia proper or from the Ukrainian forest-steppe (Ilinskaia 1968:110ff.; Kovpanenko, Bessonova, and Skoryi 1989:93ff., figs. 26–29).

As time passed, though this equipment was gradually simplified, it always retained a varied and spectacular form, which may explain the spread of this type of equipment among regions both near and far. Some items found in the North Pontic steppes are direct imports from Kuban to the Ukrainian steppes (Dniepropetrovsk region). One example, a pair of gamma-shaped cheekpieces with an openwork plaque decorated with animal heads at one end (Khanenko and Khanenko 1900:pl. XLII, 339, 342), has an analogue, recovered from the Taman Peninsula, in the collection published here (No. 258). The style and char-

acter of the ornament on these cheekpieces is typical of later 4th century BC Maeotian art. A bronze frontlet, also from this complex and generously decorated with etched detail, similarly has 4th century BC analogues from the Kuban region (Erlikh 2004:1, fig. 7), as does a rich assemblage of horse equipment, including a pair of bronze cheekpieces, seven harness plaques, and a pair of pendants (Khanenko and Khanenko 1900:pl. XLI, 334), that find comparanda among artifacts from Uliap (Leskov 1990:cat. no. 217, fig. 81), Maikop (Moshinsky 2003:36, No. 62, and the territory of Kabardino-Balkaria (Vinogradov 1972:fig. 4, 2).

Two harness plaques from the Maikop collection in the form of openwork stag heads (Nos. 171 and 218) are also similar in form to the plaques from the assemblage, with additional comparanda from the Voronezhskaie and Karagodeuashkh (Er-

Cheekpiece and frontlet in the Kuban style from the Ukrainian steppe, near Dniepropetrovsk (from Khanenko and Khanenko 1900:pl. XLII, 339, 342).

Set of horse trappings in the Kuban style from the Ukrainian steppe, near Dniepropetrovsk (from Khanenko and Khanenko 1900:pl. XLI, 334).

likh 2002:12–14, fig. 7.6; Zhuravlev 2002:no. 484) kurgans. The artifacts from the Dniepropetrovsk assemblage also support the identification of three items from the Maikop collection (Nos. 261 and 262) as cheekpiece fragments from the Kuban region.

Before leaving the subject of horse equipment, we should note the existence of the bronze cone-shaped frontlet ornaments discovered by Beglova near Tenginskaia. These items, preserved in their original context (hanging from the frontlet and breastplate), date to the 2nd century BC (Beglova 2002:299–304, fig. 6). Based on these dates, we may speculate that horse harnesses were decorated with bells from the Archaic period to the 4th century BC, but that after this date, the bells were superseded by cone-shaped ornaments. No such ornaments appear among the horse equipment typical of 4th century BC Ukrainian steppe and forest-steppe sites.

When the bronze artifacts in the Scythian Animal Style in the Kuban are compared with those of the Ukrainian steppe, it becomes clear that the Kuban objects are both more typologically varied and more numerous. Further, while there are Kuban-type artifacts at Crimean sites, especially those in the east, the reverse is not true: objects characteristic of the Ukrainian steppe are not known in the Kuban in the 5th to 4th century BC. Clear evidence of contact between the Ukrainian forest-steppe and the Kuban is also lacking, with Scythian materials not reaching the area west of the Don River; this is in contrast to the situation during the pre-Scythian period (8th to 7th century BC), when Novocherkassk horse equipment was widely known at Ukrainian sites, and the Scythian Archaic period, when the material culture of Ukraine and the Kuban was comparable.

The relationship between the Don River tribes and the Kuban peoples developed along quite different lines, as indicated by the recovered material culture: instead of forming a specific local style, the bronze harness pieces in the Scythian Animal Style from lower Don River sites appear to combine traits of artifacts typical of the Kuban and the Dniepr River basin (Perevodchikova 2000:236). Although neither the Kuban nor Don River styles are clearly predominant, the simple presence of Kuban-style artifacts in this region indicates the influence of the Kuban tribes over their western neighbors.

Goncharova (2000:51–61), who examined the Scythian Animal Style artifacts from the forest-steppe regions of the Don basin, persuasively argued ideas previously suggested by Shkurko (1976:100). She asserted that the local variant of the Scythian Animal Style was strongly influenced by art typical of 5th century BC Dniepr forest-steppe sites, mainly those on the left bank of the river. The Animal Style artifacts from 4th century BC sites of the middle Don are treated separately and identified as bearing a striking resemblance to the artistic traditions of the western Urals, thus having a stable relationship with the local Animal Style and zoomorphic art of the Kama region. While Goncharova stresses the strong cultural influence of Kuban art, related to the artistic traditions of Achaemenid Iran that is characteristic of the Don forest-steppe region, she considers the contact between the forest-steppe tribes of the Don and those of the lower Don insignificant despite the fact that the northern peoples clearly influenced those of the south. This assumption is of primary importance in the process of reconstructing the routes by which Kuban artifacts and manufacturing techniques were disseminated to the Don River's forest-steppe region. The simplest course, from the Kuban to its closest neighbors of the lower Don and thence upstream to the forest-steppe region, must be ruled out on the basis of the archaeological evidence that Scythian Animal Style artifacts clearly traveled along the Don River in the opposite direction, from north to south. Instead, we must look to the Volga region. The fact that the Volga's western bend almost touches the eastern bend of the Don River, as well as the longstanding contact between the peoples of the steppes of Eastern Europe, suggests this region was important to the dissemination of the Scythian Animal Style.

In his monograph on the Sauromatians Smirnov synthesized the local Animal Style materials and convincingly demonstrated that the Animal Style typical of the Volga Sauromatians was strongly influenced by the Scythian art of the North Pontic zone and of the Northern Caucasus (Smirnov 1964:243). Underlining the fact that already by the 6th century BC the Animal Style of the Volga River region differed from that of the eastern Urals, he noted that the difference between these two regions became even more marked in the 5th century BC, when the Volga style was distinguished by original imagery and stylistic features.

Chezhina further developed this theme in his investigation of the stylistic characteristics of the Animal Style of the Volga and eastern Ural steppes, concluding that the differences in material culture were so substantial as to suggest an ethnic difference between the Sauromatian tribes of the two regions (Chezhina 1983:27, 28). Investigation of the burial rites and artifact assemblages of the two tribes of the lower Volga River region and the southern Urals supports the existence of two different archaeological cultures and their local variants (Ochir-Goriaeva 1987; 1988). Given this data, it is interesting that Zhelezchikov (1997) supported the idea that the population of the southern Urals influenced the lower Volga tribes.

The collection of Scythian artifacts from the Khosheutovskiy assemblage on the lower Volga River, mainly 5th century BC bridle equipment, is very pertinent to this discussion; in the publication of the material the finds were compared with materials from the North

Pontic zone, the middle Don River region, the Northern Caucasus, and the southern Urals. The authors concluded that the overall association, dating to the second quarter of the 5th century BC, and various well-known sites of the late 6th and early 5th century BC, indicate close contact between the culture of the lower Volga nomads and their neighbors to the east and west. While noting the obvious cultural influence of the tribes of the southern Urals and their eastern neighbors, the authors further stressed the important cultural influences of the west and southwest, the North Pontic zone and the Kuban basin (Dvornichenko and Ochir-Goriaeva 1997:99–115). Ochir-Goriaeva (2001:129–33) noted the striking similarity between some harness plaques from Khosheutovskiy and the Maikop region, while Perevodchikova (2000:231–37) and Dvornichenko (2000:153–56) published additional parallels.

These works are primarily a response to the published abstracts of a lecture by Korolkova (1998:79–80), in which she made some important observations on the formation of the Kuban Animal Style under the influence of the nomads of the southern Urals and the tribes living east of them. These observations were published as a detailed article (Korolkova 2001:91–111), which was the first attempt, after Perevodchikova's 1980 dissertation on the Kuban variant of the Scythian Animal Style and her later publications, to develop a new approach to the study of the Kuban material.

The data analyzed by Korolkova is essentially identical to that examined by Perevodchikova, though some material from the Uliap kurgans and Kuzhorskaia has been added. The new materials published in this collection and those recovered by Erlikh in his investigations near the village of Tenginskaia on the left bank of the Kuban are not incorporated into those studies. As a result, Korolkova's conclusion that 5th to 4th century BC Animal Style art, both that of the lower Volga and that of the Kuban, developed under the dominant eastern influence of the southern Urals, western Kazakhstan, and southern Siberia (Korolkova 2001:104, 110) relies on an untenably small data set. She includes a total of nine tables illustrating objects in the Animal Style, with two of these referring to Sarmatian artifacts and the remaining seven treating a total of only 78 objects, 21 of which are from the Kuban (2 from the 5th century BC and 19 from the 4th century BC). Of the remaining artifacts she discusses, 3 are from the central Caucasian piedmont, 2 are from the eastern Caucasian piedmont, 6 are from the lower Volga River region, and 40+ derive from the eastern regions extending from the southern Urals to Mongolia and Ordos.

In addition to the immense geographical range covered by the artifacts Korolkova discusses, there is also a broad chronological range: those materials from the eastern zone date between the 7th and 4th century BC while those from the Kuban and eastern Caucasus are primarily of the Elizavetinskaia type, belonging to the later 4th century BC. Given the limited nature of the data set, the issue of the Animal Style of the Late Bronze Age Koban culture becomes pertinent. Korolkova rejects its role in the formation of the Kuban variant of the Scythian Animal Style, pointing to analogues in the southern Urals of the S-shaped harness plaque with animal-head terminals (2001:figs. 6, 10, 12). The S-shaped harness plaque is a unique artifact: it has no counterparts in the Kuban or North Pontic zone, is not typical of the Scythian Animal Style, and should be regarded as an import or as a locally manufactured artifact imitating a non-local model.

As for the analogues suggested by Korolkova, these do not bear up to scrutiny: the openwork form and abundant engraving of the gold example from the Filippovka kurgan, features characteristic of the Filippovka artifacts if not of the Animal Style of the southern Urals in general (Meliukova and Abramova 1989:tables 66, 67), distinguish it from the S-shaped harness plaque of the Kuban. In the late 2nd and early 1st millennia, however, Koban engravings on bronze axes and brooches commonly depict animals in S-shaped positions with mouths open and legs bent and crossed (Tekhov 1976:153–63, fig. 1). This type of representation continued into the Scythian period, when this type of image appeared on various bronze artifacts (Domanskiy 1984:table 106, A19, B16). Indeed, the best analogues to Korolkova's S-shaped harness plaque from the Kuban are the flat openwork plaques depicting S-shaped animals with long, bent necks, heads turned backward, and raised hindquarters leading into bent and crossed legs that appear during this period. The connection between Korolkova's Kuban example and the Koban bronzes is finalized by the former's interior decoration: the incisions, hatched lines, and dots are characteristic of the Koban bronzes, usually following the outline of the objects.

In discussing the Kobano-Scythian relationship, which is in fact vividly reflected in artifacts in the Scythian Animal Style, it should be noted that specialists in Caucasian and Scythian archaeology had by the 1930s already identified the multilateral nature of the relationship between the Scythians of the steppe and the inhabitants of the Caucasus mountains, focusing especially on the territories in this latter region that were inhabited by the Koban tribes. These territories were examined especially in relation to the Scythians' Near Eastern campaigns, as described by Herodotus (Krupnov 1960:54–75, fig. 4). In studying the Kuban basin, the focus was quite different.

Beginning in the Late Bronze Age and continuing into the pre-Scythian period, the peoples of the North Pontic steppe and those of the Kuban basin were closely interrelated thanks to favorable geographic and topographic conditions. The relations between the nomadic migrants and the local tribes in other geographic regions of the Northern Caucasus were quite different. This situation is reflected in the material culture of the Scythians, the Maeotians, and the bearers of the Koban culture. This material culture also reflects both the century-long relationship of the Pontic Scythians and Kuban Maeotians with the Classical Greek colonies, which produced numerous objects in the Scythian Animal Style to the order of the barbarian nobility, and the strong influence of Achaemenid Iran. This latter influence, which is clearly apparent in Central Asia, was disseminated through that region to the Altai and the southern Urals; it is the Achaemenid features that bind Kuban art with that of these regions (Marsadolov 1984:30–37; Perevodchikova 1994:131–35, 169). Notably, Greek art did not influence the art of the tribes in the Caucasus mountains or that of the nomads wandering the Uralian and Central Asiatic steppes in the same way. It is these factors that are responsible for the difference between the archaeological materials at Scythian sites in the Kuban and those in the central and eastern Caucasian piedmont and which preclude the consideration of the North Caucasian materials in the manner attempted by Korolkova (1998:99). The conclusions drawn on the basis of the eastern and Central Caucasus (Vinogradov 1976:147–52; Maslov and Ochir-Goryaeva 1997:62–74) should not be extrapolated to the Kuban.

In considering the Scythian Animal Style of the central and eastern Caucasian piedmont in the Scythian period, the work of Maslov and Ochir-Goryaeva is pertinent. They have proven that pottery from the central Caucasian piedmont was delivered to the steppes of the Volga-Don interfluve and to the lower Volga (Maslov and Ochir-Goryaeva 1997:66) but that Maeotian pottery was not known there. The collection of Animal Style artifacts in the piedmont is in keeping with its geographical position and includes four types of objects: (1) finds characteristic of the Koban Animal Style (a majority), (2) artifacts typical of the Sauromatian art of the lower Volga and the regions east of it, (3) generally Scythian artifacts, and (4) objects typical of the Kuban. On the basis of this data, we may conclude that local tribes of the Scythian period did not create any original variants of the Animal Style. The needs of the nomads in the piedmont were met instead by imported artifacts, with those of Volga-Ural Sauromatian origin far outnumbering those from the Kuban. Given that this inequity is exacerbated the farther a site is from the Kuban, with Kuban-type artifacts still appearing in the central Caucasian piedmont but only influencing manufactured items further east, geographical factors are clearly at work here.

In attempting to support her argument that the nomads of the southern Urals strongly influenced the Kuban Animal Style of the 5th to 4th century BC, Korolkova (1998b:91) presents the late 7th to 6th century BC Kuban materials as being unrelated to those of the later period. The only support she offers for this odd division is a mention of the work of Perevodchikova. But Perevodchikova, while noting the differences between the Kuban materials of the two periods, interprets these differences only as an indication of differing chronological origins. This is hardly remarkable given that the chronological gap separating Archaic Scythian sites such as Kelermes from Classical Scythian sites such as the Semibratnie kurgans spans at least a century and that the art of the earlier period was created under the direct influence of Near Eastern art, where the Scythians had been campaigning, while the art of the later period demonstrates clear Greek and Achaemenid influences. What Korolkova overlooked in her analysis is the group of Animal Style artifacts from the Ulskie kurgans, which date between the Kelermes and Semibratnie artifacts and connect the two, and Grach's analysis of some artifacts from the Semibratnie kurgans, which also connected the art of the two periods (Grach 1984:105–7). Just as it would be difficult to identify the cultural unity of the Semibratnie and Elizavetinskie materials without being aware of the transitional Uliap materials (and the coeval material in the Maikop collection), the relationship between the Kelermes and Semibratnie artifacts cannot be determined without taking into account the intervening Ulskie material.

The earlier frontlets, as known from Uliap kurgan No. 5 and Semibratniy kurgan No. 3 (Leskov 1990:no. 120, fig. 80; Artamonov 1966:39, fig. 74), are combined with zoomorphic images while the later examples, as found at Gyenos and the necropolis of the hillfort Tenginskaia II (Erlikh 2004:figs. 7, 1, 6, 8, 9), only bear volute decoration. Judging from this, the nose plates from the village of Gurijskaya are considered early ones (Erlikh 2004:fig. 7, 2, 5).

The 5th century BC Novocherkassk finial, though lacking the engraved decoration typical of the 4th century BC Kuban Animal Style, is thus closest in form to the early 4th century BC Kuban frontlets. In addition to the 4th century BC frontlets from the Kuban region discussed here, we must also note the existence in this period of a number of finials in the form of short, cylindrical sockets topped with stag heads. Some of these heads sprout antlers in the form of predatory heads on long necks, as known from Gyenos, and others have antlers in the form of volutes of varying shapes and sizes, as known from the Anap kurgan (Erlikh 2004:figs. 5, 7, 8, 11). These late examples clearly continue a form of finial that originated as early as the Archaic period and was first noted in the Kelermes kurgans.

In the 4th century BC, from sites of the Elizavetinskaia type as well, we find openwork plaques serving as ends on gamma-shaped cheekpieces. One plaque of this type, engraved with a profile stag's head with antlers running vertically, is compared by Korolkova to images of stags' heads with vertical antlers from objects found in the vast territory between the lower Volga and Ordos, a comparison that serves as the basis for her conclusion about the south Siberian and eastern Uralian origins of the Kuban Animal Style (Korolkova 2001:107, fig. 7).

All of Korolkova's proposed comparanda, however, pre-date the examples of Elizavetinskaia type, which belong to the second half of the 4th century BC. Further, engraved representations of stags' heads are widespread on the bronze axes and belt buckles of the 9th to 7th century BC Koban culture (Domanskiy 1984:figs. 5, 11, 16, tables VI, VII), a closer and far more likely source of inspiration for these objects specifically and for the Kuban variant of the Scythian Animal Style in general. Korolkova makes a similar leap in her identification of a Central Asian origin for swastika-shaped plaques with zoomorphic ornament and in her suggested chronology for them of the 7th to the 6th century BC (Korolkova 2001:100). This statement is all the more surprising given that two years earlier, she had more reasonably noted that zoomorphic swastikas were, to an extent, a universal motif, with their appearance at Koban sites being unrelated to the artistic traditions of the Eurasian nomads (Korolkova 1999:292). In the Kuban, where the motif is known prior to the 7th century BC, a relationship with the Iranian world cannot be ruled out (Sazonov 1997:86–90; Kantorovich and Erlikh 2006:no. 37), but the motif itself is far more likely to have been borrowed from the Koban culture.

Finally we should discuss the image of the eagle-headed griffin. Noting the appearance of this figure in the North Pontic zone from the late 6th century BC and its wide dissemination throughout that same region in the 5th century BC, Korolkova (1998b:102) asserts that coeval artifacts from West Kazakhstan find close analogues among the sewn-on gold plaques from 4th century BC sites in the Kuban. On this point it should be emphasized that the Ulskie kurgans of the late 6th and early 5th century BC have yielded over 30 iron cheekpieces with similar griffin-head terminals, all undoubtedly of local production (Leskov 1990:S.176, nos. 42, 43). To this same period belong numerous bronze harness plaques in the form of eagle-headed griffins and identically ornamented bronze cheekpieces and iron buckles. All derive from the Kuban or from closely related regions such as the Kerch Peninsula of Novorossiysk (Leskov 1990:184; Malyshev and Ravich 2001:104, figs. 1, 1–2, 2.1, 3, 1; Artamonov 1966:tables 91, 92, 115).

Given the popularity of this image in the 5th century BC, its extensive use in the 4th century BC—when it is known from Uliap, Kuzhorskaia, Elizavetinskaia, Voronezhskaia, and other sites—seems only reasonable (Leskov 1990:figs. 80, 81, 145, 147, 149, 156, 169; Korovina 1957:184, fig. 9, 5; Erlikh 2002:12ff., fig. 4, 7). The Kuban Animal Style of the 4th century BC includes in its repertoire images of eagle-headed griffins accompanied by the talons of predatory birds. This combination is also known from the 5th century BC, when circular talons are set on the ends of S-shaped or straight cheekpieces (Perevodchikova 1994:fig. 24, 1), and from the early 4th century BC, when comparable cheekpieces are adorned with three to four elongated talons bent to form circles or arches (Leskov 1990:figs. 68, 69).

In considering the nature of the contacts between the peoples of the Don, Kuban, Volga, and south Ural steppes, we cannot limit ourselves solely to a comparative analysis of the surviving art. Even given the similarity between specific items of art from territories so far apart as the Kuban and the southern Urals is no solid basis on which to propose the "penetration of certain groups of Eurasian nomads from the East to the North Caucasian piedmont" (Korolkova 1998b:99). A comparative analysis of a series of items from the Kuban and lower Volga with finds from other regions of the Eurasian steppes (Perevodchikova 2000:231–37), combined with the factors discussed above, suggests the existence of cultural relationships and mutual influence between at least some of the regions noted. While the influence of the Kuban variant of the Scythian Animal Style on the development of art in the Don and lower Volga regions in the 5th and 4th century BC is perhaps the most apparent, the nature of the relationship between the Kuban and the southern Urals is much less clear. These regions are much farther apart and could have had only indirect contact via the lower Volga region.

As early as the 1950s, Iessen discussed the contact between the southern Urals, Iran, and Asia Minor via the Caucasus from the 7th to 3rd century BC (the Scythian period). A set of Novocherkassk-type bronze arrowheads included in the burial of a warrior found in the lower Volga region (Sergatskov 1991:240–44) may indicate the route Archaic Scythian artifacts traveled, moving northward to the Volga and Kama interfluve (Kazan region) before heading east to the southern Urals. The material culture finds recovered from the Kazan region, comprising numerous pieces of weaponry and horse harness components typical of the early Scythians combined with fragments of bronze Colkhido-Koban and Urartian belts, are interpreted by Pogrebova and Raevsky (1992:215) as indicating the migration of a specific population. Herodotus (IV, 22) includes the story of a population group on a raid to the north before the turn of the 7th to 6th century BC in his discussion of the separatist Scythians.

In the southern Urals, an assemblage from the Bolshoy Gumarovsky kurgan that belonged to a rich warrior also yielded a set of bow equipment including 24 bronze arrowheads of the Novocherkassk type. A primitive stele recovered from the mound, decorated with the schematic representation of a warrior (Ismagilov 1988), is of a type known from across the Eurasian steppes from Mongolia in the east to Bulgaria in the west. Dated between the 8th and 7th century BC, such stelae are typically referred to as "stag stones," a reference to the frequent depictions of stags on the Asiatic examples. Chlenova, who has extensively studied and published on these monuments, notes interesting comparanda for the images on the stelae among the artifacts from the Kuban, where some of the earliest monuments of this type are known (Chlenova 1999:311–15, figs. 3–5). On the basis of her comparative studies, she has concluded that these stelae, especially those in the European steppes, are related to tribes with Novocherkassk-type material culture: ethnically, these people would have been Cimmerians (Chlenova 2004:220–31, figs. 5–7, 941; 1984). The example from the Bolshoy Gumarovsky kurgan is attributed to the "general Eurasian type," known further east in the Asian steppes, and apparently confirms Chlenova's suggestion that the movement of such stelae eastward from the North Caucasian piedmont is associated with the migration of 7th century BC nomadic tribes. Pogrebova and Raevsky (1992:240, n. 34) concur in this, interpreting the Bolshoy Gumarovsky discovery as an indicator of the settling of Caucasian bearers of the Early Scythian material culture in the north. Though much had changed in the lives of the East European steppe tribes by the 5th century BC, the relationships between the Kuban and the southern Urals continued despite the distance between the regions. The work of Kantorovich is of especial importance in supporting this statement. In his analysis of the "elk-goat," often depicted on gold and bronze objects of varying function, Kantorovich (2003, 2:27–29) persuasively argued that the image was created in the art of the Scythian Archaic period in the Kuban, where it was eventually transformed into a stag-goat. He also noted the existence of a pair of harness plaques in Filippovka kurgan No. 3 (south Urals) representing this stag-goat (though I prefer to consider these plaques as deer heads with bent horns ending in griffin heads). Kantorovich also associated the remainder of the assemblage from that kurgan with the Kuban.

According to the Metropolitan Museum's exhibition catalogue (Aruz 2000:nos. 102, 103), the assemblage recovered from Filippovka kurgan No. 3 comprised two pairs of gamma-shaped bronze cheekpieces with chased detail, one pair with an openwork plaque in the form of a tridactylous foot of a bird of prey and the other with three griffin heads on long necks biting each other, with analogues known from Kuzhorskaia village near Maikop (Leskov and Lapushnian 1987:nos. 22, 24) and from the Elizavetinskie kurgans (Perevodchikova 1984:fig. 3). The assemblage also included a pair of plaques in the form of stag heads, each with antlers in the form of four stylized griffin heads set in a row along the outline of the head, undoubtedly of the Kuban type, which was transmitted to Kabardino-Balkaria and the Ukrainian steppe up to Dniepropetrovsk (Aruz 2000:no.

104, though the artifacts are printed upside down); four hemispherical harness plaques bearing griffin heads on bent necks that, though they have no known analogues in the Kuban, were clearly related to that region through their use of the eagle-headed griffin; a bronze frontlet formed from an openwork plaque representing a recumbent stag, strongly resembling a representation from the Kostromskaia assemblage and from the Elizavetinskie kurgans (Perevodchikova 1994:fig. 25, 2) in the rendering of the space between its antlers and neck and between its stomach and leg, as well as in its outstretched neck and head, which sprouts antlers comprising a griffin's head; and a harness plaque in the form of a profile wolf's head with bared teeth, with comparanda known not only from the Elizavetinskie kurgans and Maikop region but also from the Maikop collection (Nos. 37, 214, 215, 295) that is distinguished by its larger size and the lack of detailing at the base of its jaw.

The overall assemblage recovered from Filippovka kurgan No. 3 is very different from those of the remaining Filippovka kurgans. Kantorovich (2003:29) is undoubtedly correct in stressing that the artifacts from kurgan No. 3 are unrelated to the local figurative tradition. The objects are clearly of Kuban character whether they were imported from the Kuban or produced locally by apprentices of Kuban craftsmen, with the latter possibility being suggested by the resemblance of the wolf's head plaque to Ananyino art and the related Sauromatian style of the south Urals. This information is notably omitted from Korolkova's work, though it clearly influenced her conclusions.

It is hoped that this brief review of the archaeological materials from and research on the interactions of the tribes inhabiting the south of Eastern Europe—in the Don, Kuban, and Volga River basins and in the southern Urals—during the Scythian period has highlighted the important role of the Scytho-Maeotian peoples in the history of that region. Indeed, artifacts of the Novocherkassk type, associated with the earliest Scythians during the period of their Near Eastern campaigns (Leskov 1975a:35-44), are already known from the southern Urals in the east to Bulgaria in the west and from the Volga-Kama interfluve in the north to the Caucasian mountains in the south, emphasizing the early date at which the Scythians influenced the history of the Eurasian peoples.

In the period following the Near Eastern raids, the Scythians maintained their leading role in the political, economic, and cultural development of the peoples inhabiting the south of Eastern Europe. They defeated the Persian king Darius's invasion of Scythia in the late 6th century and gained domination over the forest-steppe of the middle Dniepr and the Bug, forming multilateral relationships with the Greek colonies of the Pontic littoral.

It is significant that the Scytho-Maeotian relationships were permanently influenced by the accomplishments of ancient civilizations of the Near East (Assyria, Media, Urartu) and Asia Minor (Ionia) during the Archaic period, and the ancient Greek and Persian (Achaemenid) cultures of the 5th-4th century BC. During this time the Scythians and the Maeotians received metal and metal artifacts from the Caucasus, from the bearers of Koban culture. The close relationship between the Scythians and the Maeotians, however, reflected in the material and spiritual culture of the two peoples and dating back to the 7th century BC, was the greatest force behind the development of the magnificent Scytho-Maeotian Kuban variant of the Animal Style. The role and position of this style in the development of applied art of their western, northern and eastern neighbors was already discussed above.

As for the southern contacts of the Scythian period Maeotian tribes, as early as the 1950s several graves of Scythian warriors dating from the late 7th to 6th century BC were found in Abkhazia near the village of Kulanurkhva (Trapsh 1962). These have long been taken as evidence of the campaigns of the North Pontic nomads into the Near East. In the 1960s and 1970s, further discoveries in Abkhazia prompted Voronov's observation on the clear influence of the Kuban variant (Maeotian) of the Scythian culture on local artifacts, most readily apparent in the details of horse equipment (1980:218).

We turn now to a discussion of the mechanism whereby Maeotian influence spread and the chronology of its progress. In this respect, several 5th century BC bronze plaques in the Scythian Animal Style, recently recovered from Novorossiysk, are of especial interest. The subject of one of the plaques, a predatory bird tearing apart a fish (Malyshev and Ravich 2001:103–11, figs. 1, 1–2; 2, 1; 3, 1), is a popular one in 5th and 4th century BC Scythian art and has been treated by Korolkova (1998a:166–77). Currently, 14 similar representations are known, 8 in gold and 6 in bronze. Of the gold examples, 5 are likely appliqués for wooden vessels, 2 are plaques, and 1 is a circular rhyton appliqué. The 5 appliqués, all dating to the 5th century BC, include 4 from Ukraine—2 from the steppe (Mozolevskiy 1980:107–10, fig. 44, 4, 7–8) and 2 from the forest-steppe (Petrenko 1967:pls. 19, 24; Ryabova 1984:figs. 3, 9)—and 1 in the Maikop collection (No. 149). The last example is notable for its remarkable craftsmanship and its similarity to images of birds of prey from the Semibratnie kurgans (Artamonov 1966:pls. 118, 135; Korolkova 1998a:173ff.), the artifacts which reflect strong signs of ancient Greek and Achaemenid influence in the Kuban variant of the Scythian Animal Style. Later representations of this subject, specifically from the 4th century BC, are distinguished by their less skillful rendering and the outspread wings of the birds, which contrast with the folded wings characteristic of the 5th century BC.

The outspread wings characteristic of eagle images of the 4th century BC may derive from late 6th or early 5th century BC representations of eagles (lacking fish) on bronze belt buckles (Kantorovich 1997:107). The remaining three gold items are from the 4th century BC, with the two plaques recovered from Ukraine—one from the steppe and the other from the forest-steppe (Artamonov 1966:pl. 231; Petrenko 1978:pls. 19, 30)—and the rhyton appliqué coming from the Elizavetovsky kurgan on the lower Don River (Artamonov 1966:pl. 321). Of the six bronze objects, five are cast and one is hammered; all take the form of openwork plaques and, as such items are typically found in pairs, probably served as harness plaques.

The birds on all the bronze objects are rendered with folded wings, in the manner of the 5th century BC. All six artifacts are from the Northern Caucasus: one, dating from the 6th to 5th century BC, was found in the Lugovoy cemetery (Munchaev 1963:139–211, fig. 7, 1–2). Three derive from the Maikop area, with a pair found in the kurgan Zolotaia Gorka (Lunin 1939:216–17), and the third from near Shuntuk (Ilinskaya and Terenozhkin 1983:53, fig. 2). The fourth (discussed above) was found near Novorossiysk; the fifth, apparently the mate of the example from Novorossiysk, is currently in the National Archaeological Museum of France (Mohen 1989:h. 39, no. 66475) together with five more bronze plaques executed in the 5th to 4th century BC Scythian Animal Style. Four of them are typical of the Ukrainian steppes, while one undoubtedly belongs to the Kuban variant of the Scythian Animal Style; this plaque represents a stylized deer head in profile with a horn in the shape of a predatory bird's head placed on a long neck. Such plaques are present in both parts of the Maikop collection in Berlin (No. 171, Inv. No. 30.562; No. 218, Inv. No. 30.563a,b; and No. 296, Inv. No. IIId 7024), as well as at sites reliably dated to the 4th century BC: kurgan No. 19 near the village of Voronezhskaia, kurgan Karagodeuashkh, and the Elizavetinskie kurgans. As for recent excavations, kurgan No. 1 near the village of Tenginskaia is notable (see Erlikh 2002:7–16, fig. 4.1–6). In Saint-Germain-en-Laye there are two plaques of Kuban provenance; one of them shows a predatory bird pecking a fish and dates to the 5th century BC (Mohen 1989). The last is in the Maikop collection (No. 24).

In this context the finds from Novorossiysk confirm the spread of objects in the Kuban variant of the Scythian Animal Style to the Northern Caucasus Pontic littoral by the 5th century BC. From here, it seems they spread farther south to the Transcaucasus (modern Abkhazia). While only individual objects seem to have been circulated in the 5th century BC, the situation was quite different in the 4th century BC, when substantial changes in the relationship of the Maeotian tribes with Abkhazia are reflected in the archaeological record. This information was synthesized and identified by Erlikh (2004:158–72).

Toward the end of the 1970s and the middle of the 1980s, Georgian and Abkhazian archaeologists working near the town of Ochamchiri (the ancient Greek city of Gyenos) uncovered burials containing the skulls of horses with bridles still upon them. These were correctly identified by Shamba (1988) as ritual burials. Notably, as pointed out by Erlikh (2004), the bridle sets were clearly of the type known from the Kuban. It thus seems appropriate to compare them with those bridle sets recovered from Uliap sanctuaries (a new type of Maeotian monument) No. 2 and No. 5 (Leskov 1990:S.32–38), and from the sanctuary at Tenginskaia II (Erlikh 2002:7). The burial of horse heads with bridle sets is a characteristic feature of all these sites and suggests that the finds in Abkhazia (Voronov 1969:pl. XLV, 28–31; Bill 2003:pls. 152, 23–25; 154, 19; 155, 3–16), often found with horse skulls (Shamba 1988:32–34, 55–57, 64) and dating to the period of the Elizavetinskie kurgans, are the result of a Maeotian invasion into the region rather than the mere circulation or importing of goods. This theory is supported by the increasingly numerous finds typical of the material culture of the Maeotians in the second part of the 4th century BC.

As for the reason why such a campaign or invasion was undertaken, it is hoped that further research may shed some light on the matter. For the moment, however, it is worth reviewing the main points of the history of the peoples of Caucasia. It was long believed that the tribes that settled the region of what is currently Abkhazia formed a cultural and ethnic unity with the peoples of the Northwestern Caucasus. This unity has long been thought to extend back to the Copper and Bronze Ages, from the 4th to 3rd millennium BC; such a connection is indeed apparent in the material culture of the period. Later, however, beginning in the 2nd millennium BC and lasting up to the raids of the Scythians and Cimmerians on Western Asia in the 8th and 7th century BC, this similarity is no longer in evidence.

It remains unclear how exactly that lengthy period influenced the ethno-cultural processes occurring among the tribes settled in the region of Abkhazia and the Northwestern Caucasus. Current scholarship suggests that in the latter region, beginning from the proto-Maeotian period of the 8th century BC, the development of a unified tradition led to the formation of modern Adygheans. In the case of Abkhazia, the archaeological record as currently known gives us no grounds to suggest a continuous line of development from the Early Iron Age peoples to the current local population. The appearance of Maeotians or Maeotian culture bearers in the archaeological record of the 4th century BC is thus of crucial importance and must certainly play a role in the ethno-cultural processes that took place in the history of the local population, the connection of this population to the peoples of the Northwestern Caucasus, and the issue of ethnic unification or the close interaction between the predecessors of modern-day Adygheans and Abkhazians. The contribution of the Scythian and Maeotian material in the Maikop collection to art historical, archaeological, and historical scholarship thus should not be underestimated.

The artifacts from the Sarmatian period in the Maikop collection are unfortunately much less abundant, comprising a mere 20 inventory numbers from a span of four or five centuries. Of these 20 inventory numbers, 17 may be attributed to the category of ornaments and costume details (this category includes a bone amulet though the means of its attachment, and hence the evidence of whether it was ornamental as well as sacral, is lost); 2 are horse harness elements; and 1 is omitted from this section, as well as from Table 2, as it is a Celtic piece entirely unrelated to the region under discussion (No. 103).

To the Early Sarmatian period of the last centuries BC we may attribute at least 8 inventory numbers: 6 of the ornaments and the 2 harness pieces. The ornaments include 1 inventory number in glass, a glass bead (No. 268), and 5 inventory numbers in gold. The gold objects consist of several parts of ornamental details (Nos. 102, 104, and 105), possibly from intricate pendants of a type widespread in the Kuban only in the 2nd and 1st century BC. Given that the overwhelming majority of the artifacts from the de Massoneau collection published here, and particularly the part of it preserved in the Penn Museum, are of Northwest Caucasian provenance, it seems to be reasonable to attribute the ornament pieces to the last centuries BC (Leskov and Lapushnian 1987:132, fig. 58). They are known from 1st century AD sites in Ukraine and the Crimea (Kazak 1995:152, no. 128), as are two torques (Nos. 86 and 101) of types that were mass-produced during this period. While similar ornaments found in assemblages dating to this period seem to be manufactured into the first centuries AD, we should keep in mind the fact that precious items tended to remain in circulation long past the date of their manufacture, and are thus unreliable chronological markers.

As for the 2 inventory numbers representing harness elements, these are phalerae, typical harness ornaments in the Sarmatian period. Divided by Mordvinceva (2001:S.65) into three types according to where on the straps they were affixed—breast, shoulder, or head—these ornaments take a variety of forms: circular or oval, flat or convex, plain or ornamented (with chasing or relief). Those published in this catalogue include a pair of elongated ovals (No. 193), likely intended for the horse's head, and a lone example, probably for the shoulder (Mordvintseya 2001:S.66), that was likely part of the Taganrog treasure (No. 267).

Of the remaining 11 inventory numbers, 9 date to the first centuries AD and are classified as ornaments, 2 representing beads and 7 representing bronze belt buckles. Both beads are barrel-shaped and of iron covered with a layer of gold (Nos. 106 and 107). As for the belt buckles, though these are assigned to 7 inventory numbers (Nos. 269 and 301–6), they in fact total only 6 buckles, with 2 of the inventory numbers each representing half of a single buckle (Nos. 304 and 305). Overall, the 6 buckles are divided equally into two types: those with hooks (Nos. 269, 302, and 304–5) and those with tongues (Nos. 301, 303, and 306). Both types have been shown by M. Yu. Treister (2000:118ff.) to have been produced in the Bosporus under the strong influence of Roman military attire; some were indeed made in royal workshops, as indicated by the sign of the Bosporan king Tiberius Iulius Eupatorius (reigned AD 154–70) that appears on some buckles (Nos. 303 and 305–6). Further, two of these buckles are executed in high relief and set in rectangular frames, one decorated with the image of a sphinx (No. 269) and the other, now lost, with a lion (No. 302); the workmanship of both, as noted by Rostovtzeff (1931a:pls. 1, 5, 6), is typically Greek. Inventory No. 301 is the only one of these buckles in a form that was widespread across the south of Eastern Europe; silver, bronze, and iron examples found at sites ranging from the central North Caucasus to the Crimea and Dniepr basin were likely produced in a number of different centers, including some in the Bosporus.

The final 2 inventory numbers from the Maikop collection categorized as Sarmatian belong to the very end of the period and are transitional in character. The first, a silver torque (No. 108), is characterized by features both of the Sarmatian and Early Medieval periods; the second, the bone amulet (No. 109), of a type common in the North Pontic steppes but unknown in the Kuban, is similarly dated to the transitional phase, the third quarter of the 4th century AD. The identification of the latter piece as a Sarmatian artifact is based on the discovery of similar amulets at the Greek city of Tanais, situated at the estuary of the Don River. Tanais was inhabited as late as the 4th and even 5th century AD by the same mixed population of Greeks and representatives of local tribes as in the Sarmatian period. Such amulets are also known from fortified sites of the Sarmatian period in the lower Dniepr region.

The Middle Ages

The significance of the Middle Ages in the history of the region under discussion should not be underestimated. This era was marked by the formation of both the ethnic structure and the material and spiritual culture of the tribes that became the direct ancestors of the modern Caucasian peoples.

Unfortunately, this period is represented in the Maikop collection by only 43 inventory numbers (see Table 1); 22 of these are characteristic of the Early Middle Ages, dating from the 4th to the 9th century AD, and 21 belong to the High Middle Ages, dating from the 10th to the 14th century AD. Before discussing the artifacts themselves, the provisional character of the chronological division given above should be noted. For the East European steppes, the Early Middle Ages dawned with the invasion of the Huns, also marking the beginning of the Great Migration. As the Asiatic nomads overran not only the steppes but also the piedmonts of the North Caucasus and the Crimea, the local populations were driven into the mountains. The cultures of the Bosporan Kingdom, the Sarmatians, and Scythia Minor disappeared. In the period of gradual stabilization that followed, primitive state structures emerged, rapidly gaining power over large tracts of land and just as rapidly disappearing. Thus, the first Turkic kaganate, which had its center in Mongolia in the late 6th century AD, expanded over the North Caucasus and the territory of the Bosporan Kingdom at the same time as the appearance of the Avars, who then migrated to the Middle Danube. In the early 7th century, the Bulgars dominated the East European steppes; the later part of that same century saw the rise of the Alanic tribes and the capture of power by the Khazars (Artamonov 1962). The Khazar kaganate remained strong until the late 9th century, when the steppes in the Don River and Azov Sea region were invaded by the Pechenegs. As some Khazar dwellings continued to be populated into the 10th century, it is difficult to draw an exact chronological division between the Early and High Middle Ages in the region under consideration. For our purposes here, the provisional division established above will suffice.

As for the High Middle Ages, which date approximately from the 10th century with the beginning of the Seljuk migration, this period saw the Pechenegs, pressed by the Oguz tribes living on the east bank of the Volga River, cross the river and spread across the steppes of the North Caucasian foothills, the shores of the Sea of Azov, and the North Pontic zone. The Pechenegs were succeeded by the Torks and the Polovetsi in turn until the appearance in the 13th century of the Mongols and the establishment of the powerful Golden Horde, which was centered on the Volga. The Golden Horde remained powerful until the late 14th century, when it was fatally defeated by Tamerlane. This event marked the end of the High Middle Ages in the south of Eastern Europe, a period that had been characterized by the domination of and conflict between various nomadic groups who fought their battles on horseback.

Interestingly, the vicious struggles that characterized the Early and High Middle Ages are not well represented in the artifacts in the Maikop collection, the collector having been more interested in accumulating precious materials than those representative of the archae-ological record. A full 38 of the 43 inventory numbers comprise ornaments, costume ele-ments, and utensils. An additional 2 are precious objects, including a silver bowl (No. 131) and a fragment of an iron saw encrusted with gold and silver (No. 132); only 4 definitely represent weapons or equipment, including 1 arrowhead (No. 198) and 3 strap plaques (Nos. 276, 310, and 311). The latter 6 inventory numbers all date to the High Middle Ages.

The 22 inventory numbers attributed to the Early Middle Ages are thus all orna-ments, costume elements, or utensils, though they may be divided chronologically into three groups. The first, encompassing the 4th and 5th centuries AD, includes 6 inventory numbers comparable to those recovered from the contemporary stone tombs in Kerch. Four inventory numbers represent silver pins with hemispherical heads (Nos. 270, 309), 1 represents a faceted silver bead (No. 272), and 1 represents a silver belt buckle (No. 307). The second group, including objects probably from the Alanic burials preceding the Khazar kaganate, dates from the 7th to the middle of the 8th century AD. The 9 inventory numbers from this period in the Penn Museum are of special interest as a comparison with excavated assemblages, such as those from the Alanic cemetery of Klin-Iar III, indicates they may have come from a single archaeological context. A set of gold earrings (No. 113), amulets in the form of miniature mirrors (No. 118), an amulet in the form of a stag (No. 115), and an amulet representing a human figure in a circle (No. 116)—all find analogues in catacomb burial No. 20 at Klin-Iar III. Materials from catacomb No. 23 in the same cemetery display a similar likeness to the other items, such as mirrors, held in Philadelphia (Flerov 2000:35ff.). The third group comprises finds from the 8th and 9th centuries AD, when the Khazar kaganate was at its zenith. Typically identified as the Saltovo-Maiatskaia or simply the Saltovskaia culture in archaeological studies, the sites of this culture are widespread across the majority of the East European steppes and forest-steppes and the Kuban region, especially on the Taman Peninsula. Artifacts from this period existing in the Maikop collection include bronze mirrors (Nos. 119 and 120), amulets (Nos. 121 and 122), and a silver facing (No. 275).

As for the 21 inventory numbers attributed to the High Middle Ages, these are slightly more varied than those of the earlier period and may be subdivided into two chronological groups: one dating from the 10th to the 12th century AD and the other from the 13th to the 14th century AD. A total of 13 inventory numbers, including the 4 representing weap-ons or horse equipment, belong to the first group; the remaining 8 consist of ornaments (Nos. 126, 199, and 277), costume elements (Nos. 124 and 125), and a mirror (No. 123).

These artifacts broadly reflect the variety of peoples that inhabited the Northwestern Caucasus from the 10th to 12th century AD. Thus, we have silver buckles of a type associ-ated with the Hungarians (No. 24); a mirror of Alanic provenance (No. 123); a headdress ring typical of the Polovetsi; an almond-shaped pendant (No. 199) of a type subsequently developed by the Belorechenskaya culture; and a blue glass bracelet (No. 126), likely man-ufactured in Chersonesus, that may indicate the extent of the commercial connections maintained by the local tribes.

In discussing the final set of artifacts, those from the second group of the High Middle Ages, a few observations are in order on the political situation in the Kuban region specifically during this period. What is especially notable is that the territory on the left bank of the Kuban River was comparatively peaceful, being situated at a distance from the main steppe routes of the nomads. Though the Northern Caucasus was incorporated into the *ulus* of Jochi Khan and later the Golden Horde, the population inhabiting the left bank of the Kuban continued to live in open settlements, though a few fortified sites are also known. This situation is very different from that which occurred in the Volga, Don, and Dniepr River regions, which were strongly affected by centuries of nomadic struggles, as well as that in the south of Eastern Europe, which was subjugated by the Mongols in this period. The Golden Horde, which occupied a vast territory, was forced to unite two different worlds, that of the nomadic herdsmen and that of the city dwellers. Under these conditions, commerce and currency developed rapidly; new trade routes were cut and old ones, including sections of the Great Silk Road, restored, allowing significant development of the trade route into the Near East and North Pontic zone via the Caucasus. In the modern Republic of Adyghea we see the lowest mountain passes, accessible for the longest time during the year, on the shortest route from Transcaucasia to the North Pontic steppes and seaports of the Taman and Crimean peninsulas. It is not surprising that this is the region over which the Belorechenskaya culture, representing the medieval Adygheans, developed and spread. Veselovsky's excavations of kurgans of the Adyghean nobility, beginning at the end of the 19th century AD, recovered rich artifacts indicative of broad connections: there were not only masterpieces of local weaponry and ornament but also Iranian, Chinese, and Italian textiles; precious ornaments from Cilicia in Asia Minor; glazed pottery from Central Asia; Syrian glass artifacts; and Venetian silver.

The Maikop collection contains examples of locally produced precious ornaments, such as earrings (No. 278), beads, pendants (No. 127), and buttons (Nos. 128, 129, 130, 133, and 200), but also the 2 items mentioned above: the silver bowl engraved with a leopard that is a typical example of Golden Horde art and the iron saw (?) encrusted with gold and silver. This last item is especially significant, given that only one iron axe encrusted with silver was published in Kramarovskiy's monograph on Golden Horde art. That axe, decorated with images of running animals and dated to the 13th or beginning of the 14th century AD (Kramarovskiy 2001:239), is not only the closest analogue to the saw in the Maikop collection so far discovered but also links that artifact to the Golden Horde.

* * *

While examining the materials in the de Massoneau collection I could not pay equal attention to every time period, let alone every item. However, noting the scientific importance of the publication of the Maikop collection, it is worth reminding the reader that two-thirds of the collection consists of artifacts that characterize the Scythian epoch. Over half of these are executed in the Scythian-Meotian Animal Style. The wealth of the Scythian-Meotian part of the de Massoneau collection and the diversity of the items within it place it among the largest and the most important collections in the museums of Russia. Of special interest are the anthropomorphic finds that proved vital for a more general understanding of the worldview of the tribes that lived in the Kuban area during the era of the Scythians and the Meotians, at its peak in the 4th century BC.

There were 12 bronze anthropomorphic pieces, 1 located in St. Petersburg's State Hermitage and 11 in Berlin—2 in the Museum für Vor- and Frühgeschichte and 9 in the Antikenabteilung. Of the latter, 1 is an openwork plaque (No. 217) and the other 8 are figurines all depicting a warrior riding a horse (see Nos. 165–67). Without repeating the descriptions of each of these horsemen, those four that were preserved completely share an important detail, a typically Scythian gorytos worn on the left of their military belts. Gorytoi like these are examples of Greco-Scythian toreutics from the 4th century BC. A fifth, partially preserved figure depicts a warrior on horseback carrying a javelin or a spear in his raised right arm (see No. 166), a scene that is well known from gold plaques found in royal barrows from the same time. In addition, the graves of wealthy soldiers often contained gold torques, some of which are spiral shaped (Mozolevskiy and Polin 2005:333, fig. 14,1; 22,2), and we see similar torques on two of the horsemen statuettes from de Massoneau's collection.

The ethnic and cultural similarity of our horsemen is also supported by the only costume detail they share, their cone-shaped helmets. The details of the statuettes strongly suggest that the creator of these works sought to portray horse-riding warriors in possession of items typical of the 4th century BC. The primitive execution of these statuettes leaves no doubt that they are examples of local barbarian art.

The faces of all these riders are similar and represent a single anthropological type. A simple comparison of these faces with the few known depictions of Scythians made by Scythian or Maeotian artists shows that the statuettes in de Massoneau's collection were executed in a different artistic tradition.

Among thousands of artifacts characterizing all aspects of the material and spiritual life of the Scythians, only one three-dimensional anthropomorphic sculpture is known—a unique bronze pole top (finial), found near Dniepropetrovsk (Grakov 1971:84–85), in the center of which is a sculpture of a nude man standing on a pedestal. Experts have connected this image with the main Scythian god Papai, who Herodotus compared to Zeus.

While he was studying the Luristan bronzes Rostovtzeff took note of the longevity of this culture and came to believe that the later Luristan bronzes were contemporary with late Assyrian and early Persian antiquities, finding significant parallels with the designs of the early Scythian Animal Style (Rostovtzeff 1931b:46–56). Describing one of the statuettes that has not survived (which allowed us to include that description in this catalogue), Rostovtseff noted the great similarity between the heads of the Scythian horseman and a Luristan chariot driver, concluding that Luristan art had a significant influence on that of Scythia (1931b:53, fig. III, 2–3; IV,2; V,6).

At the beginning of the 1990s, Pogrebova and Raevsky also concluded that "One of the main origins of the animal imagery repertoire for this art, as well as of the methods of its realization, was the culture of Luristan bronzes" (1992:159). Hončar (1936:50, fig. 14, 1–9; Kahlmeyer 1983:57, fig. 45) had also emphasized the similarity of one of these statuettes from the Hermitage first published by Rostovtseff (1922:40, pl. V,5) to the images of horsemen typical for the Koban culture of the Caucasus mountains. Above, I had noted the appreciable influence that Koban art exerted on the Scythian-Meotian art of the Kuban region. And just as with Luristan art, this influence appears not only in the special features of the Kuban Animal Style, but also in its small anthropomorphic sculpture. Moreover, the chronological connection of late Luristan bronzes (8th–7th century BC), the late Koban culture (7th–4th century BC), and the blossoming of the Scythian-Meotian art of the Kuban area (5th–4th century BC) strongly suggests that the Luristan influence on the culture of the Scythian-Meotian tribes of the Kuban area was indirect, mediated mainly by the carriers of the Koban culture.

Another partially preserved anthropomorphic artifact is found in the Berlin Museum's holdings of de Massoneau's collection—an open ring inside of which is a small human figure (No. 217). The figure's head and body face outward, with bent legs and upraised arms bent at the elbow; two heads of birds of prey are located between the knee and elbow on each side. This plaque was cast using the same method as the horseman statuettes described above, in a now-lost form. The man's head—with large, protruding round eyes that take up half his face, a long, narrow nose, and a slightly open mouth—is very similar to the heads of the horsemen and likely represents the same anthropological type that we know from the Luristan objects. The figurine's Luristan-type body is combined with a stylized head of a bird of prey, very typical of the Scythian Animal Style of the 5th–4th century BC and unknown in the art of ancient Iran. Rostovtzeff (1931b:fig. I,1, 4, 5, 7, 9; fig. V,5) emphasized the variety of connections between Luristan bronzes and Scythian artworks, bringing out several convincing similarities between this object and the representations of Luristan deities, usually shown interacting with animals. The stylistic similarities among the bronze artifacts from the de Massoneau collection, in which two different styles—Luristani and Scythian—are intimately connected, as well as the fact that they were found in a relatively small area, lead us to believe that they were made in one workshop and, possibly, by a single master who was able to combine a familiar local Scythian Animal Style with the more ancient traditions of anthropomorphic images typical of the Luristan bronzes. Only if his customers understood the essence of the depictions—images that likely derived from a single, pan-Iranian cultural heritage—would they have been interested in items like these.

Another example, one that perhaps illustrates the close connection between the Scythian-Meotian art and the art of the Near East more vividly, is a partially preserved openwork plate or plaque from the collection of the Berlin Museum für Vor- und Frühgeschichte (No. 264). As noted before, this plate was positively identified due to the discovery of an old photograph from the 1920s that showed it completely intact: a man standing upright and holding a fantastic monster in each hand. Repeating figures of other monsters are outstretched around the man's body, those above him topped by stylized heads of birds of prey that press to his head, while those below him have heads of lions, on which the man's feet rest.

First, it is important to note that stylistically, this plate represents a now-familiar combination of the Kuban type of Scythian-Meotian Animal Style (heads of the monsters) and the Koban art of the Caucasus mountains (the figurine of the man), a combination where the interpretation of anthropomorphic images is influenced by the art of Luristan. Furthermore, a comparison of this plate with numerous other depictions of thematically similar scenes, widespread in Luristan art (Moorey 1981:Cat. NN125, 154, 155, 341, 343, 352, 386, 444), makes it clear that this is an image of a deity. His power is vividly illustrated by his opposition to the monsters, the heads of which symbolize the sky (birds of prey) and the underground kingdom (lions) according to the zoological code of the Scythian tripartite model of the world. The deity itself, shown in the guise of a man, symbolizes earth, the land of the living. Raevsky (1985) correctly notes that in some cases the image of a bird of prey, just like that of any other predator, can be understood to symbolize the underground kingdom. This means that this particular plate could be an illustration of another worldview that was less widespread in antiquity, a conception of the universe as a dichotomy, an opposition between the world of the living and the world of the dead, between light and darkness, between good and evil. This interpretation further underscores the power of the deity, which is literally trampling the heads of the lions. According to the museum inventory, this plate was found in Georgia. Today, after so many wonderful Meotian artifacts from the 4th century BC have been found in Abkhazia, such a discovery is no longer surprising. Moreover, the discovery of this plate in Georgia would represent the first evidence that the local population had contacts with the Meotians that appeared at this time in the neighboring Abkhazia.

The appearance of Meotians in Abkhazia, where the local population had experienced the presence of the Persians for over a hundred years, naturally led to a further spread of Persian influence throughout the Northern Caucasus and the steppes of the Black Sea area. At this time, new subjects, animal poses, and ornamental details become more widespread. These obvious changes were also reflected in depictions of humans. Thus, for example, a looted barrow near the Tulskaia village in the Maikop area (Mantsevich 1966:fig. 7,11) contained a golden plate depicting a deity with outstretched arms, each holding a lion by its paws. Numerous similar compositions common for Luristan art were discussed above. While emphasizing that the plate from the de Massoneau collection described above is unique, it is important to note its thematic similarity to a gold openwork plaque from the Soboleva Mogila barrow in the Dniepropetrovsk region of Ukraine. In the middle of this plaque is a man who grips the heads of two griffins and stands on top of their snake-like bodies (Mozolevskiy and Polin 2005:178–79, fig. 17,3). It appears that in the 4th century BC, during the peak of Scythia's power in southern Ukraine and that of the Sindo-Meotian kingdom in the Kuban area, there was a political and ideological demand for depictions of a man-shaped deity (or perhaps the reverse, a deity-like man) that dominates all forces opposing him, symbolized by monsters. Similar images symbolize the intimate connection of royal power with divine patronage.

In describing another plaque as a part of the anthropomorphic group, Erlikh made a very interesting discovery in the Kuban area in 2000–2001, when he examined a Maeotian sanctuary at a 4th century BC barrow. Among the skeletons of sacrificial horses were numerous horse trappings, including a unique noseband (or forehead covering) in the shape of an openwork plate (Kantorovich and Erlikh 2006:140, cat. N121). This plate depicts a man whose head is turned to the right and fully covered by a mask of a catlike predator (most likely a lion, judging from the long mane that descends to the man's shoulders). This unnatural combination of a human body and an animal head also includes a loop at the top, a detail that can be present only on a mask. The master craftsman who created this figure did not attempt to introduce a new type of image into the world view of his tribesmen, but, on the contrary, emphasized the image's artificiality, perhaps due to a familiar ritual. (It is surprising that Kantorovich and Erlikh, after describing the noseband, including the costume of the depicted man, did not pay attention to the obvious mask on the head.)

This wonderful artifact points to another find, a plaque from the de Massoneau collection in the Berlin Museum für Vor- und Frühgeschichte (No. 293). This plaque is very different from the dozens of other plaques in the de Massoneau collection. It shows a wolf-like head over a bent body, on top of which are two vertical spikes. If these spikes were closer to the ears of the head, they could have resembled a mane, typical for images of griffins in the Scythian-Meotian style of 5th–4th century BC. That is the only resemblance the body of this creature has to animals. Moreover, the contour of the body, from the neck to the tips of the legs, suggests that the image is that of a man sitting with legs bent at the knees, especially when the shape of the legs and their length relative to the upper torso are taken into account. Both legs are visible even though the figure is generally a profile (the plaque itself has not been preserved, and its description comes from an old photograph and a sketch of the plaque in an inventory book; the latter clearly underscores the toes). The strongly bent body and lowered neck, as well as the head obscured by a large mask of a predator with an oblong snout, all help depict a sitting man with a masked head resting on his knees.

This finding of these two articles, each depicting a man in an animal mask suggests a previously unknown phenomenon in the spiritual life of the Maeotians of the 4th century BC. It is not known how the above plaque was found, but the fact that Erlikh discovered the noseband in a sanctuary strongly suggests that the

Horse noseband depicting a man wearing an animal mask (Kantorovich and Erlikh 2006: 140–41).

de Massoneau plaque comes from a complex connected to a kind of religious ceremony. Unfortunately none of the written sources on them helps us understand what specific rituals required participants to wear animal masks. Written sources describing Maeotian neighbors (Scythians, Sarmatians) mention no rituals involving masked people. These masked figures are also not connected with proto-Maeotian monuments that date to the 8th–7th century BC.

The situation is quite different with the Caucasus neighbors of the Maeotian tribes from the Kuban area. Human statuettes are equally common in the Northern Caucasus, especially in Daghestan and in monuments of Koban culture (Abakarov and Davydov 1993:64–66; Domanskiy 1984:83, 84). Among the latter, only one statuette (female) is shown wearing a very simple mask. (Domanskiy 1984:73, fig. XXV). Masked anthropomorphic statuettes are noticeably more common in Armenia and Georgia (Esayan 1976:225–44; Pitskhelauri 1979:50–59), but the literature does not include detailed descriptions of the statuettes, only rarely noting that the mask shows the head of a bear, a bird, or a sheep. The vast majority of these figurines, masked or otherwise, were found within various sanctuaries.

It is plausible that the appearance of small anthropomorphic sculptures in Maeotian society resulted from enduring connections between the local tribes and those from the Caucasus and the Transcaucasus. We must also not forget the wall reliefs showing a winged deity in the shape of a man with an animal mask, reliefs that were common in Near Eastern civilizations, especially those of the Assyrians and the Hattians from the 9th–8th century BC (Crawford, Harper, Pittman 1980:24, fig.16; Rostovtseff 1931b:fig. V,13). Rostovtseff was correct in tracing the similarities among the art of Luristan, that of the Hattians, and that of the Scythians (1931b:53–55). Such similarities, which were manifested in a variety of spiritual and cultural connections, could have been formed only after the Cimmerian-Scythian raids into the Near East in the 8th–7th century BC. The chronographs of Assyria and Urartu, as well as data from Herodotus and archaeological materials, all help define the borders of the invasion zone as well as allowing us to track the movements of Cimmerian and Scythian tribes on the territory of the Near East. Thus, the Cimmerians that are moving along the Black Sea shores into Asia Minor here collide with the late Hattian kingdom, Lydia, and Ionia, while at the same time making war on Urartu and Assyria.

The main areas along the Caspian Sea shores where Scythians would have had contacts with local tribes are located in what is now western Iran and eastern Turkey, including the southern Caspian area (Iranian Azerbaijan) and farther south, in what are now Kurdistan and Luristan provinces. The military paths of Cimmerians and Scythians crossed in Urartu and Assyria. Numerous wars, during which the ethnically close Cimmerians and Scythians were often allies, would give way to peaceful periods, when the experiences and achievements of ancient Eastern civilizations could be successfully inserted in their own lives. Naturally these influences were most often expressed in material culture, first and foremost in weaponry. During this time of Cimmerian-Scythian raids, the Black Sea area nomads acquired battle chariots driven by one or two pairs of horses, and their armor became typically Scythian and began to include metal armor, helmets, and battle belts. Significant artistic changes were signaled by the appearance of various applied arts unknown among the Black Sea nomads prior to their penetration into Asia Minor and the Near East.

In the middle of the 1st millennium BC the Transcaucasus was one of the provinces of the Achaemenid Empire, during which the greatest quantity of Achaemenid imports entered the Transcaucasus and into the Maikop area, and then moved along the Kuban River to the area of the Taman Peninsula. This is the location of the famous Semibratnie barrows where Sindo-Maeotian royalty was buried. A significant number of the artifacts from these barrows are executed in the Achaemenid and Greco-Persian styles.

Apparently, not only objects but also ideas traveled to the Kuban at this time, just as they did two hundred years prior. In particular, numerous ceremonies that were believed to bring success in various activities became much more widespread. The land-owning settled Maeotians, who had had long-standing and rather close relations with the Greek inhabitants of the Bosporan Kingdom, were probably much more receptive to the ideas of ancient Eastern civilizations during the 5th century BC than the nomads of the Black Sea area steppes. Not coincidentally, over 20 sanctuaries (8th–2nd century BC) (Erlikh 2005:323–26) were discovered specifically in the Kuban area, which has greatly enriched the archaeology of the south of Eastern Europe.

Considering the discoveries made in the Kuban area in the last several decades, the materials in the de Massoneau collection help illustrate the study of the history of the Caucasus and the Black Sea regions that played such an important role in the development of many ancient civilizations of the Old World.

Mountains in Adyghea. Photograph by Dmitriy Slesarenko.

Abbreviations

AA   *Arkheologicheskii Almanakh* [Archaeological Almanac], Donetsk

ASGE   *Arkheologicheskii Sbornik Gosudarstvennogo Ermitazha* [Archaeological Collection of the State Hermitage], St. Petersburg

DA   *Donskaia Arkheologiia* [Don Archaeology], Rostov

DD   *Donskie Drevnosti* [Don Antiquities], Azov

GAIMK   *Gosudarstvennaia Akademiia Istorii Materialnoy Kultury* [State Academy of the History of Material Culture], St. Petersburg

IAA   *Istoriko-Arkheologicheskii Almanakh* [Historical–Archaeological Almanac], Armavir

IAK   *Izvestiia Imperatorskoy Arkheologicheskoy Komissii* [News of the Imperial Archaeological Commission], St. Petersburg

IGAIMK   *Izvestiia Gosudarstvennoi Akademii Istorii Materialnoi Kultury* [News of the State Academy of the History of Material Culture], St. Petersburg/Moscow

JPEK   *Jahrbuch für Prähistorische & Ethnographische Kunst* [Annual Review of Prehistoric and Ethnographical Art], Berlin

KSIA   *Kratkie Soobshcheniia Institutu Arkheologii Akademii Nauk SSSR* [Brief Reports from the Institute of Archaeology of the Academy of Sciences of the USSR], Moscow

KSIIMK   *Kratkie Soobshcheniia o Dokladakh i Polevykh Issledovaniiakh Instituta Istorii Materialnoi Kultury Akademii Nauk SSSR* [Brief Reports on the Lectures and Field Studies of the Institute of the History of Material Culture of the Academy of Sciences of the USSR], Moscow

MAR   *Materialy po Arkheologii Rossii* [Documents from the Archaeology of Russia], St. Petersburg

MIA   *Materialy i Issledovaniia po Arkheologii SSSR* [Documents and Studies of the Archaeology of the USSR], Moscow

OAK   *Otchety Imperatorskoy Arkheologicheskoy Komissii* [Reports of the Imperial Archaeological Commission], St. Petersburg

PBF   *Prähistorische Bronzefunde* [Prehistoric Bronze Treasures], Munich

RA   *Rossiiskaia Arkheologiia* [Russian Archaeology], Moscow

SA   *Sovetskaia Arkheologiia* [Soviet Archaeology], Moscow

SAI   *Svod Arkheologicheskikh Istochnikov* [Summary of Archaeological Sources], Moscow

TGE   *Trudy Gosudarstvennogo Ermitazha* [Works of the State Hermitage], St. Petersburg

TGIM   *Trudy Gosudarstvenoogo Istoricheskogo Muzeia* [Works of the State Archaeological Museum], Moscow

VDI   *Vestnik Drevnei Istorii* [Bulletin of Ancient History], Moscow

Bibliography

Abakarov, A. I., and O. M. Davydov. 1993. *Arkheologicheskaya karta Dagestana* [Archaeological map of Dagestan]. Moscow: Nauka.

Abramova, M. P. 1995. Rimskie provintsialnye fibuly IV–V vv. na Severnom Kavkaze [Roman provincial fibulae of 4th–5th centuries AD in northern Caucasus]. *IAA* N-1:140–47.

——. 1997. *Rannie Alany Severnogo Kavkaza III–V vv. n.e.* [Early Alani of northern Caucasus in 3rd–5th centuries AD]. Moscow: Russian Academy of Sciences, Institute of Archaeology.

Afanasiev, G. E. 1979. Khronologiia mogilnika Mokraia Balka [Chronology of burial ground of Mokraia Balka]. *KSIA* 158:43–51.

Alekseev, A. Yu. 1986. Nashivnye blyashki iz Chertomlykskogo kurgana [Sewed-on plaques from the Chertomlyk kurgan]. *Antichnaya torevtika–sbornik statey* [Classical touretics–collection of articles]. Leningrad: State Hermitage.

——. 2003. *Khronografiia Evropeiskoi Skifii* [Chronography of European Scythia]. St. Petersburg: State Hermitage.

Alekseev, A. Yu., ed. 2001. *Zolotye oleni Evrazii* [Golden stags of Eurasia]. St. Petersburg: Slavia.

Alekseev, A. Yu., V. Yu. Murzin, and R. Rolle. 1991. *Chertomlyk* [Chortomlyk]. Kiev: Naukova Dumka.

Alekseev, V. P., ed. 1991. *The Treasures of Nomadic Tribes in South Russia*. Tokyo: Ancient Orient Museum.

Alekseeva, E. M. 1975–1982. Antichnye busy Severnogo Prichernomoria [Ancient beads of northern Black Sea region]. 3 vols. *SAI* G1–12.

Alexander, C. 1925. Jewelry and Miscellaneous Small Antiquities. *Bulletin of the Metropolitan Museum of Art* 20, 7:180–83.

Ambroz, A. K. 1966. Fibuly Yuga Evropeiskoi chasti SSSR [Fibulae of the southern European part of USSR]. *SAI* D1–30.

——. 1971. Problemy rannesrednevekovoy khronologii Vostochnoy Evropy [Problems in the early Medieval chronology of Eastern Europe]. *SA* 2:96–123.

——. 1989. *Khronologiia drevnostey Severnogo Kavkaza* [Chronology of antiquities of northern Caucasus]. Moscow: Nauka.

Anfimov, N. V. 1951. *Meoto-Sarmatskiy mogilnik u stanitsy Ust-Labinskoy* [A Maeotian-Sarmatian burial ground in the village of Ust-Labinskaia]. *MIA* 23:155–208.

——. 1987. *Drevnee zoloto Kubani* [Ancient gold of Kuban]. Krasnodar: Krasnodar Book Publishers.

Anfimov, N. V., and E. S. Sharafutdinova. 1982. Poselenie Krasnogvardeiskoe na Kubani–noviy pamiatnik kobiakovskoy kultury [Krasnogvardeiskoe settlement in Kuban–a new site of Kobiakovsky culture]. *SA* 3:139–48.

Aricescu, A. 1965. Cazanul scitic de la Castelu [Scythian cauldron from Castelu]. *Studii şi cercetări de istorie veche* [Investigations of Ancient History] (Bucharest) 16:565–69.

Artamonov, M. I. 1961. Antropomorfnye bozhestva v religii skifov [Anthropomorphic deities in Scythian religion]. *ASGE* 2:57–87.

——. 1962. *Istoriia khazar* [History of Khazars]. Leningrad: State University Press.

——. 1966. *Sokrovishcha skifskikh kurganov* [Treasures of Scythian kurgans]. Prague-Leningrad: Artia-Sovetskiy Khudozhnik.

Artamonova-Poltavtseva, O. A. 1950. Kultura Severo-Vostochnogo Kavkaza v skifskiy period [Culture of northeastern Caucasus in the Scythian period]. *SA* 14:20-101.

Aruz, J., ed. 2000. *The Golden Deer of Eurasia.* New York: Metropolitan Museum of Art.

Babenchikov, V. P. 1957. Nekropol Neapolia Skifskogo [The Necropolis of Scythian Neapolis]. *Istoriia i Arkheologiia drevnego Kryma—sbornik statey* [History and archaeology of ancient Crimea—collection of articles]. Kiev: Naukova Dumka.

Beazley, J. D. 1956. *Attic Black-Figure Vase Painters.* Oxford: Clarendon Press.

Beglova, E. A. 1989. Pogrebalniy obriad Uliapskikh gruntovykh mogilnikov v Krasnogvardeiskom raione [Burial rituals in Uliap earthen burial grounds in the Krasnogvardeiskiy region]. *Meoty-predki Adygov—sbornik statey* [Meotian ancestors of Adygheans—collection of articles]. Maikop: Adigpoligraph.

——. 1995. Keramika Zakubania VI–IV vv. do n.e. kak istoricheskiy istochnik [Pottery of the Kuban River left bank region of 6th–4th centuries BC as a historical source]. Ph.D. dissertation: Institute of Archaeology, Moscow.

——. 2002. Kopflos und gefesselt—Bestattungen der ganz anderen Art. *Antike Welt* 3:297–304.

Belinskiy, A. B., and S. L. Dudarev. 2001. K kharakteristike nakonechnikov strel iz Mogilnika Klin-Iar III [On the characteristics of arrowheads from the Klin-Iar III burial ground]. *Materialy po izucheniiu istoriko-kulturnogo nasslediia Severnogo Kavkaza—sbornik statey* [Material for investigation of historical-cultural legacy of north Caucasus—collection of articles]. Moscow: Nasledie.

Berghe, L. vanden, I. N. Medvedskai'a', Vladimir Grigor'evich Lukonin 1992. *Drevnosti Strany Lurov* [Antiquities from Luristan]. St. Petersburg: Hermitage.

Bessonova, S. S. 1983. *Religioznye predslavlenia skifov* [Religious conceptions of Scythians]. Kiev: Naukova Dumka.

Bidzilia, V. I. 1971. Doslidzhennia Haimanovoi Mohyly [Study of Haimanova Mogila]. *Arkheologiia* [Archaeology] (Kiev) 1:44–56.

Bill, A. 2003. *Studien zu den Gräbern des 6 bis 1 Jahrhunderts v. Chr. in Georgien.* Bonn: Dr. Rudolf Habelt GmbH.

Boardman, J. 1970. *Greek Gems and Finger Rings.* London: Thames & Hudson.

Bočarev, V. S., and A. M. Leskov. 1980. *Jung- und spätbronzezeitliche Gußformen im nördlichen Schwarzmeergebiet.* Munich: C. H. Beck.

Bondar, I. V. 1975. *Drevnee zoloto iz sobrania muzeia istoricheskikh dragotsennostey USSR* [Ancient Gold from the collection of Museum of Historical Treasures of Ukrainian SSR]. Moscow: Iskusstvo.

Böttger, B. 2003. *Kontakt-Kooperation-Konflikt. Germanen und Sarmaten zwischen dem 1 und dem 4 Jahrhundert nach Christus.* Munich: Neumünster Archälogische Landesmuseum.

Brashinskiy, I. B. 1967. *Sokrovishcha skifskikh tsarei* [Treasures of Scythian kings]. Moscow: Nauka.

Bratchenko, S. N. 1976. *Nizhnee Podonie v epokhu sredney bronzy* [Lower Don region in middle Bronze age]. Kiev: Naukova Dumka.

Calmeyer, P. 1976. Iconographie und Stil urartaïscher Bildwerke. *Urartu.* Munich: Museum für Vor- und Frügeschichte.

Canessa, C., and E. Canessa. 1917. *A Catalogue of Minor Art: Collection Formed by C. and E. Canessa, on Exhibition at Their Galleries.* New York: Canessa Galleries.

Catalogue des Antiquites Grecques, Romaines et Barbares du Bosphore Cimmerien et d'une serie d'objets Persans. 1922. Paris: Hôtel Drouot.

Chaikovskiy, S. M., ed. 1992. *Scythian Gold.* The Museum of Historic Treasures of Ukraine. Tokyo: Ancient Orient Museum.

Chernenko, E. V. 1970. Pogrebenia s oruzhiem iz nekropolia Nimfeia [Burials with weapons from necropolis of Nymphaion]. *Drevnosti Vostochnogo Kryma–sbornik statey* [Antiquities of eastern Crimea–collection of articles]. Kiev: Naukova Dumka.

Chernykov, I. T. 1977. Kimmeriyskie kurgany bliz ustia Dunaia [Cimmerian kurgans near the mouth of the Danube]. *Skify i Sarmaty-sbornik statey* [Scythians and Sarmatians–collection of articles]. Kiev: Naukova Dumka.

Chezhina, E. F. 1983. Khudzhestvennye osobennosti zverinogo stilya Nizhnego Povolzh'ya i Yuzhnogo Priuralya v skifskuyu epokhu [Artistic specifics of the animal style of lower Volga region and south Urals in the Scythian epoch]. *ASGE* N23:21–30.

Chlenova, N. L. 1984. *Olennye kamni kak istoricheskiy istochnik* [Deer stelae as an historical source]. Novosibirsk: Nauka.

——. 1999. Novye dannye o svayazyakh Mongolii i Severnogo Kavkaza v skifskuyu epokhu [New data on the relationship of Mongolia and the north Caucasus in the Scythian epoch]. *Evraziyskie drevnosti–sbornik statey* [Eurasian antiquities–collection of articles]. Moscow: Institute of Archaeology.

——. 2004. Severny Kavkaz–Sintszyan–Mongolia (obsheevraziyskie olynne kamni) [North Caucasus–Sinxiang–Mongolia (General Eurasian deer stelae)]. *Arkheologicheskie pamyatniki rannego zheleznogo veka Yuga Rossii–sbornik statey* [Archaeological sites of early Iron age of south of Russia–collection of articles]. Moscow: Institute of Archaeology.

Colosanti, A. 1915. *Catalogue of Canessa's Collection: Panama-Pacific International Exposition.* San Francisco, CA: Canessa.

Crawford, V. E., P. O. Harper, and H. Pittman. 1980. *Assyrian Reliefs and Ivories in the Metropolitan Museum of Art.* New York: The Metropolitan Museum of Art.

Damm, I. G. von. 1988. Goldschmiedearbeiten der Volkerwanderungszeit aus dem Nurdlichen Schwarzmeergebiet. *Kölner Jahrbuch für Vor- und Frühgeschichte* (Cologne) 21:65–210.

Dmitriev, A. V. 1982. Rannesrednevekovie fibuly iz mogilnika na reke Diurso [Early medieval fibulae from the burial ground on the Diurso River]. *Drevnosti epokhi velikogo pereselenia narodov V–VIII vv–sbornik statey* [Antiquities from the epoch of great population movements in 5th–8th centuries–collection of articles]. Moscow: Nauka.

Domanskiy, Ya. V. 1984. *Drevniaia khudozhestvennaia bronza Kavkaza* [Ancient artistic bronze of the Caucasus]. Moscow: Iskusstvo.

Donder, H. 1980. Zaumzeug in Griechenland und Cypern. *PBF* 16,3.

Drachuk, V. S. 1975. *Sistemy znakov Severnogo Prichernomoria* [Systems of insignia of the northern Black Sea region]. Kiev: Naukova Dumka.

Dubovskaia, O. R. 1993. Voprosy slozheniia inventarnogo kompleksa Chernogorovskoi kultury [Questions about the structure of an inventory complex of Chernogorovskaia culture]. *AA* 2:137–60.

——. 1997. Zur ethnischen und kulturellen Einordung der "Novocherkassk Gruppe." *Eurasia Antiqua.* Bd. 3:277–328.

Dudarev, S. L. 1991. *Iz istorii sviazei naselenia Kavkaza s kimmeriisko-skifskim mirom* [On the history of connections between populations of the Caucasus and the Cimmero-Scythian world]. Grozny: Chechen-Ingush University Press.

Dvornichenko, V. V. 2000. Novie postupleniya v sostave Kosheutovskogo kompleksa uzdednih prinadlezhnostey [New entry in the Khosheutov complex of horse trappings]. *Skifi I Sarmativ v VII–III vv. do n.e.–sbornik statey* [Scythians and Sarmatians in 7th–3rd centuries BC–collection of articles]. Moscow: Institute of Archaeology.

Dvornichenko, V. V., and M. A. Ochir-Goriaeva. 1997. Khosheutovskiy kompleks uzdechnykh prinadlezhnostei skifskogo vremeni na Nizhnei Volge [Khosheutov complex of horse trappings of the Scythian period in lower Volga region]. *DD* 5:99–115.

Dzhaparidze, O. M. 1989. *Nasledie drevnei Gruzii* [Legacy of ancient Georgia]. Tbilisi: Metsniereba.

Ebert, M. 1909. Die frühmittelalterlichen Spangenhelme vom Baldenheimer Typus. *Praehistorische Zeitschrift* Bd. I, Heft 1:65–77.

Efimov, K. Yu. 1999. Zolotoordynskie pogrebenia iz mogilnika "Olen-Kolodez" [Golden Horde burials from burial ground of "Olen-Kolodez"]. *DA* 3-4:93–108.

Erlikh, V. R. 1992. Vooruzhenie i konskoe snariazhenie v kulture naseleniia Zakubania v skifskoe vremia [Armor and horse trappings in Kuban region population in Scythian period]. Ph.D. dissertation: Institute of Archaeology, Moscow.

———. 1994. *U istokov ranneskifskogo kompleksa* [At the source of an early Scythian complex]. Moscow: State Museums of the East.

———. 2002. Novoe meotskoe sviatilishche v Zakubanie [A new Meotian sanctuary in the Kuban region]. *IAA* 8:7–16.

———. 2004. Meotskoe sviatilische v Abkhazii [A Meotian sanctuary in Abkhazia]. *VDI* 1:158–72.

———. 2005. "Skifskiy" kultoviy nabor v meotskom svyatilishche ["Scythian" cult set in the Meotian sanctuary]. *Sbornik Statey Chetvertaia Kubanskaia Arheologicheskaia Konferentsiya* (Collection of articles Fourth Kuban Archaeological Conference). Krasnodar: Simvolika.

Esayan, S. A. 1976. *Drevnaya kultura plemen severo-vostochnoy Armenii* [Ancient culture of the tribes of northeastern Armenia]. Erevan: Academy of Science.

Eskina, A. V. 1995. Zerkalo "Olviyskogo" tipa iz mogilnika Necherziy [An "Olbian"-type mirror from Necherzi burial ground]. *Arkheologia Adygei–sbornik statey* [Archaeology of Adyghea—collection of articles]. Maikop: Meot.

Fedorov-Davydov, G. A. 1966. *Kochevniki Vostochnoi Evropy pod vlastiu zolotoordynskikh khanov* [Nomads of eastern Europe under the power of khans of the Golden Horde]. Moscow: Nauka.

———. 1976. *Iskusstvo kochevnikov i Zolotoi Ordy* [The art of nomads and the Golden Horde]. Moscow: Iskusstvo.

Fernald, H. E. 1930. The Maikop Treasure. *University Museum Bulletin* 2, 1:6–11.

Flerov, V. S. 2000. *Alany Tsentralnogo Predkavkazia V–VIII vekov* [Alani of central Caucasia in 5th-8th centuries AD]. Moscow: Institute of Archaeology.

Froehner, W. 1892. *La Collection Tyszkiewicz*. Munich.

Gabuev, T. A., and V. R. Erlikh. 2001. Dva pogrebeniia V v. do n.e. iz Predkavkazia [Two burials of 5th century BC from the Caucasus]. *Severnyi Kavkaz: istoriko-arkheologicheskie ocherki i zametki–sbornik statey* [The North Caucasus: Historical archaeological essays and paragraphs—collection of articles]. Moscow: Institute of Archaeology.

Galanina, L. K. 1977. Skifskie drevnosti Podneprovia (Kollektsia N. E. Brandenburga) [Scythian antiquities (N. E. Brandenburg collection)]. *SAI* D1-33.

———. 1980. *Kurdzhipskii kurgan* [Kurdzhips kurgan]. Leningrad: Iskusstvo.

———. 1997. *Kelermesskie kurgany* [Kelermes kurgans]. Moscow: Paleograph.

———. 2003. Zolotye ukrasheniya iz Elizavetinskikh kurganov v Prikubanie [Golden adornments from Elizavetinskaya kurgans in Kuban]. *ASGE* 36:89–99.

Galanina, L., and N. Gratsch. 1986. *Skythische Kunst*. Leningrad: Aurora.

Garanina, V. A., N. I. Limberis, and I. I. Marchenko. 2001. *Arkheologicheskie Issledovaniia na Novostroikakh Krasnodarskogo kraia* [Archaeological studies on new building sites in Krasnodar region]. Krasnodar: Kraibibkollektor.

Goncharova, L. Yu. 2000. Ikonograficheskie aspekty zverinogo stilia Lesostepnogo Podonia V–nachala III vv. do n.e. [Iconographic aspects of the animal style of the forest-steppe Don river region in 5th–beginning 3rd century BC]. *DA* 3-4:51–61.

Goshkevich, V. I. 1913. Drevnie gorodishcha po beregam nizovogo Dnepra [Ancient settlements along banks of lower Dniepr]. *IAK* 47:117–45.

Govett, E. 1919. *Illustrated Catalogue of the Canessa Collection of Rare and Valuable Objects of Art of the Egyptian, Greek, Roman, Gothic and Renaissance Periods.* New York: Privately printed for C. and E. Canessa.

Grach, N. L. 1984. Kruglodonnie sosudi iz kurgana Kul-Oba [Vessels with rounded bottoms from Kul-Oba kurgan]. *TGE* 24:100–109.

Grakov, B. N. 1971. *Skify* [Scythians]. Moscow: State University Press.

Greifenhagen, A. 1970, 1975. *Schmuckarbeiten in Edelmetall.* 2 vols. Berlin: Staatliche Museen zu Berlin.

Guliaev, V. I. 1969. Zoomorfnye kriuchki skifskogo perioda [Zoomorphic hooks of the Scythian period]. *MIA* 151:109–27.

Gushchina, I. I. 1962. Neskolko ukrashenii konskogo ubora skifskogo vremeni [Some decorations for horse trappings of the Scythian period]. *KSIA* 89:66–69.

Haskins, J. F. 1952. Northern Origins of Sasanian Metalwork. *Artibus Asiae* 15:324–47.

Hončar, F. 1936. Ross und Reiter im urgeschichtlichen Kaukasus. *JPEK*:49–72.

Iessen, A. A. 1950. O khronologii bolshikh kubanskikh kurganov [On the chronology of large kurgans of Kuban] *SA* 12:157–202.

———. 1952. Rannie sviazi Pruiuralia i Irana [Early relationships of Western Urals and Iran]. *SA* 16:206–31.

———. 1953. K voprosu o pamiatnikakh VIII–VII vv. do n.e. na iuge Evropeiskoi chasti SSSR [On the question of sites of 8th–7th century BC in the south European part of USSR]. *SA* 18:49–110.

Ilinskaia, V. A. 1968. *Skify dneprovskogo lesostepnogo levoberezhia* [Scythians of the forest-steppe left bank of the Dniepr]. Kiev: Naukova Dumka.

———. 1973. Skifskaia uzda IV v. do n.e. [Scythian bridles of 4th century BC]. *Skifskie drevnosti– sbornik statey* [Scythian antiquities—collection of articles]. Kiev: Naukova Dumka.

———. 1975. *Ranneskifskie kurgany basseina r. Tiasmin* [Early Scythian kurgans in the basin of the Tiasmyn river]. Kiev: Naukova Dumka.

Ilinskaia, V. A., and A. I. Terenozhkin. 1983. *Skifia VII–IV vv. do n.e.* [Scythia in 7th–4th centuries BC]. Kiev: Naukova Dumka.

———. 1986. Konskoe snariazhenie [Horse trappings]. *Arkheologiia Ukrainskoi SSSR* [Archaeology of Ukrainian SSSR](Kiev) 2:145–48.

Iliukov, L. S. 1999. Rostovskiy klad bronzovykh veshchey [Rostov bronze treasure]. *DA* 3–4:61–64.

Ismagilov, R. B. 1988. Pogrebenie Bolshogo Gumarovskogo kurgana v Yuzhnom Priuralie [The large Gumarovsky burial kurgan in the south Urals]. *ASGE* 29.

Ivantchik, A. I. 2001. *Kimmerier und Skythen.* Moscow: Paleograph Press.

Kahlmeyer, G. Saherwala. 1983. *Frühe Bergvölker in Armenien und im KauKasus.* Berlin: Museum für Vor- und Frügeschichte.

Kamenskiy, V. N. 1987. Pogrebalnye kompleksy iz okrestnostey Krasnodara [Burial complexes from the vicinity of Krasnodar]. *SA* 2:254–58.

Kantorovich, A. R. 1997. K voprosu o skifo-grechskom sinteze v ramkakh zverinogo stikia Stepnoy Skifii [Concerning the Scythian-Greek synthesis in the framework of animal style in the Scythian steppe]. *MIA* 1:97–113.

———. 2002. Klassifikatsiia i tipologiia elementov "zoomorfnykh prevrashcheniy" v zverinom stile stepnoy Skifii [Classification and typology of elements of "zoomorphic transformation" in animal style of Scythian steppe]. *Strukturno-Semanticheskie Issledovaniia v Arkheologii–sbornik statey* [Structural-semantic investigations in archaeology—collection of articles], vol. 1. Donetsk.

———. 2003. Evolutsiya nekotorykh obrazov skifskogo zverinogo stily i problema kontaktov Prikuban'ya, Podon'ya, Nizhnego Povolzh'ya i Yuzhnogo Priuralya [Evolution of some images of Scythian animal style and the problem of contacts of Kuban and Don regions, lower Volga, and south Urals]. *Tezisi chteniy, posvyashennie 100-letiyu V. A. Gorodtsova* [Colloquium on the 100th anniversary of V. A. Gorodtsov], part 2. Moscow: State Historical Museum.

Kantorovich, A. R., and V. R. Erlikh. 2006. *Bronzoliteynoe iskusstvo iz kurganov Adigei* [Cast bronze art from Adyghean kurgans]. Moscow: State Museum of Orient.

Kaposhina, S. I. 1956. Iz istorii grecheskoy kolonizatsii nizhnego Pobuzhia [From the history of Greek colonization of the lower Bug basin]. *MIA* 50:211–54.

Karyshkovskiy, P. O. 1982. Ob izobrazhenii orla i delfina na monetakh Sinopy, Istrii, i Olvii [On depictions of the eagle and the dolphin on coinage from Sinope, Istria, and Olbia]. *Numizmatika Antichnogo Prichernomori–sbornik statey* [Numismatics of ancient Black Sea area—collection of articles]. Kiev: Naukova Dumka.

Kazak, D., ed. 1995. *Catalogue of the Exhibition at Dal Mille al Mille. Tesori e popoli dal Mar Nero.* Milan: Electa.

Kazanski, M., and V. Soupault. 2000. *Les sites archéologiques en Crimee et en Caucase durant l'Antiquité tardive et le haut Moyen-Age.* Leiden: Brill.

Khachatrian, T. S. 1963. *Materialnaia kultura drevnego Artika* [Material culture of ancient Artik]. Yerevan: Academy of Science Press.

Khanenko, B. N., and V. I. Khanenko. 1900. *Drevnosti Podneproviia, t. III* [Antiquities of the Dniepr region, vol. III]. Kiev: Tipografiia S. V. Kulzhenko.

Kirilin, D. S. 1968. Trekhbratnie kurgany v raione Tobechikskogo ozera [The three-brothers kurgans near Tobechik lake]. *Antichnaia istoria i kultura Sredizemnomoria i Prichernomoria–sbornik statey* [Ancient history and culture of the Mediterranean and Black Sea—collection of articles]. Leningrad: Nauka.

Kolotukhin, V. A. 1982. Obsledovanie pamiatnikov Predskifskogo i ranneskifskogo vremeni v Krymu [Review of sites of pre-Scythian and early Scythian periods in Crimea]. *SA* 1:105–19.

Korolkova, E. F. 1998a. Ikonografia obraza khishchnoy ptitsy v skifskom zverinom stile VI–IV vv. do n.e. [Iconography of the image of the bird of prey in Scythian animal style in 6th–4th centuries BC]. *Istoria i kultura drevnikh i srednevekovykh obshchestv–sbornik statey* [History and culture of ancient and medieval societies—collection of articles]. St. Petersburg: State Hermitage.

———. 1998b. Kubansky zveriny stil I ego vostochnie analogii [The Kuban animal style and its oriental analogies]. *Skifi, khazary, slavyane, drevnyaya Rus–sbornik statey* [Scythians, Khazars, Slavs, Ancient Rus—collection of articles]. St. Petersburg: University Press.

———. 1999. Zoomorfnye svastiki i vikhrevye rozetki v iskusstve zverinogo stilya [Zoomorphic swastikas and whirlwind rosettes in animal style]. *Bosporsky fenomen: Grecheskaya kultura na periferii antichnogo mira–sbornik statey* [Bosphoran phenomena: Greek culture on the periphery of the classical world—collection of articles]. St. Petersburg: Institute of the History of Material Culture.

———. 2001. Kubansky zveriny stil i ego vostochnie analogii [The Kuban animal style and its oriental analogies]. *ASGE* 35:91–111.

Korovina, A. K. 1957. K voprosu ob izuchenii Semibratnikh kurganov [On the question of studies of the Semibratnie kurgans]. *SA* 2:174–87.

Koshelenko, G. A., I. T. Kruglikova, and V. S. Dolgorukov, eds. 1984. Antichnye gosudarstva Severnogo Prichernomoria [Classical states of northern Black Sea region]. *Arkheologiia SSSR* [Archaeology of USSR]. Moscow: Nauka.

Kovalevskaia, V. B. 1979. Poiasnye nabory Evrazii IV–IX vv. Priazhky [Strap sets of Eurasia in 4th–9th century AD. Buckles]. *SAI* E1-2.

———. 1981. Severokavkazskie drevenosti [Antiquities of the northern Caucasus]. *Stepi Evrazii v epokhu srednevekovia* [Eurasian steppes in the medieval period]. *Arkheologiia SSSR* [Archaeology of USSR]. Moscow: Nauka.

Kovpanenko, G. T., S. S. Bessonova, and A. A. Skoryi. 1989. *Pamiatniki skifskoy epokhi dneprovskogo lesostepnogo Pravoberezhia* [Sites of the Scythian epoch of Dniepr forest steppe right bank]. Kiev: Naukova Dumka.

Kozenkova, V. I. 1982. Tipologiia i khronologicheskaia klassifikatsiia predmetov kobanskoi kultury [Typology and chronological classification of items of Koban culture]. *SAI* B2-5.

——. 1989. Kobanskaia kultura. Zapadnyi variant [Koban culture. Western variant]. *SAI* B2-5.

——. 1995. Oruzhie, voinskoe i konskoe snariazhenie plemen Kobanskoi kultury [Weapons, military, and horse equipment of tribes of the Koban culture]. *SAI* B2-5.

——. 1998. Materialnaia osnova byta kobanskikh plemen. Zapadniy variant [Material basis of the lifestyle of Koban tribes. Western variant]. *SAI* B2-5.

——. 2002. *Mogilnik epokhi pozdnei bronzy-rannego zheleza u aula Serzhen-Yurt, Chechnia* [Burial ground from late Bronze age—early Iron age from the mountain village of Serzhen-Yurt, Chechnya]. Moscow: Nauka.

Kramarovskiy, M. G. 2001. *Zoloto Chingisidov: kulturnoe nasledie Zolotoi Ordy* [Gold of the Chingisids: cultural legacy of the Golden Horde]. St. Petersburg: State Hermitage.

Kris, Kh. I. 1981. Kizil-kobinskaia kultura i tavry [Kizil-Koba culture and the Taurian]. *SAI* D1-7.

Krivtsova-Grakova, O. A. 1949. *Bessarabskii klad* [Bessarabian treasure]. Moscow: State Historical Museum.

——. 1955. Stepnoe Povolzhie I Prichernomorie v epokhu pozdney bronzy [The Volga and Black Sea steppe in the late Bronze age]. *MIA* 46.

Kropotkin, V. V. 1970. Rimskie importnye izdeliia v Vostochnoi Evrope (II v. do n.e. V v. n.e.) [Roman imported wares in eastern Europe (2nd century BC–5th century AD)]. *SAI* D1-27.

Krupnov, E. I. 1947. Severo-Kavkazskaia arkheologicheskaia ekspeditsia [Northern Caucasus archaeological expedition]. *KSIIMK* 17:99-104.

——. 1960. *Drevniaia Istoriia Severnogo Kavkaza* [Ancient history of northern Caucasus]. Moscow: Nauka.

Kuftin, B. A. 1941. *Arkheologicheskie raskopki v Trialeti* [Archaeological excavations in Trialeti]. Tbilisi: Metsniereba.

Kukharenko, Yu. V. 1982. O Kachinskoy nakhodke V veka [On the Kachynskiy find of the 5th century]. *Drevnosti epokhi velikogo pereseleniia narodov V–VIII vekov–sbornik statey* [Antiquities from the epoch of great population movements in 5th–8th centuries—collection of articles]. Moscow: Nauka.

Kushnareva, K. Kh., and V. I. Markovin, eds. 1994. *Epokha bronzy Kavkaza i Srednei Azii* [Bronze age in Caucasus and central Asia]. Moscow: Nauka.

Kuznetsov, V. A. 1963a. *Srednevekovye pamiatniki Severnoi Osetii* [Medieval sites of northern Ossetia]. *MIA* 114.

——. 1963b. Issledovania Zmeiskogo katakombnogo mogilnika v 1958 g [Study of the Zmeiskoi catacomb burial ground in 1958]. *MIA* 114:8-47.

Kuznetsova, T. M. 1987. Zerkala iz skifskikh pamiatnikov VI–III vv. do n.e. [Mirrors from Scythian sites of 6th–3rd centuries BC]. *SA* 1:35-47.

——. 1991. *Etiudy po skifskoi istorii* [Studies in Scythian history]. Moscow: Institute of Archaeology.

Lappo-Danilevskii, A., and V. Malmberg. 1894. *Drevnosti Yuzhnoi Rossii: Kurgan Karagodeuashkh* [Antiquities of south Russia: kurgan Karagodeuashkh]. *MAR* 13.

Leipen, Neda. 1971. *Athena Parthenos: A Reconstruction*. Toronto: Royal Ontario Museum.

Leskov, A. M. 1965. *Gornyi Krym v I tys. do n.e.* [Mountainous Crimea in 1st millennium BC]. Kiev: Naukova Dumka.

——. 1967. O severo-prichernomorskom ochage metalloobrabotki v epokhu pozdnei bronzy [On the northern Black Sea center of metalwork in late Bronze age]. *Pamiatniki epokhi bronzy Iuga Evropeiskoi chasti SSSR* [Monuments of Bronze age from southern European part of USSR].

Kiev: Naukova Dumka.

——. 1968. Bogatoe skifskoe pogrebenie iz Vostochnogo Kryma [A rich Scythian burial from eastern Crimea]. *SA* 1:158–65.

——. 1970. Kirovskoe poselenie [The Kirov settlement]. *Drevnosti Vostochnogo Kryma* [Antiquities of eastern Crimea]. Kiev: Naukova Dumka.

——. 1972. *Novye sokrovishcha kurganov Ukrainy* [New treasures of Ukrainian barrows]. Leningrad: Aurora.

——. 1974a. Die Skütische Kurgane. *Antike Welt*. Kusnacht-Zurich: Baggi-Verlag.

——. 1974b. *Skarby kurhaniv Khersonshchyny* [Treasures of kurgans of the Kherson region]. Kiev: Mistetstvo.

——. 1975a. *Predskifskiy period na Yuge Ukrainy* [Pre-Scythian period in the south of Ukraine]. Moscow: Institute of Archaeology.

——. 1975b. *Zakliuchitelnyi etap bronzovogo veka na Iuge Ukrainy* [Final period of Bronze age in south of Ukraine]. Moscow: Institute of Archaeology.

——. 1990. *Grabschätze der Adygeen*. Munich: Hirmer Verlag.

——. n.d. *Ulskie Kurgany–sbornik statey* [Ulskie kurgans—collection of articles]. Moscow: Paleograph Press. In preparation.

Leskov, A. M., ed. 1985. *Sokrovishcha kurganov Adygeii* [Treasures of kurgans of Adyghea]. Moscow: Sovetskiy Khudozhnik.

——, ed. 1989. *Gold und Kunsthandwerk vom antiken Kuban*. Stuttgart: Theiss Verlag.

——, ed. 1991. *Grabschätze vom Kaukasus*. Rome: De Luca.

Leskov, A. M., and V. R. Erlikh. 1999. *Mogilnik Fars/Klady* [Burial ground of the Fars/treasure]. Moscow: Museum of the East.

Leskov, A. M., and A. Ivanchik, eds. *Ulskie kurgany* [Ulski kurgans]. Moscow: Paleograph. In press.

Leskov, A. M., and V. L. Lapushnian, eds. 1987. *Shedevry Drevnego Iskusstva Kubani* [Art treasure of ancient Kuban]. Moscow: Vneshtorgizdat.

Liberov, P. D. 1965. Pamiatniki skifskogo vremeni na srednem Donu [Sites of Scythian period in central Don River region]. *SAI* D1–31.

Limberis, N. Iu., and I. I. Marchenko. 1992. Issledovanie meoto-sarmatskikh mogilnikov Starokorsunskogo gorodishcha No. 2 [Studies of Meotian-Sarmatian burial grounds at Starokorsunskii hillfort No. 2]. *Arkheologicheskie raskopki na Kubani v 1989–1990 godakh* [Archaeological excavations in Kuban region in 1989–1990]. Ieisk.

Lordkipanidze, O. D. 1989. *Nasledie Drevney Gruzii* [Legacy of ancient Georgia]. Tbilisi: Metsniereba.

Lovpache, N. G. 1985. Mogilnik v ustie reki Psekups [Burial ground at mouth of Psekups River]. *Voprosy Arkheologii Adygei* [Questions of archaeology in Adyghea]. Maikop: Adyghean Institute of Economics, Language, Literature, and History.

Lukonin, V. G. 1977. *Iskusstvo drevnego Irana* [Art of ancient Iran]. Moscow: Iskusstvo.

Lunin, B. V. 1939. *Arkheologicheskie nakhodki 1935–1936gg v okrestnostiakh stanits Tulskoy i Dakhovskoy bliz Maikopa* [Archaeological finds of 1935–1936 in vicinities of villages of Tulskaia and Dakhovskaia near Maikop]. *VDI* 3:210–22.

Maksimenko, V. E. 1983. *Savromaty i sarmaty na nizhnem Donu* [Sauromatians and Sarmatians on the lower Don]. Rostov: University Press.

Malyshev, A. A. 1993. Pozolochennye terrakotovye medaliony s izobrazheniem Meduzy Gorgony v Prykubanie [Gilded terracotta medallions with depictions of the Gorgon Medusa in the Kuban region]. *Materialy seminara po skifo-sarmatskoi arkheologii* [Materials for the seminar on Scythian-Sarmartian archaeology]. Moscow: Moscow State University.

Malyshev, A. A., and I. G. Ravich. 2001. O nakhodkakh obraztsov skifskogo zverinogo stilia v okrestnostiakh Novorossiiska [On finds of images in the Scythian animal style in environs of Novorossisk]. *Severnyi Kavkaz: Istoriko-arkheologicheskie ocherki i zametki* [Northern Caucasus:

historic-archaeological essays and paragraphs]. Moscow: Institute of Archaeology.

Mantsevich, A. P. 1957. Riton Talaevskogo kurgana [Rhyton from Talaivskyi kurgan]. *Istoria i arkheologia drevnego Kryma–sbornik statey* [History and archaeology of ancient Crimea–collection of articles]. Kiev: Naukova Dumka.

———. 1966. Derevyannie sosudy skifskoy epohi [Wooden vessels of the Scythian epoch.] *ASGE* 8:23–38.

———. 1987. *Kurgan Solokha* [Solokha kurgan]. Leningrad: Iskusstvo.

Markovin, V. I. 1960. Kultura plemen Severnogo Kavkaza v epokhu bronzy (II tys. do n.e.) [Culture of tribes of the northern Caucasus in Bronze age (2nd millennium BC)]. *MIA* 93.

Marsadolov, L. S. 1984. Khronologicheskoe sootnoshenie Pazyrykskikh i Semibratnikh kurganov [Chronological correlation of Pazyryk and Semibratni kurgans]. *ASGE* 18:30–37.

Marshall, F. H. 1907. *Catalogue of the Finger Rings, Greek, Etruscan, and Roman, in the Department of Antiquities, British Museum*. London: British Museum.

———. 1911. *Catalogue of the Jewellery, Greek, Etruscan, and Roman, in the Department of Antiquities, British Museum*. London: British Museum.

Martirosian, A. A. 1964. *Armenia v epokhu bronzy i rannego zheleza* [Armenia in Bronze age and early Iron age]. Yerevan: Academy of Sciences.

Maslenitsina E. S. 1993. Nekortorie stilisticheskie gruppy pamiatnikov v iskusstve Prikubania v kontse V–IV vv.do n.e. [Some stylistic groups of monuments of Kuban art in late 5th–4th centuries BC]. *Grakovskie chtenia 1989–1990gg* [In memory of B. N. Grakov, 1989–1990]. Moscow: Moscow State University.

Maslov, V. E., and M. A. Ochir-Goryaeva. 1997. Ob obshchikh elementakh v culture nizhnevolzhskikh kochevnikov i Vostochnogo predkavkaz'ya v kontse VI–nachale IV vv. do v.e. [On common features in the culture of lower Volga nomads and population of central and east Caucasus piedmonts in late 6th–early 4th centuries BC]. *TGIM* 97:62–74.

Meliukova, A. I. 1964. *Vooruzhenie skifov* [Scythian armor]. Moscow: Nauka.

———. 1981. *Krasnokutskiy kurgan* [Krasnokutsk kurgan]. Moscow: Nauka.

Meliukova, A. I., and M. P. Abramova, eds. 1989. Stepi Evropeiskoi chasti SSSR v skifo-sarmatskoe vremia [Steppes of the European part of USSR in Scytho-Sarmatian period]. *Arkheologia SSSR* [Archaeology of USSR]. Moscow: Nauka.

Merhav, R., ed. 1991. *Urartu. A Metalworking Center in the First Millennium B.C.E.* Jerusalem: Israel Museum.

Miller, A. A. 1926. Kratkij otchet o rabote Severo-Kavkazskoy ekspeditsii GAIMK v 1924 i 1925 godakh [Brief report on work of north Caucasus expedition of State Academy of History of Material Culture]. *Soobshcheniya* [Information]. *GAIMK* 1:75–142.

Minns, E. 1913. *Scythians and Greeks*. Cambridge: Cambridge University Press.

———. 1942. The Art of the Northern Nomads. *Annual Lecture on Aspects of Art of the British Academy*. London: Milford.

Mitchell, T. C. 1989. *The Oxus Treasure from the British Museum*. London: Museum Riztberg Zurich.

Mohen, J.-P., ed. 1989. *Archéologie compare Europe orientale, Asie, Oceanie, Amerique sommaire illustree des collections du Musee des antiquités nationals de Saint-Germain-en Laye*. Paris: Ministere de la Culture.

Moorey, P. R. S., E. C. Bunker, E. Porada, and G. Markoe. 1981. *Ancient Bronzes, Ceramics, and Seals: The Nasli M. Heeramaneck Collection of Ancient Near Eastern, Central Asiatic, and European Art*. Los Angeles, CA: Los Angeles County Museum of Art.

Mordvinceva, V. 2001. *Sarmatische Phaleren*. Rahden: Verlag Marie Leidorf.

Moshinskiy, A. P. 2003. *Kon i vsadnik. Vzgliad skvoz veka* [Horse and rider. A view through centuries]. Moscow: State Historical Museums.

Moshkova, M. G. 1963. Pamiatninki Prokhrovskoy kultury [Sites of the Prokhorovskaia culture]. *SAI* D1–10.

Motzenbäcker, I. 1996. *Sammlung Kossnierska. Der Digorische formenkreis der kaukasischen Bronzezeit.* Berlin: Druckhaus Berlin-Centrum.

Mozolevskiy, B. N. 1973. Skifskie pogrebeniia u s. Nagornoe bliz g. Ordzhonikidze na Dnepropetrovshchine [Scythian burials in the village of Nahorne, near the town of Ordzhonikidze in Dnipropetrovsk province]. *Skifskie drevnosti–sbornik statey* [Scythian antiquities–collection of articles]. Kiev: Naukova Dumka.

——. 1979. *Tovsta Mogyla* [Tovsta Mogila]. Kiev: Naukova Dumka.

——. 1980. Skifskie kurgany v okrestnostiakh g. Ordzhonikidze na Dnepropetrovshchine (raskopki 1972–75 gg.) [Scythian kurgans in the environs of the town of Ordzhonikidze in Dnipropetrovsk province (excavations in 1972–75)]. *Skifiia i Kavkaz–sbornik statey* [Scythia and the Caucasus–collection of articles]. Kiev: Naukova Dumka.

Mozolevskiy, B. N., and S. V. Polin. 2005. *Skifskie kurgany Gerrosa IV v.do n.e.* [Kurgans of Scythian Gerros of the 4th century BC]. Kiev: "Stilos."

Munchaev, R. M. 1963. Lugovoy mogilnik [Lugovoy cemetery]. *Drevnosti Checheno-Ingushetii–sbornik statey* [Antiquities of Chechnia-Ingushetia–collection of articles]. Moscow: Nauka.

——. 1975. *Kavkaz na zare bronzovogo veka* [Caucasus at dawn of Bronze age]. Moscow: Nauka.

Murzin, V. Yu. 1984. *Skifskaya arkhaika Severnogo Prichernomoria* [Scythian archaic time in north Pontic area]. Kiev: Naukova Dumka.

Nekhaev, A. A. 1987. Veshchi iz kurganov u St Kuzhorskaia [Objects from kurgans near the village of Kuzhorskaia]. *Shedevry drevnego iskusstva Kubani* [Art treasures of ancient Kuban]. Moscow: Vneshtorgizdat.

Neverov, O. Ya. 1986. Metallicheskie perstni epokhi arkhaiki, klassiki i ellinizma iz Severnogo Prichernomoria [Metal rings from Archaic, Classical, and Hellenistic periods in northern Black Sea region]. *Antichnaia torevtika* [Classical toreutics]. Leningrad: State Hermitage.

Nikulina, N. M. 1994. *Iskusstvo Ionii i Akhemenidskogo Irana* [Art of Ionia and Achaemenid Iran]. Moscow: Iskusstvo.

Noskova, L. M. 1999. Krematsionnyi urnovyi mogilnik bliz byvshego aula Leninokhabl v Adygee [A cremation urn burial ground near the former village of Leninokhabl in Adyghea]. *Materialnaia kultura Vostoka–sbornik statey* [Material culture of the Orient–collection of articles]. Moscow: State Museum of the Orient.

OAK 1880, 1889, 1898, 1903, 1906, 1909–10.

Ochir-Goriaeva, M. A. 1987. Pogrebalny obryad naseleniya nizhnego Povolzh'ya i Yuzhnogo Priural'ya VI–IV vv. do n.e. [Burial rites of lower Volga and south Urals populations in 6th–4th centuries BC]. *Arkheologicheskie issledovaniya Kalmykii* [Archaeological investigations of Kalmykia]. Elista: Institute of Language, Literature and History of Kalmikiia.

——. 1988. Savromatskaya kultura Nizhnego Povolzh'ya VI–IV vv. do n.e. [Savromatian culture of the lower Volga region in 6th–4th centuries BC]. Ph.D. dissertation. Leningrad: Institute of the History of Material Culture.

——. 2001. Predmety konskoi uzdy iz Maikopa [Horse bridle fittings from Maikop]. *Tret'a Kubanskaia arkheologicheskaia konferentsia* [Third Kuban archaeological conference]. Krasnodar-Anapa: Simvolika.

Oliver, A. 1971. A *Bronze Mirror from Sardis. Studies Presented to George M. A. Hanfmann.* Mainz: Philipp von Zabern.

Onaiko, N. A. 1970. Antichnyi import v Pridneprovie i Pobuzhie v IV–II vv. do n.e. [Ancient Greek imports in Dniepr river region and Bug river region in 4th–2nd centuries BC]. *SAI* D1-27.

Otroshchenko, V. V. 2001. *Problemy periodyzatsii kultur seredn'oi ta piznoi bronzy Pivdnia Skhidnoi Evropy* [Problems in the periodization of cultures of middle and late Bronze ages in the south of eastern Europe]. Kiev: National University.

Perevodchikova, E. V. 1980a. Tipologiia i evoliutsiia skifskikh navershiy [Typology and evolution of Scythian finials]. *SA* 2:23–44.

——. 1980b. Prikubanskiy variant skifskogo zverinogo stilia [Kuban variant of Scythian animal style]. Ph.D. dissertation, Moscow State University.

——. 1984. Kharakteristika predmetov skifskogo zverinogo stilia [Characteristics of items of Scythian animal style]. *Arkheologo-etnograficheskie issledovaniia Severnogo Kavkaza–sbornik statey* [Archaeological-ethnographic investigations of north Caucasus—collection of articles]. Krasnodar: State University.

——. 1987. Lokalnye cherty skifskogo zverinogo stilia Prikubania [Local features of Scythian animal style in Kuban region]. *SA* 4:44–58.

——. 1994. *Iazyk zverinykh obrazov* [Language of animal images]. Moscow: Eastern Literatures.

——. 2000. K voprosu o sviazakh Nizhnego Povolzhia, Prikubania i Nizhnego Podonia (po materialam skifskogo zverinogo stilia) [On the question of connections of the lower Volga river region, Kuban region, and lower Don river region (based on material in Scythian animal style)]. *Skify, Sarmaty v VII–III vv. do n.e.–sbornik statey* [Scythians, Sarmatians in 7th–3rd centuries BC—collection of articles]. Moscow: Institute of Archaeology.

Petrenko, V. G. 1967. Pravoberezhie srednego Podneprovia v V–III vv. do n.e. [Right bank of central Dniepr river region in 5th–3rd centuries BC]. *SAI* D1-4.

——. 1978. Ukrasheniia Skifii VII-III vv. do n.e. [Ornaments of Scythia in 7th–3rd centuries BC]. *SAI* D4-5.

——. 2006. *Krasnoznamenskii Burial-ground*. Berlin: Paleograph Press.

Pharmakowsky, B. V. 1909. Archäeologische Funde im Jahre 1908. *Russland Archäeologischer Anzeiger* (Berlin):139–79.

Piankov, A. V., and V. A. Tarabanov. 1997. Mogilnik protomeotskogo vremeni Kazazovo-3 i drugie nakhodki iz chashi Krasnodarskogo vodokhranilishcha [Kazazovo-3, a burial ground of proto-Meotian period and other finds from basin of Krasnodar reservoir]. *Pamiatniki predskifskogo i skifskogo vremeni na Iuge Vostochnoi Evropy–sbornik statey* [Monuments of pre-Scythian and Scythian times in south of eastern Europe—collection of articles]. Moscow: Institute of Archaeology.

Piotrovskiy, B. B. 1959. *Vanskoe tsarstvo* [Van kingdom]. Moscow: Western Literature.

Piotrovsky, B. B., ed. 1975. *From the Lands of the Scythians*. New York: Metropolitan Museum of Art.

Pitskhelauri, K. N. 1979. *Vostochnaia Gruziia v kontse bronzovogo veka* [Eastern Georgia at end of Bronze age]. Tbilisi: Metsniereba.

Platz-Horster, G. 2002. *Ancient Gold Jewellery*. Antikensammlung Staatliche Museen zu Berlin. Mainz: Philipp von Zabern.

Pletneva, S. A. 1967. *Ot kocheviy k gorodam* [From nomads to cities]. Moscow: Nauka.

——. 1981. Stepi Evrazii v epokhu srednevekovia [Steppes of Eurasia in Medieval period]. *Arkheologiia SSSR* [Archaeology of USSR]:62–79.

——. 1989. *Na slaviano-khazarskom pogranichie. Dmitrievskiy arkheologicheskiy kompleks* [On the Slavic-Khazar border. Dmitrievskiy archaeological complex]. Moscow: Nauka.

——. 1998. *Na severnykh rubezhakh khazarskogo kaganata* [On northern borders of Khazar kingdom]. Voronezh: State University.

Pogrebova, M. N., and D. S. Raevsky. 1992. *Rannie Skify i drevniy Vostok* [Early Scythians and the ancient orient]. Moscow: Nauka.

Pokrovska, E. F. 1957. Kurgany IV st. do n.e. bilia Kholodnoho Yaru poblyzu m. Smily [Kurgans of 4th century BC near Kholodnyi Iar, near city of Smila]. *Arkheologiia* [Archaeology] 10:65–79.

Polin, S. V. 1992. *Ot Skifii k Sarmatii* [From Scythia to Sarmatia]. Kiev: Naukova Dumka.

Popov, R. 1932. Mogilniti grobove pri s. Endzhe [Burial grounds by Endzhe]. *Izvestiia na Bulgarskiy arkheologicheski Institut* [News from the Bulgarian Archeological Institute] 6:97–102.

Potratz, Johannes A. H. 1960. Skythische Kunst. *Orientalia* 29:46–62.

———. 1963. *Die Skythen in Südrussland*. Basel: Raggi-Verlag.

———. 1968. *Luristan-bronzen. Die einstmalige Sammlung Professor Sarre, Berlin*. Istanbul: Nederlands Historisch-Archaeologisch Instituut.

Pridik, E. 1911. Melgunovskiy klad 1763g. [Melgunovskyi treasure of 1763]. *MAR* 31.

Prokopenko, Yu. A. 1998. K voprosu o svyazyakh naselenia Tsentralnogo Predkavkaziya v IV–III vv. do n.e. [On the question of contacts of population of central Caucasus in 4th–3rd c. BC]. *IAA* 4:37–46.

———. 2001a. K voprosu o vydelenii v materialakh IV–I vv. do n.e. pamiatnikov Stavropolia uzko datyruiushchikhsia kompleksov IV–III vv. do n.e. [On the question of selection of materials of 4th–1st centuries BC at sites in the Stavropol area from complexes narrowly dated to 4th–3rd centuries BC]. *Tretia kubanskaia arkheologicheskaia konferentsia* [Third Kuban archaeological conference]. Krasnodar-Anapa: Simvolika.

———. 2001b. Mnogolepestkovye inkrustirovannye fibuly iz pamiatnikov Severnogo Kavkaza [Multi-petal encrusted fibulae from sites in northern Caucasus]. *IAA* 7:70–74.

Puzikova, A. I. 1964. Dva kurgana iz mogilnika skifskogo vremeni u s. Russkaia Trostianka [Two kurgans from a burial ground of the Scythian period in the village of Russkaia Trostianka]. *KSIA* 102:24–33.

———. 1995. *Skify Srednego Dona* [Scythians of central Don region]. Moscow: Praktik-A.

———. 2001. *Kurgannie mogilniki skifskogo vremeni srednego Podonia* [Kurgan burials of Scythian period in central Don region]. Moscow: Institute of Archaeology.

Raevskiy, D. S. 1985. *Model mira skifskoy kultury* [World pattern in Scythian culture]. Moscow: Nauka.

Rata, S. 1966. Cazanul scitic de bronzdin secolele VI–V Î.E.N. de la Îacobeni-Dîngeni. [Scythian bronze cauldron of 6th–5th century BC from Jacobeni-Dengeni]. *Arkheologia Moldovei* [Moldovan archaeology] 4:351–53.

Reeder, Ellen, ed. 1999. *Scythian Gold. Treasures from Ancient Ukraine*. New York: Harry N. Abrams.

Rezepkin, A. D. 2000. *Das frühbronzezeitliche Gräberfeld von Klady und die Majkop-Kultur in Nordwestkaukasien*. Rahden/Westf.: Verlag Marie Leidorf.

Richter, Gisela M. A. 1920. *Catalogue of Engraved Gems of the Classical Style*. New York: Metropolitan Museum of Art.

———. 1968. *Engraved Gems of the Greeks and the Etruscans*. London: Phaidon.

Rolle, R., ed. 1993. *Gold der Skythen*. Münster: Hamburger Museum für Archäologie und Geshichte (Helms Museum).

Rostovtzeff, M. I. 1914. *Antichnaya dekorativnaya zhivopis' na yuge Rosii* [Classical decorative paintings from the south of Russia]. St. Petersburg: Izdatel'stvo IAK.

———. 1918. *Ellinstvo i Iranstvo na Yuge Rossii* [Hellenism and Iranism in the south of Russia]. Petrograd III.

———. 1922. *Iranians and Greeks in South Russia*. Oxford: Clarendon Press.

———. 1925. *Skifiya i Bospor* [Scythia and the Bosporus]. Leningrad: Russian Academy of the History of Material Culture.

———. 1929. *The Animal Style in South Russia and China*. Princeton, NJ: Princeton University Press.

———. 1931a. Bronzeschnallen aus Südrußland. *Prähistorische Zeitschrift* 22:46–55.

———. 1931b. Some Remarks on the Luristan Bronzes. *JPEK*:45–56.

———. 1931c. *Skythen und der Bosporus*. Berlin: Hans Schoetz.

———. 1993. Sredinnaya Aziya, Rossiya, Kitay i zveriniy stil. Sbornik statey ΣΚΥΘΙΚΑ [Central Asia, Russia, China and the Animal Style. Collection of articles ΣΚΥΘΙΚΑ]. *Peterburgskiy Arkheologicheskiy Vestnik N5* [Petersburg archaeological bulletin N5] Farn:57–75.

Ryabova, V. O. 1984. Dereviani chashi z obbivkami z kurganiv skifskogo chasu [Wooden bowls with casements from kurgans of Scythian times]. *Arkheologiia* [Archaeology] 46:31–44.

Savchenko, E. I. 2001. Mogilnik skifskogo vremeni "Ternovoe I-Kolbino I" [A burial ground of the Scythian period: "Ternovoe I-Kolbino I"]. *Arkheologia srednego Dona v Skifskuyu epokhu–sbornik statey* [Archaeology of central Don area in Scythian epoch–collection of articles]. Moscow: Institute of Archaeology.

Sazonov, A. A. 1995. Rannyaya gruppa konskikh zakhoronenij protomeotskogo mogilnika Pshish [Early group of horse burials of a proto-Meotian cemetery at Pshish]. *Arkheologia Adigei–sbornik statey* [Archaeology of Adyghea–collection of articles]. Maikop: Meot.

———. 1997. K voprosu o khronologii protomeotskikh kolesnichnykh naborov v epokhu kimmeriysko-skifskikh pokhodov [On the question of chronology of proto-Meotian chariot sets in the epoch of Cimmerian-Scythian campaigns]. *Nivye issldovanya arkheologov Rossii i SNG–sbornik statey* [New investigations of archaeologists of Russia and Union of Independent States–collection of articles]. St. Petersburg: Institute of History of Material Culture.

Schiltz, V., ed. 2001. *L'Or des Amazones.* Paris: Musée Cernuschi.

Schlette, F. 1979. *Kelten zwischen Alesia und Pergamon.* Berlin: Urania Verlag.

Schmidt, H. 1927. Skythischer Pferdegeschirrschmuck aus einem Silberdepot unbekannter Herkunft. *Prähistorische Zeitschrift* 28:1–90.

Schumm, A. B. 1930. *The Ercole Canessa Collection.* New York: American Art Association, Andersen Galleries.

Sergatskov, I. V. 1991. Pogrebnie predskifskogo vremeni na Ilovle [Graves of pre-Scythian times on the Ilovle river]. *SA* N2:240–44.

Shamba, S. M. 1988. *Gyuenos* [Gyenos]. Tbilisi: Metsniereba.

Sharafutdinova, E. S. 1980. Pamiatniki predskifskogo vremeni na nizhnem Donu [Sites of pre-Scythian period in the lower Don region]. *SAI* B1–11.

Shchapova, Yu. L. 1997. Ukrasheniia iz stekla [Glass ornaments]. *Drevniaia Rus. Byt i kultura* [Ancient Rus. Life and culture]. Moscow: Nauka.

Shkurko, A. I. 1976. O lokalnykh razlichiiakh v iskusstve lesostepnoi Skifii [On local differences in the art of forest-steppe Scythia]. *Skifo-Sibirskii Zverinyi stil v iskusstve s Evrazii–sbornik statey* [Scythian-Siberian animal style in the art of Eurasian peoples–collection of articles]. Moscow: Nauka.

———. 2000. Skifskoe iskusstvo zverinogo stilia (po materialam lesostepnoi Skifii) [Scythian art of the animal style (based on the material from forest-steppe Scythia)]. *Skify i Sarmaty v VII–III vv. do n.e.–sbornik statey* [Scythians and Sarmatians in 7th–3rd centuries BC–collection of articles]. Moscow: Institute of Archaeology.

Shramko, B. A. 1976. Novye nakhodki na Belskom gorodishche i nekotorye voprosy formirovania i semantiki obrazov zverinogo stilia [New finds from the Belski hillfort and some questions regarding the formation and semantics of images in the animal style]. *Skifo-sibirskii zverinyi stil v iskusstve narodov Evrazii–sbornik statey* [Scythian-Siberian animal style in art of Eurasian peoples–collection of articles]. Moscow: Nauka.

Simonenko, A. V., and B. I. Lobai. 1992. *Sarmaty Severo-Zapadnogo Prichernomoria v I v. n.e.* [Sarmatians of northwestern Black sea region in 1st century AD]. Kiev: Naukova Dumka.

Skoriy, A. A. 1999. *Kimmeriitsy v Ukrainskoi Lesostepi* [Cimmerians in Ukrainian forest-steppe]. Kiev: Arkheologiia.

Skudnova, V. M. 1954. Skifskie pamiatniki iz Nimfeia [Scythian sites at Nymphaion]. *SA* 21:306–18.

———. 1962. Skifskie zerkala iz arkhaicheskogo nekropolia Olvii [Scythian mirrors from archaic necropolis of Olbia]. *TGE* 7:5–25.

———. 1988. *Arkhaicheskiy nekropol Olvii* [Archaic necropolis of Olbia]. Leningrad: Iskusstvo.

Smirnov, K. F. 1961. Vooruzhenie savromatov [Sauromatian armor]. *MIA* 101.

———. 1964. *Savromaty* [Sauromatians]. Moscow: Nauka.

——. 1984. *Sarmaty i utverzhdenie ikh politicheskogo gospodstva v Skifii* [Sarmatians and the establishment of their political supremacy in Scythia]. Moscow: Nauka.

Smirnov, Ya. I. 1909. *Vostochnoe serebro* [Eastern silver]. St. Petersburg: IAK.

Smirnova, G. I. 1977. O khronologicheskom sootnoshenii pamyatnikov tipa Sacharna–Soloncheni i Zhbotin (On the chronological correlation of monuments of Sakharna type–Soloncheni and Zhbotin). *SA* N4:94–107.

——. 1985. Osnoviy khronologii predskifskikh pamyatnikov Yugo-Zapada SSSR [Basis of the chronology of pre-Scythian monuments in southwestern USSR]. *SA* N4:33–53.

Sokolskiy, N. I. 1980. Tamanskiy klad bronzovykh orudiy [Taman treasure of bronze tools]. *SA* 2:144–49.

Solomonik, E. I. 1959. *Sarmatskie znaki Severnogo Prichernomoria* [Sarmatian insignia of northern Black sea region]. Kiev: Naukova Dumka.

Spier, Jeffery. 1992. *Ancient Gems and Finger Rings. Catalogue of the Collections of the J. Paul Getty Museum*. Malibu, CA: Getty Museum.

Spitsyn, A. A. 1909. Falari yuzhnoy Rossii [Phalerae from south of Russia]. *IAK* 29:18–53.

Stefani, L. 1851. *Drevnosti Bospora Kimmeriyskogo* [Antiquities of the Cimmerian Bosporus] 1. St. Petersburg.

Tekhov, B. V. 1971. *Ocherki drevney istorii i arkheologii Yugo-Osetii* [Studies in ancient history and archaeology of southern Ossetia]. Tbilisi: Metsniereba.

——. 1976. O nekotorykh predmetakh skifskogo zverinogo stilya iz pamyatnikov Yuzhnogo sklona glavnogo Kavkazskogo khrebta [On some objects of Scythian animal style from sites of the southern slope of the main Caucasian range]. *Skifo-Sibirsky zveriny stil v iskusstve narodov Evrazii–sbornik statey* [Scythian-Siberian animal style in art of the peoples of Eurasia—collection of articles]. Moscow: Nauka.

——. 1977. *Tsentralnyi Kavkaz v XVI–X vv. do n.e.* [Central Caucasus in 16th–10th centuries BC]. Moscow: Nauka.

——. 1980–85. *Tliyskiy mogilnik* [Tliyskiy burial ground]. 3 vols. Tbilisi: Metsniereba.

Terenozhkin, A. I. 1976. *Kimmeriitsy* [Cimmerians]. Kiev: Naukova Dumka.

Terenozhkin, A. I., V. A. Ilinskaia, E. V. Chernenko, and B. N. Mozolevskiy. 1973. Skifskie kurgany Nikopolshchiny [Scythian kurgans of the Nikopol region]. *Skifskie drevnosti–sbornik statey* [Scythian antiquities—collection of articles]. Kiev: Naukova Dumka.

Terenozhkin, A. I., and B. N. Mozolevskiy. 1988. *Melitopolskiy kurgan* [Melitopol Kurgan]. Kiev: Naukova Dumka.

Tolstikov, V. P., and M. Yu. Treister. 1996. *The Gold of Troy*. New York: Harry N. Abrams.

Trapsh, M. M. 1962. *Pamiatniki kolkhidskoy i skifskoy kultur v sele Kulanurkhva Abkhazskoy ASSR* [Sites of Colchis and Scythian cultures in the village of Kulanurkhva Abkhazian Autonomous SSR]. Sukhumi: Abgosizdat.

Treister, M. Yu. 2000. Mestnye podrazhaniia detaliam rimskogo voennogo kostiuma na Bospore [Local imitations of details of Roman military costumes in the Bosporus]. *RA* 3:118–24.

Valchak, S. B. 1993. O nekotorykh tselnolitykh uzdechnykh komplektakh predskifskogo vremeni na Yuge Vostochnoy Evropy [On some single-cast horse trappings of pre-Scythian period in the south of eastern Europe]. *Materialy seminara po Skifo-Sarmatskoy Arkheologii* [Materials of seminar on Scythian-Sarmatian archaeology]. Moscow: University Press.

——. 2000. Osnovnye motivy ornamentatsii uzdechnykh prinadlezhnostey Yuga Vostochnoy Evropy v nachale rannego zheleznogo veka [Fundamental motifs of ornamentation of horse trappings in the south of eastern Europe at beginning of early Iron age]. *Skify i sarmaty v VII–III vv. do n.e.–sbornik statey* [Scythians and Sarmatians in 7th–3rd centuries BC—collection of articles]. Moscow: Institute of Archaeology.

Vanchugov, V. P. 1990. *Belozerskie pamiatniki v Severo-Zapadnom Prichernomorie* [Belozerska culture sites from northwestern Black sea region]. Kiev: Naukova Dumka.

Veimarn, E. V. 1979. Skalistinskiy sklep 420 [Rock-cut crypt no. 420]. *KSIA* 158:34–37.

Venedikov, I., and T. Gerasimov. 1973. *Trakiyskoto Izkustvo* [Thracian art]. Sofia: Bulgarski Khudozhnik.

Viazmitina, M. I. 1972. *Zolotobalkovskiy mogilnik* [Zolotobalkovskiy burial ground]. Kiev: Naukova Dumka.

Viazmitina, M. I., V. A. Illinska, E. F. Pokrovska, A. I. Terenozhkin, G. T. Kovpenenko. 1960. Kurgany bilia s. Novo-Pilipivki I radgospu "Akkermen" [Kurgans near the village Novo-Pilipovka and "Akkermen" state farm]. *Arkheologichni Pamiatki URSR* [Archaeological sites in Ukrainian SSR]. Kiev: Naukova Dumka.

Vickers, M. 1979. *Scythian Treasures in Oxford*. Oxford: Ashmolean Museum.

——. 2002. *Scythian and Thracian Antiquities*. Oxford: Ashmolean Museum.

Vinogradov, V. B. 1972. *Tsentralnyi i Severo-Vostochnyi Kavkaz v skifskoe vremia* [Central and northeastern Caucasus in Scythian period]. Grozny: Knizhnoe Izdatel'stvo.

——. 1976. K kharakteristike kobanskogo varianta v skifo-sibirskom zverinom stile [On characteristics of the Koban variant in Scythian-Siberian animal style]. *Skifo-Sibirskiy zveriniy stil v iskusstve narodov Evrazii–sbornik statey* [Scythian-Siberian animal style in art of Eurasian peoples–collection of articles]. Moscow: Nauka.

Vlasova, E. V. 2002. O rogakh dlia pitia iz Ulia pskogo kurgana n.4 [On drinking horns from Uliap kurgan no. 4]. *Tamanskaia starina* [Taman Antiquities]. St. Petersburg: State Hermitage.

Voronov, Yu. N. 1969. *Arkheologicheskaia karta Abkhazii* [Archaeological map of Abkhazia]. Sukhumi: Alashara.

——. 1975. Vooruzhenie drevneabkhazskikh plemen v VI–I vv. do n.e. [Armor of ancient Abkhazian tribes in 6th–1st centuries BC]. *Skifskii mir–sbornik statey* [Scythian world–collection of articles]. Kiev: Naukova Dumka.

——. 1980. O khronologicheskikh sviaziakh kimmeriisko-skifskoy i kolkhidskoy kultur [Concerning chronological links of Cimmerian-Scythian and Colchis cultures]. *Skifia i Kavkaz–sbornik statey* [Scythia and the Caucasus–collection of articles]. Kiev: Naukova Dumka.

Yakovenko, E. V. 1970. Riadovye skifskie pogrebeniia v kurganakh Vostochnogo Kryma [Ordinary Scythian burials in kurgans of eastern Crimea]. *Drevnosti Vostochnogo Kryma–sbornik statey* [Antiquities of eastern Crimea–collection of articles]. Kiev: Naukova Dumka.

——. 1974. *Skify Skhidnoho Krymu v V–III st. do n.e.* [Scythians of eastern Crimea in 5th–3rd centuries BC]. Kiev: Naukova Dumka.

Yatsenko, I. V. 1959. Skifia VII–V vv. do n.e. [Scythia in 7th–5th centuries BC]. *TGIM* 36.

Yatsenko, S. A. 2001. *Znaki-tamgi iranoiazychnykh narodov drevnosti i rannego srednevekovia* [Insignia-tamgas of Irano-lingual peoples of antiquity and early Medieval period]. Moscow: Eastern Literature.

Zasetskaia, I. P. 1979. Bosporskie sklepy gunnskoy epokhi kak khronologicheskiy etalon dlia datirovki pamiatnikov vostochnoevropeiskikh stepei [Bosporan crypts of the Hun period as chronological standards for dating sites of eastern European steppes]. *KSIA* 158:5–16.

Zbrueva, A. V. 1952. Istoriia naseleniia Prikamia v ananynskuyu epokhu [History of the population of Prikamia in Ananynskaia period]. *MIA* 30.

Zhelezchikov, B. F. 1997. Rannie kochevniki Yuzhnogo Piural'ya I Nizhnego Povolzh'ya [Early nomads of the south Urals and lower Volga region]. Ph.D. dissertation, Moscow University.

Zhuravlev, D. V., ed. 2002. *Na krayu oikumeny* [At the edge of the oikoumene]. Moscow: State Historical Museum.

Index

Abkhazia 32, 86, 88, 117, 188, 200, 251, 255, 256, 257, 258, 264

Achaemenid Empire 183, 235, 243, 255, 267

Achaemenid style, influence 52, 53, 75, 183, 215, 243, 247, 249, 250, 256, 267

Adyghea vi, 2, 16, 62, 80, 109, 169, 171, 258, 261, 267
    Adygheans 257, 261

Adygs vii

Akhtanizovskaia settlement 150

Akkermen (near Odessa) 229

Akmolinsk district, Kazakhstan 102

Alani 88, 92, 94, 259-60

Alanian culture, sites 90, 91, 93, 94, 96, 100
    Late Alanian 96

Alanic 259, 260, 261, 262
    burials 260

Alexander the Great 60

Altai 249

American Art Association 4

amulets 86, 89-90, 91, 94-95, 238, 258, 259, 260, 261

Ananyino art 254

Ananynskaia culture 187

Andersen Galleries 4, 5

animal representations 50, 249, 262, 264, 265. *See also* bird, fish, *and* horseman representations
    animal heads 36, 46, 57, 124, 187, 189, 195, 213, 245, 248, 265
    bear 187, 266
    boar 49, 50, 118
    caprid 158
    deer 135, 254, 256
    dog 209-10
    elk 122, 127, 128, 207
    elk-goat 253-54
    feline predator 161, 176, 212
    goat 36, 110-11, 147-48, 157, 206-7, 211, 215, 240
    griffin 29, 35, 51, 52, 53-54, 62, 74, 75, 124, 142-43, 146, 161, 186, 215, 216, 224, 225, 233, 237, 251, 254-55, 265, 266
        eagle-headed griffin 251-52, 254
        winged griffin 51, 53, 62, 142, 143, 224
    hare. *See* rabbit
    hind leg 37, 49, 50, 118, 181, 192
    horse 251
    leopard 100-101, 262
        snow leopard 100-101

lion 8, 46, 49, 50, 51, 52, 53, 57, 62, 121, 123, 124, 127-28, 137, 143, 144-45, 158, 161, 181, 182-83, 194-95, 215, 216-17, 218, 224-25, 233, 237, 258, 264, 265
    winged lion 224-25

lion-griffin 52, 124, 215, 237

mule 135

panther 13, 50, 107, 108, 109, 176, 177, 190, 210, 244
    Kelermes Panther 107, 210

rabbit/hare 58, 61, 66, 143, 263

ram's head 46, 120, 128, 145-46, 157, 233, 235

sheep 266

S-shaped 249

stag 7, 53, 64-65, 89, 108, 118-19, 136, 137, 141, 161, 178-79, 186, 190, 208, 210, 212, 214-15, 224, 240, 246, 251-52, 254, 255, 260
    Kostromskoy stag 210

stag-goat 254

totemic animals 213

wolf 28, 36, 137, 159, 160, 210, 214, 254, 265

animal mask 213, 265-66

animal style. *See* Scythian Animal Style

anthropomorphic objects 262-67

Antikenabteilung, Staatliche Museen zu Berlin viii, ix, 1, 7, 10-11, 13, 28, 30, 36, 47, 48-49, 51, 52, 55, 65, 72, 73, 96, 99, 105-166, 186, 209, 214, 215, 225, 226, 235-36, 262
    Classics department 2, 5, 7, 8

Arkhangelskaia Sloboda 50, 56, 145, 238

Armenia 195, 266

armor 42, 81-82, 161, 208, 267
    helmets 39, 40, 130, 264, 267
    shields 131, 133, 242

art
    ancient Asian 2
    ancient Greek 2, 148, 249
    barbarian 59, 110, 213, 264
    Byzantine 97-98
    Caucasian (Colkhido-Koban) 82
    Greco-Scythian 81-82, 263
    Near Eastern 250

Ashmolean Museum 121

Asia, Central 231, 249, 252, 261

Asia Minor vi, ix, 55, 183, 230, 253, 255, 261, 267
    Cilicia 261

Asia, Western 257

Assyria, Assyrians vi, 230, 255, 263, 266
Athena 39–40
Avars 259
Azerbaijan 267

Balkans, Balkan Peninsula vii, ix
Bank of the Orient, Paris 1
barbarians 38, 59, 110, 213, 243, 250
barrows vi–vii, viii–ix, 263, 265, 266. *See also* kurgans
 Karagodeuashkh vi, 2, 60, 61, 64, 147, 193, 246, 257
 Kelermes vi, 2, 43, 54, 55, 57, 107, 111, 210, 224, 238, 242, 251–52
 Kostromskoy vi, 2, 210
 Kurdzhips vi, 2, 38, 60, 82, 140, 147
 Peschannoe vi
 Scythian ix
  Kul-Oba ix, 58, 65, 66, 114, 125, 132, 143–44, 145, 196, 213
 Scythian-Maeotian vi
 Semibratnie ix, 267
 Severskiy vi
 Soboleva Mogila 265
 Ul'skiy vi
 Uliap sanctuary vi
 Vozdvizhenskiy vi
 Zubovskiy vi
Bashkir 162
bells 79, 138, 177, 246. *See also* horse trappings *and* ornaments
Belorechenskaya vi, 98, 99, 100, 153, 260
Belorechenskie sites 100
Belozerskaia culture 22, 168
belt buckles 196, 198, 217–20, 252, 256, 260. *See also* buckles
belts 172, 173, 195, 196, 219, 220, 254, 256, 258, 261, 262, 267
 Colkhido-Koban 253
 Urartian 253
Berlin Museum vii, 1, 2–3, 5, 7, 8, 10, 13, 24, 36, 37, 54, 56, 58, 111, 119, 131, 162, 193, 198, 226–27, 230, 233, 235, 236, 240, 256, 263, 264. *See also* Antikenabteilung *and* Museen für Vor- und Frügeschichte
 Classical department 226, 228, 232, 233, 234, 236, 237
 inventory books 9, 10–11, 105, 106, 107, 125, 133, 152, 156, 158–59, 160, 161, 166, 168, 170, 175, 183, 188, 190, 193, 195–96, 198, 203–4, 205, 206, 207, 208, 211–12, 219, 222, 226, 240
 Prehistory department 1, 2, 5, 7, 8, 9, 36, 227, 228, 232, 233, 234, 236
bimetallic objects 7, 185, 191–92
bird representations 27, 28, 29, 35, 49, 51, 53, 65–66, 111, 114, 116, 117, 118, 119–20, 122–23, 136, 138, 140, 159, 160, 164–65, 178, 182, 188, 190, 193–95, 209, 212, 214, 215, 216, 217, 225, 245, 251, 253, 254, 255–56, 266
 bird-griffin 29, 35, 225
 birds of prey 28, 29, 36, 51, 53, 111, 114, 118, 119, 122, 127, 136, 138, 159, 160–61, 178, 182, 188, 190,

193, 194–95, 207, 208, 209, 212, 214, 215, 216, 217, 225, 252, 254, 255, 256, 263, 264
 duck 49, 84, 164
 eagle 117, 147, 233, 253, 256
Black Sea region vii, ix, 5, 8, 9, 15, 21, 22, 24, 25, 35, 37, 38, 41, 46, 47, 57, 64, 80, 83, 84, 86, 102, 104, 140, 148, 149, 153, 154, 160, 168, 172, 174, 187, 193, 195, 196, 198, 210, 211, 213, 229, 243, 264, 267
 northern Black Sea 5, 8, 9, 21, 22, 24, 25, 35, 37, 38, 41, 46, 47, 57, 64, 80, 83, 86, 102, 104, 140, 148, 149, 153, 154, 160, 168, 172, 187, 193, 195, 196, 198, 210, 211, 213, 229
Bolshaia Znamianka village 46
bone artifacts vi, 8, 86, 115, 154, 186, 209, 210, 231, 241, 258, 259
Borodinskiy treasure 16
Bosporan Kingdom vii, 59, 65, 66, 67, 69, 86, 144, 218, 219, 232, 239, 243, 258
 Bosporan elite 69
 Gorgippia 84, 151, 239
 Greek necropoleis 218
 Hermonassa 239
 jewelry centers 69
 Panticapaeum 1, 144, 199, 213, 218, 220
 Phanagoria 1, 239
 Tiberius Iulius Eupatorius 219, 220, 258
 workshops 59, 66
Bosporus region vii, 3, 141, 219, 220, 258
Bouray, France 82
British Museum 45, 144
bronze artifacts 3, 4, 7, 8, 10, 11, 13, 15–16, 17–24, 26–37, 41–42, 75, 76–80, 81–83, 88, 89–96, 105–14, 115, 117, 120, 122–24, 130–35, 136–38, 143, 148, 149–50, 151–52, 155–56, 157–63, 164, 167, 171–97, 199–200, 205, 206–9, 210–23, 227, 229, 230, 231, 233, 235, 237, 241, 242, 244, 245, 246, 249, 251, 252, 253, 254, 255, 256, 257, 259, 261, 263, 264. *See also* Luristan, bronzes
 Bronze Age 7, 9, 10, 11, 21, 167, 170, 226, 227, 228, 229, 230, 231, 233, 249, 250, 257
 Early Bronze Age 10, 226, 230
 Late Bronze Age 17, 21, 22, 167, 226, 227, 229, 230, 248, 249
buckles 28, 29, 96–97, 151–52, 187–88, 196–97, 198–99, 202, 217–21, 222–23, 252, 253, 256, 258, 261, 262
Bug River 1, 255
Bulgaria 117, 253, 255
Bulgars 259
buttons 18, 19, 20, 21, 22, 28, 29, 30, 38, 39, 40, 44, 60, 61, 99, 100, 111, 123, 125, 153, 154, 156, 157, 158, 160, 187, 237, 262. *See also* plaques, button-shaped
 gorgoneion 38, 39

Canessa, Ercole viii, 3–5, 50, 67, 68, 75, 102, 233
Carpatho-Danubian 227, 229
Caspian Sea vii, 267
Catacomb culture 227
 Late Catacomb culture site 16
Caucasia, peoples of 257

Caucasian 18, 22, 35, 82, 88, 100, 161, 188, 200, 204, 227, 249, 250, 251, 253, 254, 255, 259, 260

Caucasian art 18, 22, 35, 82, 88, 100, 161, 188, 200, 204, 227, 249, 250, 251, 253, 254, 255, 259, 260

Caucasus vi, vii, ix, 1, 2, 4, 15, 16, 18, 20, 21, 23, 24, 30, 32, 33, 38, 40, 57, 59, 84, 86, 87, 88, 89, 90, 91, 92, 93, 94, 95, 100, 101, 104, 107, 110, 111, 117, 153, 154, 165, 168, 169, 170, 171, 172, 174, 179, 185, 192, 193, 195, 196, 200, 201, 204, 210, 218, 227, 229, 232, 243, 248, 249, 250, 251, 253, 256, 257, 258, 259, 260, 262, 264, 265, 266-67
    Central 92, 232, 250
    eastern 250
    North, Northern Caucasus vii, 15, 16, 18, 20, 21, 23, 24, 30, 32, 33, 40, 86, 87, 88, 89, 90, 91, 92, 93, 94, 100, 101, 104, 107, 110, 111, 117, 153, 154, 170, 171, 172, 179, 188, 200, 201, 204, 210, 218, 227, 247, 250, 253, 254, 256, 257, 259, 261, 266
    Northwestern Caucasus viii, 2, 3, 16, 23, 25, 57, 59, 95, 100, 168, 174, 193, 195, 196, 243, 257, 258, 261
    mountains 249

cauldrons 110, 111

Celtic art 82, 83, 95, 257

Celtic ritual 82, 83, 95, 258
    decapitation 82

chariots 121, 151, 263, 267

Chechnya 171, 229

Chernogorovka-Novocherkassk period 125

Chersonesus, Crimea 1, 260
    Tauric Chersonese 149

Cherson Museum 9

Cherson region 50, 65, 238

Chertomlyk 53, 61, 111, 125, 146, 192, 216, 239, 240, 244

China 5, 231

Cilicia 261

Cimmerian-Scythian raids 266

Cimmerians 230, 253, 257, 267

Circassian tombs 1

clay artifacts vi, 4, 8, 25, 26, 38-40, 60, 165, 169-70, 235

clothing, garments 25, 60, 81, 82, 86, 99, 131, 158, 196, 237, 259, 264. *See also* belts *and* headdresses, kalathos type
    boots 196
    hats 82, 161, 193
        helmet-shaped 130, 132, 133, 262
    funerary veils 238
    military 196, 219, 259, 263
    shirt 53
    trousers 196

coins, ancient 45, 60, 89

Colkhidian culture 161, 168, 229

Colkhido-Koban influence 82, 213, 243, 253

collecting antiquities 2
    black market 2

Cologne Museum 5, 9

Copper Age 257

Crimea, Crimean viii, 1, 2, 3, 8, 18, 32, 55, 65, 72, 83, 86, 92, 120, 121, 143, 144, 145, 166, 170-71, 182, 186, 193, 195-96, 197, 204, 218, 219, 246, 258, 259, 260
    crypts 201

    piedmont 229
    steppes 232
    Taurian gubernia 65

Crimean Peninsula 1, 243, 261

Daghestan 30, 171, 229, 266

Danube provinces 87, 259

Darius I, King of Persia 232, 255

deity. *See* god

de Massoneau, M. A. Merle viii, ix, 1-9, 11, 13, 51, 52, 62, 64, 72, 80, 83, 105, 106, 119, 142, 179, 185, 186, 193, 199, 204, 207, 208, 209, 226, 227, 232, 233, 235, 236, 240, 241, 258, 262-66, 267
    sale of artifacts 2-5
    trips 1, 2

demon 149

design elements
    Athena 39-40
    concentric circles 92, 93, 94, 100, 107
    crescent shapes 42-43, 79, 94-95, 116, 154, 164-65, 199
    filigree 42, 43, 46, 47, 60, 63, 64, 65, 67, 68, 69, 70, 83, 84, 99, 100, 121, 122, 126, 128, 129, 130, 141, 144, 145, 147, 150, 153, 157, 164, 199, 201, 203, 204, 224
    fish tail 201, 202
    gorgoneion 38, 39, 165, 166
    granulation 43, 47, 62, 63, 72, 88-89, 99, 121-22, 126, 128, 129, 141, 144-45, 147, 150, 153, 157, 164
    Greek 52, 118, 119
    hatching 17, 28, 147, 157, 224, 225, 243, 249
    lotus 56, 60, 66
    Medusa's head 38, 39, 61, 165. *See also* gorgoneion
    ovolos 26, 83, 145, 146
    palmettes 25, 49, 55, 56-57, 66-67, 116, 117, 118, 119, 144, 150, 189, 207, 217
    rosettes 29, 37-38, 42-43, 51-52, 55, 60, 64, 67-68, 69, 70, 71-72, 74, 117, 148, 160, 199-200
        cruciform 160
    Siren 45, 46
    six-pointed star 90
    swastika 252
    volutes 55, 57, 66, 251

Dniepropetrovsk 115, 245, 246, 254, 262, 265

Dniepr 2, 3, 8, 30, 32, 45, 86, 167, 176, 204, 208, 211, 212, 213, 214, 216, 227, 231, 246, 247, 255, 259, 260, 261, 262

Dniepr River region 2, 3, 8, 30, 45, 86, 167, 176, 208, 211, 212, 213, 214, 216, 227, 246, 262

Don River region 2, 16, 18, 23, 32, 33, 56, 83, 86, 94, 117, 134, 135, 136, 143, 150, 187, 188, 200, 210, 229, 231, 244, 246, 247, 252, 253, 255, 256, 259, 260, 261, 262
    central Don River 56, 134, 135, 136, 143, 187, 188
    forest-steppe 210, 227, 247
    lower Don River 2, 16, 23, 83, 86, 150, 162, 200, 229, 231, 246, 247, 256
    steppes 227

drinking horns 57, 58, 126, 127, 128, 129, 130, 146, 235, 236. *See also* vessels, rhyton

Eastern Europe vi, vii, 9, 91, 140, 204, 229, 230, 232, 247, 253, 254, 259, 260, 261, 262, 267
Egypt vi, 230
Egyptian artifacts 8
electrum 44, 238
Elizavetinskaia village 37, 56, 162, 188, 190, 216, 242, 243, 244, 248, 251–52, 253
Endzhe 176
Ephesus 55
Eurasian peoples 252, 255
Eurasian steppes vi, vii, 102, 231, 252, 253, 254

Fars/Klady burial grounds 21, 23
Fedulovskiy 150
      treasure 150
female figure 25, 59, 60, 266
Fernald, H. E. viii, 5
Filippovka village 162, 249, 254, 255
finials 44, 57, 58, 114, 117, 120, 121, 124–25, 126, 127, 128, 129, 136, 138–39, 143, 144–46, 148, 155, 157, 168, 171, 176–77, 220, 227, 231, 233, 235, 245, 262
      Lukianovskiy type 168, 227
fish representations 28, 117, 136, 201, 255, 256, 257

GAIMK 130, 131. *See* State Academy of the History of Material Culture
Georgia 9, 32, 168, 171, 193, 195, 229, 264, 266
Germans, ancient 86
Getty collection 45
gilding 38, 39, 60, 114, 197, 199, 200, 201, 235, 259
glass vi, 4, 8, 35, 97–98, 140, 149, 165, 198, 199–200, 201–2, 221, 224, 258, 261
god 264
      horned 82
      man-shaped 265
      Papai 263
      winged 266
      Zeus 263
goddess 40, 59, 60, 144, 263. *See also* Athena, Nike
      snake-footed goddess 59, 144, 263
gold artifacts vii, ix, 2, 3, 4, 7, 8, 10, 11, 28, 40, 42–75, 80–84, 88–89, 94, 98, 102–4, 114, 116–22, 125–30, 132, 138, 140, 141–48, 150, 151, 155, 157, 160, 164–65, 173, 196, 197, 199, 200, 202, 223, 224–25, 226, 233, 235, 236, 237, 238, 239, 240, 241, 242, 243, 245, 249, 252, 253, 254, 255, 256, 258, 259, 261, 262, 264
      appliqués 49, 71, 117, 235, 236
      earrings 47, 236, 240, 261
      necklace 49, 151, 238, 262
      plaques 3, 7, 10, 11, 40, 53, 59, 114, 120, 132, 160, 196, 226, 235, 236, 238, 239, 240, 241, 252, 262, 263, 264
gold foil 138
gold plating 114, 140, 160. *See also* gilding
Golden Horde 102, 103, 259–61
Goliamata Mogila, Bulgaria 117
Gorgippia 84, 151, 239
      necropolis of 151

gorgoneion. *See* design elements
Gosudarstvenniy Istoricheskiy Muzey. *See* State Historical Museum, Moscow
Govett, E. 4
graves vi, 231, 235, 236, 237, 238, 240, 241. *See also* horse, burials *and* warriors, burials
      female 201, 237, 238, 240, 241
      men 241
      robbing viii, 2, 29, 240
grave goods
      Central Asian ceramics vi
      Chinese textiles vi, 262
      Genoan silver vi
      Iranian textiles vi
      Near Eastern objects vi, vii, 250, 251, 255
      Venetian glass vi
Great Silk Road 261
Greco-Persian traditions 52, 53, 267
Greece vi, vii, 2, 40, 230
Greek-Barbarian sites 72
Greek artifacts 239, 240
Greek cities of the northern Black Sea region 8, 198
Greek city-states 46, 57, 86
      Tanais 86, 220, 259–60
Greek colonies 41, 249, 255
      Greek workshops 232
Greek complexes 197
Greek imports 114, 243, 258
Greek influence 68, 243, 250, 251, 256
Greek necropoleis 5, 8, 84, 86, 218
Greeks 4, 75, 243, 259, 260
Gundestrup, Denmark 82
Gurijskaya village 251
Gurzuf 195–96
Gyenos 251, 256

handles 13, 30, 107, 108, 109, 110, 139, 140, 170, 182, 183, 204–5, 206–7, 227, 230, 231
Hattians 266
headdresses 32, 40, 52, 59, 65, 141, 144, 147–48, 200, 203–4, 237, 238, 240, 262. *See also* jewelry, diadem
      headdress rings 32, 41, 42, 200, 203–4, 261
      kalathos type 40, 59, 144
Hellenistic period 49, 148, 149, 165, 166
      Early Hellenistic period 49
Henkel Foundation vii
Heraklius II, Emperor 89
Hermitage Museum, St. Petersburg 3, 27, 45, 96, 123, 130, 131, 134, 143, 152, 161, 179–80, 182, 184, 244, 262, 263
      Classical Section 179–80, 182, 184
Hermonassa 239
Herodotus 81, 232, 249, 252, 263, 263, 266
Historical Museum, Moscow 29, 114, 162
horses 2, 7, 8, 11, 18, 24, 58, 78–79, 80, 102, 106, 107, 112, 117, 121, 125, 130–34, 138, 139, 151, 163, 173, 175, 180, 182–83, 184–85, 192, 196–97, 198, 201, 203, 211, 217, 223, 226, 237, 238, 241, 242, 244, 245, 246, 251, 254, 256, 257, 258, 259, 261

burials 78-79, 80, 125, 139, 238, 241, 245, 257
    protomes 182
    skeletons, skulls 2, 79, 257, 265
horse trappings 2, 7, 8, 11, 76, 138, 139, 151, 175, 201,
    211, 223, 237, 241, 244-46, 255, 261, 265
    bells 79, 246
    bits 18, 79, 106, 112, 131, 171, 173, 174-76, 230, 244,
        245
        Chernogorovka type 171
        stirrup-shaped 171
    breastplates 79-80
    bridles 79, 216, 217, 245, 247, 257
    buckles 29, 202, 223, 252
    cheekpieces 13, 26-27, 32-33, 75, 79, 105-6, 111-13,
        123-24, 132, 137-38, 158-59, 162-63, 175-76,
        179-82, 183-86, 188-90, 191-92, 205, 208-9,
        215-17, 226, 230, 242-43, 244-45, 252, 253, 254
        figure-8 shaft 27, 111-13, 121, 123-24, 137, 158,
            179, 180, 181, 182, 183, 184, 185, 188, 190,
            209, 216, 223
        gamma-shaped 123, 137, 158-59, 162, 188, 189,
            190, 216, 242, 244, 245, 251, 254
        S-shaped 27, 33, 85, 111, 112, 113, 137, 179-80,
            181-82, 183, 185, 209, 242, 244, 252
        Scythian 183
    facings 28, 202, 223, 261
    finials 245
    frontlets 35, 79, 136-37, 157, 159, 161, 178-79,
        195-96, 213, 216, 217, 242, 245, 246, 251, 254
    harnesses 29, 35, 82, 120, 122, 134, 157, 159, 160,
        161, 192, 193, 195, 198, 203, 208, 215, 230, 231,
        233, 234, 237, 242, 244-46, 248, 249, 253, 254,
        255, 257, 258, 259
    harness plaques 36, 37, 122, 134, 135, 136, 154, 159,
        160, 161-62, 190-91, 192-93, 208, 210-11, 214-15,
        242, 245, 246, 248, 254, 256, 257
        S-shaped 248, 249
    noseband 196, 213, 216, 217, 242, 251, 265
    Novocherkassk type 175, 176
    pendants 31-32, 35-36, 76, 79, 245
    phalerae 149-50, 197-98, 258
    rings 245
    strap plaques 202, 222, 261
horsemen, representations of 82, 130-32, 133, 196, 262,
    263
horsemen, warrior 231, 262, 263
humans, representations of 35, 40, 52, 81-82, 90, 130-34,
    149, 161, 196, 213, 243, 260, 262-66
    masked 265
Hungary, Hungarians 54, 96, 231, 261
    Zold khampushta 54
Huns 259

Iemchikha village 46
Imperial Archaeological Commission 225
imports vi, vii, ix, 33, 35, 243, 245, 251, 266
Ionia, Ionian 242, 255, 267
Iran vi, 183, 247, 250, 252, 253, 263, 264, 265, 267

influence 242, 243
iron artifacts 7, 8, 10, 27, 28, 30, 33, 40, 42, 57, 58, 84,
    102, 112, 152, 163-64, 176, 177, 178, 179, 180, 185,
    191-92, 197, 198, 218, 223, 231, 233, 244-45, 252, 253,
    258, 259, 261, 262, 263
    ironworking 233
Iron Age ix, 17, 20, 22, 171, 172, 207, 226, 230, 258
    Early Iron Age ix, 17, 20, 21, 22, 171, 172, 226, 230,
        257
Ivanovskaia village 59

jewelry 3, 69, 241
    beads 8, 18, 20, 35, 72-73, 79, 83, 84, 98, 100, 103,
        104, 140, 149, 150-51, 155, 165, 198, 200, 203,
        204, 258, 260, 262
        barrel-shaped 84, 150, 166, 258
        cruciform 18
        long 20
    bracelets 23, 34-35, 41, 46, 63, 80, 86, 97-98, 120,
        145-46, 233, 237, 238, 261
    brooches 249
    chains 47-49, 73, 81, 83-84, 120-21, 164, 236
        braided, plaited 47-49, 81, 83, 120, 164
    diadems 42-43, 49, 64, 65, 67-68, 71, 120, 141, 147,
        148, 240
    earrings 11, 47, 49, 88-89, 121-22, 147, 164-65, 200,
        204, 236, 238, 240, 260
    fibula, fibulae 83, 86-88, 200
    medallion 199-200
    necklaces 49, 60, 61, 64, 72, 73, 80, 84, 141, 151, 155,
        201, 238. *See also* torques
        Karagodeuashkh type 60, 61
        Oguz type 60, 61
    pectorals 116, 117, 236
    pendants 11, 20, 31-32, 35, 36, 40-42, 44, 46, 48,
        60, 63-64, 65-66, 67, 69, 72, 73, 81, 83-84, 98,
        103-4, 140, 141-42, 148, 149, 153, 155, 165, 187,
        201-2, 205-6, 236, 258, 262
    pins 21, 142-43, 199, 221, 240, 260
        pinhead 65, 66, 221
    rings 45, 238
        seal 45
    torques 44-45, 46, 67-68, 80, 81, 85-86, 125-26,
        144-45, 148, 193, 195, 233, 235, 237, 238, 258, 262
Jochi Khan 261

Kabardino-Balkaria 30, 94, 245, 253
Kakhovka 146
Kama region 247
Kamunta village 89
Karachaevo-Cherkessia 94
Karagodeuashkh vi, 2, 60, 61, 64, 147, 193, 245, 256
Karapet 3, 7, 8, 226, 236, 240
Kartalinia (Kartalini) 193
Karu 13, 189, 193
Kazakhstan 102, 248, 252
Kazan region 253
Kazazovo farmstead 109

Keglevich, Count 11, 121, 144

Kelermes vi, 2, 43, 54, 55, 57, 107, 111, 210, 224, 238, 242, 250, 251, 252

Kerch ix, 1, 147, 196, 197, 199, 200, 213, 221, 232–33, 237, 242, 253, 260
    crypt No. 145 199, 221
    Kerch Peninsula 147, 213, 237, 252

Kharkov Museum of History 9

Khazar 94, 202, 259–60, 261
    kaganate 94, 259, 259, 260

Khersonskaia Oblast 65

Kholodniy Iar 30

Khosheutovo 29

Khosheutovskiy, Khosheutovskiy complex 211, 247, 248

Kiev 46, 144

Kislovodsk 201

Kizil-Koba culture 170, 171, 229
    Early Kizil-Koba 170

Klin-Iar III burial grounds 22, 87, 88, 89, 90, 91, 93, 260
    catacomb burial No. 20 88, 89, 90, 91, 260
    catacomb No. 23 93, 260

Koban 18, 20, 21, 22, 23, 32, 82, 92, 135, 161, 168, 171, 185, 195, 213, 229, 243, 249, 250, 251, 252, 253, 254, 256, 264, 266

Koban culture sites 18, 20, 23, 135, 168, 171, 229, 243, 248, 250, 251, 252, 253, 256
    Isti-Su 32
    burial grounds 18, 32
    Nesterovskiy 32

Kobiakovo culture 229, 230

Kobiakovskaia-type sites 169

Konstantynovka 176

Kossnierska, A., collection of 13, 170, 227, 229

Kostromskaia village 242, 254

Kostromskoy vi, 2, 210
    Kostromskoy stag 210

Krasnodar, Krasnodar region 40, 72, 84, 102, 109, 142, 200, 215
    reservoir 84, 102

Krasnodar Historical-Archaeological Museum 215

Krasnogvardeiskii region 169

Krivaia Luka burial 208

Kuban vi, 3, 4, 5, 7, 8, 18, 21, 22, 27, 28, 32, 33, 35, 36, 37, 38, 47, 51, 52, 53, 54, 55, 56, 59, 62, 63, 64, 65, 72, 79, 81, 83, 86, 94, 96, 101, 104, 111, 113, 114, 117, 124, 128, 136, 137, 140, 142, 143, 147, 150, 156, 159, 160, 161, 162, 163, 165, 166, 167, 169, 176, 177, 178, 183, 187, 188, 189, 190, 191, 192, 193, 202, 204, 208, 213, 215, 216, 217, 218, 219, 224, 227, 229, 231, 232, 236, 239, 240, 241, 242, 243, 244, 245, 246, 247, 248, 249, 250, 251, 252, 253, 254, 255, 256, 257, 258, 259, 261, 262, 265, 266, 267. *See also* Scythian Animal Style, Kuban variant
    Kuban basin 243, 246, 248, 249, 250, 255
    Kuban River vi, 2, 33, 229, 230, 232, 262, 267

Kulanurkhva village 255

Kurdistan 266

Kurdzhips vi, 2, 38, 60, 82, 140, 147

kurgans 1, 2, 9, 24, 27, 34, 37, 40, 46, 53, 54, 55, 56, 57, 62, 64, 71, 78, 79, 96, 98, 101, 102, 111, 113, 114, 117, 120, 121, 127, 128, 135, 136, 138, 145, 150, 157, 159, 161, 173, 179, 182, 184, 188, 190, 192, 208, 214, 215, 216, 217, 224, 227, 231, 232, 237, 238, 239, 240, 241, 242, 243, 244, 245, 246, 249, 251, 252, 253, 255, 256, 257, 262. *See also* barrows
    Ak-Mechet 120
    Aleksandropol 9, 59, 62, 78, 143, 263
    Aleksandrovskiy 44
    Anap 251
    Arkhangelskaia Sloboda 50, 56, 145, 238
    Baby Kurgan 50, 119
    Belorechenskie 98, 101, 102
    Berezan kurgan No. 371 238
    Bolshaia Bliznitsa 72, 144, 184, 213, 263
    Bolshoy Gumarovsky 253
    Butenki 231
    central Don River 56
    Chastie 56
    Cherson steppes 2. *See also* Arkhangelskaia Sloboda and Oguz
        Deev 2
    Chertomlyk 216
    Chmyrev 3, 5, 116, 147, 236, 240, 241, 245
    Darievka valley 62
    eastern Crimea 2. *See* Nymphaion kurgans
    Elizavetinskaia 37, 56, 138, 159, 162, 184, 188, 190, 214, 216, 242, 243, 244, 248, 251, 252, 253, 254, 256, 257
    Elizavetovsky 256
    Filippovka 249, 254
        kurgan No. 3 254
    Gaimanova Mogila 145, 146
    Huliai-Horod 24
    Karagodeuashkh vi, 2, 60, 61, 64, 147, 193, 245, 256
    Kelermes 43, 54, 55, 111, 224, 238, 242, 251, 252
    Kholodniy Iar 30
    Konstantynovka kurgan No. 376 176
    Koshevatoie 196
    Kul-Oba ix, 58, 65, 66, 114, 125, 132, 143, 144, 145, 196, 213, 263
    Kurdzhips 38, 60
    Kvitki 231
    Maikop vii, 2, 96
    Malie Semibratnie 27, 128, 179, 182, 184, 208
    Melgunovskiy 49, 120, 242
    Melitopol 78, 140, 244
    Mordvinovskiy 53, 65–66
    Nartan 30
    northwest Caucasus 2. *See also* Karagodeuashkh
        Major Bliznitsa 2, 263
        Seven Brothers 2
    Nosachevo 231
    Nymphaion 2, 46, 121, 128, 225, 237, 238, 242
        kurgan No. 1 238
        kurgan No. 17 128, 225, 238
        kurgan No. 24 238
        kurgan No. 4 238

(kurgans *cont'd.*)
        kurgans Nos. 2, 3, and 5 238
    Obryvsky 231
    Oguz 2, 54, 55, 60, 61, 64, 65, 139, 147, 240, 244,
        245, 260
    Olshany 231
    royal kurgans 64, 65, 114, 132, 140, 143, 145, 146,
        173, 185, 244, 262
    Sarmatian vi
        kurgan No. 3 162
    Scythian 2, 9, 37, 40, 55, 56, 57, 62, 79, 117, 135,
        173, 192, 227, 240
        Aleksandropol 9, 59, 62, 78, 143
        Chmyrev 3, 5, 9, 116, 147, 236, 240, 241
        Dert-Oba 2
        First Mordvinovskyi 9
        Kulakovskyi 2
        royal kurgans 9, 64, 114, 145, 173, 244
        Talaevskyi 2, 145
    Semibratniy 27, 46, 57, 62, 113, 114, 118, 120, 121,
        126, 127, 128, 157, 179, 182, 184, 208, 225, 235,
        237, 238, 239, 242, 243, 244, 245, 250, 251, 252,
        255, 266
        kurgan No. 1 235
        kurgan No. 2 114, 120, 126, 184, 225, 244
        kurgan No. 3 62, 250
        kurgan No. 4 118, 121, 128, 157, 179, 182, 208,
          242, 244
        kurgan No. 5 244
        kurgan No. 6 238
    Sholokhovski 162
    Shulgovka 2
    Solokha 56, 114, 145, 192, 238, 244
    Strashnaia Mogila 212, 214
    Tenginskaia village 40, 79, 161, 213, 215, 217, 241, 257
        kurgan No. 1 256
    Uashkitu 231
    Uliap vi, 25, 38, 46, 53, 57, 61, 75, 79, 127, 186, 190,
        217, 235, 244, 248, 252
        kurgan No. 2 186, 190, 217, 257
        kurgan No. 4 46, 57, 127, 235
        kurgan No. 5 53, 61, 75, 79, 239, 240, 244, 250,
          257
    Ulskiy 2, 54, 57, 224, 237, 238, 250, 251, 252, 253
        kurgan No. 1 2, 224
        kurgan No. 11 27, 179, 208, 242
        kurgan No. 4 165
    Ushakovskie 2
    Vasiurina hill 150
    Verkhnerogachikskiy 53, 143
    Voronezhskaia 38, 102, 136, 162, 190, 215, 217, 243,
        244, 246, 253, 256
        kurgan No. 19 136, 257
    Zavadska Mogila kurgan No. 1 114, 118, 120, 235
    Zholtokamena Mogila 146
    Zhurovskie 24
    Zolnoe 231
    Zolotaia Gorka 44, 256

Kuzhorskaia village 162, 188, 190, 217, 241, 243, 244, 248,
    252, 254

lamps 2
Lańcut Group 25
leather 28, 42, 66, 78, 201, 224, 225, 242
leatherworking 206
Luce, Stephen B. 4
Lugovoy cemetery 256
lunulas 94–95
Luristan 161, 207, 227, 230, 263, 265, 266, 267
    deities 265
    bronzes 230, 263–64, 265, 266
Lutsenko, A. E. 2
Lydia 267

Maeotian culture 8, 21, 22, 23, 32, 35, 40, 41, 54, 115,
    156, 159, 160, 161, 163, 164, 166, 171, 172, 230, 231,
    232, 233, 235, 240, 241, 242, 243, 245, 250, 255, 256,
    257, 258, 265
    proto-Maeotian 21, 22, 23, 156, 171, 172, 230, 231,
        257, 266
Maeotians vii, 232, 243, 249, 255, 256, 258, 262, 263,
    265, 266
Maikop barrow vii
Maikop collection 8, 9, 10, 11, 15, 24, 28, 36, 37, 39, 41,
    47, 48, 49, 51, 52, 55, 58, 65, 69, 96, 111, 117, 118, 120,
    122, 140, 141, 142, 151, 152, 153, 155, 157, 159, 162,
    165, 192, 214, 215, 226, 227, 229, 230, 231, 232, 233,
    235, 236, 237, 239, 240, 241, 242, 243, 244, 246, 251,
    254, 255, 256, 257, 258, 259, 260, 261, 262
    chronological distribution of objects 234
    chronological structure 228, 232
Maikop culture vii, 15, 16, 227
Maikop region vii, ix, 82, 100, 188, 248, 256, 264, 267
Makhachkal region 30
Makhoshevskaia village 251
male figure 160, 194, 195, 213, 264, 265
    seated 213
    standing 213
marine life
    dolphin 158
    fish 28, 117, 136, 201, 256, 257
    seahorse 75, 244
Marshall, John 3, 4
Massandre 186
Mavrogordato, P., collection of 7, 13, 168, 173, 178, 182,
    195, 196, 197, 198, 207, 227
Media 255
Median style 117
Medieval period, sites vi, 1, 8, 11, 86, 91, 92, 100, 102,
    104, 142, 155, 196, 200, 202, 204, 223, 233, 259–61
    Early Medieval 92, 228, 259
    Late Medieval 10
Medusa 38, 39, 61, 165
Mesopotamia vii
metallurgy, metalworking 227, 233
Metropolitan Museum, New York vii, viii, ix, 1, 3, 7, 10, 11,

51, 55, 56, 117, 224-25, 226, 228, 232, 234, 236, 237, 254

Middle Ages ix, 86, 100, 103, 104, 153, 226, 227, 259, 260, 261, 262

    Early Middle Ages 227, 259, 260, 261

    High Middle Ages 226, 227, 259, 260, 261, 262

mirrors 13, 30-31, 75, 90-93, 95-96, 106-7, 108-9, 115, 139-40, 182-83, 23-32, 260, 261, 262, 271

    Olbian type 107, 109, 231

modern elements/composites ix, 2, 9, 67, 68, 71, 72, 75, 100, 102, 103, 233, 257, 258, 260, 262

Mokraia Balka burial 201

Moldavia 229

Moldova 229, 244

Mongolia 248, 253, 259

Mongols 260, 261

monsters 194, 195, 264, 265

Mordvinovskiy 53, 65, 66

Museum für Vor- und Frühgeschichte, Berlin vii, viii, ix, x, 1, 10, 13, 111, 162, 167, 186, 192, 229, 262, 264

    Prehistory department 2, 5, 7, 8, 9, 167-223, 227

mythological figures 45

1984 Foundation x

Nalchik 30

Nartan village 30

National Archaeological Museum of France 256

Near East vi, vii, ix, 195, 230, 232, 254, 255, 256, 261, 266

Nekrsovskaia village 231

Nike 60

Nikopol region 193

nomadic tribes vii, 195, 211, 230, 231, 248, 249, 250, 251, 252, 253, 254, 256, 259, 260, 261, 262

    Eurasian 231, 252, 253

    Black Sea 195, 211, 267

    North Pontic 230, 250, 255

    southern Urals 249, 251

nomadic burial 102

North Pontic zone 231, 232, 247, 248, 252, 257, 260, 262

    steppes 227, 229, 230, 232, 244, 245, 259, 261

Novocherkassk 18, 20, 23, 24, 106, 125, 174, 175, 176, 230, 231, 246, 253, 254, 255

Novocherkassk Museum 251

Novocherkassk period 18, 174

    Novocherkassk-type artifacts 20, 24, 106, 174, 176, 230, 231, 251, 253, 254, 255

    Novocherkassk treasure 20, 106, 174, 231

Novorossiysk 92, 252, 255, 256

    Diurso burial 92

Novosvobodnaia, village of 16

Nymphaeum 237, 238

    necropolis 121

Ochamchiri 256. *See* Gyenos

Odessa 173, 195, 229

Oguz 2, 54, 55, 60, 61, 64, 65, 139, 147, 240, 244, 245, 260

Olbia 1, 25, 109, 232, 243

    necropolis of 109

Ordos 248, 251

ornaments vi, vii, 11, 27, 29, 35, 38, 42, 43, 44, 47, 48, 49, 50, 51, 55, 64, 65, 66, 68, 69, 70, 71, 72, 73, 74, 76, 77, 78, 79, 80, 81, 83, 84, 86, 89, 100, 103, 117, 119, 120, 121, 139, 141, 147, 151, 154, 155, 158, 178, 196, 200, 201, 202, 213, 216, 217, 220, 226, 230, 233, 236, 237, 238, 240, 241, 242, 243, 246, 258, 259, 260, 261, 262

    bells 79, 138, 177, 246

    chains 47, 48, 49, 81, 83, 84, 120, 121, 164, 236

    composite ornament 64, 71, 100, 103

    personal adornments 237, 239, 242. *See also* jewelry

Ossetia 82, 89, 92, 168, 185

ovolos 26, 83, 145, 146

Panama-Pacific International Exposition, 1915 3, 4

Panticapaeum 1, 144, 199, 213, 218, 220

Pechenegs 259, 260

Pegasus 235

Penn Museum viii, ix, x, 1, 4, 5, 7, 10, 11, 13, 14-104, 111, 117, 119, 120, 122, 140, 141, 144, 146, 151, 152, 153, 155, 159, 160, 165, 175, 192, 214, 224, 225, 226, 228, 230, 232, 233, 234, 235, 236, 237, 240, 258, 260, 263. *See also* University of Pennsylvania Museum of Archaeology and Anthropology

    Mediterranean Section x, 4

Persia, Persians 52, 53, 232, 255, 263, 264

Peschannoe vi

Phanagoria 1, 239

Phoenician imports 35

Pit Grave (Iamnaia) 15

plaques 3-4, 7, 8, 10, 11, 16, 23-24, 27-28, 29, 35, 36, 37, 38, 39, 40, 42, 43, 47, 49, 50, 51-57, 58-63, 64, 65, 66, 69, 70, 71, 72, 73-75, 76, 77, 78, 79, 80, 84, 87, 96, 97, 98, 111, 114, 116, 117-20, 121, 122, 123, 127, 128, 130, 132, 134, 135, 136, 137, 141, 142, 143-44, 146-47, 148, 149, 151, 152, 154, 155, 156, 157, 158, 159, 160-61, 164, 165, 175, 178, 187, 190, 191-92, 193-95, 196, 198, 201, 202-3, 207-8, 209-10, 211-14, 215, 216, 218, 219, 220, 222, 223, 224-25, 226, 233, 235, 236, 237-38, 239, 240, 241, 242, 245, 246, 248, 249, 252, 253, 254, 255, 256, 257, 261, 262, 264, 265, 266

    button-shaped 123, 154, 160, 237, 238, 239, 241

    convex 64, 164, 165

    cruciform 56, 154, 237, 239

    deer 7, 53, 136, 161, 190, 208, 214, 237, 240, 246, 252, 254, 257

    framed lion-griffin 52, 237

    griffin 35, 51, 52, 53, 62, 74, 75, 142, 143, 146, 161, 224, 225, 233, 237, 253, 254

    harness 36-37, 120, 122-23, 134-36, 154, 159-60, 161-62, 190-91, 192-93, 208, 210-11, 214-15, 242, 245-46, 248, 249, 253, 254, 256, 257

    lotus-shaped 56, 57, 60, 237

    openwork 28, 55, 58, 59, 62, 160, 162-63, 190, 191-92, 193-95, 211-13, 216, 237, 245, 249, 251, 254, 256, 257, 264, 265

    plaque-appliqués 49-50, 117, 118, 119, 155

    plaque types 237

    strap 202-3, 222, 260

swastika-shaped 252
wolf's head 254
Polovetsi 259–61, 262
    Polovetsian sites 204
pottery 115–16, 170, 229, 230, 233, 235, 243, 250, 261
    pottery complexes 229
predators, representations of 36, 37, 62, 124, 136, 138, 158, 159, 160, 161, 162, 163, 176, 177, 185, 186, 190, 192, 212, 215
protomes 182, 183, 235
    bull 183
    horse 182
    lion 183

quiver 24, 50, 208, 242

Rhine 87
Ribbed Pottery culture 16, 227
Romanovich 198
Roman period 140, 148
Römisch-Germanisches Museum, Cologne 1, 2, 226, 233. *See also* Cologne Museum
Rostovtzeff, M. I. 5, 6, 7, 8, 25, 131, 133, 161, 199, 214, 218, 236, 240, 243, 250, 258, 263
Roztov bronze treasure 167
Russia vi, vii, viii, ix, 1, 2, 3, 4, 5, 8, 9, 37, 38, 62, 64, 72, 122, 142, 165, 167, 168, 169, 171, 172, 173, 174, 175, 176, 177, 179, 180, 181, 182, 184, 185, 187, 188, 189, 190, 191, 192, 193, 204, 205, 206, 207, 209, 216, 217, 223, 227, 241, 262
    south of Russia vii, viii, 1, 2, 3, 4, 8, 37, 38, 62, 64, 72, 122, 142, 165, 167, 168, 169, 171, 172, 173, 174, 175, 176, 177, 179, 180, 181, 182, 184, 185, 187, 188, 189, 190, 191, 192, 193, 204, 205, 206, 207, 209, 216, 217, 223, 227, 241
Ryzhanivka 55, 66

Sacae 4
Saint-Germain-en-Laye, France 256
Sakharna-type sites 229
Saltovo-Maiatskaia culture 91, 93, 95, 202, 260
Saltovskaia culture 91, 92, 93, 94, 98, 260
Saltovskiy burial 202
Sarmatian burials 83, 84, 151
Sarmatian period 5, 7, 8, 11, 33, 41, 42, 44, 63, 67, 68, 71, 80, 81, 83, 84, 86, 92, 103, 104, 150, 151, 162, 166, 204, 218, 220, 223, 227, 228, 257, 258
    Late Sarmatian 84, 86, 92
Sarmatians vi, 210, 248, 260, 266
    barrows vi. *See also* kurgans, Sarmatian
        Peschannoe vi
        Severskiy vi
        Vozdvizhenskiy vi
        Zubovskiy vi
Sarmatian tamga insignia 220
Sassanian 4, 102
Sauromatian-Sarmatian culture 81
Sauromatian culture 187, 208, 210, 250, 254

Sauromatians 210, 232, 247
Schliemann, H. 9
Scythia vii, 4, 27, 59, 71, 163, 180, 196, 232, 244, 245, 255, 260, 264
    European Scythia 27, 71, 180
    forest-steppes 163
    Scythia Minor 259
Scythian-Greek sites 140, 148, 149
Scythian Animal Style vi, 5, 7, 8, 36, 54, 71, 107, 114, 118, 119, 124, 134, 135, 136, 137, 157, 158, 159, 162, 163, 186, 187, 188, 189, 191, 192, 195, 210, 211, 217, 226, 241, 242, 244, 246, 247, 248, 249, 250, 251, 252, 253, 256, 257, 263, 264, 265
    Elizavetinskaia type 243
    Kuban variant 36, 54, 134, 157, 158, 159, 162, 163, 186, 188, 189, 191, 192, 195, 210, 217, 248, 250, 251, 252, 253, 255, 256, 257, 263
Scythian art vi, 4, 5, 36, 187, 247, 256, 265
    Scythian gold 7
Scythian burial 46, 53, 74
Scythian period vi, vii, ix, 1, 2, 4, 5, 7, 8, 9, 11, 18, 20, 21, 22, 24, 28, 30, 36, 37, 38, 40, 41, 42, 44, 45, 46, 49, 50, 52, 53, 54, 55, 56, 57, 59, 61, 62, 63, 64, 68, 69, 71, 74, 75, 78, 79, 80, 81, 82, 84, 86, 107, 111, 113, 114, 115, 116, 117, 118, 119, 123, 124, 125, 134, 135, 136, 137, 138, 140, 142, 145, 146, 148, 149, 150, 154, 156, 157, 158, 159, 160, 161, 162, 163, 166, 173, 174, 178, 179, 181, 182, 183, 184, 186, 187, 188, 189, 191, 192, 193, 195, 196, 205, 206, 210, 211, 216, 217, 226, 227, 228, 230, 231, 232, 233, 235, 237, 238, 239, 240, 241, 242, 243, 244, 246, 247, 249, 250, 251, 252, 253, 254, 255, 256, 257, 258, 262
    Archaic 30, 57, 107, 117, 178, 181, 186, 195, 210, 231, 232, 242, 243, 246, 250, 253, 254
    Classical 232, 250
    Early Scythian 18, 20, 45, 117, 174, 187, 254
    Late Archaic 108, 117
    post-Scythian 8
    pre-Scythian 1, 2, 7, 8, 11, 20, 21, 41, 125, 154, 156, 160, 206, 227, 228, 230, 243, 246, 249
Scythians vi, vii, 4, 28, 59, 144, 178, 230, 232, 248, 250, 251, 253, 255, 256, 258, 262, 263, 264, 265, 266, 267
    elite 46, 56, 57, 69, 71, 78, 125, 241, 242
Scytho-Maeotian 54, 164, 254, 255, 256, 262, 263
Scytho-Sarmatian archaeology 5
Scytho-Sarmatian period 8, 104, 166
Sea of Azov 2, 259, 260
Seljuk migration 259
Semibratnie 27, 46, 57, 113, 127, 128, 157, 179, 182, 184, 208, 237, 238, 239, 241, 242, 243, 244, 245, 250, 251, 256, 267
Serzhen-Iurt burial grounds 171
Severskiy vi
Shuntuk village 191, 192, 211, 256
Siberia 101, 231, 248, 250, 251, 252
silver vi, vii, 2, 3, 4, 8, 50, 82, 85, 86, 87, 94, 96, 97, 98, 99, 100, 102, 103, 104, 114, 116, 124, 128, 135, 138, 139, 146, 149, 151, 152, 153, 155, 156, 197, 199, 200, 201,

202, 203, 204, 218, 221, 223, 233, 235, 236, 239, 245, 259, 260, 261, 262, 263
Simferopol 197
Sind state 239
Sirens 45–46
Smith, William Hinckle viii, 5
snake 59, 94, 144
snake-footed goddess 59, 144, 263
Soboleva Mogila barrow 264
socket 16, 17, 22, 23, 24, 34, 42, 46, 57, 87, 88, 127, 128, 144, 145, 146, 155, 156, 168, 171, 172, 176, 206, 207, 229, 251. *See also* terminals
sphinx 147, 198, 199, 240, 258
spindle whorl 166
Srubna culture 229
stamp 37, 38, 169
    cogged stamp 169
State Academy of the History of Material Culture (GAIMK), St. Petersburg 130, 131
Stavropol, Stavropol region 54, 79, 232
stele, stelae 253
Sukhumi, Abkhazia 188
Sul River region 176
swastikas 252
Syrian glass artifacts 261

tableware 229
tacks 49, 57, 58, 70, 71, 72, 117, 118, 119, 201, 202
Taganrog treasure 197, 198, 258
Taman vii, ix, 1, 2, 3, 121, 145, 178, 182, 183, 184, 188, 189, 193, 198, 199, 200, 201, 202, 203, 204, 208, 209, 210, 211, 212, 213, 214, 215, 216, 217, 218, 219, 220, 221, 222, 223, 232, 233, 240, 243, 245, 262
Taman Peninsula vii, ix, 1, 3, 121, 145, 178, 182, 183, 184, 188, 189, 193, 198, 199, 200, 201, 202, 203, 204, 208, 209, 210, 211, 212, 213, 214, 215, 216, 217, 218, 219, 220, 221, 222, 223, 232, 233, 240, 245, 261, 267
Tamerlane 259
Tanais 86, 220, 258, 260
Taurian sites 32
Taurian tribes 195
Tenginskaia village 40, 79, 161, 213, 215, 217, 241, 243, 244, 246, 248, 251, 256
terminals 46, 124, 244, 248, 251, 252, 253
terracotta 38, 40
textiles vi, 242, 261
Thrace 50
Thracian site 117
Tiberius Iulius Eupatorius 219, 220, 258
    royal insignia 220
Tiligulskoe village 207
Tizengauzen, V. G. 2
Tliiskiy burial grounds 18, 168
Tli village 82
tombs, stone 261
tools vi, 11, 16, 206, 233. *See also* utensils *and* weapons
    adze 167
    chisel 16, 206, 227

saw 102, 260, 262
whetstone 125, 172, 173, 207, 227, 230, 234
work tool 206
toreutic artifacts 131, 196, 262
Torks 259
Transcaucasia vi, ix, 33, 169, 183, 195, 261
Transcaucasian 229
Transcaucasus 256, 266, 267. *See also* Abkhazia
Troy 9
Tulskaia village 56, 264
Turkey 267

Uashkitu 231
Ukraine viii, ix, 1, 9, 15, 18, 21, 22, 27, 30, 33, 38, 47, 55, 56, 59, 61, 62, 63, 64, 72, 79, 81, 84, 86, 111, 114, 117, 143, 156, 164, 165, 171, 177, 179, 187, 201, 209, 213, 218, 223, 229, 231, 235, 236, 239, 240, 241, 244, 246, 256, 258, 265
    forest-steppe 113, 117, 136, 143, 164, 165, 182, 192, 208, 209, 231, 244, 246, 255, 256
        Sul River region 176
    southern Ukraine 1, 15, 21, 59, 62, 72, 79, 86, 114, 218, 231, 235, 240
    steppes 55, 59, 114, 145, 147, 164, 165, 168, 192, 208, 209, 232, 239, 240, 243, 245, 246, 254, 255, 256, 257
    western 201
    Zaparozhye region 236
Uliap village 25, 38, 46, 51, 53, 57, 61, 62, 75, 79, 127, 128, 157, 163, 166, 186, 190, 217, 235, 239, 240, 241, 243, 244, 245, 248, 251, 252, 253, 257
    sanctuaries vi, 257
Ulskiy Aul 131
unity of collections 7
University of Pennsylvania vii, viii, x, 1, 6, 7, 15, 51, 226
    Center for Ancient Studies x
    History of Art Department x
University of Pennsylvania Museum of Archaeology and Anthropology vii, viii, 1, 7, 14–104
    Archives 7
Ural Mountains 34, 187, 188, 231, 247, 249, 250, 251, 252, 253, 254, 255
Urartu vi, 230, 255, 266, 267
    Urartian style 55, 116, 117, 254
Ust-Labinskiy burial grounds 32
Ust-Labinskiy district 40
utensils 233, 234, 260

Verkhnerogachikskiy 53, 143
Verkhniy farmstead 150
Veselovsky, N. I. 2, 243
vessels vii, 2, 13, 25, 26, 28, 49, 67, 71, 97, 114, 116, 117, 118, 119, 120, 127, 128, 146, 148, 169, 170, 229, 233, 235, 236, 237, 238, 239, 242, 243, 256, 263
    amphora 134, 243
    ancient Greek 235
    bowl 100, 101, 102, 114, 148, 235, 260, 262
    cauldron 82, 110, 231
    cup 4, 170, 227, 229, 230
    goblet 101

jar 169, 229, 230
kylix 25
metal 235, 243
pelike 26
phiale 114, 116, 235, 236, 239
Red-figure 26
rhyton 46, 121, 129, 130, 145, 156, 157, 235, 255, 256
skyphos 7, 25, 239
wooden 49, 67, 71, 114, 117, 118, 120, 236, 255
Vettersfelde treasure 44, 125
Virkhov, R., collection of 7, 185, 192
Vochepshiy village 109
Volga 15, 29, 34, 81, 187, 188, 204, 208, 210, 211, 227, 247, 248, 250, 251, 252, 253, 254, 255, 260, 262
Volga-Don interfluve 250
Volga-Kama interfluve 255
Volga-Ural regions 81, 227, 250
Volga River 29, 34, 187, 188, 204, 208, 211, 248, 250, 253, 255, 260, 261
Vornezhska province 102
Voronezhskaie village 38, 136, 162, 190, 215, 217, 243, 244, 246, 252, 256
Vovkivtsi 192
Vozdvizhenskiy vi

warrior, representations of 81, 82, 125, 139, 172, 196, 231, 253, 254, 262, 263, 264
warriors 238, 255
burials 125, 172, 231, 238, 253, 255, 262
weaponry 231, 233, 238, 253, 261
weapons vi, 1, 2, 11, 131, 230, 233, 234, 237, 260, 261
arrowheads 11, 22, 23, 24, 30, 33, 34, 42, 152, 153, 156, 163, 164, 230, 231, 233, 237, 253, 254, 260
bilobate 22, 23, 24, 42
Novocherkassk-type 23, 253
trilobate 34, 156, 163

axes 11, 102, 168, 227, 229, 230, 249, 252, 262
Colkhido-Koban type 168, 229
bilobate blade 22, 23, 24, 155, 171, 172
bow 253. *See also* quiver
dagger 178
gorytos, gorytoi 130–31, 133, 161, 196, 208, 242, 262
javelin 132, 233, 262
knife-daggers 16
knives 15, 16, 227
handled 227
mace, macehead 16, 18, 227, 229
Maeotian swords 235
spear 58, 132, 134, 171, 196, 262
spearheads 155, 156, 171, 172, 229, 230, 231, 233
swords 231, 233, 235
akinak 178, 233
scabbards, sheaths 44, 50, 55, 242
whips 71
wire 31, 46, 47, 48, 49, 63, 64, 65, 70, 71, 72, 76, 77, 78, 79, 80, 83, 84, 85, 86, 88, 100, 102, 103, 104, 121, 122, 127, 128, 130, 140, 141, 144, 145, 146, 147, 148, 150, 151, 153, 157, 164, 165, 199, 201, 203, 204, 224
World War I 3
World War II 7, 8, 9, 10, 106, 142, 155, 164, 170, 203, 226, 236

Yalta 1, 2, 186

Zabelin, I. E. 2
Zahn, R. 1, 7, 10, 11, 49, 107, 125, 133, 134, 136, 158, 160, 163, 166
Zaporozhskaia Oblast 46, 65
Ziwiyeh 116
Zmeyskiy catacomb 96
zoomorphic 124, 181, 186, 211, 247, 251, 252
Zubovskiy vi

SPORTS

VIPs

MEET
STEPHEN
CURRY

JOE LEVIT

Lerner Publications ◆ Minneapolis

SPORTS THRILLS *MEET* RESEARCH SKILLS

Lerner SPORTS

Free Database Trial: **lernersports.com**

Lerner Publications Company
An imprint of Lerner Publishing Group, Inc.
241 First Avenue North
Minneapolis, MN 55401 USA

For reading levels and more information, look up this title at www.lernerbooks.com.

Main body text set in Aptifer Slab LT Pro. Typeface provided by Linotype AG.

Designer: Kim Morales

Library of Congress Cataloging-in-Publication Data

Names: Levit, Joseph author.
Title: Meet Stephen Curry / Joe Levit.
Description: Minneapolis, MN: Lerner Publications, [2023] | Series: Sports VIPs (Lerner Sports) | Includes bibliographical references and index. | Audience: Ages 7–11 years | Audience: Grades 2–3 | Summary: "Golden State Warriors point guard Stephen Curry is a three-time NBA champion, two-time NBA MVP, and the league's greatest long-range shooter. Learn about his athletic family and how he sinks so many clutch shots"—Provided by publisher.
Identifiers: LCCN 2021055024 (print) | LCCN 2021055025 (ebook) | ISBN 9781728458151 (Library Binding) | ISBN 9781728463346 (Paperback) | ISBN 9781728462325 (eBook)
Subjects: LCSH: Curry, Stephen, 1988– —Juvenile literature. | Guards (Basketball)—United States—Biography—Juvenile literature. | African American basketball players—United States—Biography—Juvenile literature. | Basketball players—United States—Biography—Juvenile literature. | Golden State Warriors (Basketball team)—History—Juvenile literature. | Basketball—Records—Juvenile literature.
Classification: LCC GV884.C88 L49 2023 (print) | LCC GV884.C88 (ebook) | DDC 796.323092 [B]—dc23/eng/20220201

LC record available at https://lccn.loc.gov/2021055024
LC ebook record available at https://lccn.loc.gov/2021055025

Manufactured in the United States of America
1-50845-50182-2/23/2022

TABLE OF CONTENTS

>>>>>>>>>>>>>>

RUNNING WITH THE BULLS 4

FAST FACTS 5

CHAPTER 1
BORN TO PLAY BASKETBALL 8

CHAPTER 2
A WARRIOR ON THE RISE 12

CHAPTER 3
CHANGES AND CHAMPIONSHIPS 18

CHAPTER 4
REMAKING THE GAME 22

STEPHEN CURRY CAREER STATS 28

GLOSSARY 29

SOURCE NOTES 30

LEARN MORE 31

INDEX 32

RUNNING WITH THE BULLS

The 2015–2016 season was magical for Stephen Curry and the Golden State Warriors. Curry scored 118 points in the season's first three games. No one had scored that many points so quickly since superstar Michael Jordan did in 1989–1990.

On November 24, 2015, the Warriors won their 16th straight game to start the season. That was a new NBA record. They pushed their record to 24 wins in a row before losing to the Milwaukee Bucks in December.

FAST FACTS

DATE OF BIRTH: March 14, 1988
POSITION: point guard
LEAGUE: National Basketball Association (NBA)

PROFESSIONAL HIGHLIGHTS: chosen with the seventh overall pick of the 2009 NBA Draft; won three NBA championships; is the NBA's all-time leader in three-point shots made

PERSONAL HIGHLIGHTS: has three children; attended Davidson College; started the Eat. Learn. Play. Foundation with his wife to provide education and food for kids

Michael Jordan led the Chicago Bulls to six NBA championships in the 1990s.

By the All-Star Game break near the middle of the season, the Warriors had 48 wins and only four losses. That gave them the best record through 52 games in NBA history.

Led by Michael Jordan, the Chicago Bulls finished the 1995–1996 season with 72 wins and 10 losses. Their record was the best in NBA history. In 2015–2016, Golden State had a chance to challenge Chicago's record.

Over the season, Curry scored 50 or more points three times. He became the first NBA player to make 300 three-point shots in a season. And in the final game of the year, he also became the first to make 400!

Curry's scoring helped the Warriors win their final game and finish the season 73–9. Golden State had set a new record for wins. Many basketball fans were happy for the team, including former US president Barack Obama. "Congrats to the [Warriors], a great group of guys on and off the court," Obama wrote on Twitter. "If somebody had to break the Bulls' record, I'm glad it's them."

Curry (*right*) celebrates another three-point basket with teammate Andre Iguodala.

CHAPTER 1

BORN TO PLAY BASKETBALL

Stephen Curry and his younger brother, Seth, both play in the NBA. They come from a sports-loving family. Their father, Dell Curry, was the all-time leading scorer for the Charlotte Hornets when he retired from the NBA. Their mother, Sonya Curry, played three sports in high school and was a volleyball player at Virginia Tech University.

Stephen's parents could tell that he had the desire to win from a young age. "He was always the smallest kid on every team he played, but he was one of the hardest workers," Dell Curry said. Stephen led his high school team to three conference titles.

Stephen wanted to play basketball at Virginia Tech. That's where his mother and father had played college sports. But the team did not offer him a scholarship. So he chose Davidson College in North Carolina instead.

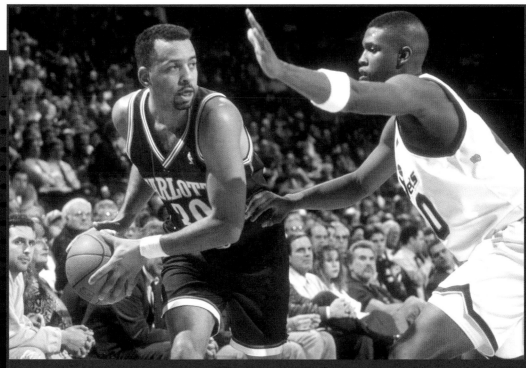

Dell Curry (*left*) scored 12,670 points in his NBA career. Stephen Curry surpassed his father's point total in 2017.

Curry was one of the top scorers in the US as a freshman in 2006–2007. He led his team to a fantastic 29–5 record. In the men's NCAA tournament, he scored 30 points against Maryland. But his team lost by 12 points.

The next season, Curry's scoring skills helped Davidson reach the NCAA tournament's Elite Eight.

Curry (*right*) takes a shot over a University of Kansas defender during the 2008 men's NCAA tournament.

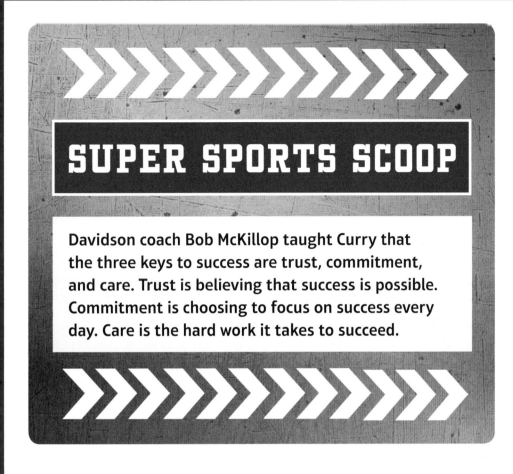

SUPER SPORTS SCOOP

Davidson coach Bob McKillop taught Curry that the three keys to success are trust, commitment, and care. Trust is believing that success is possible. Commitment is choosing to focus on success every day. Care is the hard work it takes to succeed.

They finally lost to the University of Kansas by two points. Curry became just the fourth player to score 30 or more points in each of his first four NCAA tournament games.

The team didn't make the tournament in Curry's junior year. But he still had a great season. He averaged 28.6 points, 5.6 assists, and 2.5 steals per game.

CHAPTER 2

A WARRIOR ON THE RISE

The Warriors selected Curry with the seventh overall pick of the 2009 NBA Draft. He was a long-range sharpshooter right from the start. Curry made 166 three-point shots, setting a new record for a first-year player. He also had five games with at least 30 points and 10 assists, tying Michael Jordan's first season. In Curry's second season, he made a team-record 212 of 227 free throws attempted.

Curry injured his right ankle several times in 2010–2011. After the season, he had surgery to repair it. That summer, Curry married longtime partner Ayesha Alexander. The couple had a daughter, Riley, in 2012. Their second daughter, Ryan, was born in 2015. Their son, Canon, was born in 2018.

Stephen Curry and Ayesha Curry in 2013

SUPER SPORTS SCOOP

Curry won the NBA Sportsmanship Award for the 2010–2011 season. Every year, the NBA gives the award to a player who shows fair play and honor on the court. The NBA gave $10,000 in Curry's name to Habitat for Humanity East Bay, a group that helps build homes for people in need.

Curry's ankle took a long time to heal. He missed 40 games in 2011–2012. After the season, Curry had a second ankle surgery. "I feel like I've been doing nothing but rehabbing for two years," he said. "I feel like I'm never going to be able to play again." But his ankle slowly got healthier and stronger. Going into the 2012–2013 season, his ankle felt good. He also signed a new four-year contract worth $44 million.

That season, Curry scored 22.9 points per game, his best average yet. He also set a new NBA single-season record for three-point shots. He made 272 three-pointers, beating the previous record by three.

Curry and teammate Klay Thompson were both fantastic long-range shooters. Together they earned the

Curry and Klay Thompson reach for the ball. Thompson was the 11th overall pick in the 2011 NBA Draft.

Curry talks about his work with Nothing but Nets at an event in San Francisco, California, in 2016.

nickname Splash Brothers. Their deep shots were often so perfect that the ball would hit the net without touching the rim. The net would move the way water splashes when you drop a rock into it.

Curry led the Warriors to their first playoff appearance since 2007. The team won their first series against the Denver Nuggets in six games. Then they lost to the San Antonio Spurs four games to two.

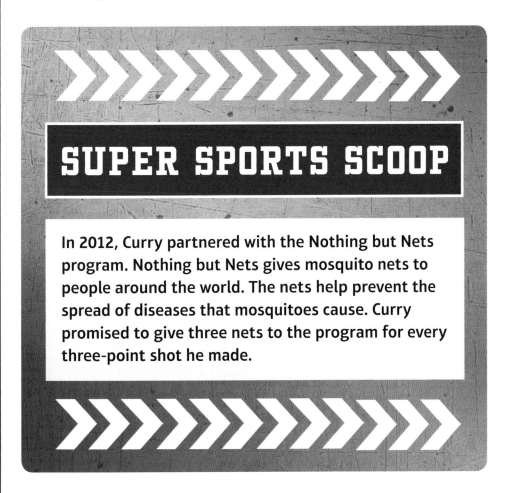

SUPER SPORTS SCOOP

In 2012, Curry partnered with the Nothing but Nets program. Nothing but Nets gives mosquito nets to people around the world. The nets help prevent the spread of diseases that mosquitoes cause. Curry promised to give three nets to the program for every three-point shot he made.

CHAPTER 3

CHANGES AND CHAMPIONSHIPS

The Warriors made the playoffs again in 2013–2014, but
they lost in the first round. The team was ready for a
change. Before the 2014–2015 season, the Warriors hired
Steve Kerr to coach the team. Kerr had won five NBA titles
as a player.

Kerr wanted the Warriors to play with a faster style. Curry raced up and down the court and led the team to 67 wins. He took home the league's Most Valuable Player (MVP) award.

The Warriors beat three teams to reach the NBA Finals. Then they topped the Cleveland Cavaliers four games to two. The victory was the team's first championship in 40 years!

After winning the 2015 NBA Finals, Curry (*front row, second from right*) and his teammates celebrated with the league's championship trophy.

SUPER SPORTS SCOOP

Curry visited the White House in 2015 to talk about the fight against malaria. The deadly disease is spread by mosquitoes. Curry also met then president Barack Obama. "Meeting the president in the Oval Office is a dream come true," said Curry.

Curry had a fantastic 2015–2016. He became the first player to make at least 300 three-point shots in a season. He finished with an amazing 402. Curry also won his second MVP award.

Curry led the Warriors all the way to a two-game lead in the 2016 NBA Finals. But then LeBron James and the Cavaliers took over the series. They won three straight games and the championship.

The tough loss in the Finals hit the Warriors hard.

To improve the team, they added superstar Kevin Durant. He and Curry led Golden State to another great year. They finished the season in first place in their conference.

Curry and James met again in the 2016–2017 Finals. This time, the Warriors beat the Cavaliers in five games for their second title. A year later, the Warriors faced the Cavaliers in the Finals for the fourth straight season. Golden State swept the series 4–0. The victory meant three titles in four years for Curry and company!

Curry (*left*) dribbles the ball away from LeBron James during the 2016 NBA Finals.

CHAPTER 4

REMAKING THE GAME

Curry and the Warriors advanced to the Finals again in 2018–2019. But this time, they faced a different team. The Toronto Raptors played with a tough style. In Game 5,

Durant went down with a serious injury. Curry and his teammates kept fighting. They forced the series to six games, but Toronto took the title.

Curry (*left*) rests on the bench during the 2019 NBA Finals. He led all players with 183 points in the series, but it wasn't enough to beat the Raptors.

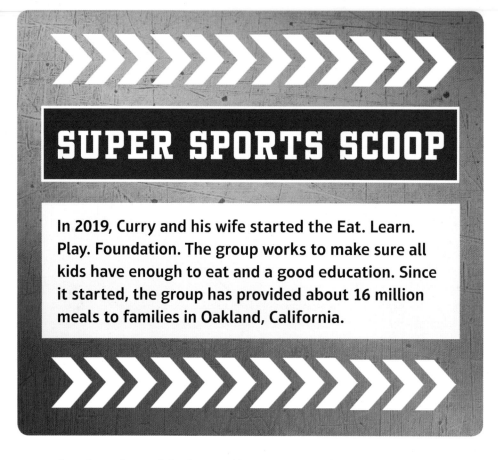

SUPER SPORTS SCOOP

In 2019, Curry and his wife started the Eat. Learn. Play. Foundation. The group works to make sure all kids have enough to eat and a good education. Since it started, the group has provided about 16 million meals to families in Oakland, California.

A broken hand led to a down year for Curry in 2019–2020. But in 2020–2021, he was back. Curry scored a career-high 62 points in a game against the Portland Trail Blazers. He averaged 32 points per game that season, the best of his career.

In 2021–2022, Curry set an incredible record. In a victory against the New York Knicks, he sank the 2,974th three-point shot of his career. Curry passed superstar Ray Allen for the most three-pointers in NBA history.

Curry's quick shots are difficult for defenders to block.

"I saw my teammates [celebrating]," Curry said. "I felt the whole buzz of the whole arena. So it was special."

Curry's long-range skills have changed the game. NBA players take more three-point shots than in the past because of his success. He is one of the NBA's all-time

Curry makes almost half of the three-point shots he takes.

Curry led the Warriors to one of the best records in the NBA in 2021–2022.

greatest players. Curry led the NBA in points per game in 2015–2016 and 2020–2021. He has been voted to seven NBA All-Star Games. He set an NBA record by making at least one three-point shot in 157 straight games. Fans can't wait to see what he does next.

STEPHEN CURRY CAREER STATS

STEALS:

1,335

ASSISTS:

5,211

POINTS:

19,427

POINTS PER GAME:

24.3

ASSISTS PER GAME:

6.5

GLOSSARY

assist: a pass that leads directly to a score

conference: a group of sports teams that make up part of a league

draft: when teams take turns choosing new players

Elite Eight: the final eight teams in the men's and women's NCAA basketball tournaments

free throw: an open shot taken from behind a set line after a foul by an opponent

NCAA tournament: a series of games played each year to decide college basketball's champion

rehabbing: working to restore health after an injury

scholarship: money that a school or another group gives to students to help pay for their education

sharpshooter: a good shooter in basketball

steal: when a basketball player takes the ball from an opposing player

three-point shot: a shot taken from behind the three-point line on a basketball court that counts for three points

SOURCE NOTES

7 Associated Press, "Steph Curry Shoots Warriors to 73rd Win, Breaking Bulls' Mark," *ESPN*, April 14, 2016, https://www.espn.com/nba/recap?gameId=400829114.

9 "Before They Made It: Stephen Curry," USA Basketball, updated May 4, 2015, https://www.usab.com/news-events/news/2015/05/before-they-made-it-stephen-curry.aspx.

14 Pablo S. Torre, "How Stephen Curry Got the Best Worst Ankles in Sports," *ESPN*, February 10, 2016, https://www.espn.com/blog/truehoop/post/_/id/74078/how-stephen-curry-got-the-best-worst-ankles-in-sports.

20 Diamond Leung, "Warriors' Stephen Curry Meets President Obama," *San Jose (CA) Mercury News*, updated August 12, 2016, https://www.mercurynews.com/2015/02/25/warriors-stephen-curry-meets-president-obama/.

26 Michael C. Wright. "Steph Curry Overtakes Ray Allen for NBA's All-Time 3-Point Lead," NBA, updated December 16, 2021, https://www.nba.com/news/stephen-curry-tracker-all-time-3s-record.

LEARN MORE

Flynn, Brendan. *Golden State Warriors All-Time Greats*. Mankato, MN: Press Box Books, 2020.

Golden State Warriors
https://www.nba.com/warriors/

Levit, Joe. *Basketball's G.O.A.T.: Michael Jordan, LeBron James, and More*. Minneapolis: Lerner Publications, 2020.

Sports Illustrated Kids—Basketball
https://www.sikids.com/basketball

Stephen Curry
https://www.nba.com/player/201939/stephen-curry

Walker, Hubert. *Stephen Curry: Basketball Star*. Lake Elmo, MN: Focus Readers, 2021.

INDEX

Cleveland Cavaliers, 19–21

Curry, Ayesha, 5, 13, 24

Curry, Dell, 8–9

Curry, Seth, 8

Curry, Sonya, 8

Davidson College, 5, 9–11

Durant, Kevin, 21, 23

Eat. Learn. Play. Foundation, 5, 24

high school, 8–9

James, LeBron, 20–21

Kerr, Steve, 18–19

NBA Draft, 5, 12

NBA Finals, 19–22

Nothing but Nets, 17

Obama, Barack, 7, 20

three-point shot, 5, 7, 12, 15, 17, 20, 24, 26–27

PHOTO ACKNOWLEDGMENTS

Image credits: Ezra Shaw/Getty Images, pp. 4, 12, 15; Mitchell Layton/Getty Images, p. 6; Nhat V. Meyer/MediaNews Group/Bay Area News/Getty Images, pp. 7, 19, 21–22; Jonathan Ferrey/Getty Images, p. 8; Focus on Sport/Getty Images, p. 9; Gregory Shamus/Getty Images, pp. 10, 23; Thearon W. Henderson/Getty Images, p. 13; Scott Strazzante/San Francisco Chronicle/Hearst Newspapers/Getty Images, p. 16; Frederic J. Brown/AFP/Getty Images, p. 18; Carlos Avila Gonzalez/San Francisco Chronicle/Hearst Newspapers/Getty Images, p. 25; Stephen Lam/The San Francisco Chronicle/Hearst Newspapers/Getty Images, p. 26; Allen J. Schaben/Los Angeles Times/Getty Images, p. 27. Design elements: The Hornbills Studio/Shutterstock.com; Tamjaii9/Shutterstock.com.

Cover: AP Photo/Jeff Chiu.

Lerner SPORTS

When point guard Stephen Curry joined the National Basketball Association (NBA) in 2009, he quickly made the Golden State Warriors one of the best teams in the league. Curry is the greatest long-range shooter in NBA history. He holds many scoring records, including the most three-point shots made in a game and in a season. Curry's incredible scoring made him a seven-time All-Star and a three-time NBA champion. Learn about his life and find out how he became such an incredible long-range scorer.

SPORTS VIPs

ALLYSON FELIX

CRISTIANO RONALDO

GIANNIS ANTETOKOUNMPO

JESSICA LONG

KEVIN DURANT

LIONEL MESSI

PATRICK MAHOMES

STEPHEN CURRY

SYDNEY MCLAUGHLIN

TOM BRADY

Lerner
www.lernerbooks.com
GRL: R

ISBN 978-1-7284-6334-6

50999

9 781728 463346